'*Xinjiang Year Zero* provides an analysis of the processes of dispossession being experienced by Uyghurs and other indigenous peoples of China's Uyghur region that is sorely needed today. Most politicians and their followers today, whether on the left or the right, view what is happening to the peoples of this region through a twentieth-century lens steeped in dichotomies that are obsolete in describing the nature of states today—those of capitalism vs socialism and democracy vs totalitarianism. The contributors to this volume explore what is happening in Xinjiang in the context of the twenty-first century's racialised and populist-fuelled state power, global capitalist exploitation, and ubiquitous surveillance technology. At the same time, they invite the reader to reflect on how the processes of dispossession in the Uyghur region during the twenty-first century are repeating the colonial practices of the nineteenth and twentieth centuries that have shaped our current global system of inequality and oppression. The result offers an analysis of what is happening in Xinjiang that emphasises its interconnectedness to what is happening around us everywhere in the world. If you believe that the repression in this region is a fabrication to 'manufacture consent' for a cold war between the "West" and China, you need to read this book. Afterwards, you will understand that if you want to stop a return to the twentieth-century geopolitical conflicts embodied in the idea of a cold war, you must establish solidarity with the Indigenous peoples of China's northwest and call for the end to the global processes fuelling their dispossession both inside China and outside.'

—Sean R. Roberts, Director of International Development Studies, The George Washington University's Elliott School of International Affairs, and author of *The War on the Uyghurs*

'*Xinjiang Year Zero* provides a highly readable and utterly necessary account of what is happening in Xinjiang and why. By showing how the mass detentions of Uyghurs and other Xinjiang Muslims are linked to both global capitalism and histories of settler colonialism, the edited book offers new ways of understanding the situation and thus working toward change. A must-read not only for those interested in contemporary China, but also for anyone who cares about digital surveillance and dispossession around the globe.'

—Emily T. Yeh, University of Colorado Boulder, author of *Taming Tibet: Landscape Transformation and the Gift of Chinese Development*

'The crisis in Xinjiang has engendered its own crisis of interpretation and action at a time of growing geopolitical rivalry: how to condemn the atrocities without supporting hawkish voices, particularly among US politicians, who seek to Cold War-ise the US relationship with "Communist China"? How to critique China for colonialism, racism, assimilationism, extra-legal internment, and coerced labour when many Western nations are built on a history of those same things? *Xinjiang Year Zero* not only provides non-specialists a thorough, readable, up-to-date account of events in Xinjiang. This much-needed book also offers a broader framing of the crisis, drawing comparisons to settler colonialism elsewhere and revealing direct connections to global capitalism and to the rise of technological surveillance everywhere.'

—James A. Millward, Georgetown University, author of
Eurasian Crossroads: A History of Xinjiang

Xinjiang Year Zero

Edited by Darren Byler, Ivan Franceschini,
and Nicholas Loubere

Australian
National
University

ANU PRESS

Australian
National
University

ANU PRESS

Published by ANU Press
The Australian National University
Canberra ACT 2600, Australia
Email: anupress@anu.edu.au

Available to download for free at press.anu.edu.au

ISBN (print): 9781760464943
ISBN (online): 9781760464950

WorldCat (print): 1289469184
WorldCat (online): 1289458546

DOI: 10.22459/XYZ.2021

Cover: Images by Lisa Ross, Black Garden, Qadam Jai Mazar, Maralbeshi, Xinjiang, 2006; and Alpata Khojam Mazar, Turpan, Xinjiang, 2011. Design: Tommaso Facchin

This book is published under the aegis of the China in the World Editorial Committee of the ANU Press.

The publication of this book is generously supported by the Per Anders och Maibrit Westrins Stiftelse.

Thinking about the cemetery full of flowers,
I remember my ancestors even though they are gone.
I know they will not come back to this world.
I will remember them every day for the rest of my life.
I am a humble human of merciful *khuda*.

—Anonymous inscription from the shrine to Alpata Khojam, Turpan, Xinjiang, 2011 (as photographed by Lisa Ross in the image used for the cover of this book).

Contents

Part III: Global connections   173

Abbreviations

AI	Artificial intelligence
ASPI	Australian Strategic Policy Institute
BCI	Better Cotton Initiative
BRI	Belt and Road Initiative
CCP	Chinese Communist Party
CNPC	China National Petroleum Corporation
CVE	Countering Violent Extremism
FSG	Frontier Services Group
GMD	Guomindang
J&K	Jammu and Kashmir
PRC	People's Republic of China
XUAR	Xinjiang Uyghur Autonomous Region

Figure, map, and plates

Tables

Preface

Andrea Pitzer

The harm done to millions of civilians in China's Xinjiang Uyghur Autonomous Region in recent years is unique yet perfectly familiar. The crisis is familiar in part because the situation the Chinese Government has created in Xinjiang fits a pattern that has played out dozens of times across the globe over the past century. From Chile to Myanmar, from the United States to North Korea, the phenomenon of the concentration camp has shown itself to be both predictable and universal—and dangerously flexible.

No country preemptively detains the people it values. Instead, nations lock up members of groups they wish to 'reform', defeat, or exterminate. When population categories are rounded up, the group in question is targeted by identity: who they are or the people they associate with rather than any actual crimes they might have committed. A small number turning to violence within a group is enough to brand an entire people as suspect.

But the reason whole groups are implicated is often less about the specifics of their identity and more about the security theatre, controlling demographic shifts, a demand for labour, or a need for a societal scapegoat. In each case, the government is asserting its ability to mistreat part of the population as a display of authority, to maintain its hold on power.

Detained without trial, real evidence, or legal representation, members of the target populations are typically held communally and subject to arbitrary, quasi-legal, or extrajudicial treatment by authorities, mostly out of view of the public—except when a show can be put on to suggest that what is happening is not actually happening.

China is currently targeting Uyghurs and other Turkic Muslims. The essays in this book reveal that events in Xinjiang today draw on established traditions, both international and domestic. In the first concentration camps that unfolded as a public spectacle, Spain carried out an imperial genocide in the 1890s in Cuba. During World War I, brutal colonial camp systems were rehabilitated into the more anodyne framework of internment, which lulled the world into thinking that some forms of indefinite detention might be acceptable.

Those internment camps were nonetheless still part of the concentration camp universe and, by the end of the Great War, they had paved the way for camp bureaucracies worldwide. Decades later, when Nazi extermination camps industrialised mass murder, the possibilities of camps had simultaneously evolved and degenerated to include a new possibility: not just isolating and punishing a whole category of people, but erasing them from existence.

In the wake of Auschwitz, countries have avoided the label 'concentration camp' while running precisely the same kinds of detention systems that led to the death or torture of millions in locations other than Nazi Germany long before and long after World War II.

Xinjiang is among the most recent of these vast enterprises. Across history, the majority of concentration camps have *not* been extermination camps. Yet, even systems not deliberately optimised for murder have managed to kill hundreds of thousands of people or more and warp whole societies. From colonial Kenya to the Soviet Gulag, camps devoted to the indefinite detention of civilians without trial are a deeply damaging experience for the individual, the community, and the nation. The threat of being disappeared can poison every human interaction.

Due to Cold War pressure towards a binary distribution of global power, two broad international traditions rose in postwar concentration camp systems: the colonial model and the Soviet model. The Soviet model emphasised the remoulding or reeducation of citizens through forced labour and collective training. The colonial model, adopted more frequently by Western imperial powers, typically targeted specific ethnic or racial groups tied to independence movements in colonial outposts, and often trafficked in the active dehumanisation of people by ethnic or racial identity—a latent, and sometimes active, form of eugenics. In Xinjiang, China has borrowed from both traditions.

What are the common features of both types of modern mass detention? The preemptive warehousing of humans in inhumane settings. The use of propaganda to shape a political narrative that justifies and benefits from the mass detention of a segment of the population. The injection of military language and tactics into civilian society. The assertion that special measures are necessary because of the emergency threat represented by the target group. The alteration or erasure of the identity of a distinct group of people.

Events in Xinjiang incorporate all these horrors. The approach to minority populations in the region repeats many elements we have seen for more than a century. But newer aspects are present as well—elements rooted firmly in the twenty-first century.

Though its long history of building concentration camps was influenced most heavily by the gulag model, in more recent years, the Chinese Communist Party (CCP) has embraced and bent to its own ends the anti-Muslim rhetoric rooted in Western nations' response to 9/11 and the ensuing 'War on Terror'. America's open justification of torture, black sites for interrogation, and places like Guantanamo Bay encouraged other states less invested in even the public appearance of justice to double down. Counterinsurgency tactics employed in non-battle settings have proliferated. US and European demonisation of Muslim populations leave Western governments opposed to what is happening in Xinjiang unable to denounce China's actions without facing charges of hypocrisy.

In recent years, the similarities have expanded. The Trump administration's push for a ban on Muslims entering the country, its criminalisation of asylum-seekers, its willingness to separate immigrant parents and children, and its explicit efforts to limit the expanding minority demographics of the country provide more than enough rationale for a Chinese Government hoping to accomplish parallel goals.

In this sense, Xinjiang is just the nightmare extension of concentration camp tactics already adopted in other parts of the world. Camps in border regions are on the rise around the globe, from the US detentions that exploded into public awareness in 2018 and 2019, to India, Myanmar, and elsewhere. It is no accident that with the disappearance of most colonial possessions, borderlands are becoming twenty-first-century colonial settings. Since 9/11, China has embraced a world vision in which the Xinjiang Uyghur Autonomous Region has become an experimental lab in which to preemptively punish civilians.

Technologies for surveillance and detention have likewise evolved in this century. From automatic weapons that allowed a small guard force to control vast numbers of people to barbed wire patented and mass-produced in the nineteenth century, technology has always been the spark that makes mass civilian detention possible.

Advanced tools for twenty-first-century detention operate in their own international economy, without loyalty to any nation. Today, we see surveillance equipment developed in and outside China being used to monitor targeted groups. New technologies project a sense of objectivity and authority, isolating these groups and formalising bigotry. Networks spread pseudo-scientific propaganda to even remote areas at the speed of light, making dehumanisation both a goal and a by-product of innovation. As with camps throughout their history, technologies for projects of mass detention often cross borders more easily than people.

Following a familiar pattern, the assertion of intellectual, physical, or moral superiority by the dominant cultural group—in this case, Han Chinese—is used to imply that by detaining whole groups of people based on ethnicity, religion, political affiliation, or race, the government is taking on a paternal, civilising role. The project of Han guidance and control over minority groups has a long history and continues to undergird Chinese detention tactics.

If these are the global elements of the Xinjiang project, what are the local ones? Every camp system is a combination of international norms and inspiration combined with cultural traditions and exploitation of the fault lines in a nation.

While conscript labour has existed in China for millennia, Nationalists embraced brutal labour camps in the 1930s, using forced civilian labour for rural land reclamation. In 1941, Nationalist forces established a modern concentration camp at Shangrao in Jiangxi Province. During the Chinese Civil War itself, Nationalist and Communist forces alike made use of detention camps and reeducation efforts for both combatants and civilians.

After winning that war, the CCP's use of the systems of reform through labour (*laogai*) and reeducation through labour (*laojiao*), as well as internal exile, swept millions into a punitive state apparatus that for decades changed and adapted along with Chinese society. Both *laogai* and *laojiao* would meet an official end—the first in 1994, and the latter only in 2013. But forced labour and reeducation through labour did not vanish. And other forms of arbitrary detention persist, even outside northwestern China, in a wide range of settings, from 'black jails' to rehab centres and psychiatric facilities.

For many nations that have used concentration camps, military defeat or a regime's fall from power forced an end to their camp systems and occasional accountability for the people behind them. Yet, though the CCP has changed over time, it has never lost power. The government's willingness in the current era to impose detention on more than a million residents of Xinjiang shows that there has been no hard break with the prior, much larger Chinese concentration camp system. This tool remains available for use by the government. The existence of what are now widely recognised as concentration camps has become the defining feature of the plight of minority groups in Xinjiang—particularly Uyghur residents—for much of the world. These camps feel like a concrete, discrete, and recognisable thing. We believe we know how to think about them. But observers of camp systems often miss the fact that any nation that has built a camp system is already far down a path on which many other things are happening simultaneously. The camps are only one part of a larger effort.

In China, the local strategies are bound up with a long history of population control. In addition, millions of people never held in detention have nonetheless been forced into reeducation programs. As illustrated in this volume, the destruction of religious and cultural buildings and the reconfiguration of physical spaces down to the level of individual homes extend the government's project into every aspect of life. Forced labour, family separations, and an inability to speak freely in almost any setting further fracture families and communities. The distinctions between each level of punishment begin to blur, and the concentration camp phenomenon becomes a much larger, more ambitious plan than just the detention of a million or more people.

Yet what China has been doing for some time in Xinjiang should not be denounced as some set of exotic tactics only a communist state might adopt. The roots of Chinese concentration camp policy pre-date the existence of the People's Republic of China itself, and its branches include strategies and tools grafted on from the West in recent decades.

This kind of detention, this kind of targeting of whole groups based on identity, is part and parcel of a phenomenon that is expanding in dangerous ways around the globe today. *Xinjiang Year Zero* reveals the specifics of what is happening in the region without falling back on political tropes or generalisations, and makes clear that other countries also have a role to play in ending the space in which nations have the ability and the fig leaf of legitimacy to impose these horrors on generation after generation, both within and outside Xinjiang.

Xinjiang year zero: An introduction

Darren Byler, Ivan Franceschini, and Nicholas Loubere

Even before mass internment in Xinjiang became a major point of international contention in the late 2010s, the plight of Uyghurs and other Muslim minorities in northwestern China was the focus of considerable attention. As early as the 1990s, China's rise as the 'factory of the world' led to a massive influx of Han settlers to the region, attracted by opportunities in sectors as diverse as oil and natural gas, and, eventually, cotton and tomatoes. In documenting this economic boom, scholars and journalists, both Chinese and foreign, showed how native peoples were largely excluded from the most lucrative opportunities—a situation that fostered dispossession and marginalisation, fuelling a resentment that was already lingering for a variety of historical reasons (Cliff 2016; Millward 2021; Byler 2022). This resentment came to a head in late 2013 and early 2014, with a spate of violent attacks carried out by Uyghur civilians that directly targeted Han civilians, the most notable of which took place in urban centres such as Beijing, Kunming, and Ürümqi. Unlike many previous attacks, which were often spontaneous and targeted state representatives, these were planned and coordinated, utilising knives, vehicles, and explosive devices to wreak havoc among innocent civilians. In response, the Chinese authorities launched the 'People's War on Terror' (反恐人民战争).

However, the 'Strike Hard' campaign of the People's War on Terror ended up targeting many more people than the criminals who carried out the attacks and those who directly supported them. Instead, it precipitated a general criminalisation of religious and cultural practices. Initially, only religious leaders were sent to camps, but by 2017, the Party-State began to assess the entire adult Muslim population. It was not simply about preventing terrorism; rather, the People's War on Terror had become a program of preventing Uyghur, Kazakh, and other peoples from 'being' Muslim and, to a certain extent, from practising the way of life of their ancestors. In the years since, hundreds of thousands of people have been detained in prisons and camps, while hundreds of thousands of their children have been placed in residential boarding schools where they receive 'patriotic' non-Muslim training. Many of the relatives of detainees have been assigned to work in factories far from their homes.

The program is enforced through a comprehensive biometric surveillance and checkpoint system, as well as an army of police contractors. It is a camp and factory system at the forefront of 'smart' control, a limit case in the co-construction of colonial and capitalist frontiers. If that were not enough, at the same time, many of the sacred landscapes of these peoples—from cemetery shrines to mosques—have been demolished or transformed.

This edited volume sets itself three goals in relation to these developments. First, it attempts to document the reality of the surveillance state and how the state and its proxies strive to capture the social institutions of Uyghurs and others through processes of dispossession and occupation. It shows how a relationship of domination is established and reproduced. Second, it aims to shed light on the workings and the root causes of this system by examining its linkages to past political campaigns, global counterterrorism logics, and the expansive drive of global capital. And, finally, it argues for the need for an epistemological shift in how the progressive left engages with Xinjiang if it wants to live up to its vocation to change the world and not just analyse it.

Framing the debate

As we have written elsewhere (Franceschini and Loubere 2020, forthcoming), recent discussions surrounding developments in China have largely been dominated by two competing frames, which we have termed 'essentialism' and 'whataboutism'. The essentialist approach is characterised by an obstinate refusal of any attempt to find similarities and linkages between dynamics in China and elsewhere. This form of argumentation tends to emphasise the set of attributes specific to a certain context as its defining elements and takes China as a discrete unit separated from the rest of the world. In particular, today's essentialist arguments mostly centre on the idea that authoritarian China cannot be compared with liberal-democratic countries because they represent fundamentally different political systems—and any suggestion that there may be commonalities is immediately and vociferously denounced as whataboutism and moral relativism. The whataboutist approach, instead, dismisses any criticism of the Chinese authorities as hypocritical on the faux moral premise that they are doing nothing more and nothing less than what everyone else is doing. While essentialists hold that the camps in China are an exclusive manifestation of the authoritarian or totalitarian nature of the Chinese Communist Party, whataboutists usually ask how anyone in the West can put forward any criticism of Xinjiang given the long colonial history of their own countries, the grim situation in their prison systems, the mass detention of refugees, and the disasters unleashed by the global War on Terror.

The mass internment in Xinjiang has probably done more than anything else to strengthen essentialist views of China today. Indeed, it is easier to place all the blame on the leadership of the Chinese Communist Party (and certainly it deserves blame) and forget how the Xinjiang camps as carceral infrastructure aimed at reinforcing a colonial presence represent the culmination of a century-long global process in which concentration camps were first conceived by the Spanish in Cuba in the late 1890s, expanded by the British in South Africa during the Boer War, normalised by all warring factions during World War I, and finally manifested in the extreme variants of the Soviet gulags and Nazi lagers, before lapsing into the more familiar forms of 'black' detention sites that became common in Latin America in the 1970s (Pitzer 2017). It is equally easy to neglect the connections that link these camps to global brands and multinational corporations, or how the technologies that have made the camps possible have been spearheaded in Western universities.

This volume starts from the assumption that both essentialist and whataboutist frames are inadequate to either explain the current situation or lay the foundation for meaningful political action. As such, we turn our analysis to the economic factors that have produced both protest and violence in northwestern China. Using a materialist mode of analysis, these essays argue that the process of removal of Uyghurs and others from their land, combined with the physical and digital enclosure of their societies, constitutes an ongoing process of 'original accumulation'—or capitalist frontier building. Because state authorities have framed minority peoples as a threatening, yet detainable, subject population, their existence offers technology companies the space and funding that are unavailable in other parts of China to develop new technologies. Importantly, these technology-assisted forms of social control do not simply identify preexisting forms of criminality that had not yet been detected. Instead, they actually *produce* what the state and private corporations categorise as 'precriminal' offences of thought and action or 'terrorism and extremist crimes that were not serious' by criminalising normative religious behaviours and social relations. These new technologies can then be used to assist in the 'legal' theft of pre-terrorist workers' labour when they are assigned to work in unfree conditions. The dispossession of Uyghurs and others should be thought of as linked to processes of labour exploitation in eastern China and forms of state capital–driven development in other spaces in the country. The key premise of the book is that state power is channelled through private and public infrastructure and institutions to intensify ethno-racialisation and produce a contemporary colonial system at a frontier of global capitalism—something we refer to elsewhere as 'terror capitalism' (Byler 2022).

Zeroing in on the logics that drive and justify these processes of accumulation allows us to examine the way the strategies and technologies that are being used borrow not only from the Chinese historical experience, but also from global discourses of counterterrorism, technologies of biometric surveillance, and consumer-driven industries that seek to maximise profits. This not only rejects the false binaries set up by proponents of whataboutist arguments, but also allows us to challenge the questionable essentialist claim that democratic states in North America and Europe are somehow free from responsibility for human rights abuses, while China is uniquely susceptible to them due to its political system. Disrupting this binary by making these interconnections explicit also helps to prevent research on Xinjiang from being taken up by right-wing politicians who wish to exploit and exacerbate growing Sinophobia around the globe to push forward geopolitical conflict that can only end in disaster.

In short, this kind of approach underlines global linkages and connections. Through these essays, we emphasise that highlighting the colonial processes at work requires that decolonial and anti-racist refusal in Xinjiang be linked to other instances of contemporary colonisation in places like Hong Kong, Taiwan, Kashmir, and Palestine, and ongoing settler colonialism in North America and Australia. Likewise, the struggle against labour malpractice, mass incarceration, and police brutality in North America and Europe must be thought of alongside the systems of enclosure in Xinjiang. Anti-imperialism means standing in opposition to imperialism and all its subimperial derivations, and standing with the colonised and unfree wherever they may be.

Key controversies

In compiling this book, we have been mindful of three key controversies that have held sway in debates about Xinjiang in recent years. The first is whether we should resort to the term 'genocide'. While particular aspects and effects of the post-2017 system in Xinjiang do meet legal definitions of the term—namely, the transfer of children from one ethnic group to another that is facilitated by a widespread residential boarding school system and a negative eugenics program named 'Complete Inspection and Handling of Illegal Births' (全面彻底处理清查违法生育) that along with widespread family separation has produced a dramatic decrease in birth rates (Li 2021)—the system does not seem to be one of intentional mass death. Rather, it seems to be premised on a biopolitics of 'making live' as docile, submissive workers, detainees, and prisoners. This is not to say that the system, like all settler-colonial structures, is not focused on eliminating key aspects of what makes Uyghurs and others who they are—which is the reason we chose *Xinjiang Year Zero* as the title for the book, as we will explain shortly. However, rather than centring our attention on legal debates concerning the term genocide, we have focused primarily on analysing the logics and effects of the system, and on documenting the lived reality of the people who are experiencing it.

Another key controversy is the exact number of people detained. Although the Party-State has said that more than 533,000 individuals have been prosecuted in Xinjiang since 2017 (Byler 2021b), Chinese officials have declined to publicly say exactly how many individuals whose terrorism and extremist crimes 'were not serious' or 'were serious but not malicious'—the state definitions used for those sent to camps rather than prisons—were detained. State officials have, however, estimated that as many as 30 per cent of adults in some areas were 'infected' with extremism—another description of 'untrustworthy' behaviour. Internal police documents obtained by *The Intercept* and the Xinjiang Victims Database confirm that a minimum of 8–20 per cent of Muslim adults in locations with the most available data, such as areas of Hotan, Aksu, and Ürümqi, were in some form of detention, ranging from house arrest to imprisonment (Xinjiang Victims Database 2021; Byler 2021a). These state data, combined with open-access analysis of the construction of new detention facilities, interviews with former detainees from across the region who spoke about levels of crowding in facilities, as well as researcher visits to the region as recently 2021, give us some confidence that as many as

10 to 15 per cent of the adult population of Muslims—some 900,000 to 1.5 million people—have been, or are, in some form of detention. Since this estimate is not yet conclusive, throughout the text we have tended to refer to the numbers detained as hundreds of thousands.

Finally, there is considerable controversy regarding the naming of the ancestral homelands of approximately 12 million Uyghurs, 1.5 million Kazakhs, and several hundred thousand Kyrgyz, Sarikoli Tajiks, and others in contemporary northwestern China. The name 'Xinjiang'—literally, 'new frontier'—appeared as the definition of 'colony' in Chinese dictionaries published in the late nineteenth and early twentieth centuries. This colonial name was adopted first by a Manchu emperor near the beginning of the Qing Dynasty and codified as the legal name of the region in 1884 following what the Turkic peoples of the region referred to as a military massacre by the armies of Zuo Zongtang. As such, the name Xinjiang evokes a settler-colonial past and present, in a manner like that employed in British Columbia or Australia to mask the placenames of the aboriginal peoples.

The most strident voices when it comes to renaming these homelands are from Uyghur advocacy organisations based in North America and Europe who wish to reclaim the term 'East Turkestan'—the historical name claimed first by a short-lived Islamic republic in the 1930s and then by a Soviet-backed republic in the 1940s. However, since many of the advocates of East Turkestan appear to be exclusively Uyghur and appeal to a type of right-wing ethnonationalism rather than an inclusive democratic and decolonial ethos, we have decided not to use this name. Furthermore, because the term East Turkestan is associated in Chinese media discourse with small Uyghur militant groups in Syria and Pakistan, the name carries with it associations that act as obstacles to solidarity for many non-Uyghurs and Chinese citizens who otherwise may stand in solidarity with oppressed peoples in northwestern China.

In the absence of a name that addresses the concerns of hundreds of thousands of native peoples who would be excluded through the adoption of the name East Turkestan, we have used the colonial name Xinjiang as a reminder of the prohibition of formal decolonial political formations inside China. In some cases, we also use local naming traditions like 'homeland' or terms that emerge from Maoist multiculturalism such as 'autonomous region'. We have also striven to emphasise that these indigenous peoples claim a precolonial *priorness*—particularly in the case of the Uyghurs and Kazakhs, which are the two largest groups in the region—in their attachment to their homelands. This, in turn, allows us a way of thinking beyond the nation-state when considering future decolonial pathways.

About this book

Why did we choose the title *Xinjiang Year Zero*? Even though the term 'year zero' (as well as 'year one') has been used with more positive connotations in relation to both the French Revolution and the year 1945, we are obviously aware that it is more recently associated with 1970s Cambodia, when the Khmer Rouge, after seizing power, proclaimed the advent of Year Zero and proceeded with systematic brutality to erase all Cambodian culture and traditions with the aim of creating a new revolutionary individual. Are we suggesting a direct comparison between what is happening in Xinjiang today and the ominous precedent of the Cambodian killing fields? No, because as far as we know, there is no evidence of mass killings in Xinjiang today; one could even argue that mass murder becomes somewhat superfluous when one has at their disposal pervasive surveillance tools that leave almost no room for dissent. A direct comparison with the Cambodian genocide is also inappropriate because the ideological underpinnings of the Chinese Party-State today are the opposite of the revolutionary fervour displayed by the Khmer Rouge; if anything, as we have argued, the Chinese authorities are attempting to create a new, cheap workforce ready for capitalist exploitation.

But there are at least two uncanny resonances that, after much deliberation, prompted us to choose this title. First, as in Cambodia decades ago, the Chinese authorities have embarked on a quest to radically reshape the subjectivities of Uyghur, Kazakh, and other peoples, imprisoning them en masse and preventing them from practising their traditional ways of life in an attempt to clean the slate and engineer a new type of docile and 'civilised' (proletarianised) citizen. Whether they will succeed remains to be seen, but 'year zero' seemed to us a very apt term to define this ambition to manufacture a historical rupture. Second, what is happening in Xinjiang today is unfortunately being met with scepticism among certain groups on the left. This recalls the way many prominent leftists questioned the horrific tales of Cambodian refugees in Thailand in the 1970s and systematically attacked those who dared denounce the crimes of the Khmer Rouge. This leftist support for the Khmer Rouge, despite all the evidence of what was happening in Cambodia, later served to discredit the left and deeply undermined leftist causes. We see the same dynamic unfolding today. In this sense, this book represents our attempt to frame the possibility of a critique of China from the left in a bid to avoid repeating the mistakes of the past.

The book is structured in three broad sections. In the first, we explore the historical roots of the current repression in Xinjiang, as well as its discursive framing and justification. In the opening chapter, Ye Hui situates the repression of Turkic Muslims in Xinjiang in the long-run history of global imperialism, outlining how the dispossession of populations in Xinjiang today is an effect of secular nation-building. This is followed by Zenab Ahmed's analysis of assimilationist policies targeting Uyghur spirituality and mythic storytelling. Next, Guldana Salimjan traces how conceptions of racial purity and authenticity have shaped national consciousness throughout the history of the People's Republic of China. In this section's final two chapters, David Brophy examines how Beijing taps into global discourses of counter-radicalisation emerging from the US-led War on Terror, and Darren Byler digs into how counterinsurgency strategies developed in the United States, Israel, and Europe have been adapted for 'community policing' in Xinjiang.

Section two situates the case of contemporary Xinjiang in a longer-run history of Han settler colonialism. We start with a photo essay by Tom Cliff depicting the lives of Han settlers in Xinjiang, followed by a detailed examination by Guldana Salimjan of the ongoing human transfer project in Xinjiang through the banal language of recruitment and employment. Next, Sam Tynen explores multiple forms of everyday dispossession and displacement of Uyghurs, and Timothy A. Grose outlines the ways in which Uyghur spaces are being reorganised, resulting in the disruption of conceptions of home. We then turn to Rian Thum, who details the meaning and implications of the destruction and desecration of three of the most revered sacred and historical sites in Xinjiang, followed by Guldana Salimjan's explanation of how the discourses and practices of ecotourism are used to justify the removal of Kazakh communities. The section closes with a chapter by Darren Byler elaborating on how the internment camps are producing cheap labour for the factories moving to Xinjiang to take advantage of the situation.

In the final section, we shift to the global nature of mass detention and the emergence of a high-tech surveillance state in Xinjiang. In the first chapter, Nicholas Loubere and Stefan Brehm draw connections between experiments with 'social credit' and broader global processes of financialised inclusion, reflecting on what this means for social control. Next, Darren Byler explores how Xinjiang's 'Safe Cities' are facilitating forms of surveillance and digital enclosure. Gerald Roche examines the role of an international private security firm in Xinjiang, considering how the global security industry precipitates the circulation of methods and technologies of control in China and beyond. In the final two chapters of the book, Séagh Kehoe looks at the plight of women and ethnic minorities in Tibet and Xinjiang from the perspective of the Chinese and international feminist movements, and Nitasha Kaul compares China and India in their treatment of 'othered' populations in Xinjiang and Kashmir, respectively.

This volume is an outgrowth of the *Made in China Journal*—which we edit—and many of the chapters have been previously published in the journal's pages. The *Made in China Journal*, and the many projects associated with it, is rooted in the belief that the scholarly community needs to reappropriate academic research through open-access publishing models, and that academic research should be accessible more broadly to the public. It is with these commitments in mind that we have curated this volume, with the aim of helping the international community conceptualise what is happening in Xinjiang in the context of longer-run histories of settler colonialism and as a facet of the rapid expansion of repressive technologies of social control emerging from global capitalist entanglements. We thank the Per Anders och Maibrit Westrins Stiftelse for generous funding to assist with the design and production of the volume, and ANU Press for its unswerving commitment to open-access publishing.

Part I: Discursive roots

1
Nation-building as epistemic violence

Ye Hui

Since the People's Republic of China (PRC) declared a 'People's War on Terror' (反恐人民战争) in 2014 in the wake of a series of violent incidents perpetrated by or associated with Uyghurs, the Chinese authorities have built an extensive surveillance, internment, and forced-labour regime to control the non-Han peoples in Xinjiang. In a sweeping fashion, the Chinese Party-State has criminalised the everyday lives of Muslims in Xinjiang (Byler 2019). In profiling entire non-Han peoples as potential 'terrorists', the campaign has been an act of Han-majoritarian state violence. While this has often been interpreted in an essentialist fashion, as indicative of the authoritarian nature of the Party-State, transnationally minded scholars (many of whom have contributed to this volume) have shown that this perspective obscures the violence of Islamophobia and global racial capitalism, neither of which is unique to China (Brophy 2019; Byler 2021; Liu 2020). We cannot understand the particular repression of Muslims in Xinjiang without investigating the globalised logic of the modern age: capitalism and so-called progress often mean policing, exploitation, and dehumanisation for those on the receiving end.

However, while it is crucial to situate the current state violence towards Turkic Muslims at the intersection of postsocialist neoliberal development in inner Asian frontiers since the 1990s and the heightening of Islamophobia due to the West's 'War on Terror', I suggest we also view the tragedy as part of the centuries-long global imperial history. The epistemic infrastructure for this political violence was established through modern imperialism and has been reproduced by the nation-state—even when the latter was born of a history of anti-imperialism, such as the PRC. The Chinese state's dispossession of Turkic Muslims today is an effect of secular nation-building. The nation-state is an incessant, violent project that began to be globalised in 1492 with two simultaneous developments: within Europe, the Castilian monarchy forced exile and conversion on Jews and Muslims to build a pure nation-state for Christian Spaniards; overseas, the same Spanish state conquered the Americas through genocide and conversion (Mamdani 2020). In other words, ethnic cleansing and conquest lie at the heart of the myth of national progress. While the violence in Xinjiang is particular to both the postsocialist context and China's role in a post-9/11 global security regime that targets racialised bodies, it must also be understood as continuous with technologies of imperialism that have transposed non-nationalist polities, such as Qing China, into nation-states.

This essay traces a paradigm shift in political rationality from the late Qing Empire to modern China with respect to the 'new frontier' (新疆). In the Qing's violent encounters with Western and Japanese imperial powers, and as the Manchu emperors of the Qing struggled to maintain authority, an emergent group of Han elites in the multiethnic empire began to reconceptualise the political community. Territorial integrity and a cultural—if not racial/ethnic—homogeneity, for the first time, became the principal conceptual grids through which early nationalists imagined a political community of 'China', the nation-state (Duara 1995; Millward 1998; Mosca 2013). This epistemic shift is paradoxical: it enabled Chinese nationalists to articulate anti-imperialist self-determination, but only on imperially conscripted terms. It was only on this altered epistemic ground of the nation-state that Chinese nationalists came to perceive Turkic Muslims in Xinjiang as a problem. As the nationalist pedagogy has hardened since the 1990s, it becomes increasingly difficult for Turkic Muslims—their inherited life-worlds and political actions—to be taken seriously on their own terms. Dissent is narrowly interpreted as a threat to national unity and territorial sovereignty, thereby justifying auto-mated, widespread systems of surveillance and dispossession. Yet this violent positioning is not inevitable. By focusing on the epistemic (and material) violence of the nation-state, my intention is not to reinscribe closure, but to scrutinise the paradoxes, contingencies, and tragedies of nation-building. This is also an invitation to unlearn the progressive temporality on which colonial and nationalist regimes of violence have been founded, so we can look for other ways towards collective action.

Territory and population as the sovereign body

After the Qing annexation of what became Xinjiang in 1759, the empire did not imagine itself as a civilising project to bring 'Chinese' order and virtues to the Muslim peoples of Altishahr. Rather, the Qing imperial house, not 'China', was at the centre of this premodern political imagi-nation, under which Han, Manchu, Mongol, Tibetan, and Muslim were the five main cultural blocs equal 'under Heaven' (天) and 'in great unity' (大同) (Millward 1998: 197–201). Until 1864, Manchu and Mongol officials governed local communities through alliances with local Muslim elites, serving as intermediaries and seeking to shield locals from the destabilising influence of Han merchants and settlements (Millward 1998). However, as the Qing became encircled by sprawling British and Russian imperialisms in Asia from the mid-eighteenth century, and later the French threat from the southwest and the Japanese menace from the coast, their old way of comprehending the frontiers became unworkable. They could no longer see frontier crises as place-specific, discrete, and too complex to be standardised into a centralised lexicon, especially when the British Empire operated simultaneously on multiple frontiers (Mosca 2013). Pervasive geopolitical upheavals pushed Han scholars and officials who later dominated the high offices of the Qing to reconceptualise the empire, for the first time, as an integrated territorial entity in need of 'grand strategies' to be on par with what came to be perceived as its rival states (Mosca 2013: 11).

The shift towards imagining the Qing as a self-contained entity among other hostile geopolitical entities is reflected in an important debate in 1874 between two Han statesmen, Zuo Zongtang (1823–1901) and Li Hongzhang (1812–85), which led to the reconquest and integration of Xinjiang into a modernising Qing state. Both sides deployed a metaphor of the sick body to convey the danger of foreign imperial threats, although they disputed which threat (inner frontier or coastal) constituted a disease of the heart and hence directly endangered the life of the state (Millward 2007: 126–27). Corporeal metaphors had long been deployed in traditional Confucian political thought; they were embedded in a premodern mode of social organisation—what Benedict Anderson (2006) has termed 'the religious community' and 'the dynastic realm'. Under such a premodern form of sovereignty, society is organised vertically around 'a high centre whose legitimacy derives from divinity, not from populations' (Anderson 2006: 19); nor does political legitimacy derive from territory. We can see the importance of territory emerge in the changing conceptualisation of the body politic. In Confucian cosmopolitical order, the political body would be considered ill because of immoral and corrupt rule. It would be the duty of the Confucian literati to restore it to health. However, in response to China's encounter with Western and Japanese imperialisms, the metaphor of the body was *territorialised*. According to the then emergent nationalist rationality, losing claim to a frontier territory amounted to political dismemberment or even death. Overlapping and changing sovereignty over the borderland hence became problematic. Territory must be permanently defended. As Chinese President Xi Jinping expressed to then US Defence Secretary Jim Mattis in 2018: 'We cannot even lose one inch of territory left behind by our ancestors. What is other people's we do not want at all' (Stewart and Blanchard 2018).

While this new political rationality enabled Qing scholars and officials to comprehend and respond to foreign imperialist challenges, it also subjugated complex spaces and overlapping sovereignty to empire-wide strategic considerations. Conceptualising the Qing Empire (hence 'China') as a self-contained territory unambiguously demarcated from its rival states has had devastating effects on the frontier peoples and places, for their complex, and hence impure, orientations and loyalties became objects of permanent suspicion and surveillance. The point of foregrounding this epistemic disjuncture is not to idealise the early Qing and its conquests. Rather, I seek to show that, for centuries before modern imperialism globalised the nation-state paradigm, people were not required to have the same culture, language, or values to share a world; the land they lived on did not have to be permanently reified as a fixed, sovereign geo-body for sociopolitical life to be meaningful.

While Han scholars had presented economic arguments for integrating Xinjiang to ease the burden of overpopulation in China proper as early as 1826 (Millward 1998: 243), the proposal was only given new legitimacy under the epistemic paradigm of the modern state. As the Qing was shuffled through the era of New Imperialism (1870–1914), its emergent epistemic infrastructure of the modern state engendered not just discursive shifts, but also material and institutional reforms. After the 1878–81 reconquest, Zuo Zongtang proposed establishing a Xinjiang province. The court authorised Zuo, with his Han officials and armies, to replace the multiple indirect systems of local authorities with Chinese-style administration (郡县), to integrate Xinjiang into China proper (Millward 2007: 132). The assumption underlying the series of integrationist policies across multiple frontiers—such as promoting Han migration and training non-Han elites in Confucian schools for magistrate positions—was that, to make frontier regions governable, they had to be demographically and culturally more like the Han-dominated China proper (Millward 2007: 138). At this moment, the Muslimness of the Turkic peoples was not seen as oppositional to 'Chineseness'. The Sinicising agenda was to make

Turkic-speaking peoples—first, the elites and, later, the commoners—into morally Confucian Muslims, so they could become more loyal to the throne (Schluessel 2020). The Confucian pedagogy was short-lived and unsuccessful, lasting only until the Qing was overthrown in 1911. But the Sinicising and modernising mission pioneered by Zuo Zongtang continued into the twentieth and twenty-first centuries, and acquired new, deadly force when married with a change in temporal horizons. As linear, progressive time swept through the epistemic ground of late-Qing elites via new social-scientific concepts, and the concept of *minzu* (民族, usually translated as 'nation', 'nationality', 'race', or 'ethnicity') arrived from Japan, the Central Asian Muslims and their temporalities came to be rendered distant and Other, while the territory in which they lived was being integrated into an imagined sovereign body of China.

The social scientific and the aporia of *minzu*: Separate and the same

The ambiguity of the concept *minzu* has long haunted Chinese nationalism. The term was first introduced from the Japanese word *minzoku* (itself a neologism for the German word *Volk*, meaning 'people' or 'nation') in the early 1900s, after the Qing's alarming defeat in the First Sino-Japanese War (1894–95) (Leibold 2006: 213). Han revolutionaries in the late Qing began to use this concept as a new epistemic ground for their anti-Qing activism. The old culturalist distinction between Han and Manchu was insufficient to justify their opposition to a royal house that had successfully assimilated itself into the Confucian and other ritual institutions (Mullaney 2010: 23). Revolutionaries promoted the concepts of *Hanzu* (汉族) and *Manzu* (满族) as unassimilable racial categories and framed their opposition as a majority race's struggle against a conquering minority race (Duara 1995: 37). After the Qing were overthrown in 1911, the Nationalists of the Guomindang (国民党, GMD) found the discourse of a racially pure Han China inexpedient, as the same nation–race equation had fuelled growing self-determination movements in the former inner Asian frontiers, which they had no intention of relinquishing. The solution for the GMD under the stewardship of Sun Yat-sen (1866–1925) was to extend the recognition of *minzu* status to the Manchu, Mongol, Hui, and Tibetan peoples alongside the Han and unify them into one people, so the frontier regions in which they lived could be incorporated into the new nation-state.

Sun Yat-sen's theory of *minzu* offers a glimpse into the constitutive paradox of *minzu* and its propensity for majoritarianism. As Foucault has pointed out, modern statecraft in eighteenth-century Europe depended on 'the emergence of the problem of population', through which statistics and other social-scientific practices became central to the legitimation and exercise of political power (Chakrabarty 2002: 83–91). The very idea of good government—fairness and justice in political representation—relies on mathematical notions of enumeration and proportionality. In the age of calculability, a numerically larger community carries more political weight. In Sun's famous 1924 lecture on nationalism, he maintained that *minzu* was a community that shared five common traits: blood, religion, language, economy, and customs. What about the Tibetans, Mongols, Manchu, Turkic, and other peoples who might not share these traits with the Han? Sun dismissed them as numerically insignificant: 'The "non-natives" [外来] merely make up less than ten million. We can say that the four hundred million Chinese people are entirely *Hanzu*: sharing a common blood, common language, common religion, and common customs—a single, pure *minzu*' (Sun 2006). Measured through the statistical apparatus of population, the theoretical equality between *minzu* promised by the new Republic of China failed to bring real equality. Rather, because everyone was equal regardless of *minzu*—that is, statistically the same—the numerical majority became politically privileged.

As the Japanese invasion and annexation of Manchuria broke into a full-scale war with the Republic of China in 1937, the GMD and the Chinese Communist Party (CCP) came to a critical convergence through which the theory of *minzu* and its contradictions began to be put into practice. Before 1937, the CCP, under the tutelage of the Communist International, was committed to the rights to self-determination of non-Han peoples, setting itself apart from the GMD's 'great Han chauvinism' (大汉族主义). This period marked a pivotal transformation of the CCP from a marginal oppositional movement that had been critical of the GMD's assimilationist *minzu* policies, to a nationalist rival with similar goals as the GMD. During the Second United Front (1937–45), the two parties agreed on the notion of China—that is, the sovereignty of the Republic of China over all former Qing territories except the already independent Mongolia—and the imperative to defend it against Japan. They also agreed that during the war, it was necessary to centre the representation of the Chinese nation (中华民族) both despite (from the communist internationalist perspective) and through (from the CCP and GMD nationalist perspective) the unambiguous privileging of the Han in this imagination. It was the only way to mobilise the numerical majority to join the resistance movement (Liu 2018: 122).

Hence, they faced a challenge: how to stretch the narrow skin of an apparently Han-centric representation over immense ethnocultural and political diversity? Meanwhile, Japanese scholars and agents were tirelessly coopting non-Han elites in the frontier regions to install anti-Han nationalist regimes under Japanese imperial patronage (Leibold 2006). Their persuasive strategies relied on theories of ethnic-racial distinction between the Manchus, Mongols, Hui, and so on, on one hand, and the Han on the other, drawing on modern scientific disciplines such as history, anthropology, and archaeology to authenticate their claims of different national origins from the Han (Leibold 2006).

This strategy of divide/define and conquer incited seemingly opposite but equally nationalistic responses from the GMD and the CCP as both sought to derive legitimacy from the social sciences. The Nationalist regime blended the scientific theory of race with a revised myth of ancestry according to which the Mongols, Manchu, Tibetans, and Muslims, along with the Han, were all descendants of the mythical Yellow Emperor (黄帝), who was (and is) commonly believed to be the progenitor of the Han. By stretching the narrative of a common ancestor, the GMD regime justified assimilationist policies as a project of reunion (Mullaney 2010: 28).

The Communists objected to this single-race theory as unscientific and Han chauvinistic (Chen 1943, quoted in CCP UFWD 1991). Yet having recognised the sovereignty of the Nationalist regime over all former Qing territory, the CCP was ultimately constrained. It could advocate only for a plural singularity of the nation-state by recognising non-Han communities as 'the minority *minzu*' (少数民族) and not plural political formations such as federalism. This was evident in their discursive shift on the minority question. In the 1931 Constitution of the Chinese Soviet Republic, the CCP proclaimed that it 'categorically and unconditionally recognizes the right of minority minzu to self-determination', which included the right of independence (quoted in Mullaney 2010: 26). In 1938, Mao Zedong announced in his report titled 'On the New Phase' (论新阶段) that the CCP allows the Mongol, Hui, Tibetan, Miao, Yao, Yi, Fan, and other *minzu* to have equal rights as the Han, and based on the principle of a united anti-Japanese front, have the rights to manage its own affairs, and to ally with the Han to build a unified state. (Mao 1938)

The CCP in 1938 was no longer a marginal revolutionary movement that acceded to the minority right of self-determination to undermine the legitimacy of the Republican state. Under duress from the GMD onslaughts, the Soviet reluctance to provide aid, the alienation in non-Han communities during the Long March (1934–36), and Japanese imperialism, the CCP changed strategies and positioned itself as a spokesperson of the state and official nationalism: it conditionally granted the minority *minzu* recognition and autonomy, but only if they performed the required duties as national minorities, meaning, conditionally sovereign and less-than-sovereign minorities.

Furthermore, the CCP's anti-imperialist struggle was imperially conscripted in its very efforts to recognise 'the minority *minzu*' as distinct categories and build an inclusive, progressive nation. In addition to statistics, the CCP shared another set of social-scientific premises with the imperial powers it sought to subvert. The epistemic ground that enabled modern practices of definition (such as the *minzu* classification) is well articulated by the anthropologist Johannes Fabian's (2014: 27) genealogy of naturalised Time in European conceptual–colonial history—that is, 'the classification of entities or traits which first have to be separate and distinct before their similarities can be used to establish taxonomies and developmental sequences'. This presupposed essential separation and distance between 'primitive' and 'civilised' societies have been the justification for colonial plunder and conversion. What is more tragic is that communist regimes reproduced such violence in the name of anti-imperialism. In 1949, Joseph Stalin urged the CCP leadership to occupy Xinjiang immediately to keep the British from activating the Muslims against the Chinese communists, 'for there are large deposits of oil and cotton in Xinjiang, which China needs badly' ('Memorandum …' 1949). While repudiating the crude racism of the West, the Soviet and Chinese communists upheld the same 'primitive or civilised' distinction. Like European colonists, the communist state-builders viewed indigenous peoples as incapable of self-rule, their land available for occupation, and their resources ready for extraction.

When this boundary-drawing exercise is recruited to do the work of imperial domination and, ironically, anti-imperial nationalism, the aporia for the colonial civilising mission and national incorporation is continuous. Hui, Mongol, Uyghur, and Han had to be first objectified as distinct, self-contained entities (the non-Han represented as backward vis-a-vis the Han) before their contacts and exchanges could be used to establish developmental sequences of ethnic melding and unity, thereby establishing the necessity of the CCP leadership in bringing about the historically inevitable progress (CCP UFWD 1991). Unity, therefore, no matter how passionately represented, is always subjected to suspicion. How can fundamentally separate and distinct entities be truly unified as one? Surely some Tibetans or Mongols or Uyghurs still harbour their parochial loyalties and must be constantly surveilled and purified into transcendent citizens of China? The impossible task of the nation-state is to define permanent difference and rule it to its extinction. By accepting separation as the premise of diversity and progress as the universal temporality, the Communists did not just appropriate imperial tools for emancipatory ends. Their political formations were too powerfully altered by the imperial epistemic infrastructure. Tragically, since the CCP came to power in 1949, their imperially constrained political rationalities have reproduced the hierarchical distinction between the self and the Other, the majority and the minority—an underlying epistemic infrastructure that has made conceivable the mass detention, surveillance, and control of Turkic Muslims in Xinjiang today.

Unlearning progress

In a press conference on 26 March 2021, China's Foreign Ministry spokesperson Hua Chunying denounced the US charge of genocide in Xinjiang by invoking precedents of US imperial wars waged in the name of human rights:

> [The United States'] true intention is to undermine China's security and stability and stop China from growing stronger. We solemnly inform the US side that today's China is neither Iraq nor Syria, still less the late Qing Dynasty downtrodden by the Eight-Power Allied Forces ... We have full resolution, determination and capability to firmly defend national sovereignty, security, dignity, and honour. (Hua 2021)

I am deeply pained by this statement because my ancestors were survivors of imperial and nationalist wars. This proud proclamation of counterhegemony is authorised by progress. Yet progress is entangled in separation, competition, and domination. Must China be not Iraq, not Syria, and not the late Qing to defend 'sovereignty, security, dignity, and honour'? Do the multitudes of communities in and of Iraq, Syria, and the Qing not deserve safety and sanctity? Do the displacement and destruction of their life-worlds—which are also our shared, entangled life-worlds—not demand outrage and mourning? How are some of us infuriated only because China has become the second strongest yet still cannot win the game, but not because the game of the nation-state itself is unjust and rooted in long-run imperial histories?

As Talal Asad (2003) has argued, secular modernity has to do with a radical change in the distribution of pain and the rationality that justifies it. Modern cruelties of warfare, colonisation, incarceration, and forced labour are normalised by 'a secular calculus of utility and a secular dream of happiness' (Asad 2006: 508). Just as the US invasion of Afghanistan was justified by the mission to 'save' Afghan women from (allegedly anti-modern) Islamic patriarchy, the PRC has rationalised its cruelties towards the Turkic Muslims today as 'saving' the Muslim masses (women and children in particular), who are seen as pawns of 'separatism, extremism, and terrorism'—simply because they have been defined as not Han, and hence, not safely Chinese. Since the ascendancy of the modern state, the pain inflicted by secularism and nation-building has been justified as necessary for the elimination of what is seen as excessive, backward 'religious' and 'traditional' pain. Yet, as made evident by both the US occupation of and withdrawal from Afghanistan and the Xinjiang camps, the violence of civilisation is enmeshed in—and hence deserves no less scrutiny than—the violence of so-called backwardness. Ultimately, liberal and communist regimes are not so far apart on the secular calculation of pain and gain.

In situating the present state terrorism in Xinjiang within the longer-run history of imperial epistemic violence that has underpinned Chinese nationalism and modernity, I seek to de-exceptionalise China and gesture to the difficult yet not impossible task of decolonising the political. While early Chinese communism has its specificities, its reproduction of imperial technologies of violence should be viewed as part of the shared paradoxical struggles in many postcolonial contexts. The CCP's impasse is not unlike how European settler-colonial regimes first denied colonised subjects the recognition and rights of nationhood, and then granted them the recognition, but without altering colonial regimes of domination (Massad 2018). As David Scott (1999: 45) has noted in another context, as in the seventeenth-century colonial reforms in Ceylon (present-day Sri Lanka) that allowed certain colonised subjects to participate in representative institutions,

> the crucial point here is not whether natives were included or excluded so much as the introduction of a new game of politics that the colonized would (eventually) be obliged to play if they were to be counted as political.

As important as it is to hold the Chinese state accountable, my goal is less to critique the PRC than to reflect on how the political itself—namely, nation-state formation—is an effect of colonisation. Perhaps, by revealing the peculiar epistemic apparatus of imperially conscripted nationalism—that territory must be defended, the population homogenised, and communities separated and objectified—we are able to see China's anti-imperialism as reenacting the founding epistemic and material violence of the modern nation-state. It is time to look for another way.

2
Revolution and state formation as oasis storytelling in Xinjiang[*]

Zenab Ahmed

No-one can say the world is ignoring Xinjiang. In October 2019, at the American Association of Christian Counsellors, US Secretary of State Mike Pompeo likened China's treatment of more than a million Uyghur Muslims in the Xinjiang Uyghur Autonomous Region to George Orwell's *1984* (Reuters 2019). This was while the Trump White House began placing sanctions on Chinese governmental and business organisations involved with the now infamous reeducation camps in the region. In June 2020, Pompeo went further to condemn alleged mass sterilisations and, the following month, the US Departments of State, Commerce, and Homeland Security issued a joint 'Xinjiang Supply Chain Business Advisory' targeted at forced labour in the province (South China Morning Post 2020; US State Department 2020). China has been condemned by representatives from more than 20 countries, with the notable exception of Muslim-majority states that have important trading relationships with Beijing such as Pakistan, Uzbekistan, Iran, and Iraq (AFP 2019; Shams 2019; Kerimkhanov 2019; Liu 2019; Calabrese 2019).

Yet, in the current political climate, with the United States and China engaged in a protracted trade war and the War on Terror evolving into rapidly intensifying Islamophobia and the use of concentration camps the world over, important details about Chinese objectives in Xinjiang have been poorly discussed in the mass media. Academics, journalists, and politicians are right in noting that Beijing is using the camps as a tool for social reengineering, to force Xinjiang's 'integration' into the Chinese political and cultural mainstream. Nevertheless, this analysis, while correct, risks overlooking long-term economic goals in the region—most notably, Xinjiang's importance to the Belt and Road Initiative (BRI), as well as the CCP's existential opposition to the ideological threat of Uyghur ethnic,

*A slightly different version of this essay was published in the *Made in China Journal* (vol. 5, no. 1, 2020), doi.org/10.22459/MIC.05.01.2020.03. The article has been revised and updated for inclusion in this volume.

cultural, and spiritual distinctiveness. Ultimately, what is often left out is that the CCP's social engineering appears to be creating a new kind of post-communist and post-Islamic society in Xinjiang that will likely be on the cutting edge of similar pushes for mass surveillance and ethnic cleansing all over the world.

The new frontier

First, it is useful to give a brief overview of Xinjiang. Xinjiang literally means 'New Border' or 'New Frontier' and demarcates a territory that was conquered by the expanding Qing Dynasty in the 1760s. The region represents about one-sixth of China's total land area and includes 5,600 kilometres of international borders with eight countries, including Russia, several former Soviet republics in Central Asia, Pakistan, India, and Afghanistan. Xinjiang has two distinct subregions: Dzungaria, which is north of the Tianshan Mountains, and the Tarim Basin, which is largely a desert to its south. Most Uyghurs live in the Tarim Basin, which has half a dozen major cities on the edges of the Taklamakan Desert—hence the Turkic name 'Altishahr', which means 'Six Cities' and which will be used stylistically throughout this article as a synonym for indigeneity. After the Chinese Revolution in 1949, 10 ethnic groups were classified as 'Muslim' minorities, including the Uyghurs in Xinjiang.

Before the Qing Dynasty, the Altishahri economy prospered from complex trading networks along the Silk Road, with merchant commerce reinforcing highly cosmopolitan and only loosely hierarchical readings of Central Asian Sufism that are difficult to assimilate into modern state institutions without alteration. Following the Qing Dynasty's conquest, local rulers led frequent revolts against Beijing during a period of Chinese expansion, population growth, and prosperity that would start to decline shortly before the Opium Wars. It was the violent suppression of these revolts that began to shift ruling-class attitudes towards Muslims in China, and Uyghurs in particular. The region's Muslims were treated with hostility during the Republican era (1911–49), and particularly so due to continued violence from loyalist Muslim members of the Guomindang, who fought in China's western provinces throughout the 1950s (Jacobs 2016).

Apart from its geopolitical significance, Xinjiang has been cultivated as a major food production centre in China, serving as the country's second-largest pastureland (including major sheep farming and wool production), and its largest growing base for cotton, hops, lavender, and other important crops. Xinjiang is also rich in energy resources, with the country's largest oil, natural gas, and coal reserves, in addition to 130 different kinds of minerals. Many of these resources are being exploited by the Bingtuan (兵团), which is shorthand for the Xinjiang Production and Construction Corps (see Cliff's photo essay in Chapter 6 and Salimjan's Chapter 7 in this volume). While the Bingtuan employs about 12 per cent of Xinjiang's population, more than 80 per cent of its workforce are Han Chinese. The Bingtuan has been operating since 1954 as a paramilitary development organisation, and reports directly to Beijing, rather than the local government. While its original objectives were to ensure the settlement of Han Chinese immigrants, to change the province's demographic balance, to maintain security internally and along international borders, and to project the power of the 'centre', the Bingtuan has developed a complex, multisectoral economy based on food and agriculture. The Bingtuan also controls important technological, cultural, health, and judicial infrastructure and, in many cases, was responsible for building it.

Many of today's problems in Xinjiang were severely exacerbated by Beijing's Open Up the West Campaign (西部大开发) in the 1990s, which aimed to increase Han Chinese immigration to Xinjiang through a system of economic and social incentives. It was in the 1990s that the CCP first began to promote people moving to Xinjiang with rhetoric about ethnic unity, national integrity and stability, religious activities being opposed to the state, and anti-separatism, among other things. The campaign resulted in huge wage and labour gaps between Han Chinese and Uyghurs and other local minorities, especially in the professional and managerial class. Uneven access to state institutions and jobs created, and then reinforced, spatial divisions in cities, worsening ethnic apartheid and gaps in living standards. Since the 1990s, China has adopted a policy of 'creative destruction', whereby it destroys cultural religious sites, but also funds educational, religious, and tourist infrastructure to integrate the non-threatening remnants of 'Altishahri' indigeneity (see Thum's Chapter 10 in this volume). The global outcry has tended to focus on the more destructive parts of Beijing's approach—for understandable reasons—but this ignores how the CCP is simultaneously creating a new kind of post-communist and post-Islamic society in Xinjiang that is driven as much by technological advances as by its own conventional and managerial world view.

Altishahri integration

While Beijing often accuses Uyghur political agitators of separatism (though it has steadily updated this rhetoric over the past 20 years to be more about 'fighting terrorism'), 'separatism' as a term is very reductive and does not fit the complexity of Altishahri spiritual and political thought. Indeed, its unique reading of Islam, legends, and history reflects a dynamic cosmopolitanism produced in part by Silk Road merchant commerce that is often hard to define for bureaucratic and managerial purposes. This is largely the reason 'Islam' often means so many different things with respect to the Uyghurs. It is common to hear Beijing, or workers in the Bingtuan, label anything from language to ethnicity to diverse spiritual rituals as 'Islamic'. Xinjiang is unique, with multiple sources of Muslimness and seemingly 'non-Islamic' markers like the Turkic language that are nevertheless attached to Islam in popular and institutional consciousness. It is important to fully appreciate this cosmology and understand it within the local context rather than from the standpoint of conservative and statist ideologies—if only to avoid unintentionally reinforcing the CCP's efforts to brand 'Uyghur' as a neatly bounded identity that is essentialised for administrative and bureaucratic ease. Indeed, even Uyghur exiles and political activists risk adopting the language of separatism, nationalism, and even Islamism, in a manner that reshapes local understandings of politics and struggle while sidelining a properly Altishahri approach.

Altishahri ideas about resistance are rooted in a blend of Silk Road cultural traditions shaped by the active veneration of Sufi saints and community-authored manuscripts. It is this tradition that China seeks to crush in favour of ideas that are more compatible with a centrally managed approach to religion and identity. The local vocabulary is heavily influenced by Sufi Naqshbandi Islamic orders that arose in Central Asia in the fourteenth century, with Semitic, Iranic, and Turkic influences (Thum 2014). By the 1930s, this mixture became roughly equal to a 'Uyghur' identity strongly affected by Sufi cosmology. Traditionally, local history is taught at the tombs of important figures ('shrines') where *shaykhs* tell pilgrims different stories about them. This storytelling has a great deal of spiritual legitimacy, often because it is literally about the same ground on which these figures walked. There are also political consequences because, when pilgrims go to the shrines and remember these figures, they go over the historical record and meditate on the 'higher' values associated with them. This puts them in the position of noting the gap between these values, such as freedom and justice, and the world around them, which can potentially lead to utopian thinking that is represented in the memory of the figures themselves. Important manuscripts, written by the local community, also encourage utopian thinking in a similar process. It is useful to consider Altishahri thought as a kind of 'active mysticism' through which meditation and worship start to blend with political activity, without strict distinctions between the secular and the religious.

It is important to distinguish 'active mysticism' from the kinds of mysticism with which Western observers are normally familiar, which is seen as something a worshipper does in isolation from the rest of the world. Indeed, while local Islamic practice does contain these forms, mysticism can also mean a variety of activities that are explicitly rooted in the ways one deals with society. Mysticism is not only about one's personal spiritual needs outside the community. It is also explicitly about how those needs are expressed through interactions with the community (which is what makes it 'active'). Worship can take many different forms, only one of which is private apolitical meditation. In Xinjiang, one person may tell a tale about a Sufi mystic, at their shrine, with that storytelling being an expression of worship in a similar way to a pilgrim hearing that tale. More radically, a pilgrim may hear that tale and be inspired to interact with the community in ways that correspond to the spiritual themes of the story. Such actions could be anything from marrying a suitable partner and treating one's elderly relatives with respect, to giving money to the poor and waging armed struggle against the Chinese state. Behaviour in the real world reflects the sorts of ideals drawn from the story.

Beijing has shut down shrines and ended Uyghur Islamic practice, but also reshaped activities at other shrines and inserted itself into the regulation of manuscripts, because it is threatened by the political ramifications of this active mysticism. It coopts local spirituality by controlling the *shaykhs* who lead it and emphasising the kind of storytelling that gives rise to forms of community interaction more aligned with its strategic objectives in the region. As a result, Beijing effectively positions itself to rearticulate the local transmission of knowledge and spirituality, with a significant impact on its political landscape. It is like changing the textbooks students use to make them think a certain way.

Rian Thum (2012) explains this process through the example of Afaq Khojah. Afaq was the founder of a line of rebellious Sufi leaders in the seventeenth century and, over the past three centuries, narratives about him have been occasionally reshaped based on changing politics and shifting definitions of what is considered properly 'local' to Xinjiang. Starting in the 1930s, Afaq's tale was reconfigured as an ethno-national history of rebellion and independence from China, which is often portrayed as a 'distant city' in the local manuscript tradition. Beijing has made dramatic changes to how Afaq is understood, whether in the manuscripts themselves (CCP officials confiscate or destroy copies of the popular historical novel *Apaq Khoja*) or the oasis history about which pilgrims hear at his shrine. Indeed, CCP-appointed *shaykhs* and the local tourist industry tend to place more emphasis on his descendant Xiang Fei (香妃), who is also buried at his shrine and was known as the 'fragrant concubine'. Legend has it that the Qianglong Emperor was so enamoured with Xiang's beauty that he brought her from Xinjiang to be a consort at the Royal Court. Effectively, therefore, rather than values of liberation and resistance associated with the story of Afaq Khojah, pilgrims and tourists now learn to value the Han–Uyghur cultural fusion at the core of this romance. As such, the shrine has largely been neutralised, with the role of gender in reconfiguring the spiritual tale being particularly significant, since the Uyghurs are now represented by a passive and seductive female who captures the emperor's benevolent attention, rather than her male ancestor who violently pushed back against the Chinese Empire.

Clearly, the takeaway is that Uyghurs need to be seen and not heard. They are allowed to be exotified by middle-class tourists but can never be political subjects in their own right. As Afaq's tale and shrine have always been reformulated based on changing political and economic forces, they have now morphed in respect to Beijing's new regional and global ambitions. For their part, Chinese officials often say they are attempting to guard Xinjiang from foreign influence and are seeking to prevent Islamic extremism. Yet, the reality is that Beijing often seeks to redesign Uyghur Islam to make it more compatible with the needs of modern China. Prominent Uyghur activists, as well as international observers, often participate in this redesign by simplifying Altishahri resistance as separatism by a culturally distinct population, a nationalistic backlash to human rights violations, or an internal problem of Islamic extremism and terrorism. These framings often reflect the intricacies of the foreign powers and institutions being lobbied, whether in Ankara, Washington, Geneva, or at the United Nations. These interpretations of the province's cultural and political landscape are often more about the observers and their need to impose certain historical and geopolitical narratives on the situation. Ultimately, the Uyghurs are the ones who lose the most, as Altishahri cosmology is largely deleted and reorganised to fit within the authoritarian requirements of China's emerging imperial model.

Communism as forced baptism

Integration is necessarily a process of deletion and substitution as the target population is shaped to be more manageable by the ruling class. The War on Terror has created a global climate in which Muslim minorities face unprecedented scrutiny—including in long-established democracies like France, the United States, and the United Kingdom—and in which government agencies root out 'extremists' and appeal to moderate Muslims who profess loyalty to the state. Yet, it would be misleading to characterise Beijing's conduct as the latest chapter in a period of worldwide Islamophobia. Rather, the integration of Xinjiang is a heavy-handed push to wipe out all but a sliver of the Altishahri backdrop that preceded the current period, while leaving fragments that can be assimilated into state administration (in addition to important tourist and cultural production industries in the province).

Like other post-communist states, China does not ban Islam outright. Indeed, such a move would be counterproductive, given its ambitions as a global actor and its strategic partnerships with majority-Muslim countries. Instead, Beijing pushes to create a distinctly 'Chinese Islam' that trims perceived Altishahri excess, at the same time as wiping out the basis for its independent existence as a social form. Xinjiang's surveillance and concentration camp infrastructure serves both purposes—simultaneously crushing and reorganising the Uyghurs—to create a new human landscape in the area. While not anti-Muslim, this landscape will confine Islamic practice to a few tolerated spaces and forms, with a new, implicitly Han Chinese and CCP-controlled, secular culture dominating the region.

Since 2017, hundreds of thousands of Uyghur Muslims (out of a population of about 11 million) have moved through holding cells in the Xinjiang prison system before being handed long sentences or indefinite internment in concentration camps that push 'transformation through education'. The camps effectively function as medium-security prisons, with 'vocational training' that seems directed at teaching Uyghurs to disavow Islam and embrace secular allegiance to Beijing. Since there is no clear definition of what 'Islam' even means with respect to the Uyghurs, the word 'allegiance' should be understood as a euphemism for the forced adoption of irreligion under duress. When the CCP or institutions linked to Beijing speak of 'integration' and 'fundamentalism', they are referring to this process of rooting out beliefs and practices. The approach parallels that of other major powers in previous centuries—the assimilation policies of the United States, Canada, and Australia towards their indigenous populations immediately come to mind—with the notable addition of huge technological advances.

Speaking at the Left Forum 2019, Darren Byler cited a spokesperson from Leon Technology—an information technology company providing services to the government in Xinjiang—to show how this tension projects a racialised desire for control on the issue. Byler said the spokesperson, who was at the Ürümqi security trade fair in 2017, noted: 'Anyone who has been to Kashgar will know that the atmosphere there was really thick and imposing' (Zhang 2017). The words 'thick' and 'imposing' mean 'Uyghur' in this context, and Leon Technology was building an artificial intelligence (AI) project to learn from this 'thick and imposing atmosphere', to make it more manageable and legible to Beijing. Indeed, the spokesperson went on to say: 'Through the continuous advancement of the project, we have a network of 10,000 video access points in the surrounding rural [Kashgar] area, which will generate massive amounts of video. This many images will bind many people.' It is difficult not to see what is really going on.

Leon Technology is one of many firms working with Beijing on the mass surveillance and incarceration projects that have been set up in Xinjiang at an accelerated rate since the declaration of the People's War on Terror in 2014 (see also Byler's Chapter 14 in this volume). Reports from the camps themselves—officially called 'Vocational Education and Training Centres' (职业技能教育培训中心)—often shock audiences with descriptions of how Beijing's goals are enforced by state-of-the-art technology. TV monitors are used to deliver the state curriculum in cells and classrooms, while detainees are closely monitored. They are disciplined via speaker systems if they sleep at the wrong times, express what are seen to be Islamic traditions, speak Uyghur, or otherwise behave 'improperly'. Technology is also used to terrorise the Uyghurs outside the camps, with transnational corporations like Google, Huawei, Facebook, and Hikvision interlinking with venture capitalists from the major powers—including the United States—to build a sprawling AI-based policing infrastructure for the Chinese state. Millions of people in the region are now subjected to smartphone scans, wiretaps, location tracking, and regular 3D facial and voice scans at local police stations that create biometric databases for Chinese intelligence agencies (see also Loubere and Brehm's Chapter 13 in this volume). It is very likely that as President Xi Jinping pushes China towards becoming a 'cyber superpower', the slow erasure and rewriting of Uyghur Islamic practice will be touted as a pioneering victory for social control to be repeated elsewhere.

Towards a new Altishahri resistance

While this combination of mass incarceration, the tech sector, ethnic erasure, and discussions of Islamic terrorism and extremism may seem new, it relies on a classical imperial push to control and neutralise difference that has led to concentration camps under every other major global power. Indeed, there is not much difference, in terms of state behaviour, between China's activities in Xinjiang and the Spanish Empire's in Cuba, the British Empire's in South Africa, and so on (Pitzer 2017). The history of concentration camps is one of societal anxieties leading to undesirable populations being caged and then stripped of what is seen as making them threatening. As China builds the military and trading infrastructure to compete with the world's richest countries, it is also building its equivalents of the migrant detention centres on the Australian, European, and US–Mexico borders and colonial prisons in Abu Ghraib, Guantanamo Bay, and Bagram Air Base. The danger is that this is just the beginning, and these versions of the authoritarian policing technology being used in Xinjiang will eventually be exported throughout the BRI, whether in northwestern Pakistan or eastern Europe. Notably, several private Chinese security companies have joined the Frontier Group, which is affiliated with Erik Prince, in Central Asia, making clear the intertwined global reach of both Chinese and US counterterrorism forces—something made possible despite Beijing facing a torrent of popular criticism and international pushback due to its policies in western China.

Beijing is in the process of creating a new kind of Xinjiang, in which Uyghur cultural, spiritual, and political expression are severely limited and placed below the needs of a new secular (and multicultural) polity. While it is tempting to believe that oppression of the Uyghurs will limit its ambitions—particularly considering the international outcry—the likely reality is Chinese internal imperialism and social reengineering will mark the beginning of a new phase of capitalist governance. Certainly, the technology being used in Xinjiang will become more widespread, but the same goes for the way that local culture and distinctiveness are being destroyed and violently brought in line with the CCP's ideas about top-down management and social control. One could argue that the techniques on display in Xinjiang are more refined versions of tactics initially fine-tuned during European imperialism, with particularly fruitful comparisons possible with the settlement of Australasia and the Americas. Obviously, the questions of genocide and population settlement are different in the two cases, but the shared point is a new world being built on the colonial frontier that erases its indigenous precursors and serves as an exemplar for future governance.

Left-wing observers of Xinjiang have the chance to use Beijing's oppressive policies as an excuse to consider Uyghur spiritual and cultural material as a source of political resistance, including outside the region itself. This will likely be a prolonged process in conjunction with Uyghur scholars, and risks being counterproductive due to how academic and governmental requirements are likely to also reshape Altishahri consciousness. As Xinjiang goes global, it is unlikely that one will find a pure form of the complex societal medley that emerged from Silk Road trading across Central Asia. Nevertheless, it is certainly possible to appreciate how the Uyghurs may continue to be subjects of their own history, inspired by the manuscripts, oasis storytelling, and 'active mysticism' that alarm Beijing and the CCP. Certainly, this is a helpful approach to countering the War on Terror in general, as David Brophy has written with reference to the simplified rhetoric of 'good Muslim' versus 'bad Muslim' in his chapter in this volume. Yet even beyond the need for Uyghur agency, as Brophy writes, it is worth considering whether Altishahri resistance in the future can be a source of inspiration for resistance against models of state authoritarianism. Indeed, the reliance on storytelling and religious activity in the mould of Islamic Neoplatonist philosophy is far more likely to hit mass appeal in several BRI countries (especially Pakistan) than established left-wing traditions. It is a question of exploring Altishahri thinking as something that has value outside museums, tourism, and the niche interests of academics—as a source of political understanding that regards history as mythic and inspirational, and storytelling as on the same plane as large-scale insurrection.

3
Blood lineage*

Guldana Salimjan

The concept of blood lineage, or blood line, has been a political ideology of many monarchical regimes and aristocratic societies throughout history. The rise of nationalism in Europe in the seventeenth and eighteenth centuries paralleled the discourse about purity and the authenticity of one's blood/race. In the context of national formation, blood is a metaphor for race, ethnicity, and sexuality that enacts loyalty, belonging, and national consciousness. Blood lineage can be a malleable narrative explaining the Self and the Other, a rigid disciplinary tool reinforcing hierarchy, or a fluid signifier for social groups seeking belonging and protection. This chapter delineates the political ideology of blood lineage in China through different historical periods, with particular attention paid to its modern evolution from facilitating class struggle as a tool of social control during the Cultural Revolution, to a racialised system of securitisation that is currently occurring in the Xinjiang Uyghur Autonomous Region.

Imperial China's rulers adopted the use of blood-based ties to clarify the hereditary rights of power and property, and as a tool for social management to distinguish between royalty, civilians, and slaves. For example, the imperial Chinese punishment of collective responsibility (株连九族, literally, 'guilt by association of nine of a group/clan') and the politics of lineage, or blood relations, played an important role in moulding, disciplining, and confining people to the social roles prescribed for them. People were expected to stay in their place in society, and transgression of the boundaries of their socially or politically ordained blood lines could be met with severe punishment. In Chinese, 氏族 or 宗族 represents a group tied by blood relationships as a family or a clan, led by lineage heads (族长), with its family history and genealogy recorded as 族谱. In the late nineteenth and early twentieth centuries, 族 (zu) took a

*This essay was originally published under the pen-name Yi Xiaocuo in Christian Sorace, Ivan Franceschini, and Nicholas Loubere (eds), *Afterlives of Chinese Communism: Political Concepts from Mao to Xi* (Canberra: ANU Press and Verso Books, 2019), doi.org/10.22459/ACC.2019.

nationalistic turn when the founding father of the Nationalist Party, Sun Yat-sen, indicated that people of the Han or Chinese race had 'common blood' and should stand together as a 'Chinese nationality' (中华民族) facing the threat of extinction under Western imperialism (Dikötter 2015: 78). After the turn of the century and the May Fourth Movement in 1919, the Republic of China was founded under the famous slogan 'Five Races under One Union' (五族共和) to unify Han Chinese and Manchus, Mongols, Tibetans, and Muslims—the major non-Han groups of China as perceived by the Nationalists. Following the Communist victory in 1949, the state's ethnologists classified 55 non-Han peoples and stressed a unified nationality comprising the Han as a majority ethnicity and non-Han as minorities (少数民族) (Bulag 2019). Official discourse aside, popular memories and heroic narratives centred on blood lineage also thrived. For example, the Han nationalist imagination proposed a linear history of ancient China in which an immutable Han racial identity continually existed by identifying themselves as descendants of the mythological Yan and Huang emperors (炎黄子孙).

The 1950s: Building a new nation

After the Chinese Communist Party (CCP) took control of mainland China in the 1950s, the discourse on blood lineage temporarily shifted away from national or racial concerns to struggles over class identity, but the notion of heritability remained. Under Mao Zedong's guidelines for class struggle, individuals were labelled with a class identity according to birth or family relationships. Despite contradicting the socialist goal of eradicating imperial practices, reckoning by blood was effectively institutionalised by those in power through the practice of class struggle, as it justified the monopoly over social and political resources of the privileged while disenfranchising and suppressing vulnerable groups, such as those who did not comply with or challenged such arrangements.

During the early 1950s, Mao's land reform and class-motivated purge of landlords virtually removed the authority of reproductive ties between powerful lineage groups within rural communities. Throughout China, previously ruling classes saw massive socialist transformations: land was confiscated from landlords and distributed to landless and poor peasants and private merchants and capitalist industries gradually became state-owned. Blood became a form by which to assess one's revolutionary subjectivity through family background (出身) or class labels (阶级成分).

The 'good ones' were reproduced and circulated as revolutionary agents within the national body, and the 'bad ones' were identified as reactionary or bad-blooded and outcast. A person's class or family background not only haunted his or her own life, but also the lives of their spouse, children, and other relatives. In Michael Dutton's (2004: 168) words, the class-related political problems recorded on personal dossiers can 'spread like a virus' to the files of their family members, marking them also as untrustworthy, and in this way class becomes a 'blood-borne disease'. The unfavourable classes were labelled the 'Four Black Categories' (黑四类): landlords, rich farmers, counterrevolutionaries, and bad-influencers. After the Anti-Rightist Campaign in 1957, 'rightists' were added to the list, making Five Black Categories.

In non-Han peripheral regions such as Inner Mongolia, Tibet, and Muslim-populated Xinjiang, local political groupings, religious authorities, and hereditary leaderships were also dismantled during the socialist reform. Following Western intellectual traditions of social evolutionism, party cadres and ethnologists depicted the Inner Asian pastoral aristocracy's houses of power as a primitive tribal kinship society (in Chinese, 部落 or 氏族), but also denounced them as 'capitalist' since the rich herders were accused of accumulating capital in the form of livestock and thereby reproducing oppressive class relations in pastoral production. State power materialised in omnipresent institutions in these native communities, such as the 'pastoral office' and the 'pastoral production cooperative', with Han administrators promoting the Communist Party's work and policies in non-Han regions. The discourse on blood lineage in these regions was used to depict pastoral people simultaneously as backwards or stuck in time and having advanced the pastoral economy to a stage of economic modernity in which capitalists could exist, and therefore worthy of persecution.

When necessary, the Party-State was tactical and flexible in instrumentalising lineage as a political tool among the pastoralists; at other times, the state obliterated those lineages when they threatened perceived national interests. As the denunciation of local authorities continued, CCP cadres also reflected on their lack of understanding of pastoral social structure, especially the great social power and influence of lineage heads. They realised pastoral lineage heads were crucial targets for cooptation after careful indoctrination. This method effectively assured the mobilisation of powerful local leaders to assist in the dissemination of party policy, propaganda, and new modes of socialist animal husbandry. For example, in northern Xinjiang, Han ethnologists surveyed the Chinggisid lineage of the Kazakh noble Tore clans in detail and evaluated their productivity, eventually restructuring them into major production brigades as a form of state 'socialist primitive accumulation'.[1] On the eve of Mao's Great Leap Forward (1958–62), interethnic relations became tense due to the expanding people's commune system and a huge influx of Han settlers into traditionally non-Han regions. As the overwhelming scale of socialist transformation in ethnic minority borderlands led to resistance in these regions at the end of the 1950s, the CCP simply denounced the resistance as 'local nationalism' (地方民族主义)—a 'counterrevolutionary' crime to be purged. The ever-shifting target of blood lineage in Xinjiang exemplifies the malleable nature of blood lineage in twentieth-century Chinese politics.

The politics of communist lineage in the Cultural Revolution

During the Cultural Revolution, the idea of blood lineage (血统) was revamped and gained a sinister level of national popularity. At the same time, Mao's notion of the class line (阶级路线) opened a path away from one's background based on one's revolutionary devotedness and political behaviour. Those from good family backgrounds—called the 'Five Red Categories' (红五类): poor and lower–middle peasants, workers, revolutionary soldiers, revolutionary cadres, and revolutionary martyrs— declared they were the legitimate successors of the socialist revolution and 'red by birth' (自来红). The Five Black Categories were expanded to nine, with new additions being capitalists, capitalist roaders, traitors, and spies. In 1966, a couplet began to circulate after appearing at the Beijing Aeronautical Engineering Institute. It read: 'A hero's son is a real man; a reactionary's son is a rotten egg' (老子英雄儿好汉; 老子反动儿混蛋).

At first, high officials in the CCP criticised this blood lineage idea and stressed that one's political behaviour or expression (政治表现) was also important. However, in practice, the hierarchical categorisation and political naming prompted discriminatory policies aimed at

---

1   There are multiple terms to describe genealogical and political groupings in Kazakh society (for example *ulus, ru, juz*) and they are inconsistently translated in English and Chinese sources—a result of early British anthropology's ideological perceptions of 'tribes' and 'clans' in Africa. The Chinese sources for this material used 部落, which in modern Chinese can be loosely translated as clan or tribe. However, as Morton Fried (1966) and Daniel Biebuyck (1966) argue, 'tribe' simplifies the innate complexity of a group's terms for social organisation.

innocent individuals with bad family backgrounds or class labels. It stamped indelible institutional marks on the countless bodies of the Nine Black Categories (黑九类), whose children were euphemistically referred to as 'teachable offspring' (可教育好的子女). In fact, they were deprived of any rights to political or social participation. Under this regime, they had to earn leniency or better treatment through good 'political behaviour' such as making a clean break with their reactionary parents and family backgrounds. Some cases resembled the imperial penal style of 'implicating associates' when the class labels of up to three generations were scrutinised. The 'teachable offspring' were often excluded from opportunities such as joining the army or acceptance into schools. They were subjected to unequal pay and reform through labour, and their unbearable humiliation and torture led to numerous unnatural deaths.

Yu Luoke, a young worker from Beijing, made a powerful counterargument to the Red Guards' principle of blood lineage. Having suffered from the negative impact of his father's 'rightist' background, in 1967, Yu published the essay 'On Family Background' (出身论). Quoting Marxist and Maoist theories, Yu pointed out that one's family background should not be equated with one's political identity and revolutionary consciousness. Moreover, the principle of blood lineage could not justify violence against people without a good family background; in this sense, the Five Red Categories were the oppressors. Yu's argument shook the foundation of the party's revolutionary legitimacy by rendering illegible the categories of class struggle. Without a clearly identified set of heroes and villains, the machinery of class struggle would break down. The party became desperate for a consolidation of self-identity, ideological control, and epistemological certainty. The principle of blood lineage came in handy because it isolated people into different categories and stratifications and screened the political disloyalties of those who could challenge the CCP's status quo. As a result, top officials chose not to follow through with their criticism of blood lineage but instead exploited it as a social governing mechanism. Yu's calls for equal human rights as intrinsic to socialism eventually touched a sensitive nerve with the party authorities. In 1970, he was executed for the crime of 'organising counterrevolutionary groups'.

For non-Han pastoral societies during the Cultural Revolution, the system of class labelling established new hierarchical political categories that replaced previous ones and significantly frayed the fabric of society and individual families. Mongol landlords who leased land to Han peasants were denounced and disenfranchised in the name of class struggle (Bulag 2000). In Tibet, class struggle heightened internal divisions and led to tens of thousands being killed in 'struggle sessions' or sent to reform through labour (Woeser 2020). In northern Xinjiang, nomadic pastoral nobility had formerly protected their lineages by not allowing their women to marry men of lower status, at least in principle. This was reversed after CCP cadres conducted struggle sessions denouncing landlords and aristocrats, and they went as far as forcing marriage across class differences.

Ghosts of blood lineage today

After the Cultural Revolution, the CCP abandoned the principle of blood lineage, but the generation who benefited from it had already attained high positions in powerful national-level political and economic organs. Many have gone on to generate profits for their entire family from corrupt practices and abuses of power, capturing the prosperity produced through the privatisation of public goods during the reform era. Numerous cases have been exposed illustrating the ways in which these second-generation elites and bureaucrats enjoy above-the-law lifestyles and hold billions of dollars in offshore accounts. It has been an unspoken rule in China that the offspring of elite groups inherit their father's privilege; they have been given nicknames such as 'officialings' (官二代), 'red second generation' (红二代), and 'princelings' (太子党).

The ghosts of blood lineage continue to haunt non-Han regions in the twenty-first century as a new era of state racism dawns. While pseudo-traditional symbols of 'Chinese culture' such as the Han costume movement, Confucian memorial ceremonies, and virtue training schools for women mushroomed in mainland China, Tibet and Xinjiang have been increasingly subjected to state-led exploitative development projects at the expense of native peoples and lands. Temporary pluralism and multiculturalism in the reform era have given way to Han-centred empire-building aimed at rooting out ethnic, religious, and cultural differences as social deviancy and disease. This is simultaneously shaped by Western discourses fostered by the US-led War on Terror and global Islamophobia (Roberts 2020). China's use of this discourse has fostered its own industrial complex of 'terror capitalism' (Byler 2021): high-tech Orwellian social control targeted mainly at Turkic Muslim and Tibetan populations. So far, hundreds of thousands of Uyghurs, Kazakhs, Kyrgyz, and other ethnic minorities have been detained indefinitely in 'concentrated reeducation and transformation centres' (集中教育转化中心), without indictment or fair trial. Echoing the West's 'War on Terror' and racialisation of Muslims, Chinese authorities have also framed Uyghurs as 'bad Muslims' (see Brophy's Chapter 4 in this volume) who need to be reengineered through forced political indoctrination and labour. This view of Uyghurs as a dehumanised, racialised Other is clear in a speech by a Han official in Xinjiang:

> You can't uproot all the weeds hidden among the crops in the field one by one—you need to spray chemicals to kill them all. Re-educating these people is like spraying chemicals on the crops. That is why it is a general re-education, not limited to a few people. (Hoshur 2018)

The CCP initially shifted away from the racial/nationalist discourse of mid-twentieth-century political movements, but it has rekindled those flames by explicitly combining the discourse on blood lineage with ethnicity in places like Xinjiang. Blood as a metaphor of social differentiation and guilt by association are implied in leaked official party documents from Xinjiang, in which a point system is utilised to criminalise family members, both in and outside the camps. In this document, officials are instructed to tell students whose parents have disappeared into the detention camps:

> Family members, including you, must abide by the state's laws and rules, and not believe or spread rumors … Only then can you add points for your family member, and after a period of assessment they can leave the school if they meet course completion standards. (Ramzy and Buckley 2019)

This process of hyper-criminalisation is unprecedentedly aided by cutting-edge technologies in biodata collection and surveillance networks. Since the end of 2016, a military technology used for national defence has been applied in Xinjiang, called the Integrated Joint Operation Platform (一体化联合作战平台). This security system instantly gathers data on individuals from multiple sources such as banks, medical providers, and travel histories to analyse, make predictions, and generate lists of suspects. Human Rights Watch (HRW 2018) reports that, under this system, Uyghurs who have been arrested or are deemed 'unsafe' are differentiated from others and their personal dossiers are tagged in a different colour. Xinjiang residents also have been required to fill out a Population Data Collection Form (see Figure 3.1) and report whether they are Uyghur, whether they are 'persons of interest' (beyond a scale of one to five, there exists an extra 特, or special security level), whether they are relatives of a detainee or of someone being subjected to crackdown and punishment, whether they are tagged by the Integrated Platform, and whether they have contacts abroad and how they are related (Chin and Bürge 2017). They also must submit detailed information including their religious habits, whether they have a passport and have travelled abroad, and so on. Moreover, Chinese AI companies such as SenseTime, Hikvision, and CloudWalk have developed facial recognition cameras and DNA tracking to automatically detect Uyghurs by their phenotypes (Mozur 2019). Blood samples and images of irises were also unethically collected from Uyghurs and other targeted groups to aid the development of such DNA phenotyping technologies (Wee and Mozur 2019). The Party-State's population-control measures have metamorphosed into a highly organised blood lineage classification system with layers of class, political, racial, and geographical inputs. Based on the collected data, officials then categorise people in terms of reliability into three groups: safe, average, and unsafe. The collected family information enables the authorities to track down and terrorise people even when they are outside China.

While Uyghur and Kazakh masculinity were ostensibly tamed through carceral governance in Xinjiang, women's bodies became the next frontier for the state to deploy its settler politics in sexuality and reproduction. In its initial nation-making process in the early 1950s, to solve the gender ratio imbalance, the paramilitary settlers of the Xinjiang Production and Construction Corps recruited thousands of female students, soldiers, and prostitutes from Hunan and Shandong provinces to populate the settlements. Following Mao's dictate about 'anti-Han chauvinism' and maintaining border stability, interethnic marriage between Han settlers and local Muslims was strictly prohibited. Though the Han population has continued to increase in the past decades, low rates of Han–minority marriages are seen as an indication of ethnic tension in Xinjiang, while Uyghurs view the avoidance of such interethnic marriages as a type of resistance (Smith Finley 2013). In 2014, the state changed its policy and started to offer incentives to encourage interethnic marriage (Wong 2014). From 2015, propaganda depicting secularised mass weddings as 'new fashion weddings' to delegitimise Islamic *nikah* ceremonies and other indigenous marriage customs as a form of 'counterterrorism' work has become prevalent.

From the debate about blood lineage and class labelling to today's detention of Muslim minorities in Xinjiang, blood is a powerful symbol the Party-State uses to envision and sometimes cleanse its political and national body. As the CCP no longer needs to mobilise ethnic minorities as a united front, it has embarked on a mission to establish itself as an ever-expanding Chinese nation focused on Han interests. From imperial China to revolutionary movements and the War on Terror, the discourse on blood lineages remains a flexible political tool for the state. As the marriage of biotechnological surveillance techniques with Mao-era political ideas about blood lineage in Xinjiang suggests, the principle of blood lineage is still an important concept for understanding Chinese politics and society, and will remain so for the foreseeable future.

人口信息采集表

基本信息	房屋地址			采集事由	□居住 □商户/务工 □访客	重点标签
	房屋性质	□自购房 □自建房 □出租房 □公租房	居住性质	□家庭居住 □合租	商用性质 □业主 □雇工	系重点人员
	姓名		性别	民族		系特殊群体
	身份证号		出生日期		照片	系收押人员亲属
	户号		与户主关系			系打击处理人员亲属
	户籍信息	□辖区 □本地 □外地 □国外	户籍详址			一络记比中标签人员
	文化程度		婚姻状况	政治面貌		
	职业 □有 □无		职业名称	务工地详址		
	流动人口婚育证明号		现有子女数量	儿童是否预防接种 □是 □否		关键信息
	是否为学龄儿童 □是 □否		是否就学 □是 □否	学校名称与班级		年龄段 15-25 26-40 41-55
	是否有医社保 □是 □否		医社保所在地	社保类型		
	联系方式		在乌社会关系人 关系: 联系方式:	姓名:		维吾尔族
活动轨迹	来乌日期		来乌事由	最近一次流动轨迹		无业人员
宗教信仰	宗教信仰	□无 □伊斯兰教 □儒教 □基督教 □其他	是否礼拜 □是 □否			持有护照
	每日礼拜次数 □1次 □5次 □2-4次		礼拜地点 □家 □清真寺 □其他	是否主麻 □是 □否		每日礼拜
	蓄去清真寺名称		是否朝觐 □公 □私 □摆队 □否	是否有教职 □有 □无		有宗教学识
	是否有宗教学识 □是 □否		学经地	教经人		去过26国
护照持有情况	是否持有护照 □有 □统管 □否		护照编号	护照种类 □因公 □因私		系滞留入境人员
	是否出过境 □是 □否		年内出境次数 ___次	近一次出境时间和国家		有境外关系人
	出境事由 □朝觐 □旅游 □公务 □探亲 □求学 □其他			是否有境外关系人 □是 □否		家有辍学儿童
	境外关系人姓名		境外关系人所在国家	与境外关系人关系		
	前往26国次数 ___次		国家名称	最近一次回国时间		
涉稳情况	是否为重点人员、特殊群体 □是 □否		被列类别 1□ 2□ 3□ 4□ 5□ 特□	一体化比对结果 □无 □比中 □有标签		人员分类
	是否为被打击处理人员亲属 □是 □否		是否为收押人员亲属 □是 □否	与被打击处理收押人员关系		放心人员
	是否参加过集中教育转化 □是 □否		参加集中教育时间、地点	集中教育时长		一般人员
驾照车辆情况	是否有驾驶证 □是 □否		驾照类别 □A □B □C	驾驶证号		不放心人员
	是否有车辆及车辆类型 □否 □小车 □客车 □货车		车牌号	车辆用途		
备注						

采集人:　　　　社区（村）民警 审核签字:　　　　社区（村）领导 审核签字:　　　　15岁以上 被采集人签字:

Figure 3.1 The Population Data Collection Form that Xinjiang residents are required to fill out. Form provided by Tahir Hamut.

4
Good and bad Muslims in Xinjiang*

David Brophy

A huge network of internment camps for those displaying the slightest sign of 'extremism', where, according to some former detainees, Muslims are encouraged to renounce their religion. Closure and demolition of mosques, with intense surveillance of those still functioning. Severe restrictions on the observance of ritual fasting—enough to dissuade all but the most devoted to the faith. These form part of the charge that the People's Republic of China (PRC) is conducting a sweeping campaign against Islam—what some activists decry as a total ban on the religion. For its part, China has responded with a mixture of indignation and incomprehension, with PRC authorities maintaining they are only following international norms of counterextremism and de-radicalisation. Spokespeople for the Chinese Government point to what they see as a worldwide consensus on the need to combat radicalisation through preemptive measures that identify, isolate, and rehabilitate potential extremists. A recent propaganda film on Chinese state television cited de-radicalisation centres in France and Britain as precedents for China's own efforts in Xinjiang (CCTV 2019). While Chinese experts acknowledge that the scale is different, they can explain this, too: Western counterextremism policing, focusing only on select individuals, has not done enough to prevent ongoing acts of terrorism (Doyon 2019). China's more sweeping approach is not only justified, but also the logical extension of Western methods.

This is the terrain on which the war of words over the Xinjiang question is likely to be conducted for the foreseeable future, and it is worth reflecting on how best to navigate it. It may be uncomfortable to admit this, but the Chinese position has its own underlying logic. Yes, China's efforts to reengineer Islamic religious life are on a scale that seems to undermine the very foundations of the faith. But there is no denying that these policies embody a widely held view about the need to bring Islam into line

*This essay was originally published in the *Made in China Journal* (vol. 4, no. 2, 2019) doi.org/10.22459/MIC.04.02.2019.05.

with 'modern' social norms and expectations. It was former US President Barack Obama who said in 2016 that 'some currents of Islam have not gone through a reformation that would help people adapt their religious doctrines to modernity' (Goldberg 2016). The CCP's vision of a Sinicised Islam compatible with socialist modernity mirrors Obama's invocation of an idealised Christian path of religious evolution.

China's party-state system allows for the swift implementation of an elite consensus on a massive scale, while Western liberal democracies are partly, though by no means sufficiently, constrained by concerns about civil liberties and possibilities for resistance. We should be thankful that such constraints still exist. But criticism of China's policies should not dwell on these systemic differences for too long. For those outside China, a robust critique of China's approach, and one that provides a blueprint for an effective response, must extend to the philosophical underpinnings that its policies continue to share with the domestic War on Terror in the West. Failure to do so carries considerable risk. After all, the West's own unwillingness to confront the political causes of terrorist violence is likely to end up validating the point on which China rests its case—that the West's more circumscribed counter-radicalisation strategy will fail to end terrorism. In the absence of a more radical critique that attacks the terms of this debate, China's foreign critics may end up losing it.

How the Uyghurs became Muslims

A heightened focus on Islam in discussions of Xinjiang—with much reporting emphasising the Muslim identity of the Uyghurs, or simply describing China as oppressing 'Muslims'—is new. I will argue that this is justified, but we can also acknowledge extraneous factors that contribute to this framing. Outside China, freedom of religion sits alongside human rights as one of the most widely recognised and well-received registers of international lobbying. As Elizabeth Shakman Hurd (2015) has observed, since 9/11, the institutionalisation of this discourse has led to the reinterpretation of various global conflicts in religious terms. Emphasis on the 'Muslim' identity of China's victims also provides a convenient entry point for Western actors hoping to persuade Muslim-majority countries to take a stand against China's policies. Equally, the religious identity of the Uyghurs gives the United States an opportunity to claw back some of its own lost credibility as a defender of Muslim interests. As Benny Avni (2018) put it in the *New York Post*, the Uyghurs are 'a model pro-American Muslim community'.

Some Uyghurs resent this emphasis, arguing that this is not a question of religion, but of nationality. In part, this response reflects a longstanding tendency of Uyghur intellectuals to downplay the role of Islam in Uyghur identity and treat their predicament as the product of conflicting, even irreconcilable, *national* claims to the territory of Xinjiang. Concomitant with this, a generally anticommunist political orientation has often led Uyghurs to disassociate themselves from causes that pit Muslims against US imperialism, such as the issue of Palestine. Interestingly, such sentiments persist even among those Uyghurs drawn to join jihadist militias in Syria. As reported by Gerry Shih (2017), Uyghur fighters in Syria express admiration for Israel and 'how the Jews built their country'. But setting these considerations aside, the Uyghur critics seem to have a point: if China was pursuing an anti-Muslim policy, wouldn't we expect it to also sweep up the Sinophone Hui Muslims in Xinjiang? Uyghurs seem to be ending up in internment camps not because they are Muslims, but because they are Uyghurs.

This objection is best dealt with by reference to our experience in the West. Twenty years since the launch of the War on Terror, we have become familiar with the idea of the 'racialisation' of Muslims. This is what has made it possible for police and politicians to refer to people as being 'of Muslim appearance'. It has led to a spate of attacks on turban-wearing Sikhs—mistaken for Muslims by their Islamophobic assailants. The converse of this association of religious identity with visible identifying features has been the 'Islamisation' of national identity. In the wake of 9/11, people have described how they came to be seen first as Muslims, and only second as members of a particular nationality. Self-ascription carries little weight in the face of the ability of the state and the media to construct social groups.

White converts to Islam in Australia or the United States (depending on how they dress) may face little to none of the stigmatisation and discrimination directed at fellow Muslims who conform to the stereotype of the brown-skinned Muslim. Simply put, they will not be racialised as Muslim. Similarly, we might posit that in Xinjiang the Uyghurs have become *racially Muslim* in ways that the Sinophone Hui have not. Their Central Asian features increasingly signify the category 'Muslim'—that is, more so than they do the category 'Uyghur', which is a classification that is losing its salience at administrative levels as the promises of China's *minzu* (民族) system (the national, or ethnic, rights enshrined in the constitution) fall by the wayside. In the more homogeneous Chinese interior, of course, the situation differs. There, despite their high degree of acculturation, the communal life of the Hui singles them out as different, and we see a climate of Islamophobic suspicion growing around them. Racial and cultural distance are not things that can be measured objectively. Visible marks, or distinguishing customs, take on significance only in specific political contexts.

Thinking of the Uyghurs as racialised Muslims is compatible with analysis that emphasises the sense of a deepening racial divide in Xinjiang (for example, Hunerven 2019), but has the advantage of allowing us to engage with China's justifications for its policies on their own terms. These justifications centre not on race or ethnicity, but on extremism and terrorism—the two guiding categories of the State Council's most recent White Paper on Xinjiang (State Council Information Office 2019). In the process of turning Uyghurs into racialised Muslims, the figure of the 'terrorist' clearly plays an outsized role. Chinese officialdom now describes all Uyghurs involved in violent actions as terrorists. In the 2009 communal riots in Ürümqi, the White Paper claims, '[t]housands of terrorists attacked civilians, government organs, public security and police officers'. In its crackdown since 2014, China claims to have 'arrested 12,995 terrorists'. In a global climate in which the archetypal terrorist is the brown-skinned Muslim, the editorial choice to subsume all Uyghur violence in Xinjiang into the category of terrorism entrenches, in the most prejudicial way possible, a view of the Uyghurs as Muslims.

Superficially, China looks to be doing the exact opposite of what I am arguing. Indeed, the March 2019 White Paper goes to great lengths to downplay the Islamic identity of the Uyghurs:

> Islam is neither an indigenous belief of the Uygurs and other ethnic groups, nor the sole one of the Uygur people. Today in Xinjiang, a fairly large number of people do not believe in religion or believe in religions other than Islam. (State Council Information Office 2019)

But of course, this desire to enforce the correct line on the contingency of Islam's preeminence in Xinjiang is itself a reflection of the state's preoccupation with the Muslim identity of the Uyghurs. This insistence on the only recent and incomplete Islamisation of the Uyghurs historically has the paradoxical effect of heightening the rhetorical Islamisation of the Uyghurs in the present.

China's liberal Islamophobia

It is possible, therefore, for an Islamophobic climate to take hold and inform policymaking, while visible marks of difference continue to shape the way that climate is experienced by different groups of Muslims. We can, and should, therefore, situate our discussion of the repression meted out to Xinjiang's Turkic-speaking minorities within an analysis of Islamophobia. That is not the only possible context for this discussion, of course, but it will be the focus of this essay.

Alongside its ongoing racial dimensions, it is important to consider the dynamics of Islamophobia itself. Islamophobia is not always expressed in the form of a blanket hostility towards Muslims. In *The Muslims Are Coming!*, Arun Kundnani (2014) describes how, in the wake of the War on Terror, Western anxieties surrounding Islam took on two forms. The first was a conservative discourse that posited an incompatibility between Islam and the West—that is, Islam as inherently backward, with Muslims predisposed to violence by virtue of their religion. The second was a liberal discourse, which set up a distinction between the 'good' Islam that can be reconciled with Western society and the 'bad' Islam, which fosters alienation from, and hostility towards, the West. While this 'bad' Islam can act as a catalyst for radicalisation, 'good' Islam can serve as an ally against it. While this liberal discourse is ostensibly more enlightened, Kundnani shows how it has licensed state interventions in Muslim religious and social life that are equally, if not more, far-reaching as its conservative form.

At various points in Chinese history, the view has been expressed that Islamic customs, or theological precepts, are at some deep level incompatible with Chinese culture. In the eighteenth century, some Qing officials called on the emperor to suppress the doctrine on these grounds. The court usually repudiated such views, though it did eventually implement certain discriminatory statutes against Chinese-speaking Muslims in the interior, which reflected a view of them as particularly prone to violence. Still, even in times of conflict, it was rare for officials to attribute anti-state or anti-Han violence to any inherent flaw in the Islamic faith. While often disparaging of non-Chinese religions, China's intellectual tradition had no 'Orientalist' discourse comparable with that of the West, which furnished explanations of Muslim anticolonial violence in terms of a congenital 'fanaticism'. To this day, Chinese analysis tends to attribute the high points of resistance in pre-PRC Xinjiang not to religious fervency but to the meddling of foreign imperialists. In a recent essay on China's western frontiers, for example, Wang Hui (2017) revives claims that a Sufi-led rebellion in the 1820s was part of a British imperialist plot. China's March 2019 White Paper conveys a similar message in describing Republican-era pan-Islamism as the creation of 'former colonialists'.

If one logs on to Chinese social media today, it is certainly possible to find self-styled 'Muslim-haters' (穆黑) articulating what Kundnani describes as the 'conservative' view—that Islam is irredeemable and has no place in modern society. Much of this Chinese hate speech thrives in a pernicious feedback loop with Western online Islamophobia. Analysts such as James Leibold point out that in China's highly censored media environment, the ability of such views to circulate with relative freedom may reflect a certain connivance with them on the part of the state (Leibold 2016). At the official level, however, one is hard-pressed to find Chinese pronouncements that could compare with the stridence of the West's conservative anti-Islamic rhetoric. Among candidates for the recent Australian Senate elections, for example, Pauline Hanson has said that 'Islam is a disease, we need to vaccinate ourselves against that', while Fraser Anning called for a 'final solution' to the 'problem of Muslim immigration' (Remeikis 2017; Karp 2018).

Rather, China's official discourse on Muslims is almost exclusively of the liberal variety, drawing a dichotomy between what is acceptable and unacceptable, between 'good' and 'bad' Muslims. Chinese counterextremism experts sound exactly like their Western counterparts: they warn against Islamophobia, of the need to disassociate 'extremism' from any religion, and to avoid subsuming anti-extremism measures within a discourse of counterterrorism (Wang 2018). The CCP's intention to 'Sinify' Islam implies a normative view of shortcomings in the religion as currently practised but is couched in optimistic terms that posit remedies and a bright future for a healthier, more Chinese-looking version of the faith.

One way this dichotomy of 'good' and 'bad' manifests in Xinjiang today is in the divide between Turkic-speaking minorities and the Chinese-speaking Hui. This association of Xinjiang Muslims with potentially subversive foreign influences, in contrast to the more domesticated Hui, has historical precedents, but it is worth noting that the line between 'good' and 'bad' Muslims has not always been drawn in this way. One hundred years ago, Xinjiang's Governor Yang Zengxin tended to view Hui religiosity as deviant and undesirable. He drew a contrast between what he saw as the Hui's clannish devotion to local 'Eastern' *shaykhs*, and the more Muhammed-centred religiosity of the Uyghurs ('devout believers in the teachings of the Western Prophet') (Brophy 2013: 279). Writing in the shadow of the Qing Empire, Yang's views capture a moment in time before Chinese nationalism made proximity to Chinese culture a standard by which to take the measure of a citizen. And he was writing before the first of two pro-independence uprisings in the Republican period, which led to the identification of the Uyghurs, and not the Hui, as the chief threat to Beijing's hold on Xinjiang. These twin perceptions of cultural difference and propensity for militancy now single out the Uyghurs as Xinjiang's 'bad' Muslims.

Yet importantly, the distinction applies within the Uyghur (or Kazakh, Kyrghyz, and so on) community as well. The premise of the liberal view is that when 'extremist' ideology penetrates the Muslim community, it puts some, but not all, of its members on to a path towards radicalisation. Descriptions of this pathway vary in the emphasis given to either theological deviations or individual psychological considerations; the two are usually hard to disentangle. From this premise, an elaborate discourse has arisen, purporting to scientificity, which allows security agencies to identify 'at-risk' individuals and take steps to rehabilitate them. As other commentators have noted (for example, Jamshidi 2019), China's lists of warning signs of radicalisation—growing a beard, donning religious dress, or even quitting smoking—immediately call to mind those applied in Countering Violent Extremism policing elsewhere: Britain's Channel program is a classic example, as is the New York Police Department's surveillance of Muslim communities in New York.

For China, the upshot of all this is something of a contradiction. On the one hand, liberal counter-radicalisation theory tends to describe extremists as distorting the true meaning of Islam. This often commits the terrorism expert to a certain fundamentalism of his/her own, and China is no exception. The task of de-radicalisation, according to a Chinese scholar in Kashgar (Liu 2018), is to 'restore the basic message of the religion's teachings' (还原宗教教义本身的主旨). On the other hand, talk of 'Sinicisation' seems to imply that Islam became something different on reaching China and partaking of the common Chinese culture (中华文化). That is, Islam in China has features that distinguish it from Islam as originally conceived, and as practised elsewhere (Zhang 2017).

The intellectual gymnastics required to reconcile these two contradictory impulses will likely keep China's Islam specialists busy, but these contextual specificities should not obscure their common mission with War on Terror Islamologists in the West. The 'reformist war on terror', as Kundnani (2014: 107) describes it, is 'one in which governments tell believers what their religion really means, and back that up with the power to criminalize alternatives'.

Western commentary on Islam in China

Because the PRC's discourse is so enmeshed with that of the West, foreign commentary on the Chinese state's relationship to Islam often finds itself in something of a bind. While striving to be critical of China's policies, it tends to reproduce certain assumptions that drive these policies. In its most crude form, this commentary simply buys into major elements of the Chinese narrative. Although the high tide of post-9/11 counterterrorism collaboration between China and the West has receded, it has left a residue of low-quality punditry that more or less endorses China's claim to be fighting a serious domestic terrorist enemy. An article published by the Hoover Institute in 2018, for example, while critical of Chinese repression, describes the 'East Turkmenistan [*sic*] Islamic Movement' as 'the largest domestic extremist group in China', and parrots China's evidence-free accusations that this organisation has carried out more than 200 attacks (Auslin 2018). The author's view of 'irreconcilable tensions' here predicts a long-running fight to the end between China and organised Uyghur terrorists.

Most writers these days are more sceptical of such claims, and critical of the Bush administration's acquiescence in deeming the nebulous East Turkestan Islamic Movement a terrorist organisation. The instinct of these commentators is to be sharply critical of China's efforts to play up the scale of the terrorist threat in Xinjiang. But at the same time, the terms of China's counterextremist discourse are so familiar and so like the West's own way of framing its domestic Muslim populations that they are difficult to entirely escape. The most well-meaning critiques can easily lapse into them.

Take, for example, a recent article in *The Economist* on the Hui Muslims of the southwestern province of Yunnan, in which the author criticises China's 'crude attempts to sinicise the faith' as counterproductive (Chaguan 2019). Holding up the example of patriotic Chinese Muslim politicians of the early twentieth century, the author faults today's PRC officials for their ignorance of this existing Sinicised Islam. But then, the author encounters Hui Muslims who fail to conform to his preferred image of them. These Hui reject the *hadith* that 'love for the homeland is part of faith' (*hubb al-watan min al-iman*), thereby distancing themselves from the patriotic, Sinified Islam that the author valorises. For this, they are deemed 'historically ignorant'. What starts off as a critique of China's Sinification of Islam campaign thus ends up reinforcing one of the campaign's basic assumptions: that there exists a historically authentic, patriotic Chinese Islam, and that Muslims who think otherwise are getting their religion wrong.

In the case of Xinjiang, one often reads of the 'moderate Sufi' Islam that the Uyghurs practice—usually intended as a rebuke to China's depiction of Xinjiang as a region rife with extremism. True enough, Sufism—and associated practices of shrine pilgrimage, meditation (*zikr*) circles, and so on—has long been an important part of religious life in Xinjiang. But these invocations carry the baggage of a distinctly Western discourse on Sufism as a meditative, new-age form of Islam, making it a perfect foil to extremist ideology. There is, in fact, little in this Western mythology surrounding Sufism that stands up to historical scrutiny. Sufis in Xinjiang have proven themselves perfectly capable of religious dogmatism and of engaging in violence against their political enemies. It was Sufis who led the anti-Qing resistance of the nineteenth century and, judging by references to 'ishanism' (依禅派) in early PRC accounts, it was Sufis who put up some of the stiffest resistance to the arrival of the People's Liberation Army in the Tarim Basin in the 1950s (National People's Congress Ethnic Affairs Committee 1956). Criticising China's crackdown by reference to the region's Sufi traditions will likely make little sense to a Chinese audience, therefore. And more importantly, upholding the notion of a native 'moderate' Islam implies the acceptance of its converse: a foreign, non-Sufi, 'extremist' or maybe 'Salafist' Islam. This is precisely the dichotomy on which China's policies rest, and PRC officials make use of it in explaining these policies to the world. In a meeting with religious affairs officials in 2018, for example, China's Ambassador to Pakistan told them: 'The Chinese government is the bearer of Sufi and moderate thought' (Hussain 2018).

Obviously conscious of the use to which the frame of moderate Sufi versus radical Salafist can be put, James Millward's otherwise excellent article in *The New York Review of Books* nonetheless relies on it, but with a twist. Instead of viewing the decline of a native Sufistic Islam and the emergence of more austere forms of religiosity as a trend arising from within the Muslim community itself, he pins the blame for this on the Chinese state: 'Chinese policies have tended to undermine indigenous Uyghur Islam and to enforce, through the party-controlled Islamic Association of China, an idealized version of Islam modelled in part on Sunni practice as promoted by Saudi Arabia' (Millward 2019). A better appreciation of Xinjiang's religious traditions—something Uyghur scholars of religion might provide—would have obviated the need for the Chinese state's misguided interventions.

Today, in its aversion to shrines and ornate mosque architecture, it is possible to see a certain convergence between Chinese policy and the prescriptions of Wahabbi Islam. Arguably, the logic behind this convergence has been present in the modernising PRC since its founding. But there is no evidence for the role of any deliberate Beijing–Saudi nexus in supplanting a shrine-centred Islam in Xinjiang. There is far more evidence to show—as we would anticipate—that scripturalism and its accompanying critique of Sufism had native roots, while also gaining sustenance from ongoing exchange between Xinjiang Muslims and the wider Islamic world, and all of this well before the communist revolution. Questionable from a historical point of view, Millward's narrative also keeps us firmly within the moderate/extremist paradigm, drawing a contrast between indigenous Uyghur Islam and something alien to it. Shifting the blame for a malignant Saudi-style Islam from Xinjiang Muslims themselves to the Chinese state simply does not pack the rhetorical punch it is intended to. After all, many in the West acknowledge the past role of the United States in sponsoring jihadism in Afghanistan and elsewhere, while still endorsing the need for invasive counterterror policing to root out extremist forms of Islam today.

These are examples of ways in which analysis of Xinjiang reproduce the reformist discourse of 'good' Sufis and 'bad' scripturalists. But at times, the effort to critique China's repression in Xinjiang draws authors into something approaching the 'conservative' discourse of the essential incompatibility between China and Islam. As I have discussed, this view is not a major feature of the Chinese intellectual tradition. Confucian literati could be highly disparaging of all non-Chinese faiths, but their prejudice did not lead them to envisage an inevitable showdown between China and its Muslims. This perspective, though, has had a prominent place in scholarship outside China. It emerged first in the nineteenth century, in the period of Muslim rebellions against the Qing, when the notion took hold that Islam was a rising force in China, and one that might eventually endanger Western (and Russian) interests. The discourse was revived in the 1970s, as commentators in the West became increasingly conscious of Islam as a global political force. In a 1977 article titled 'Muslims in China: The Incompatibility between Islam and the Chinese Order', Israeli intelligence analyst-cum-historian Raphael Israeli argued that the

> Muslim presence in China … has always posed a challenge, at times even a threat, to the Chinese establishment. This was due to [the fact] that Islam, far from willing to acculturate into Chinese society, on the contrary nurtured its distinctive traits and stressed its own superiority, something almost unheard of in other minority cultures in the Middle Kingdom. (Israeli 1977: 296)

In 1978, Harvard historian Joseph Fletcher offered a similar analysis of the Turkic-speaking Muslims of Xinjiang, arguing that they could only temporarily accept the rule of a non-Muslim emperor and they therefore lived under the 'obligation of jihad' (Fletcher 1978).

Today, most scholarship on Islam in China looks askance at these views, but the deteriorating situation in Xinjiang has led them to resurface, only now in a more anti-CCP form. In a recent contribution, also in *The New York Review of Books*, Ian Johnson (2018) presents a bleak picture of the possibility for coexistence between Muslims and non-Muslims in Xinjiang. Focusing on the Qing Dynasty, he highlights what he sees as the Chinese state's inability to accommodate pluralism, which was manifested at that time in the 'Qing's Buddhist political-religious utopia', but derived ultimately from 'older, deeper problems in the Chinese worldview'. Yet in the same article, Johnson also references Abrahamic theology's 'monolithic view of truth'—a phrase that carries more than a hint that there have been cultural impediments to tolerance and coexistence on both sides. He claims that militant resistance was an immediate response to Qing rule in Xinjiang and was motivated by the fact that Xinjiang's Muslims 'did not feel Chinese, look Chinese, speak Chinese, share Chinese values and myths and stories, or, by and large, want be part of China' (Johnson 2018).

Once again, an argument that sets out to provide a critique of China's policies in Xinjiang ends up losing much of its force. Johnson cites historian Johan Elverskog for the view that '[w]e can't say that Islam is incompatible with China or Chinese culture'. But as he describes it, the fault line in Xinjiang ends up looking a lot like a Huntingtonian clash of civilisations. From that perspective, whether the Chinese state or Islam is ultimately to blame starts to become more of a question of emphasis. And regardless of where we might come down on that question, Johnson's paradigm offers little scope to think about solutions to the crisis facing Xinjiang today; if the confrontation has such deep historical and cultural roots, what can anyone hope to do about it?

Towards a defence of religious freedom

There are obviously grounds for pessimism in viewing the present situation in Xinjiang. Thankfully, though, Johnson's narrative does not provide us with the complete picture. While the Qing Empire was merciless towards its enemies among Xinjiang's religious elite (mostly Sufis who claimed descent from the Prophet Muhammed), one can in fact tell a story of the eighteenth century as a period of considerable accommodation towards the region's Muslim population. Of course, whether the Qianlong reign of the high Qing provides a workable model for today's PRC is debatable. My point here is simply that history is far from univocal, and we should not allow it to dictate a particular view of the present.

On taking control of Kashgar in 1759, Qianlong immediately commissioned the restoration of the city's chief Sufi shrine. While wary of the influence that remaining members of Xinjiang's elite religious families wielded, his approach was to accommodate them in luxury in Beijing, from where they kept up contact with the Muslim society of the Tarim Basin. Johnson is correct when he writes that there was no mosque inside Beijing's Forbidden City—in his view, an indication of its exclusion from the Qing's 'religious system'. But there was a mosque directly opposite— a well-appointed compound built to house this community of Xinjiang Muslims—and we know the emperor paid it annual visits. While probably much more knowledgeable of, and interested in, Tibet's Buddhist traditions, Qianlong was equally keen to find out what Xinjiang's Muslims had to offer the dynasty in terms of spiritual capabilities, and he recruited ritualists from among them to conduct rainmaking ceremonies in and around the capital. When Naqshbandi Sufi networks loyal to the dynasty's enemies were rediscovered in Xinjiang in the late eighteenth century, Qianlong's response was not to launch a bloody inquisition, but to disperse the network by appointing its members to low-ranking official positions. It was not until the 1820s, 60 years on from the Qing conquest, that dissident religious elites were able to mobilise serious resistance to the Qing, and these efforts were far from unanimously welcomed by the locals.

From Beijing's point of view, of course, all this is of secondary importance. In official rhetoric, it was the arrival of 'pan-Turkism' and 'pan-Islamism' at the turn of the twentieth century that laid the foundations for today's violent extremism. But here, too, history can complicate things. These twentieth-century ideologies did not automatically bring with them a critique of Chinese rule in Xinjiang, and more frequently expressed hope for anticolonial collaboration with China. The 2019 White Paper cites Masʿud Sabri and Muhämmämd Imin Bughra as representatives of these radicalising trends, but both men spent considerable portions of their lives working alongside Chinese nationalists in the Guomindang— hardly the CV we would expect from a pair of diehard extremists. A third much-maligned villain of this period is Sabit Damulla, who served as prime minister of the short-lived East Turkestan Republic in 1933–34. Yet, although he was obviously inspired by 'Salafist' theology, there is nothing in his writings to indicate that he felt religiously obligated to engage in anti-Chinese resistance. On a trip to the Middle East in the early 1930s, Sabit Damulla penned articles describing the Muslims in Xinjiang as enjoying almost complete freedom of religion, directing most of his complaints towards the activities of European missionaries. His views were in accord with those of prominent Arab theorists of political Islam such as Rashid Rida, who held that while China lay outside the Islamic world and was technically *Dar al-Harb* (the 'Abode of War'), this did not impose on Muslims any obligation to contest Chinese rule (Halevi 2019). The preferred course of action, he believed, was to engage in proselytisation of the faith.

The point to be drawn from all this is that no straight line can be drawn from theological standpoints to political prescriptions. Just as Sufism did not necessarily cultivate a pluralistic pacifism, nor was the call to return to Islam's founding texts—the Quran and the *Hadith*—invariably accompanied by a rigid anti-Chinese militancy. In the changing political circumstances he encountered on returning to Xinjiang, Sabit Damulla endorsed the province-wide rebellion that gave birth to the East Turke-stan Republic and justified this bid for independence in religious terms. But his participation in this act of resistance was not a function of his interpretation of Islam. The intellectual genealogy that China seeks to provide for its campaign against 'extremist ideology' cannot do the work it is designed to do.

This need to separate our analysis of political violence from a typology of Islam is as true today as it was in the past. Whether couched in terms of theological deviations or psychologising talk of alienation and identity crisis, explanations that rely on notions of 'extremist ideology' do not provide a convincing diagnosis of the origins of terrorist violence, and therefore cannot inform effective remedies for it. Already, many experts have spoken out against the ill-founded assumptions that inform Countering Violent Extremism policing, arguing that the empirical research on terrorism simply does not support its guiding assumptions (Ross 2016). At best, these theories provide vague correlations, which count for little in the absence of more rigorous control-group studies. When given voice, almost all justifications for terrorist violence centre on political grievances that have failed to find alternative outlets for expression.

Arguing that political factors are what spur some Uyghurs to acts of violence will provoke little objection among a Western audience predisposed to acknowledge China's policy failures. But pointing this out to China is likely to be ineffective if our own practices of policing Muslims obscure this basic truth. This is not to mention the prestigious, well-funded institutions that sustain the theory behind these Western policing practices, and which have contributed to disseminating a dubious counter-radicalisation doctrine to China. Critics should therefore rethink the reflex calls on China to comply with 'international norms'. The international norms on this issue are precisely what we should be challenging. Instead, we should be working to rescue the principle of genuine religious freedom from the damage it has sustained through the global War on Terror. Muslims in China deserve the freedom to be shrine-worshipping Sufis or not, as they see fit. They should be free to insist on the exclusive validity of Islam's original texts or not, as they see fit. And if they wish to argue among themselves as to the best way of being Muslim, they should be free to do so, without the Chinese state, China's non-Muslim experts, or foreign critics intervening in that debate to pick sides, promoting preferred voices while slighting others as alien and inauthentic. To reshape the discussion in this way, we need to free ourselves from our own ingrained paradigms of good versus bad and moderate versus extremist Islam, which, even when invoked in a critical spirit, can serve to sustain state interventions into Muslim communities.

5

Imprisoning the open air: Preventive policing as community detention in northwestern China*

Darren Byler

ometime in May 2017, an ethnic Kazakh woman was detained in Ürümqi, the capital of the Xinjiang Uyghur Autonomous Region. Perhaps this woman, a Chinese citizen, had travelled to Kazakhstan in the past or had relatives there. Perhaps she had become part of a Quran study group on WeChat. It may not even be clear to her what 'micro-clue' of her potential 'extremism' resulted in her detention. In any case, once she was in custody, a scan of her smartphone revealed that she had been in contact with a Uyghur woman in Kazakhstan. Eager to please her interrogators, whose priority was to capture 'returning terrorists', she placed a call to the woman in Almaty. She told this woman, Gulbahar Jelilova, that her mother, Gulbahar's partner in a shuttle trade business, was in hospital so Gulbahar would need to travel across the border to Ürümqi to pick up the products she had ordered for export to Kazakhstan. Gulbahar was suspicious at first, because she had heard about the mass detention of Turkic Muslims that had begun earlier that year, but because she knew her partner had a heart condition, she thought perhaps the story of her illness was true. Since she was a Kazakhstani citizen born in Kazakhstan, she thought she had nothing to worry about despite her Uyghur ethnicity.

The morning after she arrived in Ürümqi, she found out how wrong she was. She said:

> At 8 am, the police knocked on my door. They showed me their badges and then said they had a few questions to ask me. I thought they really would just ask a few questions, so I went along with them [without any attempt to resist]. As soon as we arrived at the police station, they checked my phone. When they couldn't find

*This essay was originally published in the *Made in China Journal* (vol. 4, no. 3, 2019), doi.org/10.22459/MIC.04.03.2019.13. The article has been updated for inclusion in this volume.

anything, they showed me the picture of my friend and asked if I knew her. Then I realised they had already detained her. They had found my phone number in her cell phone and pressured her daughter to call me. Then they accused me of wiring 17,000 *yuan* to Turkey. I said, why would I do that? They said: 'Take your time, think it over.'[1]

As it turned out, Gulbahar was given plenty of time to think about this. For the next year, three months, and 10 days, she was held in a series of detention centres in Ürümqi. The conditions in these holding centres, where detainees were investigated for potential connections to terrorism, were horrific. She and the more than 30 other Turkic Muslim women who shared her 14-square-metre cell were forced to take turns sleeping because there was not enough room for everyone to stretch out. The lights were never turned off. Their movements and speech were recorded by cameras and microphones.

Gulbahar, who spoke no Chinese, learned to say 'thank you' (谢谢) and 'here' (到) and to sing the Chinese national anthem, *The March of the Volunteers*. Every day she watched political speeches on TV monitors mounted high on the wall. This was the 'reeducation' (再教育) component of her detention.

Her interrogators showed her a brand-new Chinese ID card and made her memorise her new 18-digit citizenship number. They told her she was not Gulbahar Jelilova, she was a Chinese citizen now, and she should confess her crimes.

Gulbahar had been caught up in the reeducation system that explicitly targets Turkic Muslims. She was one of as many as 1.5 million people who had exhibited the 'early warning' (预警) signs of terrorism. This preventive policing system was built on modes of counterinsurgency that emerged from the United States, Israel, and Europe, but was adapted to 'Chinese characteristics' (中国特色) that came from China's Maoist past. Together, these modes and technologies have produced a coercive internment camp system that is implemented by an army of more than one million non-Muslim civil servants and police (Byler 2018; see also Salimjan's Chapter 7 in this volume). The project is supported by a

---

1   This quote is an extract from a video interview conducted by the Uyghur-language TV channel in Turkey called *Pidaiylar Ekrani* (2018). The interview was translated by the author and an anonymous viewer. The interview is available from: www.youtube.com/watch?v=VILgyCn-gS0.

comprehensive, AI-assisted biometric and digital surveillance system. The scale of detentions and the use of technology make the Chinese counterinsurgency unprecedented. It is the American war in Iraq without organised, weaponised insurgents and without mass killing; a Countering Violent Extremism (CVE) program with purpose-built internment camps and state-run residential schools. It has adapted counterinsurgency to produce a new form of contemporary settler colonialism. The political and material structure of this colonialism partition Uyghur and Kazakh communities, removing and dispossessing them of their land and their remaining social institutions: their language, faith, family, and cultural traditions. The technology-assisted forms of policing that characterise this system produce a racialised relationship of state and settler domination over their lives.

A global shift in counterinsurgency

The experiences of Gulbahar Jelilova and others in her social network are indicative of a broader shift in policing and detention in northwestern China and counterinsurgency around the world. As David Brophy has shown in his chapter in this volume, since 2014, Chinese authorities have adopted forms of Islamophobia and counterinsurgent militarism that are similar to those of the post-9/11 United States and other nations. As in the US-led occupation of Iraq and Afghanistan in the mid-2000s, Chinese police have transformed Xinjiang into a space of exception—a counterinsurgent war zone where active militants are thought to be hiding among the 'neutral population' (Harcourt 2018). In the American case, the only way to detect and uproot these terrorists-in-hiding was through full-spectrum intelligence encompassing all inhabitants in the war theatre. Once knowledge dominance was achieved, the networks of the insurgency could be traced and fractured through processes of removal and isolation. The final step in counterinsurgency implementation was winning 'the hearts and minds' of a targeted population through humanitarian aid, infrastructure building, and job training. This, it was thought, would legitimise and solidify a 'regime change'.

A key element of the American experiment in Iraq and Afghanistan was the construction of a 'human terrain system'. At its height, this system employed 27 teams of social scientists, specialists on Islam and Arabic or Pashto and Dari, to enter people's homes and map out Iraqi and Afghan social relations as participant-observers, creating a database that would chart the communities and ideologies of the population (Kelly et al. 2010). This system—what the geographer Derek Gregory (2008) referred to as 'armed social work'—was thought to produce a knowledge network that would anticipate insurgent threats. Ethnography aided in the targeted assaults necessary for the selective removal and internment of insurgent leaders in a network of camps. By 2008, Camp Bucca, the largest of these camps, had as many as 18,000 detainees—including Abu Bakr al-Baghdadi, the future leader of the Islamic State (Enders 2008).

Since 2016, a similar system has been put in place in Xinjiang (Mahmut 2019). Unlike in Afghanistan or Iraq, there is no organised, armed insurgency, yet Uyghurs and other Turkic Muslims have been targeted as 'pre-terrorists' in similar ways. Chinese authorities use many of the same 'enhanced interrogation' techniques used by the Bush administration. An important distinction, however, is that the Chinese Government pathologises nearly all forms of Turkic Islamic practice as expressions of mental illness, and strives to transform Muslims through psychiatric treatment, language education, political indoctrination, and coercive factory labour in an internment camp system much more extensive than the camps in Iraq or Afghanistan (Grose 2019). In Xinjiang, the police are not attempting to produce political regime change; the institutions of state are already fully within their grasp. Here there is something more. As in settler-colonial systems around the world (Wolfe 2006), they are attempting to produce deep epistemic and social elimination by detaining and retraining the entire population. This is accomplished through increasingly restrictive nested systems of biometric and digital surveillance checkpoints—ending in the tight constraints of the camps and prisons themselves. All Uyghurs and other Turkic Muslims are detained to varying degrees in what many describe as the 'open-air prisons' (*sirttiki türme*) of their communities.

Adapting a Western framework

State media and policing theorists in China noticed the shift in US militarism as early as 2007, when discussions of the 'Petraeus Doctrine'—the new counterinsurgency manual named for US General David Petraeus—signalled a transformation of military science around the globe (Yang 2007). Over the next several years, scholars at elite police academies across China began to examine counterinsurgency theory—first, as practised by the US military and then, the way it was adapted and technologically assisted in Israel (Lu and Cao 2014). In the space of less than a decade, this new theoretical paradigm was adapted in practice in Xinjiang.

Much of the impetus behind this shift from academic research to policy implementation emerged from the tragic events of 2013 and 2014 in Beijing and Kunming, respectively. In the first of the two incidents, a family of Uyghur attackers drove a vehicle into a crowd of tourists in Tiananmen Square on 28 October 2013; in the second, on 1 March 2014—an episode often referred to as 'China's 9/11'—Uyghur attackers killed dozens of Han travellers in the Kunming railway station (Doyon 2019). Within a year, the new forms of policing that had been observed in Palestine, Afghanistan, and Iraq coalesced into a series of Chinese National Science Foundation policing theory projects, such as 'The Anti-Terrorism Mode of Community Policing with Chinese Characteristics' (Lowe 2017).

One of the leaders of this new paradigm of Chinese policing, which stresses 'prevention' (预防) through 'preemptive strike' (先发制人), is a young scholar from Shenyang named Cao Xuefei. Named to the project while still a PhD student in police science and antiterrorism at Charles Sturt University in Australia, Cao and a colleague named Lu Peng published an influential article on the way Israeli counterinsurgency theory should be used as an inspiration for counterterrorism in Xinjiang. As his thinking continued to evolve, Cao and another colleague translated a book called *Policing Terrorism* by CVE expert David Lowe (2017). Their award-winning Chinese translation of the book provided an 'empirical basis' from which to expand Chinese antiterrorism activities in relation to the Islamic State, which many suspected was connected to the Uyghur attacks in Beijing and Kunming. Lowe's book, which analysed the methods used by Islamic State affiliates in Britain to 'radicalise and recruit people to their causes', also stressed 'critical' methods of gathering intelligence through surveillance and community informants.

In an article that was published in the summer of 2016, Chinese policing theorists Ji Yantao and Yin Wei (2016) began to describe the way this turn in policing could be adapted in a Chinese context by emphasising the need to move to prevention rather than 'passive reaction' (被动反应). Ji and Yin argued that this new form of policing should supplement the military-style 'intervention' (干预) and 'harsh punishment and suppression' (打击和严格的惩罚) that had typified earlier 'Strike Hard' (严厉打击) campaigns in Xinjiang. Yet, although they were suggesting a broader approach, they were careful to note that terrorism in China was rooted in social causes such as 'education, religion, ethnicity, and economic factors' and was 'not directly proportionate to police presence' (Ji and Yin 2016: 144). As per the position of the Chinese Communist Party (CCP)—which resonated with that of CVE advocates around the world—they claimed that Uyghurs were terrorism-prone because of their social and cultural systems and failed to acknowledge the role of police brutality and colonisation. In any case, they argued for the key focus of antiterrorism activities to shift to 'preemptive strikes' facilitated by civilian intelligence workers. At the core of this mode was a term Ji and Yin repeated 58 times in the space of 12 pages: 'prevention' (预防).

From their perspective, prevention encompassed three interlinked domains: 'strike prevention' (打击性预防), 'controlled prevention' (控制性预防), and 'protective prevention' (保护性预防). Strike prevention refers to the 'real-time control of key high-risk populations' (Ji and Yin 2016: 150) such as people like Gulbahar—that is, 'returning' (回流) terrorism suspects. Uyghurs who had lived abroad in Muslim-majority environments with open access to information, especially those for whom there was evidence linking them to other suspects, needed to be 'preemptively attacked'. Once the terrorism suspect is in custody, they are moved into 'controlled prevention'. In this domain, people for whom there are not enough clues or evidence of terrorist intent need to be 'controlled' (控制) to reduce the possibility of them committing a crime and to eliminate the 'unfavourable' (不利) aspects of their behaviour and thinking. The third form, protective prevention, refers to the prevention of potential terrorism through comprehensive intelligence-gathering and intervention in the 'breeding and spreading' (滋生和蔓延) of terrorist thought among the general population.

In a striking departure from non-Chinese counterinsurgency, all this intelligence-gathering was to be run through a *shequ* (社区), a term that refers to a state-directed neighbourhood watch unit in urban areas, or through village-level neighbourhood brigades (大队)—the most grassroots forms of party-facilitated policing in China. In Xinjiang, a *shequ* is staffed by mostly Han CCP members and police, but also employs Uyghur auxiliary police and mostly Han volunteer informants mobilised in the fight against terrorism through a weekly intelligence report quota system. Although Chinese community policing echoes the rhetoric of Euro-American counterterrorism, Ji and Yin argued that 'the people' (人民) must be pressured to report on their neighbours to fill in the blind spots in the intelligence system. In practice, the way this community policing is accomplished is by watching the Muslim population for 75 signs of 'extremist' (极端主义) Islamic practice, ranging from mosque attendance and Quran study to use of the common greeting '*Assalamu alaikum*' (Buckley 2018; Greer 2018).

Special attention is focused on unauthorised religious knowledge and practice, and relationships to other suspects (Hunerven 2019). Unlike non-Chinese counterinsurgencies, each state-run watch unit is supported by a People's Convenience Police Station, which conducts 'seamless' (无缝) surveillance of Muslims within their jurisdiction through video monitoring, digital media history searches, biometric tracking, and human surveillance at mandatory political activities (Zhang 2016).

At the time when Ji and Yin were writing their 2016 article, the 'reeducation camps' in Xinjiang had not yet been fully built and sweeping purges of Uyghur and Kazakh societies had not yet begun. Less than one year later, Gulbahar and 1.5 million other Turkic Muslims began to be pushed through these domains of 'prevention' and subjected to the accompanying forms of social elimination.

The Xinjiang mode

In November 2016, a new article appeared, written by Wang Ding and Shan Dan, who were theorists in a Xinjiang police academy. The authors argued that the mode of preventive policing proposed by other policing theorists needed to be adapted in an explicit 'Xinjiang mode' (新疆模式) that would not only transform religion, but also lead to a 'deep fusion' (深度融合) of Turkic minorities into Chinese culture. They wrote that this new mode would combine the full-spectrum intelligence 'war mode' (战争模式) used by the US Army with a 'criminal mode' (犯罪模式) aimed at eradicating the root of terrorism—that is, 'extremist' religious ideology. These two aspects of preventive policing would be brought together with a 'governance mode' (治理模式) focusing on 'achieving a normal social order' (把社会秩序恢复到常态).

But what exactly was the 'normal' social order that Wang and Shan had in mind? As they put it: 'In the contemporary era there is no future for a religion without "culture"' (Wang and Shan 2016: 25). Therefore, they suggested, there must be an acceleration of 'the deep fusion' of Chinese culture in Xinjiang—a process they argued was in fact the 'most distinctive aspect of the Xinjiang mode' of counterterrorism. They suggested that these adaptive approaches to counterterrorism were necessary due to the context of Xinjiang. Because it was a frontier region that was not yet fully settled by Han people, the local population generally lacked market integration. The deeper issue though remained religion, which, as Wang and Shan put it, was a 'personality problem' (个性问题). They wrote that the only way to deal with this was to be resolute in preventing people from being 'brainwashed' (洗脑) by a religion that had 'no culture' (没有文化). The implication was that because Turkic Muslims dangerously lacked 'culture'—a term that referred explicitly to 'Chinese culture'—there must be an acceleration of 'the deep fusion' of Chinese culture in Xinjiang.

Since Islam was so deeply integrated in the Xinjiang way of life, Wang and Shan argued that Turkic Muslims would need to unlearn nearly every aspect of their lives. The only way this could really be accomplished was if the entire population of non-Muslims in the region was brought into the process. They argued that people who possessed Chinese culture needed to 'occupy the positions of public opinion, the positions of cultural and social media platforms' throughout Xinjiang society (Wang and Shan 2016: 26). In writing this, they implied that Uyghur cultural leaders needed to be replaced through the full implementation of settler colonialism. Only then would 'unstable factors' be 'nipped in the bud' (把各类不稳定因素消灭在萌芽状态).

When Gulbahar Jelilova was lured back to Xinjiang as a suspected 'returning terrorist' in mid-2017, much of what these scholars had advocated had been operationalised. Like hundreds of thousands of others, Gulbahar was targeted with a 'strike prevention' arrest. From there, she moved into 'controlled prevention' until she was eventually released into 'protective prevention'. Although she was found to be guilty of nothing other than being Uyghur and Muslim, the Xinjiang mode of counterinsurgency radically upended her life.

Communities as prisons

Those with the least amount of social power suffer the most in counterinsurgent war. According to the independent researchers at the organisation Iraq Body Count, there have been nearly 200,000 documented civilian deaths in Iraq since 2003 (IBC 2019). In some periods of the war in Afghanistan, the US military and its allies killed more civilians than the Taliban (Zucchino 2019). The cascading effect of these deaths and the widespread fragmentation of social life that has been produced through surveillance and removal in these spaces have produced tremendous forms of violence as social networks are broken and families are separated. The pain of counterterrorism is carried by those who remain into future generations and across communities.

As Arun Kundnani and Ben Hayes (2018) have shown, in Europe and North America, Muslim communities have been asked to carry the brunt of the social violence that is tied to CVE programs. Families, mosques, employers, and teachers are tasked with assessing their friends, relatives, and students as 'pre-criminals'. As in China, in Britain, extremism is 'pictured as a virus' and, counter to empirical evidence, religious ideology is assumed to be the primary cause of violence (Kundnani and Hayes 2018). Instead of considering the role of structural violence, colonialism, and institutionalised Islamophobia, it is simply assumed that Muslims— especially those who practise their faith in public—are potential terrorists.

Yet, despite all these similarities, it is important to note that in liberal societies civil rights and free speech can produce a hedge against the implementation of mass extrajudicial detention and death. This was not the case in Iraq and Afghanistan. And it is not the case in China. As a Xinjiang official put it recently, what is happening to Uyghurs is 'not about human rights violations. Uyghurs have no rights' (ITV 2019). This framing resonates with a common interpretation of human rights in China: human rights mean the right of the majority Han people to be free from terrorism (Liu 2019). This in turn means they have the right to be free from their fear of Turkic Muslims—the only population in the country that is placed in the terrorism slot.

The violence of the process that confronted Gulbahar Jelilova was signi-ficantly lessened by the relative privilege of her Kazakhstani citizenship. Without it, she would still be in some form of detention like hundreds of thousands of others. Racialised religious discrimination, intrusions of privacy, political censorship, disappearances, detention without due process, and lack of personal and collective autonomy are institutionalised in Xinjiang. For most Uyghurs and Kazakhs, there is no foreseeable end to their detention. Their communities themselves have become their prisons.

Part II: Settler colonialism

6
Oil and water

Tom Cliff

ost Han in Xinjiang, northwestern China, have settled—or *been settled* by state decree—in the region since the Chinese Communist Party won the Civil War and took control of China in 1949. Since that time, the proportion of Han in the population has risen from 6 per cent to at least 42 per cent and is now roughly equal to the other major population group in Xinjiang, Turkic Muslim Uyghurs. The massive project of cultural, economic, physical, and personal transformation in which these migrants are involved is rightly described as a 'colonial endeavour'.

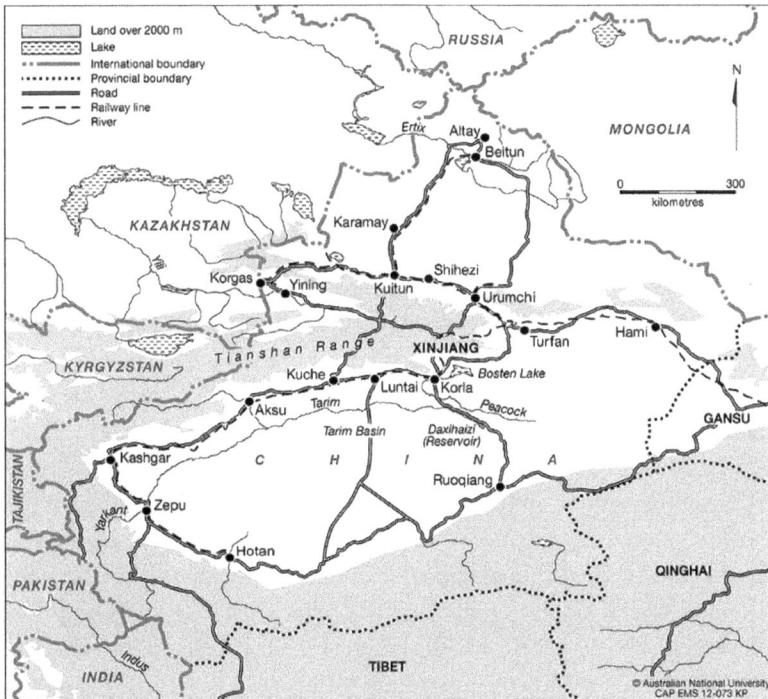

Map 6.1 Xinjiang.

Since I first lived in Xinjiang for eight months in 2001–02, I have been asking myself: 'What is it like to be a Han person living in Xinjiang?' I asked myself this question because I felt it was not the same as being a Han person who lives in the core area of China. Perhaps the question came to me because, as an Australian-born child of European parents, I felt some sort of affinity with these settlers on the edge of their empire. Xinjiang was both alien and strangely familiar to me.

I returned to Xinjiang from July 2007 until February 2010 to conduct research on the experiences of Han settlers, centring my project on the oil city of Korla. The resultant book was published in June 2016 by the University of Chicago Press. The following photo gallery contains some highlights from an exhibition held at The Australian National University in early July 2016.

Time

On 5 July 2009, Ürümqi's streets were witness to some of the worst interethnic communal violence to hit Xinjiang since 1949. Angry and frustrated Uyghurs protested, were met with police violence in response, and then rioted. They burned buildings and vehicles, and randomly beat any Han person unlucky enough to be in their path. Thousands of Han retaliated two days later, destroying Uyghur property and beating—often to death—any Uyghur witless enough to be present on the deliberately lawless streets.

A massive crackdown from the embarrassed and embattled Xinjiang authorities was imminent, violence past and violence-to-be hung heavily in the thick summer air, and fear and loathing were visible on the eerily quiet streets of Xinjiang's cities. The only thing in Xinjiang that was not at least semiparalysed was rumour, which spread like wildfire.

The period from July 2009 to February 2010 was a crucible of politicised storytelling, fired by heightened emotions and unconstrained by the mannered niceties of peacetime. A certain kind of talk became briefly allowable as the assumptions of settler loyalty to Xinjiang and the precepts of Han occupation of the region lost their hold on public discourse. The uncertain months following 5 July 2009 can be seen as a 'decisive moment' in Xinjiang's recent history.

Plate 6.1 Friday morning, 10 July 2009. The supermarkets in Korla open for the first time since the Uyghur riots on 5–6 July and Han retribution riots on 7 July. Despite repeated official warnings to avoid crowded public places, all these people seem to want (aside from food supplies) is the comforting, familiar feeling of a supermarket crush.

Migration

Migration and colonial settlement are core elements of the experience of being Han in Xinjiang. Most Han in Korla are migrants within a generation or two who came to the region in a series of waves since 1949. The first major wave of Han in-migration to Xinjiang began in the 1950s; it was state-sponsored and directed towards a quasi-military agricultural colony called the Xinjiang Production and Construction Corps (兵团, or Bingtuan). The second major wave began in the early 1990s and continues; it is economically motivated and self-sponsored migration, but shaped and strongly encouraged by state actors. The second wave brought Han settlers into more direct contact with Uyghurs in Xinjiang, partly because of a much stronger emphasis on migration into Uyghur-majority areas of southern Xinjiang.

The very act of migration into the 'behindness' that is Xinjiang infects the Han migrant with behindness, although at the same time, the movement often helps to raise their relative social status. Military officers and bureaucratic cadres posted to Xinjiang during the early Mao era (1950s) were typically promoted one level; self-sponsored farmer-settlers today are often granted land packages that provide an income far greater than what they could earn in rural eastern China.

Civilians and bureaucrats are the frontline soldiers of the colonial endeavour, yet by becoming 'Xinjiang people'—settlers, not just sojourners—they distance themselves from the cultural core and become themselves subject to this civilising project.

Mao-era settlers

Plate 6.2 Dr Pei in the backroom of his acupuncture and massage clinic, early August 2009. We were having a robust argument about domestic and political violence. Like many Chinese, Dr Pei was offended and angry that the Melbourne International Film Festival was showing a film about exiled Uyghur businesswoman Rebiya Kadeer, and that Australian authorities had refused Chinese demands to drop the film from the festival program and deny Kadeer a visa. The Chinese Government blamed Kadeer for instigating the riot on 5 July 2009, and very few Han people had any cause not to believe that the riots were premeditated and Kadeer was the mastermind. Dr Pei wrung out his towel over and over, occasionally clenching his fist, and insisting that it was absolutely right to govern Uyghurs and women with violence or the threat of violence.

Plate 6.3 Pei Jianjiang (centre) with his two best friends from the transport company school. Mid-1970s.

Plate 6.4 Pei Jianjiang (left), posing in a local photographic studio with the same two best friends, early 1980s. Soon after this photograph was taken, Pei began studying traditional Chinese medicine and martial arts.

Plate 6.5 Ms Gu at the market garden she runs with her husband. Ms Gu was laid off without a pension from her job as a kindergarten teacher at the 'Third Front' factory, where her husband also worked his whole life. The Third Front was an industrial policy (1964–80) that relocated urban factories deep inland, supposedly to make them harder to bomb in the event of war. Ms Gu and her husband were relocated from where they lived in eastern China to a remote valley north of Korla. In 2008, Ms Gu was knocked off her bicycle by a passing motorcyclist, sustaining head injuries and suffering memory loss and mild brain damage. The effects of the accident put a strain on her relationship with her husband.

Plate 6.6 Ms Gu at the factory in the mountains, 1979.

Plate 6.7 Ms Gu with her husband and son, ca. 2005.

Plate 6.8 Mr Jia in his oil company Land Cruiser in January 2010, looking at the Bingtuan high school from which he graduated in the early 1980s. According to him, at that time, Bingtuan children's greatest wish was to get into university—to shake off the Bingtuan, because life on the Bingtuan was very hard: 'At the same time, [non-Bingtuan] people looked down on you and discriminated against you. So, we studied hard; it was the only way out.'

Plate 6.9 Mr Jia's parents after arriving in Xinjiang for his father to take up a company commander position in the Bingtuan, 1963. The Bingtuan was set up as a military-agricultural colony in the early 1950s. Demobilised soldiers of both the Communists and their civil war enemies, the Nationalists, settled marginal arid lands, building extensive irrigation networks with hand tools and sheer force of numbers.

上海文革

Plate 6.10 Mr Jia, aged four, and his younger sister. He holds Mao's Little Red Book. It is 1969, a few years into the Cultural Revolution. The original photo was hand-coloured by the studio.

Plate 6.11 Teachers awaiting a negotiation. It is Friday morning and some teachers are sitting in the often-absent principal's office. They have just heard that their working conditions—hours, shifts, responsibilities, calculation of salary, and so on—have once again been changed by their boss, the investor. One month they may have to work or be on-call at the small private boarding school all day every second day; the next month it is back to 12 hours a day, six days a week. They do not like it, but teachers are common, and many new ones are produced every year. These older teachers have little chance of permanent employment in a government school; if they did, they would not be here. They wait and prepare themselves for yet another asymmetrical negotiation.

Recent settlers

The Bingtuan began as a system of military-agricultural colonies and was the main force behind Han in-migration to and the cultural transformation of Xinjiang until at least the end of the Mao era. Today, the Bingtuan is almost entirely civilian, but it is still seen by the central government as playing an important role in maintaining social and political stability in Xinjiang—largely because the Bingtuan's population, 94 per cent of whom are Han, occupies key peri-urban, rural, and border regions. Moreover, the legal parameters governing this settler population remain different to those that govern non-Bingtuan populations throughout the rest of rural China, including Xinjiang. These differential modes of governance result in a significant socioeconomic and politico-legal divide between the Bingtuan population (especially the newcomers) and the non-Bingtuan population.

Plate 6.12 Exploited tenant farmers on the Bingtuan.

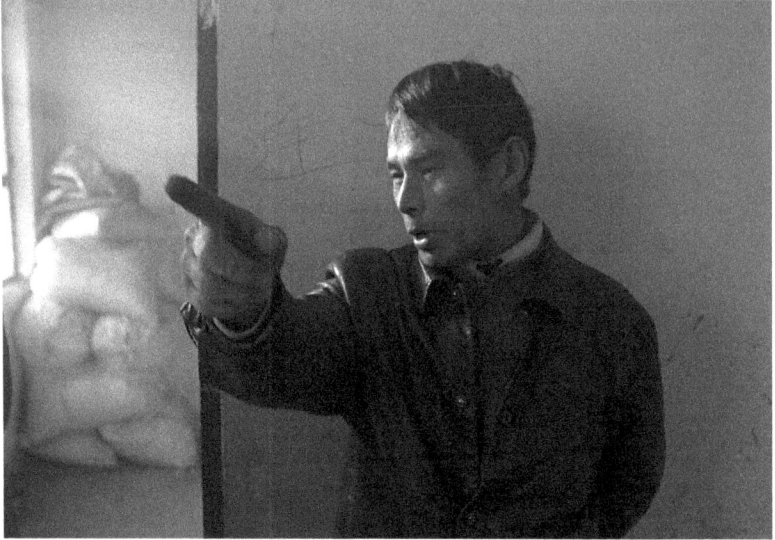

Plate 6.13 Another exploited tenant farmer on the Bingtuan.

Plates 6.12 and 6.13 depict tenant farmers on the Bingtuan, in winter 2007. Their village in inland China was hit by a natural disaster a few years previously, so they opted to come to Xinjiang to start a new life. The conditions of their employment on the Bingtuan as told to them before they came were apparently vastly different to the reality of how they are treated: 'What we have is not even enough to support a family and send a kid to school.'

They were promised 600 *yuan* a month as a minimum, whether they worked or not, but this has not been paid. Instead, they receive 15 *yuan* per day, but there is always work arranged for them by the Bingtuan authorities, so 'days off' do not really exist. Their house was apparently to be given to them, but after five years they are expected to pay 'over 10,000 *yuan*' and if they do not they will be taxed five years of rent for their house. The house is bare, clammy, unheated, unpainted, and small to boot. The man told me the table and wardrobe—both made from cheap plywood and not in good condition—cost 3,000 *yuan* of their pay and were a mandatory purchase. In this way, the Bingtuan authorities justify holding back their pay. They have 2.6 hectares and must invest 10,000 *yuan* in agricultural inputs each year. The poor land they work is more costly than that on which earlier arrivals work because the tax rate is fixed at the beginning of the land contract with the Bingtuan.

The disparity between their income and their needs for investment means they owe money to creditors in their old home in Henan.

Their household registration, which gives them access to basic health care and allows their child to attend school, has been transferred to the village in Xinjiang where they now live. If they returned to their old home, they would effectively be 'non-citizens', because they would not have these rights. Despite this, two-thirds of the people they originally came with have fled the Bingtuan.

Plate 6.14 Train series. Migrant track workers returning home after a day's work. North of Korla, October 2009.

Plate 6.15 Han on the squatter periphery of Korla, July 2009.

Plate 6.16 A due-for-demolition corner of old Korla, May 2008.

Empire

Water and oil are the liquid foundations of empires past and present. Karl Wittfogel famously coined the term 'hydraulic empires' in reference to the 'feudal' formations in which the centre commanded the coercive power to mobilise the population, through corvée or slave labour, to build extensive networks of transportation canals and irrigation channels. Control over water, in a rather different sense, was also the basis of expansionist European colonial empires from the Spanish and Portuguese to the British. These empires relied on their naval prowess—exporting their early modern technologies of power (bureaucracy, culture, and gunpowder-based armaments) into a spatial context in which these technologies conferred an insuperable advantage over the 'natives'. In Xinjiang, the Bingtuan established the irrigation that became the basis on which extensive Han settlement beyond the oases could be sustained—thus transforming, throughout most of the region, the frontier of control into a frontier of settlement.

Water remains important, but oil now flows through the channels of the imperial landscape. Many wars and invasive manoeuvres of the recent past have been motivated by the desire for oil. Oil also fuels and lubricates the global economy and supports and maintains the global status quo. Oil pipelines trace the linkages between political blocs, simultaneously blurring and affirming their boundaries and loyalties. Xinjiang is both an oil and gas-producing base and an essential transit point for hydrocarbons extracted in Central Asia and consumed in China's eastern metropolises. Despite being a domestic company, China National Petroleum Corporation (CNPC) is increasingly involved in offshore investment and oilfield development, as well as being the majority player within the PRC. CNPC is the parent of the Tarim Oilfield Company. The trope of 'oil and water' thus references the liquids that motivate and enable Han activities in Xinjiang, the oil company and the Bingtuan (as the formal institutions most closely associated with these respective liquids), and, more generally, the resources that have played and continue to play the key roles in the expansion and maintenance of imperial formations. Last but certainly not least, 'oil and water' metaphorically express the diverse experiences of Han people in Xinjiang.

Plate 6.17 Mausoleum in a Mongol autonomous county.

Plate 6.18 Apartment buildings in Korla's New City District.

Plate 6.19 Abandoned cinema in a former 'Third Front' factory south of Korla.

7
Recruiting loyal stabilisers: On the banality of carceral colonialism in Xinjiang[*]

Guldana Salimjan

While Uyghurs, Kazakhs, and other Turkic Muslim peoples are secretly transferred into prisons all over China (Bunin 2019; Kuo 2019; Jiang 2019), or reemerge as bare-minimum wage workers on the 'reeducation camp' factory floors (Byler 2019), China's settler institution, the Xinjiang Production and Construction Corps (兵团, Bingtuan), is facilitating new waves of Han influx from inner China (内地, *neidi*) to settle as farmers, civil servants, prison guards, police officers, and teachers. The totalitarian nature of such a massive human transfer is neutralised by the banal and procedural language of recruitment and employment—disguising the continued occupation and colonisation of Xinjiang.

State-sponsored Han migration into Xinjiang has been an important element in the militarisation and securitisation of the region since the founding of the People's Republic of China (Seymour 2000; Zhu and Blachford 2016). After October 1949, demobilised People's Liberation Army soldiers were recruited into production teams to establish mechanised state farms and ranches all over Xinjiang. In 1954, the Bingtuan was founded. Its development needs justified its grip on the region's vast grasslands and waterways, as well as the huge influx of ethnic Han migrant labourers. While early Bingtuan work was aimed at consolidating Communist Party power among the Kazakh population along the Sino-Soviet border (Moseley 1966; McMillen 1979), today's Bingtuan has expanded into a multi-billion-dollar urbanised corporation with its own jurisdiction and media that controls most agricultural industries in Xinjiang (Cliff 2009).

[*]This essay was originally published in the *Made in China Journal* (vol. 4, no. 3, 2019), doi.org/10.22459/MIC.04.03.2019.08.

Since Chen Quanguo, the current CCP secretary of the Xinjiang Uyghur Autonomous Region, established his carceral regime in 2017, Bingtuan recruitment notices have frequently appeared on the websites of provincial governments, colleges, and universities in inner China. With the ever-expanding detention centres and camps (Doman et al. 2018), there has been a growing need to recruit assistant police staff in Xinjiang (Zenz and Leibold 2019). Unlike civil servant recruitment materials in other provinces, Bingtuan advertisements utilise propaganda discourse typically reserved for Xinjiang and Tibet, such as 'ethnic unity, national integrity and stability, anti-separatism, and illegal religious activities' to get politically obedient and manageable individuals to settle in Xinjiang (see Advertisements Nos 1, 2, 3). The new recruits—usually college graduates and underemployed youths—are thus disengaged from the consequences of their settler-colonial practices. All parties involved in China's carceral colonialism in Xinjiang—Bingtuan, exam tutors, universities, state media, and new settlers—engage in an Orwellian 'newspeak' that comprises thoughtless teleological communist vocabularies of development, production, and employment. It is through such newspeak that the Bingtuan legitimises itself as a perpetual settler institution in Xinjiang and serves to cultivate colonial ideology and a sense of belonging for incoming generations of settlers.

Choreographed loyalty

As one of the major recruitment streams for civil servant positions (公务员) for various Bingtuan regiments, these advertisements are often seen on the 'career' webpages of Chinese universities (see Advertisements Nos 1, 2). Civil service positions are popular among college graduates in China as they offer stable income and better welfare than jobs in the private sector or self-employment. These Bingtuan recruitments are particularly systematic, targeting recruits from specific provinces or cities, aiming to ensure long-term settlement by providing attractive social benefits packages.

Unlike civil servant recruitment in other provinces, these Bingtuan recruitments put extra emphasis on the evaluation of the applicants' 'practical performance in safeguarding national unity, ethnic unity, and social stability' (其在维护祖国统一、维护民族团结、维护社会稳定中的现实表现) (see Advertisement No. 3). According to a recruitment advertisement posted in December 2018, the Bingtuan was calling for

237 civil servant applicants from the provinces of inner China (excluding Tibet and Qinghai) (see Advertisement No. 4). The recruitment targeted college graduates under 30 years of age for positions at various Bingtuan regiments in southern Xinjiang, including the 1st Division in Aral City in Aksu, the 2nd Division in Tiemenguan City in Korla, and the 3rd Division in Tumshuk City in Kashgar. The applicants would undergo interviews and background checks in inner China in cities such as Shenyang, Zhengzhou, Changsha, and Lanzhou. The recruiting personnel would examine the applicants' eligibility, including their 'political quality' (政治素质), 'thought quality' (思想品质), 'adaptability' (适应能力), 'psychological quality' (心理素质), 'volunteering spirit' (奉献精神), and 'discipline and law-abiding quality' (遵纪守法). The minimum service period was five years. Successful applicants would be reimbursed for the cost of their round trip to Xinjiang.

Among the following recruitments from Gansu, Jilin, Inner Mongolia, Anhui, Hebei, and Shanxi, applicants for the positions in Hotan were not even required to sit a written exam (see Advertisement Nos 5, 6). Successful applicants were promised a high salary, housing, official rank, and social security benefits. The state even offered to reimburse their graduate school tuition at the rate of 8,000 *yuan* per year (see Advertisement Nos 5–8). Eligibility once again depended on political performance. Applicants had to be college graduates with membership or preliminary membership of the CCP (see Advertisement Nos 5–9).

To prepare for these political performance interviews, applicants can sign up for online training courses streamed on mobile phones by scanning a QR code and logging into an official WeChat site. The courses teach applicants to mimic the tones and gestures of Communist Party cadres during an interview. For instance, in one of these videos, a tutor teaches the applicants to perform an enthusiastic endorsement of 'Xi Jinping Thought' like an actor: 'The key is to speak nonsense in a serious manner [一本正经的胡说八道] [see Advertisement No. 12]. You need to act like someone who belongs to the system. It is all about acting skills [拼演技].' Speaking to the broader audience from inner China, this tutor is grooming politically apathetic college graduates to participate in everyday political performances of loyalty in Xinjiang, where Communist Party 'nonsense' is a serious matter.

Table 7.1 Examples of Bingtuan civil servant recruitment notices

Date published	No. of people	Recruited from	Recruited to	Advertisement no.
3 Jul 2017	113	Sichuan Province	Various Bingtuan divisions: 6th, 8th, Ürümqi (i.e. Changji, Shihezi)	17
8 Dec 2017	80	Provinces of inner China	Various Bingtuan divisions: 1st, 2nd, 3rd, 14th (i.e. Aksu, Bayingol, Tumshuk, Hotan)	18
11 Aug 2018	1,348	Provinces of inner China	Various Bingtuan prison systems	19
19 Mar 2019	524	All police school graduates in China	Various Bingtuan divisions: 1st, 2nd, 3rd, 14th (i.e. Aksu, Bayingol, Tumshuk, Hotan)	20
15 Apr 2019	49	Provinces of inner China	Bingtuan 2nd division (i.e. Bayingol)	21
10 May 2019	330	Hebei Province	Bingtuan 2nd division (i.e. Bayingol)	22

Online tutorials also disseminate official settler-colonial ideology about Xinjiang in relation to securitisation and ethnic integration. In another video, a tutor shares with his viewers a real question that was asked during a Bingtuan job interview (see Advertisement No. 13):

> Xi Jinping said: 'Make Bingtuan the stabiliser of the frontier, the melting pot of different ethnic groups, and the exemplar of advanced productivity and modern culture.' Please discuss your thoughts on this quote considering the practical situation of Bingtuan and explain the relationship between the three aspects.

Fully costumed like a China Central Television anchor, the tutor gives a model answer in perfect Mandarin pronunciation:

> Stabiliser, melting pot, and exemplar region are strong indications of our party's work in land reclamation and border reinforcement, [and] also an excellent summary of our Bingtuan mission. To be the frontier stabiliser is the basic requirement for Bingtuan's land reclamation and border reinforcement. Well known for its large

scale, numbers, and strong ability, combining military police in battle in quelling separatist and unrest activities, Bingtuan is an important force to maintain border stability and security. Unifying different ethnic groups in a melting pot is another role Bingtuan is playing. For a long time, Bingtuan has implemented the party's ethnic policy, and stressed the unity, development, and prosperity of all ethnic groups, promoting harmonious living and peaceful coexistence … In my future work, I will also practise these three points. I will lead by example by staying close to the border masses, close the gap between us, and integrate with the masses.

Loyal education and police spirit

As can be seen in Table 7.2, prison guard positions constitute another rising employment stream into southern Xinjiang, where many 'reeducation camps' are located. Among all civil servants recruited by the Bingtuan in 2018, prison personnel made up more than one-third of the total prospective employees (see Advertisement No. 14). For these positions, the 'political quality' (政治素质) criterion was more concrete and even family members were under scrutiny. People with criminal or correctional records were not allowed to apply. If the applicants had a relative within three generations who had been sentenced to death, endangered state security, incited ethnic separatism, conducted illegal religious activity, or practised Falun Gong, they were not eligible.

A Bingtuan recruitment drive for 500 prison guards in 2019 did not require a written exam, only a face-to-face interview (see Advertisement No. 15). Such an exemption is rare and indicates to some degree the state's growing need for security forces in Xinjiang. In another video, a tutor introduces the eligibility requirements for the positions in the regiment's prisons, as well as which cities they are in (see Advertisement No. 16). At minute 19:30, he casually says:

> Many of you might have looked up the specific locations of these prisons on Baidu Maps but couldn't find them. Prisons are supposed to be secretive. Of course, we can't mark the location of the prisons otherwise it would look like there are prisons everywhere; it's not good, right?

It is worth mentioning that once selected for the position, applicants for prison guards must receive systematic political indoctrination. At the end of 2018, the Bingtuan prison system initiated a series of 'loyalty education programs' (忠诚教育) to reinforce 'loyal police spirit' (忠诚警魂), which included the compulsory study of 21 essays on Xi Jinping Thought, the Communist Party Constitution, Xinjiang history, and the history of Bingtuan land reclamation (Ministry of Justice 2018). Police and prison guards must study for at least one hour every day and always carry with them the *Bingtuan Prison Police 'Loyalty Education' Study Manual* (兵团监狱民警'忠诚教育'应知应会手册). Employees must establish 'four kinds of consciousness' (四个意识)—that is, political consciousness, overall situation consciousness, core consciousness, and unification consciousness—regularly write reflections, participate in patriotic red song choruses, watch patriotic films, participate in 'Inheriting Red Genes, Practising Bingtuan Spirit' (传承红色基因.践行兵团精神) speaking contests and seminars, and so on. There is a monthly examination and those who fail are criticised. Employees must also denounce 'two-faced people' (两面人) among their ranks and participate in the 'Becoming Families' campaign (访民情、惠民生、聚民心), which is aimed at spying on the ethnic minorities in the Bingtuan regiments in southern Xinjiang.

Table 7.2 A selection of Bingtuan police recruitment notices since 2017

Date	No. of people	Recruited from	Destination	Advertisement no.
9 Nov 2018	111	Anhui, Henan, Shanxi	Regiments of the 14th Division, Kunyu City (Qurumqax in Hotan)	3
9 Nov 2018	61	Hubei, Gansu	1st Division, Aral City, Aksu	10
9 Nov 2018	48	Hebei, Shanxi	2nd Division, Tiemenguan City, Korla	9
18 Dec 2018	237	Provinces of inner China	1st, 2nd, 3rd, 14th Divisions, Aral, Tiemenguan, Tumshuk, Qurumqax in Hotan	4
26 Mar 2019	620	Provinces of inner China	Various Bingtuan regiments and police stations	11

(Un)transferrable belonging: Farmers and workers

Another stream that absorbs a huge number of Han labourers from inner China is the 'employment transfer' (转移就业) program, which targets less-educated farmers and workers under 40 years of age. Households of Han settlers are particularly welcome. Unlike the above-mentioned civil servant and prison guard recruitment streams that focus on political conformity and reliability, this stream's recruitment advertisements clearly explain levels of agricultural production, land area, working seasons, and annual income for the farmers, and offer full packages of social welfare that are unfathomable in the hometowns of the potential applicants.

According to a 2018 recruitment campaign targeting farmers from Henan Province, holders of agricultural *hukou* (household registration) would be given non-agricultural *hukou* once they were settled in Xinjiang and their trip fares would be reimbursed (see Advertisement No. 23). New employees are provided rent-free accommodation for four years in apartments equipped with electricity and heating. Couples will both receive registered positions to grow cotton on 35 *mu* (2.3 hectares) of land each and are given land at the end of their first year in Xinjiang. For China's vast population of economically precarious farmers and migrant workers, social and medical insurance are among the most attractive benefits for settling in Xinjiang. The new employees and all their family members are fully covered by health, unemployment, and retirement insurance.

Neighbouring provincial governments such as Gansu and Ningxia are collaborating with the Bingtuan to transfer their impoverished farmers to various regiments in Xinjiang. After a 'farewell ceremony' (欢送大会), impoverished people are finally out of sight, out of mind for the officials of the sending governments. A single county in Ningxia had a quota of 900 people to be transferred to Xinjiang in 2017 (see Advertisement No. 24). In a video recruitment advertisement for the Bingtuan 1st Division in Aral City, Aksu, where more than 99 per cent of the population is Han, the narrator stresses the local population is scarce and the need for labour input is urgent and necessary (see Advertisement No. 25). She then sets out the recruitment plan for each regiment as part of the Thirteenth Five-Year Plan in the region. To take a few examples from a long list: the 14th Regiment is planning to recruit 9,000 people; the 224th Regiment is planning to recruit 5,600 people; the 14th Division is planning to recruit 650 households (Bingtuan recruitments favour households over individuals, as whole families are more likely to settle down), and so on.

Again, the benefits for settlers are astounding. Each settler will receive 20 *mu* (1.3 hectares) of land for each type of crop cultivated by the regiment. The settlement's housing is equipped with living supplies and rent is subsidised for the first three years. Each settler couple can earn 1,500 *yuan* in housing subsidies per month, including social security and *hukou* transfer procedures. Some regiments even provide apartments to households with six or more people. Their rent is subsidised as well and can be used towards a mortgage with the aim of eventually owning the property. Settlers' children can attend local schools without having to pay for tuition for 15 years and can enjoy added points on their college entrance examination scores (高考加分)—an affirmative action policy that has historically been directed towards Uyghurs and other ethnic minorities in Xinjiang. However, despite all these benefits, many households are not interested in moving and, according to a report from Dingxi, Gansu (Li 2019), some poor households have been threatened and coerced into relocating—with those refusing cut off from the social guarantees for impoverished families. The local government ensured relocated households did not return to Gansu by revoking their *hukou* and confiscating their land and houses. Villagers also revealed that, in some cases, the promised benefits did not materialise.

Despite all this, *Sina.com* (2018) painted a rosy picture of one farmer's employment transfer from Dingxi in Gansu to Xinjiang, titled 'Make a Home Across 3,000 Kilometres'—an experience almost too good to be true and starkly different from the stories of manipulation and coercion reported by independent sources (Li 2019).

The protagonist of *Sina.com*'s report is Cao Yongping. His hometown, Bailu village, is the poorest in the whole province. Environmental deterioration in recent years has pushed many of his fellow villagers to find work in the cities, and Cao himself has made several attempts to leave the countryside and get out of poverty. A few years ago, he took out a 100,000-*yuan* loan and purchased a long-haul truck to transport vegetables between Lanzhou and Chengdu. In 2016, he broke his ribs in a traffic accident and was unable to continue this work. He has since been in debt and has been unable to repay his loan.

In February 2017, various divisions of the Bingtuan began to recruit workers from Dingxi. The slogan for the recruitment campaign was 'Relocation employment in a systematic, organised, and scaled manner' (有计划、有组织、有规模地进行转移就业). Cao learned that if he chose to relocate to Xinjiang, he could immediately move into an apartment of

80 square metres with 70 *mu* (4.7 hectares) of allotted land, plus 15 years of free education for his children. Many farmers like Cao were recruited by the Bingtuan to cultivate land and settle as long-term farm employees. Cao had to learn from his father how to do agricultural work. After much preparation, Cao took his wife and children to Xinjiang first, leaving his elderly father behind to take care of the rest of the relocation work.

In 2018, Cao's family arrived in Tumshuk County on the outskirts of Kashgar, 3,100 kilometres from his home village. They became the first household of the Bingtuan 'employment transfer' program. Unlike previous waves of migrant workers to Xinjiang, workers enrolled in this program are required to settle down. Cao's family was to settle in the 50th Regiment in Tumshuk. Fellow villagers from Dingxi picked them up and registered them at the regiment's office. Cao was given the option of living in an apartment or in a one-storey house close to his allotted land. Since he planned to bring his parents as well, he chose the house, which had three bedrooms, a living room, and a courtyard.

In their new residence, all the necessities of life and furniture were already installed. The regiment leader told Cao that their regiment's renovation fee was the highest among all regiments, as water, electricity, the gas stove and hot water, and even food and cleaning supplies were all provided. Cao's family was assigned to one of dozens of traditional Chinese Hui style houses, with an 85-square-metre courtyard, where they could live rent-free for six years. Cao thought he would have to work for more than 10 years to achieve these kinds of living conditions in Dingxi. Although he worried about safety issues in Xinjiang, his fellow Dingxi compatriots told him this place was now safer than anywhere in China. Two weeks later, Cao's parents arrived after selling their pigs back home. Cao's children have registered in local schools. A new life has begun for them.

Epilogue

Like a drop of water disappearing into a vast sea, Cao and his family faded into the state machine of human transfers in China. At the first dinner after settling down at the regiment, Cao commented that the potatoes in Xinjiang are not as delicious as in Dingxi. *Sina.com*'s journalist allowed this humanistic moment of recalcitrance in Cao's story. On a broader scale, state-sponsored Han settlement in Xinjiang is normalised by this kind of triumphant narrative of poverty-alleviation campaigns, burying the inconvenient truth that sees the dilution, incarceration, and replacement of native populations in Xinjiang. Cao would not be burdened by the thought of benefiting from stolen land. He has settled permanently in Xinjiang, just as countless Uyghurs and Kazakhs have been indefinitely imprisoned behind the barbed wire just a few miles away, in reeducation camps staffed by other hopeful new migrants from inner China.

The continued challenge facing the Bingtuan lies in cultivating a sense of loyalty and belonging among the newest waves of Han immigrants from inner China, who are different from both the older generations of Han settlers who arrived after the 1950s and the economically motivated migrant subalterns who arrived in the 1990s, such as those described by Tom Cliff (2016) in his recent ethnography of Bingtuan Han settlers, *Oil and Water*. These new waves of incoming Han add biopolitical fuel to Chen Quanguo's carceral regime, which in return provides solid ground for the political and economic legitimacy of the Bingtuan. Through the CCP's banal, technocratic discourses of employment and political loyalty, the Bingtuan fulfils the state's mission of securitising Xinjiang. Yet, at the same time, it also securitises the potentially unstable situations created by the surplus of underemployed Han youth in the countryside and cities of inner China—a problem continuously exacerbated by ongoing land dispossession and wealth disparity.

8
Triple dispossession in northwestern China

Sam Tynen

I n Xinjiang today, most Uyghurs remain outside the detention camps
but still live in a type of open-air prison. Their phones are monitored
and censored. Their passports are confiscated. Their movements are
tracked, and bodies checked and scanned constantly. The Chinese state
security agenda has targeted Uyghurs since Islamophobia really took hold
in the country after 11 September 2001 (Hessler 2006; Roberts 2020).

In this essay, I demonstrate what oppression and marginalisation mean
outside the camps in broader Uyghur society. I argue that there are many
kinds of state violence that are invisible and insidious. The visible types
of state violence that will be explored are housing demolition, eviction
from homes, and incarceration or detainment. These aspects are all very
much present in media and government reports about the Xinjiang
region. However, this recent focus on the strikingly visible aspects of
Chinese state power in the region overlooks acts of everyday and invisible
violence that are part and parcel of the region's current political economy
of development. My goal is to shed light on the inherent violence of the
nation-state, especially for targeted minorities and the undocumented.

Building on Das (2007), I use ethnographic fieldwork to study 'ordinary'
state violence. What do I mean by 'everyday', 'ordinary', and 'invisible' state
violence? I refer to those mundane events that occur so frequently that
one does not think about them—for example: ID cards being stamped
with a fixed ethnic identity; being called a 'minority'; housing registration
forms only being available in Chinese, with no translation; Chinese as the
dominant language of television and government; movement controlled
by police and bureaucratic red tape; being compelled to move to the city
for work; and needing a passport for mobility. Indeed, refugees and the
undocumented will be the first to tell you how passports are a type of
ordinary state violence, preventing free passage and granting rights and
access only to certain people.

ID cards, language, and minority categories might not look like violence because nobody is forcing anyone to do anything and no-one is being physically harmed. However, on further investigation, one can see that conditions that remove agency from the subject are a type of violent control. These aspects of state monitoring are not based on choice but are compulsory; having an ID card that labels the person a certain race and gender is not optional. Invisible state violence is often the precondition for more obvious forms of explicit violence. In the Uyghur case, managing and monitoring ID cards and residency permit applications for Uyghurs later allowed the state to efficiently locate and displace hundreds of thousands of Uyghurs from various parts of China, ultimately channelling them into internment camps.

While the media and some foreign governments focus on internment camps for Uyghurs in China, questions remain about the invisible violence of the state: How do dispossession and displacement occur for rural migrant Uyghurs in Xinjiang on an individual scale? What is the role of their dispossession in securing state territorial control? To explore these questions, I focus on 22 Uyghurs and their rural-to-urban migration experiences. Their stories illustrate their dispossession even before the internment camps became widespread. According to my interviews, the three stages of dispossession are displacement from the countryside, alienation in the city, and ultimately eviction from the city. This triple dispossession helped create the conditions for the mass internment.

This essay draws on ethnographic participant-observation over the course of living in Ürümqi, in Xinjiang, for 24 months from 2014 to 2017.[1] All names used are pseudonyms. Note that to protect the identity of my informants, I do not include specific demographic information when quoting from conversations. The figures in this chapter are composites of several female rural migrant informants and provide a thick description of Uyghur migrant women's experiences in Ürümqi. The remaining quotes are a sample collection from all 22 Uyghur rural migrants whom I interviewed in 2016–17, most of them women. I also spoke to an additional 26 Uyghurs who grew up in cities, who informed my analysis but are not quoted here. In addition, I had informal conversations with 52

---

1   For more information on state surveillance, knowledge production, and methods during that time, see Ryan and Tynen (2019).

Uyghurs from urban and rural areas who gave informed consent to quote them. Some of those 52 conversations from rural migrants informed the figures and are quoted here.

Defining displacement and dispossession

Uyghurs live in a settler-colonial context (Byler 2018; Roberts 2020). Colonisation is about extracting resources from a place for profit. Settler colonialism takes it to the next level by bringing people from the colonising place into the colonised one to live there permanently. The United States, Canada, and Australia are examples of colonies where large numbers of settlers came to the new land, decimated the native populations, and became the dominant society (Coulthard 2014).

State-subsidised Han Chinese migration to the Xinjiang region, especially since the 1940s, represents a clear pattern of settler colonialism in the Uyghur homeland (see also Cliff's Chapter 6 in this volume). According to official data, the Han Chinese population grew from 200,000 residents in 1944 to 9.5 million in 2015 (Xinjiang Statistics Bureau 2016). The Chinese Communist Party continues to use Han migration as a tool of state control in the region (Cliff 2009, 2016). Estimates from the *Xinjiang Statistical Yearbook* of 2019 say there are close to 12 million Han migrants in Xinjiang today, although the accuracy of these numbers is questionable.

In addition to migration, there is a long history of Han appropriating land, oil, natural gas, jade, and other resources from Xinjiang that goes back to the early eighteenth century but took off from the 1880s (Perdue 2005). Uyghurs have long experienced colonisation via 'development', through which the Chinese state claims to provide economic 'assistance'. The boom in private industry in the 1990s and 2000s also removed Uyghur ownership of land and capital (Byler 2018). As one example, Dautcher (2009: 57) records that there were 'discriminatory zoning regulations and the coerced sale of Uyghur-owned land to Han in-migrants' in Xinjiang during the 1990s. Settler colonialism systematically removed the Uyghur relationship to land, livelihood, and knowledge (Schluessel 2016).

Dispossession is the opposite of possession (Moreton-Robinson 2015), and dispossession is a primary theme in the colonisation of Xinjiang. If possessing property and resources is the advantage of the coloniser, the colonised experience the inverse. Dispossession can be accomplished through various means—for example, the changing of placenames or redrawing of maps to ignore native land possession. Other examples include the destruction of knowledge systems, ways of life, or modes of thinking—for instance, in North America, the native idea that 'land cannot be owned' was transformed under colonisation into 'you must have a title to use this land'. The concept of 'dispossession' used in this essay aids in investigating the inequality and social relations that underlie the process of Uyghurs claiming a homeland.

Epistemic dispossession is at the heart of the settler-colonial process. In colonial contexts, epistemic dispossession destroys a way of thinking and being without offering a replacement or substituting with an unwanted replacement. Coulthard (2014) argues that dispossession is not as simple as land seizure and compensation in a context where that concept of ownership never existed. Rather, dispossession is the introduction of a new episteme that brings forward a different relationship to property. New ways of thinking, knowing, and being deprive natives of prior forms of sociality. The present-day dispossession of Uyghurs—through the introduction of Chinese ways of thinking and being, a novel sociality, as well as new private property relations—occurred during their movements between rural and urban areas. A triple dispossession has occurred since 2014 as Uyghurs left the countryside, found alienation and unemployment once they reached the city, and were later forced from the cities and into internment camps (see also Tynen 2019, 2020).

Stories of epistemic dispossession highlight the invisible forms of violence inflicted by state-led development, as well as palpable incidents of state terror. Uyghur life stories highlight the marginalisation of bodies left behind by development and disappeared by the state. Uyghur narratives of desire and fear demonstrate the way the vectors of dispossession move between the epistemic and the material. In addition to loss of land and livelihood, they experience loss of personal autonomy and sovereignty over their own bodies, homes, and families. Control over the domestic sphere and bodies is a key goal of state territorial control. As such, territorial control comes to encompass not simply land, but also the economic, political, and cultural networks that shape a certain place.

Part 1: Displacement from the countryside

The people I interviewed claim agency in their decision to move to the city, but their narratives reveal a fine line between consent and coercion. The invisible violence associated with economic development played a major role in dispossession and displacement. All the rural migrants came to the city for work or to accompany family members who had migrated to look for work or to study. However, they also repeatedly claimed that 'economic development' had caused negative effects in their rural hometowns, as 'the [rural] economy has got worse' (*iqtisad tovenlep ketti*). It is important to note that this recurrent theme in the interviews reflected a measure of how Xinjiang's economy was doing for categories of the population—indeed, according to the numbers, Xinjiang's economy has only improved in the past 10 years. However, for Uyghur people in rural areas, economic opportunities have decreased while the cost of living has increased. Their stories are evidence of the way inequality is being exacerbated by economic development. For these interviewees, dispossession in their rural hometowns occurred because of development projects that were supposed to increase the standard of living, but instead made homes and other goods unaffordable.

In addition, interviewees reported experiencing surveillance in rural areas that pushed them to find political and cultural freedom in the cities. Some spoke about the relatively intense surveillance in their hometowns that went beyond restrictions on religious practice alone: 'The local politics has made [my hometown] a difficult place to live. It's not free like Ürümqi is.' 'There are police and roadside checkpoints everywhere, people are afraid to leave their homes for fear of getting arrested for no reason.' 'We came with high hopes for a new life. Everybody in [my hometown] wants to leave and come to Ürümqi, and our relatives told us not to come home and to stay in Ürümqi for now, at least until the situation [*veziyet*] gets better.' *Veziyet* was often used as a seemingly neutral euphemism to refer to the government or to mean 'political situation'. 'Everybody in [my hometown] wants to leave and come to Ürümqi because it's a lot freer here.'

This tightening of surveillance and control in rural areas ultimately enabled forms of dispossession that exceeded simple land seizure. This dispossession included restrictions on a people's identity and way of life. By eliminating daily practices—such as mosque attendance, ritual performance, language education, and travel to regional markets—the state undermined the cohesiveness of Uyghur society and thus established stronger territorial control. All this was part of an Islamophobic policy targeting Uyghur bodies. These projects, in conjunction with state and community surveillance, drove Uyghurs to the city. The economic dispossession by the state and market combined with ethnic discrimination and dispossession of homeland in a colonial project to control and eliminate

Plate 8.1 A typical Uyghur living room, with carpet, decorated mat, and a tablecloth for eating, while a child sleeps in the corner. Photo by the author.

Uyghur culture and society. It is against this backdrop that the next two phases of dispossession—that is, alienation in and eviction from the city—have taken place.

Part 2: Alienation in the city

Aygul quickly swept the carpet with a hand broom, pulled out the guest mat with gold trim, folded it over double for me, and urged me to sit.

Flustered, she apologised profusely for not having any tea on hand: 'We just don't have the conditions for luxuries like tea right now.' She then brought in *naan* bread, hot water, and tiny clementine oranges from her shop for us to share.

I asked Aygul about her life in the city. She had moved to Ürümqi 13 years earlier from a rural village in Xinjiang. 'When I first moved here, for me, Ürümqi was awesome [*peyzi*]. There was every kind of person and every kind of opportunity, and a lot more freedom,' she told me.

Aygul had a round face and was almost always smiling, despite the fact one of her favourite activities was complaining. She vented to me about her poor housing conditions—they did not have a toilet or proper heating—her husband and kids, and the Chinese Government. Aygul spoke fast—so fast that sometimes I could not catch all the words as they jumbled together and on top of one another. But even when she was angry or upset, she usually still managed to slip in jokes, even if they were at the expense of her husband.

'I'm so tired and worn out. I'm a mother of two young kids, so there's no such thing as rest for me,' she said, sighing.

Her jolly chortles made her large belly shake and her chubby cheeks stick out. When she was tired—as she so often was—she put her head in her hands and her eyelids drooped, and she talked a little slower, telling me about the pressures of trying to run the shop and raise two young children without the resources, such as a washing machine, that she desired and envied others for having.

The story of Aygul illustrates some common sentiments expressed during my 22 interviews with rural migrants. All my interviewees came to the city for work or accompanied their husbands or parents who had come to the city looking for employment or to study. Economic dispossession played a major role in their displacement from rural to urban areas in Xinjiang because there was no work in the countryside.

People felt compelled to move to the city to find a job or to pursue an education. For rural migrants, a phrase that came up at least once in all my interviews was 'amal yoq', which literally means 'there is no way/method', and is used in Uyghur to mean 'there is nothing to be done' or 'I have no other options'. The Chinese equivalent of this phrase is 'mei banfa' (没办法). Often their stories of moving to the city were couched in the terms of amal yoq, and the lack of alternatives spoke to the depth of economic dispossession that many experienced in their hometowns, which eventually drove them to the city and kept them there.

While some Uyghurs talked of the freedom of the city, they also spoke of a further dispossession after relocation from the jobless countryside. They struggled with loneliness in a new culture in the city. They often complained about the pollution and felt stress and alienation from their community due to wage labour. These feelings of being trapped in hourly wage jobs were couched in terms of the pervasive selfishness imbued in urban social relations. They also talked about a loss of community practices, such as hosting visitors or being a guest in the home of others (mehman bolush/qilish). One woman told me: 'We hate the city, but we have no choice but to move here for the jobs and for political and cultural freedoms.' While most interviewees in 2016—before the camps opened— said they disliked the city, about half said they did not plan to return to their hometowns for the reasons cited above: lack of jobs and freedom. As such, their narratives of urban existence were shrouded in hopelessness and depression.

That rural migrants who came to the city seeking a better life were met with alienation and dispossession reveals the political and economic implications of dispossession from urbanisation and development projects. Their insistence that they had no choice but to stay and could not return to their hometown in the countryside for economic and political reasons foreshadowed the demolitions, evictions, and incarcerations that began in 2017.

Part 3: Eviction from the city

Aygul was sitting on the carpet in the front room playing on her phone. When I approached, she stood up to greet me with two kisses, one on each cheek, and her eyelids were drooping with sleep.

'How are things?' I inquired.

'Well … They are kicking everyone [the Uyghurs] out of Ürümqi. I can't go back to rural Kashgar … The politics, the economic situation—it's so much worse than here. So, I don't know what's going to happen,' she said with a wavering voice, tears pooling in her eyes.

'We just got word today that all the shops on this street will be demolished in three days. So, our shop will be gone soon. There's nothing we can do about it.'

'Where are you moving to?' I asked.

'There is no place to move to!' she said, as though she was talking to an incompetent child. 'But now they are evicting *all* migrant Uyghurs from the city. They [government agents] are all so evil, they are breaking up families and they don't even care.'

I told Aygul I was sad to hear this, but my words sounded flat as my heart sat in my throat. She said to me:

> All of us here have broken hearts, eh? We can't do anything here; they won't rent to us [Uyghur people], they won't let us buy a house, they won't let us live here or work here, nothing. They just want to send us away. So, they're evil. There's nothing to be done.

(Left) Plate 8.2 Notification of demolition by the local government. Both strips of paper say the same thing: 'Victory Road Management Committee, Nanliang Neighbourhood Committee Letter.' Photo by the author, May 2017. (Right) Plate 8.3 The 'chai' symbol of demolition marks a Uyghur restaurant in Ürümqi. Photo by author, May 2017.

All the shops on the street were shuttered, locked and marked with big white Xs to prevent anyone getting back in. I saw through the window of Aygul's shop that there were some abandoned blankets inside. The white Xs bore the name of the neighbourhood community centre office.

I noticed a white X taped firmly across the front doors of the neighbouring noodle restaurant. I walked up to the window and looked inside. The display case for cakes was still illuminated and half a watermelon was sitting inside. Tables and chairs were stacked on top of each other, there was a metal basin filled with white porcelain cups, and a container of spicy chilli peppers and a basin of vinegar on the table closest to the window. It was as though the occupants had not been informed of the demolition with enough time to clean out the shop.

A street that was once bustling with activity now sat silent.

By the end of the first week of May, the entire neighbourhood had been demolished.

In mid-May 2017, I met up with Aygul, who was still in Ürümqi. 'I tried delaying going back to Kashgar as long as I could. But the situation is just out of control,' she explained, shaking her head. 'They are cracking down like never before. I have to leave. I have to go back to Kashgar now or else I'll be arrested. They might arrest me or send me to a "re-education" training school.' She shook her head and raised her eyebrows while pursing her lips.

That was the last time I saw or heard from her.

This story illustrates the way poor, rural migrants were evicted from the city through a slow escalation and tightening of rules. The evictions were carried out as targeted neighbourhood policing that profiled rural Uyghurs and used demolition for the purpose of redevelopment as a pretext to economically and politically force Uyghurs from the city and into internment camps.

Implications of Uyghur migrant dispossession

In some ways, the process of Uyghur migrant eviction is similar to the experiences of Han migrant workers in other urban areas of China (Zhang 2001). Some scholars have argued that, historically, migrant workers have been treated as 'minorities' and 'outsiders' even if they have 'Han' on their ID card (Honig 1992). Some contemporary scholars compare the *hukou* regime to a form of apartheid (Alexander and Chan 2006). Others speak of discrimination as a kind of classism in terms of the 'quality' of migrants (Pun 2005; Yan 2008). Meanwhile, other scholars talk about migrants from certain provinces being 'racialised' (Han 2009). Thus, important similarities exist between Han migrants and Uyghur migrants, particularly regarding the economic forces that push migrant workers to be less attached to their land and livelihood (Tynen 2019).

However, the situation in Xinjiang is also distinct. Han migrants are generally able to move to other parts of the city or to other cities, while Uyghurs are criminalised wherever they go due to an Islamophobic discourse of terrorism and violence that follows them everywhere (see Brophy's Chapter 4 in this volume). Once evicted, Uyghurs in Ürümqi and all over China were forced to return to their rural hometowns. Furthermore, the Uyghur case is different in its context of a colonial power seizing indigenous land and claiming sovereignty. Especially for the Uyghurs, the ethnic differences between themselves and their colonisers define an inequality that is irreversible and unforgivable. The gap between cultures, religions, and languages leaves a gulf so wide it cannot be mended. This is the difference between urban cleansing in the Han case and racial banishment in the Uyghur case (Roy 2019).

The camps in 2017

Aygul's experience was a common one during the spring of 2017. At that time, no-one knew what was going on. The rules kept changing. It was confusing and scary. We did not realise it then, but the purpose of demolishing Uyghur homes and shops, and eventually evicting Uyghur migrants from the city, was to force them back to the countryside, where they would be met with internment, held without trial or criminal conviction, never to return.

After Aygul, many of my friends started disappearing. The confusion and fear were palpable in the whispers and looks exchanged and in the shake of a head. Words did not need to be exchanged to know that a relative or friend had been interned for 'reeducation'.

According to a state report published in 2013, Xinjiang authorities believed ethnic-minority migrants in the region needed to be targeted and 'transformed' (转变) through a range of legal education and training measures (Wu 2020). In line with the hierarchical policy implementation that is common in China, it appears that, over time, each county was made responsible for carrying out this project and given quotas and targets. To meet these, they had to call people back from the city—a process that had begun in 2014 with a passbook system (The Economist 2016). Underlying this system was a discourse of danger. The Uyghur migrants were seen as a threat to the safety and security of the city and Han populations, and therefore had to be detained and re-educated because of their extremist beliefs. The camps were part of this re-education effort. They were built primarily in rural Xinjiang. Many rural Uyghurs who were sent back to the place of their original household registration were placed in camps in that location. According to interviews with a former camp worker in the city (Byler 2021), urban Uyghurs were also detained in city camps. The entire process of asserting social control was originally underpinned by rather banal ID cards and registration forms.

Warning signs

The life experiences of Uyghur rural migrants in the city show how economics and security work to exploit and displace minority bodies. First, they were displaced from their homes in the countryside due to poor economic development policies. Second, they struggled in the city, and were often left unemployed and alienated. Third, they were evicted from the city because of the Islamophobic discourse of Uyghurs as extremists and terrorists. They were seen as a danger to safety and security, and were evicted, arrested, and detained on a scale that far outweighs that of any other ethnic group in China. These stories offer us warning signs for other parts of the world that might be heading towards state violence. The pattern is economic crisis combined with an oppressive political environment. The evictions were not simply displacement for the sake of demolition and redevelopment of the cities. The evictions were about forcing Uyghurs to leave the city for 'safety' reasons, which justified their incarceration in internment camps. The triple dispossession created the conditions for the mass internment: large numbers of unemployed Uyghurs, dissatisfaction with their lives in the cities, and eviction based on narratives of Islamophobia.

9
Replace and rebuild: Chinese colonial housing in Uyghur communities*

Timothy A. Grose

From Khan Tengri to the Kunlun Mountains, Uyghur homes are being transformed from the inside out. Snaking alleys connecting *mähällä* ('communities') are being buried beneath rows of high-rise apartments and tract-housing developments. Walls that once displayed beautiful woven *giläm* ('rugs') and delicate fabrics are now covered by Chinese national flags and images of President Xi Jinping. Raised platforms, or *supa*, which were used for eating, sleeping, and entertaining, are being smashed to clear space for chairs, sofas, and tables. Officially, the Chinese Communist Party boasts that these changes help rescue Uyghurs from poverty and propel them into modernity. However, these measures betray the hallmarks of colonisation: they are part of a process that destroys indigenous cultures to replace them with the values, sensibilities, and practices of the colonisers (Wolfe 2006).

Domestic colonisation

This strategy is neither new nor distinct to the CCP; it is critical to all colonial projects. Indeed, expanding empires and nationalising states have routinely regarded indigenous spaces as disorderly, unhygienic, and unsafe, and therefore in need of transformation (Glover 2007; Mitchell 1991). Meanwhile, cities, parks, courthouses, government housing, and public spaces of the metropole are inscribed with symbols of state authority, which legitimise its power to rule over communities (Dovey 1999: 10–13). Colonial configurations of order are also imposed at the family level. From French designs of Egyptian villages that were 'very neat' (Mitchell 1991: 44) to the construction of concrete structures for Aboriginal families in

---

*This chapter is based on the article 'If You Don't Know How, Just Learn: Chinese Housing and the Transformation of Uyghur Domestic Space', published in *Ethnic and Racial Studies* (vol. 40, no. 11, 2021: 2052–73).

Victoria, Australia (Healy 2019), and the introduction of 'practice cottages' to Native American boarding school students in Flandreau, North Dakota (Child 1998: 80–81), control of domestic space is critical for the imposition of colonial projects—often carried out by politically and economically disadvantaged members of the metropole—and provides opportunities for indigenous resistance (Stoler 2010).

Despite uneven outcomes, these historical examples reveal common motivations among colonisers: they attempt to regulate daily life. Foucault (1991) defines this general process as 'government rationality' or the social and political structures that create, mould, and groom upstanding citizens. Within the domain of the home, Timothy Mitchell (1991: 44) proposes thinking of these policies and practices as 'enframing' or 'dividing up and containing, as in the ... rebuilding of villages, which operates by conjuring up a neutral surface or volume called "space"'. Enframing instils order through two steps: 1) imposing microphysical power or regulation of behaviour brought about from the reordering of space, and 2) creating metaphysical power or instilling the deeply held belief that *this* order is natural and eternal (Mitchell 1991: 93–94). Put another way, enframing controls physical mobility and conditions the mind to accept these constraints as normal. Mitchell's theory can be aptly applied to Chinese state-mandated changes to Uyghur homes.

Uyghur homes before Chinese colonisation

The CCP is in the process of eliminating and replacing Uyghur configurations of the home. Before the peoples and places of the Tarim and Junggar basins—modern-day Xinjiang—were incorporated into the People's Republic of China, the region's residential architecture changed in line with cultural currents (Mähsut and Mähsut 2000). As the area's peoples sedentarised, urbanised, and converted en masse to Islam, their physical dwellings began to reflect their faith as well as their incorporation into a Central Asian milieu (Tursuntohti 2013: 46–50).

A mental blueprint of a typical rural Uyghur house illuminates a matrix comprising intersecting physical and cultural boundaries (Dautcher 2009: 11–22). Family members and guests enter the courtyard (*hoyla*) and outdoor pavilion (*aywan*) from adjacent roads through a large, often two-door, wide gate (*därwaza*). The house's interior is commonly divided and arranged into formal entertaining rooms (*saray/mehmanxana*), common rooms (*dalan*), bedrooms (*yataq öy*), and kitchens (*ashxana*).

In some houses, *mehrab* (arches or niches) are carved in the wall facing the direction of Mecca—that is, the *qibla*—and are used to store bedding (*orun-körpä*) and religious articles (Tursuntohti 2013: 48).

The *saray* is reserved for formal gatherings and special occasions. Marking a home's place of prestige, the *saray*'s construction is distinct from other rooms and it is usually equipped with alcoves (*oyuq-täqchä*) that store and display delicate porcelain, vases, and linens. Meanwhile, the *dalan* functions to strengthen bonds among the immediate family, distant relatives, and neighbours. Reflecting this purpose, the *dalan* is animated with constant activity (Dautcher 2009: 13–14).

The *supa* stands at the centre of domestic life and hospitality. It also marks the house's *tör*, or place of honour (Tursuntohti 2013: 55). Interior *supa* are built of earth—or, less often, lumber—and raised 40–50 centimetres from the ground. The *supa* fulfils essential roles for extending and strengthening social networks beyond the genealogical family to more indigenous concepts of local belonging such as relatives (*tughqan*), neighbours (*koshna*), and community members (*hekemsaye*) (Steenberg 2014: 174–75). Often the site of naming ceremonies, *sünnät* circumcisions, *nikah* marriage vows, and other life-cycle rituals (*toy*), the *supa* also effectively blurs divisions between the sacred and the profane.

Rapidly 'beautifying [Uyghur] spaces'

CCP officials regard Uyghur homes and local domesticity as impediments to Han-defined secular modernity. A branch party secretary in Qaghliq County, Kashgar, insisted:

> In the past, the situation of rural households was relatively poor: they didn't cultivate good living habits, most houses lacked beds, not to mention any other furniture. Families just slept on the floors or on mats on their *supa*; some didn't even wash them regularly. These habits are unhygienic, unhealthy, and contrary to a modern, civilised lifestyle. (China Kashgar Net 2018)

In a policy framed as 'poverty alleviation' (扶贫), the CCP has insisted on moving Uyghur families into Han-style homes to 'improve' their lives.

Although these efforts began in the 1980s and 1990s (Dautcher 2009: 29; Kobi 2016: 126–29, 2018: 214), the CCP has acted with greater urgency since 2017. Of course, that year witnessed the incarceration of Xinjiang's

Turkic populations at alarming rates (Zenz 2019). Outside these reeducation centres, China's top brass set in motion a series of policies that have demolished and rebuilt Uyghur spaces. During his opening address at the Nineteenth Congress of the CCP on 18 October 2017, President Xi announced his 'Beautiful China' (美丽中国) initiative, which intended, among other goals, to raise environmental awareness and improve basic sanitation practices across the country (Beh 2017).

Officials in Xinjiang invoked Xi's speech to justify several 'beautification' programs in Uyghur communities. A government brief from Yarkand County cites Xi's call to 'accelerate the reform of [China's] ecological civilisation system, [and] build a beautiful China', before adding that 'beautifying rural villages is an important part of building a beautiful China' (Ma and Lin 2018). This abstract pledge solidified into concrete action before the 2018 Lunar New Year, when cadres introduced the 'Three New' campaign (三新活动). At the core of this multifaceted endeavour is 'advocating a new lifestyle, establishing a new atmosphere, and constructing a new order' (People's Daily 2018).

'Three new' to replace the 'old'

The 'Three New' campaign's 'Establishing a New Atmosphere' (树立新气象) initiative inspired the 'Beautifying Spaces' (美丽庭院) program. The first step in this beautification campaign is rearranging residential structures in a floorplan with 'three separate spaces' (三区分离). This model demands constructing clearly defined living quarters (生活区), spaces for small gardens (种植区), and areas for rearing domesticated animals (养殖区) to replace current house designs (Ma and Lin 2018). The standardised blueprint replicates government-built housing in rural Han-majority villages in eastern and central China. In fact, the *Khotan Daily* (2018) compares the results of its city's housing projects—displayed with before and after photographs—with those carried out in Han areas.

Reframing Uyghur homes into discrete domestic compartments requires the absence (or removal) of the structure that blurs physical, social, and religious-cultural boundaries: the *supa*. Some officials have even called for all *supas* to be 'demolished' (拆除) (Zero Distance Kashgar 2018). A Uyghur-language post from the county government in Maralbeshi County demanded that residents 'smash up' (*qeqish*) their *supa* and refuse to lay out mats and rugs (Zero Distance Maralbeshi 2018). Unquestionably, the *supa* has been singled out as a symbol of backward Uyghur customs, even though, in northern China, Han families regularly use the similar *kang* (炕) fixture in their homes. Yet in Xinjiang, interior *supas* have been deemed unhygienic, inconvenient, and detrimental to physical and mental wellness.

The destruction of the *supa* allows us to revisit Mitchell's discussion of 'enframing' or the colonial process of elimination and replacement. According to Mitchell's theory (1991: 93–94), when Han cadres remove the *supa*, they effectively eliminate the space that connects the sacred and the profane. They then replace the *supa* with tables and chairs—that is, discrete (and secular) spaces designed for individuals and only a few activities. In the end, these Han workers, through the introduction of furniture, impose a new ordering of space.

The project also aims to eliminate important symbolic markers that orient Uyghurs towards the Islamic world. Newly built and renovated houses are also devoid of *mehrab* arches/niches. Radio Free Asia (2019) reports that residents in Ili, Kashgar, and Khotan prefectures have been forced to either destroy *mehrab* carvings or fill them in because officials have deemed them 'extremist'; houses are demolished if the *mehrab* is part of a weight-bearing wall and cannot be removed. Although I have been unable to find government documents to corroborate this claim, I can confirm that *mehrab* cannot be found in the dozens of photographs depicting newly built and renovated living spaces.

Furniture provided by the nearly 1.1 million 'big brothers and sisters' sent to rural Xinjiang to live among Uyghur families fills otherwise empty concrete rooms (Byler 2018). According to the CCP, dining tables, coffee tables, sofas, and beds assume the power to acquaint residents with a 'new life' (Zero Distance Konashähär 2018) and establish 'scientific, civilised, and healthy' (*ilmiy*, *mädäniy*, and *saghlam*) living standards (Zero Distance Maralbeshi 2018). Officials in Kona Shärä even proclaim that 'civilisation begins at the dinner table' (Ma and Lin 2018)—a reference to interiors *sans supa*.

Dismantling Uyghur space, regulating Uyghur pace

The three-separate-spaces arrangement drastically alters Uyghur templates of domestic spatial organisation. Drawing on Glover's (2007: 139) analysis of the reordering of houses in Lahore, Pakistan, we learn that clearly delineating areas for living, farming, and animal rearing serves to isolate specific activities and objects to specialised spaces to increase domestic efficiency. The result, according to Glover (2007: 139), is 'the formation of new domestic sensibilities, habits, and sentiments that would be cultivated and disciplined in the newly remade spaces of the home'. Newly remodelled homes and the rearrangement of domesticity introduce a Han-dominated, government-defined rationality of space and movement.

Similarly, new furniture is not meant to merely update aesthetics; rather, these fittings are meant to act on Uyghur world views. Glover (2007: xx) argues that colonisers 'shared an assumption that the material world embodied immaterial qualities that were both tangible and agentive'. According to this logic, material objects—as something that can be seen, touched, moved, and so on—affect and can even make predictable the behaviours of the agents who manipulate them. Seemingly informed by this belief, officials in Yarkand proclaim that 'modern furniture not only gives home interiors a brand-new look, it functions more to greatly elevate the quality of living' (Yarkand County Radio and TV 2018b).

These remarks bring into sharp relief the greater purpose of the program: 'civilising' Uyghurs. Government-mandated transformations of Uyghur domestic space are a part of the CCP's broader efforts to increase 'civilisation' (文明) in society and improve the individual quality (素质, or *suzhi*) of its citizens. Construction projects in China specifically seek to enhance the interconnected concepts of material (物质) and spiritual (精神) civilisation and *suzhi* (Cliff 2016: 34). From the perspective of the CCP, state-built housing, replete with modern amenities, can help propel all communities towards the nation's 'epistemological centre of civilisation': urbanite Han people (Moreno 2018: 28–29). In other words, the furniture, according to this official, creates the 'civilised' (Han) environment that enhances the *suzhi* of local Uyghurs.

Invisible violence, visible punishments

As a 'project of improvement'—both material and individual—colonial housing is meant to appear less violent than other assimilatory programs (Mitchell 1991: 44). Glover (2007: xxi) is unequivocal: the introduction of new material objects in Lahore houses was 'largely meant to persuade, rather than force social change', thus distinguishing this method from Foucault's (1984: 179–87) 'disciplinary' practices, or the various programs of physical and mental subjugation imposed on a population to increase human efficiency. Yet, CCP housing policies in Uyghur communities fuse these two methods of inculcating compliance. That is, the state is using new materials—introducing standardised construction plans, beds, desks, and so on, while removing indigenous orderings of space, such as *supa* and *mehrab*—as tangible and agentive objects that seek to 'modernise' Uyghur lives. Put another way, the 'Three New' project—along with other colonial campaigns—destroys to replace (Wolfe 2006). However, as human agents of the state, the more than one million sent-down 'relatives' enforce compliance, document infractions, and punish insubordination (Byler 2018).

Those failing to conform to the party's standards are ostracised and punished. A party branch deputy secretary in Tage'airike village, Khotan, reports that village cadres conduct random inspections each week to determine compliant and deviant households, which are then marked with, respectively, red or black banners (Zero Distance Päyzawat 2018). In Maralbeshi County, weekly village meetings announce blacklisted households, who are given a deadline by which to correct violations. Families placed on the blacklist three times are paraded on stage (亮相) in front of their peers, where they promise to rectify their faults. Officials are confident that public shaming will help villages establish a morality system under which 'poverty is disgraceful, wealth is honourable, laziness is shameful, and diligence is glorified' (Livestock Office of the XUAR 2018). The fear of incarceration will coerce families into conformity; otherwise, they will be removed from society.

Eliminating the native

This essay has introduced and examined the CCP's 'Three New' campaign as colonial practice. Although publicly described as poverty elimination, these construction projects impose immediate and, from the CCP's calculations, permanent changes on Uyghur perceptions of order, domestic space, and modernity. These spatial transformation programs are often essential components of centralised, comprehensive strategies to 'eliminate' the native. In other words, Wolfe (2006: 388–89) urges us to analyse cultural and racial elimination as a 'structure, not an event'—that is, an ongoing project that destroys, rebuilds, replaces, and renames. State-led housing projects in Uyghur communities destroy indigenous orderings of space and replace them with newly built structures originally designed for Han nuclear families. The physical, social, and conceptual changes spurred by the Three New campaign decode the Uyghur homeland and remap it more legibly into the CCP-imagined 'Xinjiang'.

(Top) Plate 9.1 Kashgar's 'Old Town', 2013. (Bottom) Plate 9.2 New housing developments in Kashgar, 2013.

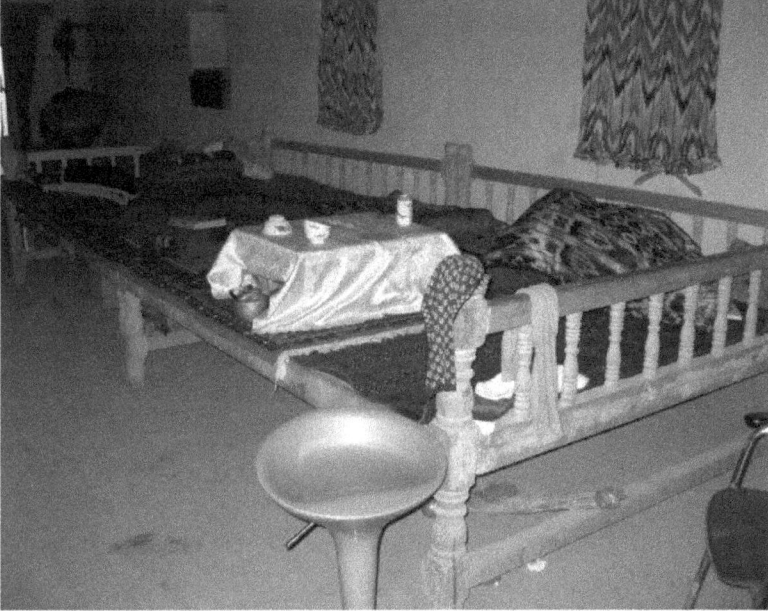

(Top) Plate 9.3 Family interior *supa* in rural Turpan. (Bottom) Plate 9.4 Newly built interior family room with picture of President Xi.

(Top) Plate 9.5 Mehrab in rural Turpan home. (Bottom) Plate 9.6 A work team destroys family *supa*.

10
The spatial cleansing of Xinjiang: *Mazar* desecration in context[*]

Rian Thum

S
ometime between 10 and 17 March 2018, on a high sand dune
75 kilometres from the town of Niya, a beloved historical monument
disappeared (Kuo 2019). For at least 450 years, the site had drawn
pilgrims from across the expanse of Altishahr—the southern half of
what is now known variously as Eastern Turkistan or Xinjiang (Dūghlāt
1996: 190). Pilgrims came to be in the presence of Imam Je'firi Sadiq, a
founding father and hero who had died there 1,000 years earlier while
bringing Islam to their homeland. At his tomb, they wept, prayed, and
gained blessings from contact with the physical structure.

The white-painted tomb had the shape of an ordinary grave marker, but
on the scale of a giant, like a grave for someone 6 metres tall, resting on
a platform 15 metres square. Some pilgrims wrote graffiti in a wooden,
box-like prayer house erected in the sand nearby, recording their shared
presence with the saint in the very location where their society and their
history were born. All around, flags and strips of cloth whipped loudly
in the wind—thousands of offerings tied to various sacred structures,
testifying to the crowds of fellow Uyghurs who had come over the years
to venerate this point of historical origin and connection to the divine.
In the early autumn, pilgrims came in especially large numbers, cooking
communal meals in a gigantic pot and sleeping near the site. All of this
disappeared in the middle of March 2018, leaving an empty dune.[1] In
the ensuing two years, the Chinese state has destroyed and desecrated
Uyghur historical and holy places at a scale unprecedented in the history
of Eastern Turkistan (Altishahr, Xinjiang) as a Chinese-dominated region.
Among the demolished places were mosques, which have received the

---

1   This description is based on the author's visit during the pilgrimage festival of 2007. Other
shrine descriptions throughout the article are based on the author's fieldwork in 2003, 2004–05,
2007–08, 2010, 2013, 2015, and 2017.

*This essay was originally published in the *Made in China Journal* (vol. 5, no. 2, 2020),
doi.org/10.22459/MIC.05.02.2020.04.

bulk of international media attention. But another kind of sacred site, less legible to outsiders, has arguably been a more significant crux of desecration. This is the *mazar*, a point on the landscape that holds particular numinous authenticity, a connection to and presence of the divine that surpasses the sacredness even of the mosque as a physical structure.

For many Uyghurs in urban contexts, *mazars* have become peripheral, irrelevant, or entirely forgotten. But most Uyghurs live in rural environments, where *mazars* have commonly functioned as community resources, historical archives, arenas of dispute, and independent social actors. At a *mazar*, one can seek fertility or healing. The pilgrim can learn about the history of the shrine's buried saints, and thus of her own land. Local religious leaders can promote their understandings of right behaviour against the claims of others. And the shrine itself can intervene in the everyday lives of its constituencies by entering their dreams or bringing rain.

Mazars are nearly always marked by some physical construction, ranging from high domes with green, glazed tiles to nothing more than a few flags on crooked twig poles (Dawut 2001). Most are graves, purported to hold the physical remains of an individual whose accomplishments in life— whether scholarly, heroic, or miraculous—are thought to grant his or her immortal personage a closeness to God that can be shared with the living. *Mazars* can also be other points of transcendent contact: sacred trees or springs, the footprints or stopping places of holy people, or the locations where sacred personages disappeared. Such non-burial sites represent a tiny minority of *mazars*, but they demonstrate the capaciousness of the term and the potential for points on the landscape to become sacred by multiple means. Whatever the physical and narrative form of a particular *mazar*, in practice, '*mazar*' denotes the most immediate, tangible manifestation of the sacred in physical and geographical form.

The miraculous power of a *mazar*'s substance is visible in the habits of pilgrims. Women who seek to become pregnant will sometimes reach into a crack in a *mazar*'s walls or a hole in the earth on which the *mazar* sits, grasp the first thing they touch, such as a small clod of dirt or mortar, and swallow it. Such faith in the power of the *mazar*'s physical material has been prominent enough to earn the condemnation of reform-minded Muslims in the region, as in the case of the early twentieth-century critic Abdu Vali Akhon, who complained about 'common' pilgrims who 'rub their faces and eyes on the shrine's walls' (Abdu Vali Akhon 1905: 162). Another reformist of that era, visiting Kashgar from Ottoman lands, similarly complained about people 'rubbing their faces on sheep horns …

and on cow tails' kept at the shrines (Kemal 1925: 94). Especially devoted pilgrims, such as a man I met at a tomb in Yarkand in 2007, will sometimes sleep inside a *mazar* structure itself, in the hope of receiving miraculous inspiration in their dreams.

These properties of the *mazar* stand in some contrast to attitudes towards mosques. I have not been able to document any similar interactions with the physical structure of a mosque, even when the mosque is attached to a *mazar*. This is not to say that mosques are not sacred. They provide a space of purity where worshippers can engage in devotions towards God, and the collective acts of devotional prayer can generate miraculous effects. In Kashgar in the 2010s, women would line up at the exits of the Id Kah Mosque and hold out food for departing worshippers to blow a puff of air upon, lending the food curative properties. But here the curative power was generated by the activities and personal traits of other worshippers, not the physical substance of the mosque.

The nature and goals of desecration

Authorities in Xinjiang clearly share some awareness of the power of *mazars*. The circumstances of the destruction of Imam Je'firi Sadiq's tomb show that it was the *mazar* itself that attracted the authorities' attention, not the economic value of the land. The remote and barren dunes on which the *mazar* stood have no other use. Elsewhere, some aspects of China's assault on sacred spaces have involved economic incentives. More than 100 graveyards have been destroyed across Xinjiang in the past three years, in some cases making valuable urban land available to developers or the state (Xiao and Yiu 2019; Rivers 2020). But the destruction of Je'firi Sadiq's tomb paved the way for precisely nothing. Destruction seems to have been the point, not a sacrifice to some economically valuable end.

For decades, authorities have been nervous about the large festivals (*seyla*) that some *mazars* inspire. Officials across China tend to be wary of potential for independent gatherings to create alternative sources of political power or develop into protests. Across those decades, however, the state demonstrated that complete destruction of a *mazar* is not necessary to prevent gatherings. For more than 20 years, authorities have prevented mass pilgrimage to the only site more revered than Je'firi Sadiq's *mazar*: the Ordam Padishah *mazar*, in the desert outside Yengisar. The occasional lucky or connected party slipped through the police net around the site from time to time (I was arrested when I tried), but the famous festivals of Ordam Padishah, with their tens of thousands of attendees, were successfully killed off (Harris and Dawut 2002). Based on my own visits, I can confirm the same for Chūje Padishahim *mazar* (near Yengisar), Ujme *mazar* (near Khotan), and, more recently, Imam Asim *mazar* (also near Khotan). Even the Je'firi Sadiq *mazar* had already been closed to all pilgrimage sometime after my successful 2007 visit, and I was turned away when I returned in 2015. The destruction was not needed to prevent pilgrimage; destruction appears to have been an end in and of itself.

Even when locked behind police roadblocks and roadside informants, *mazars* wield power. They enter people's dreams and give them guidance. One can petition them from a distance or send personal prayers (*du'a*) in their direction, as I witnessed a man do after being turned away from Imam Je'firi Sadiq *mazar* in 2015. Simply knowing that the *mazar* is standing out there between the Uyghur-inhabited oases maintains a community tie to history and the land. I met one of the handful of lucky Uyghurs who managed to reach Ordam Padishah long after it had been closed, and she told me what happened when she mentioned her good fortune, standing outside a village mosque, weeks later. The men to whom she was talking began weeping and begged to collect some of the dust of the *mazar* from her jacket. To judge from publicly available satellite imagery, Ordam Padishah is now gone, too (Google Earth 2020: 38.9144°, 76.6567°).

After the Notre-Dame cathedral in Paris was partly destroyed by fire in April 2019, the French government began a billion-dollar remediation that continues today. Fallen stones are cleaned with lasers. Previously inaccessible materials are examined for clues that can shed new light on the monument's history. Scientists analyse lead from the fallen spire and trace its environmental impact on the Seine River and beyond. And a team of anthropologists studies the emotional trauma that the monument's damage has inflicted on Parisians and visitors from around the world (Lesté-Lasserre 2020).

The many Uyghurs whose relationship to Ordam Padishah parallels the Parisian and global attachments to Notre-Dame would surely welcome a similar effort. The rubble of Ordam's destruction holds abundant clues to its history. Archaeologists could undertake tree-ring dating of the sort that scientists have planned for Notre-Dame's fallen timbers. Ancient refuse and offerings left by pilgrims could reveal changes in patterns of worship over the centuries. Because many of Xinjiang's desert shrines sit on or near older Buddhist sites, Ordam's destruction may have revealed traces of even earlier sacred monuments. It is unlikely that many Uyghurs inside Xinjiang have learned yet about the destruction of Ordam Padishah, but when they do, the emotional trauma will be no less acute than in Paris after the cathedral fire.

Of course, in the case of Ordam Padishah, the cultural destruction is not accidental. The shortest distance from Ordam Padishah to cultivated land is 14 kilometres, over soft sand and high dunes. The expense and effort required to bring equipment capable of obliterating Ordam's network of monuments, mosques, rest houses, and mounds in the open desert must have been substantial. The recent pattern of government activity thus suggests that further destruction and desecration in Xinjiang are far more likely than the kind of state-led effort at recovery, remediation, and reparations occurring in Paris. As at Je'firi Sadiq *mazar*, the land around Ordam Padishah is remote and barren, and the shrine has been replaced with nothing; destruction of the Uyghurs' most sacred site seems to have been the goal, as part of the government's broader efforts to define and control Uyghur material culture and history.

Full obliteration of the sort that Je'firi Sadiq and Ordam Padishah suffered is not the only attack that Uyghur holy places have suffered. The wave of *mazar* closures of the past three decades was already a form of destruction. *Mazars* are continually created and recreated through pilgrimage. Their structures accumulate mass as pilgrims bring flagpoles, lengths of cloth, sheep horns, oil lamps, animal skins, and other ephemeral offerings. The offerings pile up and the accumulated flagpoles sometimes reach 10 metres high. The slow deterioration of wood, cloth, and skin testifies to the age and continuity of pilgrimage. The constant replenishing of the flags and skins manifests the continued power of the *mazar* over its constituencies and reminds the pilgrim that his or her devotion embeds them in a community larger and less knowable than the circles of their home village. Shrine closure interrupts this continuous production of the sacred site.

At the *mazar* of Imam Asim, near Khotan, it almost looks like local authorities share this understanding of continual incarnation through pilgrimage. Recent photos show that the mudbrick structure of the tomb itself was unharmed as of 2018 (MarcelTraveller 2018). But the site is unrecognisable. The associated mosque has been demolished; the *mazar* proper has been denuded of its flags, offerings, and wooden railings. The grave marker, which sits atop a low mudbrick building, was previously invisible behind a forest of pilgrims' flags, their poles affixed to the wooden fence on the building's roof. It now stands naked, motionless, and monochrome, shorn of the colourful, flapping attire of sacred offerings. Authorities have stopped short of total obliteration. But they have crossed the wooden fence into a zone that is forbidden even for most believing pilgrims and desecrated the *mazar* by denuding it of its external display of community veneration.

For officials who came into close contact with them before the closures, *mazar* activities and pilgrimage festivals made otherwise hidden troubles visible. Particularly at times of mass pilgrimage, shrines revealed themselves as alternative sources of legitimacy and authenticity outside the control of the state. The crowds of pilgrims in group prayer demonstrated— not just to observers, but also to pilgrims themselves—the emotional power of collective action. The mixing of devotees from far-flung regions circumvented the ubiquitous state control of long-distance communication. Even outside of the large pilgrimage festivals, daily, small-scale devotions revealed the state's tenuous hold on life-cycle rituals, knowledge production, and medical care. In a more general way, the architectural, sonic, and overall aesthetic qualities of the shrine made it immediately clear that it was a world entirely alien to the self-consciously modernist, 'harmonious', and totalitarian society pursued by the Chinese state.

The history and scope of desecration

Although the acts of extreme desecration and demolition described above seem to have begun in 2018, states have always been interested in Uyghur *mazars* as centres of economic and political power. When the Qing Dynasty's Qianlong Emperor (1711–99) conquered Eastern Turkistan in 1759 and incorporated it into the new administrative entity of 'Xinjiang', he issued an order to protect and even repair the region's *mazars*. However, in the succeeding 150 years, the Qing state would frequently confiscate *mazar* landholdings in the wake of rebellions, targeting particular *mazars* that were associated with rebel factions (Zhang 2016: 130–31). Nonetheless, beyond the occasional economic dispossession of *mazars*, the Qing did little to disrupt pilgrimage or physical structures. On the contrary, their system of indirect rule gave local elites latitude to perpetuate and, in some cases, even promote *mazars* (Brophy and Thum 2015). The tombs of some Qing client-administrators themselves became *mazars*.

Chinese officials ended the system of indirect rule in the late nineteenth century and began to introduce assimilationist policies, but even then *mazars* seem to have largely escaped notice. The earliest attempt to control sacred sites on a systematic scale may be the efforts of warlord governor Sheng Shicai (who ruled from 1933 to 1944) to bureaucratise the landholdings of *mazars*, all of which he confiscated in the mid-1930s (Sugawara 2016: 155; Zhang 2016: 132). Landholding again brought *mazars* under state scrutiny in the 1950s, as the newly arrived Chinese Communist Party confiscated their land and turned their religious personnel into state employees (Wang n.d.). Personnel were gradually reduced until, during the Cultural Revolution, *mazars* throughout Xinjiang were closed completely.

With the loosening of restrictions on cultural and religious practices in the 1980s, *mazars* sprang back to life in two different ways. Some, like Ordam Padishah, enjoyed a grassroots revival of festivals and ordinary pilgrimage. Others—most notably, Afaq Khoja in Kashgar—were transformed by the state into museum-like tourist attractions. This museumification was the earliest wave of *mazar* disruption in reform-era China.

The museumification of Afaq Khoja—once a site of large gatherings—kept pilgrimage to a trickle. The few members of the *mazar*'s rural constituency who could afford the high-priced entry ticket discovered a sacred site with no religious authorities, a secularised environment denuded of visible offerings, and sanctuaries full of Han Chinese tourists, souvenir sellers, and guides. Pilgrimage festivals and overnight activities were prevented entirely. Similar efforts at the Altunluq ('golden') cemetery in Yarkand, the Sultan Sutuq Bughrakhan *mazar* in Artush, and the Yusup Khas Hajip *mazar* in Kashgar lacked the resounding tourist success of Afaq Khoja, but similarly curtailed pilgrimage. The important *mazar* of Eshabulkehf, near Turpan, continued to receive somewhat more pilgrims (though no large gatherings), perhaps due to looser and more affordable ticketing policies that exempted some locals.

In the late 1990s and early 2000s, as pilgrimage festivals expanded at *mazars* that had escaped museumification, authorities began imposing restrictions. They levied entry fees at Imam Asim (2 *yuan*) and Imam Je'firi Sadiq (50 *yuan*), adding strict identity registration procedures at the latter. The closure of Ordam Padishah in 1997 is the earliest documented for the post-reform period, but others followed. By 2008, authorities had closed the shrines of Ujme (Khotan) and Chūje Padishahim (Yengisar), both of which had hosted large festivals. By 2015, there were no shrine festivals taking place anywhere in Xinjiang.

The demolitions and desecrations that began in 2018 have so far left most minor *mazars* unscathed. Hundreds or perhaps thousands of small *mazars* punctuate the sacred geography of Xinjiang. These provide some of the same devotional and miraculous functions of the famous *mazars*, without the large gatherings or regional community-building effects. Satellite photos suggest that a handful of more historically significant *mazars* with impressive domed structures have also been spared—notably, Yarkand's two most famous holy sites, Chilten and Muhemmed Sherip. In the early 2000s, Chilten drew a steady flow of pilgrims on market days and holidays but did not host large gatherings of the type that led to the closures of other *mazars*. However, given the criminalisation of most religious activities, all *mazars* are likely to be under some level of restriction or de facto closure.

Full demolition and desecration have so far been aimed at *mazars* that have drawn large crowds, have region-wide reputations, and have not been museumified. My fieldwork among pilgrims conducted between 2003 and 2017, combined with historical documentation, suggests that among the hundreds or thousands of Uyghur *mazars*, five have exceptionally strong and historically deep regional reputations for holiness (Table 10.1). The destruction of Imam Jafiri Sadiq and Ordam Padishah has now taken two of those most widely revered *mazars* off the map. The remaining three have physically survived as museumified destinations for Han Chinese and foreign tourists. Among these five sites, the newly demolished Ordam Padishah was often described—both by living pilgrims and by historical sources—as the holiest site in Eastern Turkistan (Jarring 1935).

Table 10.1 Status of *mazars* that once hosted large gatherings of pilgrims (*seyla*)

Shrine name	Nearest town	Status as of 2020
Imam Je'firi Sadiq*	Niya	Demolished
Turt Imam	Khotan	Unknown, standing
Imam Asim	Khotan	Closed and desecrated
Ujme	Khotan	Closed, physical status unknown
Ordam Padishah*	Yengisar	Demolished
Chūje Padishah	Yengisar	Closed, standing
Afaq Khoja*	Kashgar	Museumified
Eshabulkehf*	Turfan	Museumified
Sultan Sutuq Bughrakhan*	Artush	Museumified

Note: Asterisks denote the five most sacred *mazars* in the Uyghur region—my subjective determination based on fieldwork among pilgrims conducted between 2003 and 2018 and historical accounts. Imam Asim is a borderline case. It attracted exceptionally large numbers of pilgrims, but historical sources do not present it as one of the region's most sacred places.

While authorities have destroyed Uyghur historical monuments, they have promoted their own shrine-like structures—built from the 1980s onward but often claiming antiquity. For example, in 1994, they built Kashgar's 'Ban Chao Memorial Park' (班超纪念公园), which was expanded in the 2010s into the 'Pantu City Scenic Area' (盘橐城景区), a park with statues, reliefs, and architectural imitations of ancient Chinese fortifications. It commemorates the period between 73 and 102 CE, when the Eastern Han dynasty conquered and briefly controlled the region under the Chinese general, Ban Chao (Millward 2009: 24). The memorial and park are claimed to occupy the site of Ban Chao's original fortifications. Chinese tourists from throughout the country are encouraged to visit this 'patriotic education base' (爱国主义教育基地), where they learn about the state's vision of a Han-dominated national community, in much the same way that Uyghur pilgrims once learned about their community's history at Ordam Padishah *mazar*. Recognising that entry fees can disrupt the functions of a pilgrimage site, authorities recently made entry to the park free of charge (Xu 2018).

Contemporary context

Mazar desecration is part of a larger set of policies that raze the Uyghur built environment, reconfigure Uyghur geography, and eradicate the spatial underpinnings of Uyghur culture. Though a comprehensive enumeration of Chinese spatial reengineering policies is not practicable here—they are simply too numerous—a few examples will demonstrate the extraordinary scope of state efforts to replace Uyghur built environments and uproot geographically embedded expressions of Uyghur culture. As these examples show, almost no part of Uyghur life is untouched by state destruction of the Uyghur built environment, suggesting that state attacks on apical cultural nodes like prominent *mazars* are part of a larger effort to disconnect Uyghur experiences and identities from the landscape.

The recent spate of prominent mosque demolitions and desecrations—including the most important mosques of Karghalik and Keriya—followed a large 'rectification' campaign from late 2016, which 'demolished nearly 70 per cent of mosques in the city' of Kashgar, according to Wang Jingfu, the head of Kashgar's Ethnic and Religious Affairs Committee, along with an unknown number of mosques in other parts of Xinjiang (Hoshur 2016). The mosque destructions closely followed the introduction of bans on praying in public, which had left homes and mosques as the only remaining spaces where religious devotions were permitted. This means the destruction of mosques has achieved an even greater constriction of religious space than it would have under ordinary conditions.

Both homes and mosques eventually became unsafe for prayer due to the combination of surveillance and arbitrary internment. The *fanghuiju* program (访惠聚 being an abbreviation of 访民情、惠民生、聚民心, which means 'inspect the situation of the people, improve the welfare of the people, gather the hearts of the people'), which sent more than one million Han Chinese government workers into Uyghur houses, enabled direct monitoring of Uyghurs' religious devotion at home (Byler 2018; Xinjiang United Front Work Department 2017b). Surveillance cameras in mosques further tightened the net on those who prayed. Authorities used the frequency of prayer as an indicator of (un)trustworthiness, ultimately sending people who prayed frequently to the internment and indoctrination camps. One leaked document shows that simply having family members who engage in too many religious activities can lead to internment (Zenz 2020).

As Timothy Grose describes in his essay in the present volume, homes were also transformed in more physical ways. Chinese state media outlets have published multiple reports of official efforts to change Uyghur household furnishings. These usually explicitly target the *supa* (土炕), a raised platform, often heated from below, on which many Uyghurs eat meals and sleep. However, many reports also mention other types of furniture throughout the house and complete transformations of household interiors as part of the 'beautiful courtyard' (美丽庭院) campaign. Because *supas* are often built into the structure of houses, their removal is labour intensive. In addition to serving as large communal beds, shared by numerous family members, *supas* are often used for activities that range from hosting guests to doing school homework. The shift to Western-style beds dedicated to sleeping singly or in pairs substantially changes the everyday interactions within a household. Authorities are aware of this, noting that children and adults will need to sleep separately (Xinjiang Minsheng Net 2018) and commanding Uyghurs to 'abandon the bad customs of laying out carpets, eating and sleeping on the *supa*, and getting on the *supa* to do homework' (Zero Distance Awat 2019).

Several ethnic groups across rural areas of northern China, including Han Chinese, use *supas*, and the province of Gansu has seen its own 'supa reform' (土炕改造) campaign. The different ways officials both execute and portray 'supa reform' in Gansu and Xinjiang show how

Xinjiang officials enlist and reframe wider government policies as tools for transforming Uyghur culture. In Gansu, *supa* reform is pursued as an environmental policy, designed to reduce emissions from the coal fires that heat the *supa* (Zheng 2017). In most cases, the goal is to convert coal-heated *supas* to electric-powered *supas*, often through subsidies (Gansu Daily Net 2019).

In Xinjiang, on the other hand, the environmental justification is largely absent, and *supas* are removed rather than converted. Instead, as Timothy Grose (2020) has shown through his analysis of state media reports, officials have adopted a civilising discourse that presents Uyghur household furniture as backward and uncivilised. Xinjiang's highest-ranking Uyghur official, Shohret Zakir, modelled this attitude in his comments to state media, saying:

> Only by having farmers, especially farmers in poor areas of Southern Xinjiang [where most Uyghurs live], personally experience the benefits of a modern way of life, can we make modern civilised life deeply penetrate farmers' souls ... Grassroots leaders and cadres should ... guide farmers, step by step, to abandon backwards customs and live a modern lifestyle. (Xinjiang Daily 2018)

Meanwhile, in a pattern similar to the museumification of *mazars*, the state has made a tourist attraction out of the very object it is destroying in Uyghur villages. *Supas*, transformed into odd shapes, now stand along the roads of the tourist simulacrum that replaced Kashgar's old city. Before the demolition of Kashgar's Uyghur urban core between 2001 and 2017, typical homes were mostly featureless on the outside, with small windows and little in the way of decoration. The interiors, by contrast, featured lush courtyards, elaborate woodwork, colonnades, and interior reception rooms with intricate niches holding display ceramics. The new Kashgar has turned the Uyghur home inside out. Above one of the new roadside *supas* are shelves holding jars and a teapot. An old column—likely salvaged from a demolished interior courtyard—now stands in front of an exterior door. Supposedly 'backward customs', increasingly off limits to Uyghurs themselves, are now on display for the primarily Han tourists who are driven through the new 'old city' on electric carts.

(Top Left) Plate 10.1 *Supa*-like platform and mock hearth outside houses in the new Kashgar Old City, 2015. (Top Right) Plate 10.2 Interior column repurposed for exterior use along a public street in the new Kashgar Old City, 2015. (Bottom) Plate 10.3 Tourists entering the new Kashgar Old City, 2015. Photos by the author.

Between 2000 and 2016, Kashgar was the only historic Uyghur urban core to suffer such wholesale obliteration and replacement. In other towns, piecemeal development slowly transformed and eroded the Uyghur built environment (Kobi 2016), but there was little evidence of state-directed demolition of historic Uyghur neighbourhoods on the scale of Kashgar. However, satellite images reveal that in the years after 2016, authorities oversaw the destruction, in whole or in part, of the old cities of Khotan, Yarkand, Kargalik, and Keriya.[2] The most common type of replacement structure is the multistorey apartment building.

The example of Kashgar, which has been studied in detail elsewhere, gives a sense of what is involved in the replacement of Uyghur neighbourhoods (*mähällä*) with apartment blocks. Many residents had no choice but to relocate to multi-storey apartment blocks outside the city, and the change has involved disruptions to a wide range of social phenomena, including inheritance practices, life-cycle rituals (funerals, weddings, and so on), elder care, neighbourhood solidarity (*mahalladarchiliq*), sleeping arrangements, patterns of cohabitation, and networks of reciprocity (Pawan and Niyazi 2016; Liu and Yuan 2019). In short, the move from *mähällä* to apartment compound represents a shift to an entirely new way of life. Detailed information about the demolition and replacement of other old cities from 2016 is unavailable as yet, and research in the affected towns is almost impossible for outsiders. However, the dislocation and cultural disruption that Kashgar's old-city residents have experienced gives a sense of the changes that residents of demolished neighbourhoods in Khotan, Yarkand, Karghalik, and Keriya likely face.

Seen in the context of the comprehensive reengineering of Uyghur spaces, the destruction of prominent *mazars* represents one extreme on a spectrum. On one end are sites of daily, highly localised, and sometimes mundane interactions with the built environment, for example furniture, house plans, and street layouts. On the other end, famous *mazars* are sites at which people connect on rare occasions with a transregional, transtemporal, and transcendent community. For those who make pilgrimages in person, forgiveness, merit (*sawab*), healing, and the intermingling with strangers tie these weighty communitarian meanings to their personal lives. For those who cannot make the pilgrimage, the *mazars* exert such powers from a distance. Chinese state interventions across the spectrum

---

2   Google Earth (37.1133°, 79.9369° [Khotan]; 38.4218°, 77.2654° [Yarkand]; 37.8805°, 77.4153° [Karghalik]; and 36.8501°, 81.6706° [Keriya]).

of the built environment threaten a disruption of Uyghur lifeways and understandings that straddles the symbolic and the practical, the sacred and the mundane, transforming geography and space as they intersect with practices, discourse, and knowledge.

Graveyards

At graveyards, the widespread state cleansing of intimate spaces with individualised or highly local significance intersects with the *mazars'* political and symbolic power. Because *mazars* are most often tombs, the boundary between ordinary graves and *mazars* is permeable. That line is also blurred by the widespread desire to be buried near a *mazar*. The tombs of saints—famous and parochial—are often surrounded by the graves of those who were prominent enough in their communities to access prime sacred land for their final resting places. The eminence of these figures, and the prominence of the saints beside whom they lie, often leads to their graves being treated as parts of the *mazars* themselves. A grave with a large enough marker, near enough the saint's tomb, will accumulate substantial offerings of its own, even from pilgrims who profess ignorance of the tomb's occupant. An inverse phenomenon also appears, which is that physically remarkable graves in a cemetery are often treated as, and thus become, *mazars*, possibly through the general association between *mazars* and graveyards.

As discussed above, the most widely renowned *mazars* appear to have been disproportionately targeted for destruction. However, many very minor *mazars* have also been destroyed, not because they are *mazars*, but because they sit in one of more than 100 Uyghur graveyards demolished by the Chinese state since 2017. Many Uyghurs have thus witnessed, in one act of destruction, the simultaneous desecration of their family members' graves and the demolition of their local *mazars*—sites that, despite not attracting substantial numbers of long-distance pilgrims, held similar connections to the divine and to community history at a local level.

For the moment, I only have access to the reactions of Uyghurs in exile, but the desecrations appear to have had predictably devastating effects on local communities. Some of these are documented in interviews by journalists and by Bayram Sintash (Rivers 2020; Sintash 2019). The phenomenon is widespread. *Agence France-Presse* documented the destruction of 45 cemeteries and *CNN* more than 100 (AFP 2019; Rivers 2020).

The reasons given for graveyard destruction vary. The central Uyghur graveyard and shrine in Khotan were demolished for the 'city's development' and to create 'open spaces' (Khotan Government 2019). Authorities in the Yili region cited the need for a new fire station as the reason for destroying another graveyard (Zero Distance Yining 2019). Much like the case of '*supa* reform', the graveyard destructions align with a nationwide program—in this case, 'funeral and burial reform' (殡葬整治) (Ministry of Civil Affairs 2018; Xinjiang Civil Affairs Department 2018). Outside Xinjiang, this campaign targets the unapproved burial of individuals in forests, the construction of 'luxury' tombs, and the creation of new, unapproved cemeteries. It is often framed as an environmental effort (She County People's Government 2020). Overall, the national campaign is aimed primarily at controlling the creation and expansion of cemeteries, rather than destroying longstanding, often historically significant, cemeteries as has happened in the Uyghur case.

The political and symbolic ramifications of this uprooting of Uyghur bodies and history from the land are interwoven into strains of Uyghur historical consciousness that are shared widely today. A story told to me by a young Uyghur man in a southern oasis gives a sense of the significance of death and burial, and the connection they enact between communities and the land.

Perhat, who is most likely still alive, was an urban and, in the context of his largish oasis town, urbane man in his late twenties when he volunteered a fictional tale he said came from a book. I did not record his telling in audio or written form, thinking it must be a well-known written tale I would track down later. I asked where he read it, but my subsequent searches in the books he named as possibilities have not turned up a close match. The terminology he used suggested a story from the famous 1996 novel by Memtimin Hoshur, *Sand Buried City* (*Qum Basqan Shahr*), which describes the fall of a Uyghur city to a conquering king, but I have been unable to find the tale there. I paraphrase here from memory, hoping the imprecision of my recall is outweighed by the explanatory value of his recounting. If it does have a written precedent, I hope a reader will inform me:

> The Sun King desired our homeland. He sent his vizier here. The vizier did not engage in any political machinations, but instead set up a home, took a wife, and lived a modest life. The people welcomed him, treating him as a guest. Eventually, he died and

was buried here, in our land. This was, in fact, precisely what the Sun King had hoped for. The vizier's tomb became a foothold for the Sun King, a claim upon the land. Before long, the armies of the Sun King followed, and our land became a part of the Sun King's empire. The Sun King had taken the land by sending someone to die here.

This story illustrates not just the political significance of graves, but also an awareness of their power to connect living people to the land. The Sun King's soldiers could have conquered the land with or without a grave. But the basis of sovereign ownership preceded conquest and was effected instead by the linking of death to the landscape. It is a Uyghur story about the primacy of tombs in connecting community and political power to geography.

Different symbols, same grammar

The rootedness of Uyghur communities in land and the built environment is hardly unique. Though individual phenomena described here may be particular to Uyghurs, and may need some explanation for outsiders, Uyghur geographies are hardly exotic expressions of human relations to land and space. Similar patterns play out across the world. Even the Chinese state shares some Uyghur understandings of space and place. As much as China's settler-colonial regime depicts Uyghur–land relationships as backward, it seeks to create analogous interments of its own. Uyghur-style graves are replaced with 'modern' graves that mark the state's control and new, shrine-like monuments to Chinese control are erected, such as the Ban Chao Memorial in Kashgar. This is one message of the Sun King story. The symbols are different, but the grammar is familiar. The actions of the Chinese state suggest that *mazars* are just as significant as Uyghur pilgrims believe they are.

As the Chinese state works to coopt and disrupt Uyghur geographies, it also embeds itself further in the global history of settler-colonial regimes. The desecration of shrines, the forced reordering of household space, and the demolition of cities in the name of modernity, civilisation, and development have all been common tactics of conquering empires and, especially, settler-colonial projects around the world. To this list we may add the coerced movement of Uyghurs to factory work outside Eastern

Turkistan (see Byler's Chapter 12 in this volume). There could hardly be a more literal and explicit example of Tuck and Yang's argument that 'everything within a settler colonial society strains to destroy or assimilate the Native in order to disappear them from the land' (2012: 9).[3]

The Chinese state's program of arbitrary internment, which has swallowed up a million or more Uyghurs, has no doubt facilitated the cleansing of Uyghur geographies and sacred sites. When Uyghurs can be abducted into camps for activities like refusing to watch state television, using foreign mobile phone apps, or being related to someone who wanted to travel abroad, protesting the destruction of a *mazar* is unthinkable. Many of the *mazars*' constituents were likely already victims of the internment program, because *mazar*-related activities have been designated as 'illegal religious activities' or 'signs of potential extremism', sometimes retroactively (Xinjiang United Front 2017a). And the most renowned Uyghur scholar of *mazars*, Rahile Dawut, has been disappeared since late 2017. Uyghurs are unable to even document the destruction, much less resist it.

One historically deep strain of Uyghur thought on sacred places offers a possible future for the desecrated and destroyed *mazars*. In the *tazkiras*— manuscript texts that act as explanations and sometimes liturgy for famous *mazars*—the *mazar* is often figured as an enduring point of significance on the landscape, independent of human-made structures. It can even be argued that the sacredness of the place preceded the saint's arrival on the spot (Thum 2014: 126 ff.). This increases the likelihood that future generations of Uyghurs, perhaps living in a postcolonial or at least less repressive reality, will return to the dunes of Imam Je'firi Sadiq and Ordam Padishah to build new memorial structures, and pilgrims will renew their visits, bringing new accretions of offerings. In this possible future, the *mazars*, no less sacred than they were before the Chinese state's attacks, have the potential to again serve as nodes for a Uyghur geography linking Uyghur pasts, presents, and futures to Uyghur lands.

However, this is only one possible future among many. And it is remote from the present reality of destruction. In a 2012 interview, before the shrine demolitions and before her own disappearance, Rahile Dawut described what the erasure we are now witnessing would mean:

---

3   I am grateful to Darren Byler for pointing out this passage.

If one were to remove these material artifacts and shrines, the Uyghur people would lose contact with the earth. They would no longer have a personal, cultural, and spiritual history. After a few years we would not have a memory of why we live here, or where we belong. (Manzi 2013)

In that interview, Dawut also pointed to the words of a Uyghur beggar she once met: 'When the *mazar* is at peace, the people are at peace. When the people are at peace, the rulers are at peace.'

11

Camp land: Settler ecotourism and Kazakh removal in contemporary Xinjiang[*]

Guldana Salimjan

On a summer day in 2015, at Tianshan's Bogda Lake with a friend who had come to visit Xinjiang, I felt out of place in my home-land. At the bus terminal by the lake, which Chinese tourists refer to as Tian Chi (天池) or 'the basin of heaven', the tour guide drew on romanticised cultural stereotypes to introduce my people to the tourists. 'The Kazakhs', she said, 'are nomads who move the most in the world' (世界上搬家最多的民族). Ironically, in the past decade, Kazakhs, along with many other mobile pastoral groups in China—Tibetans, Mongols, Kyrgyz, Tuvans, and Evenks—have been pressured by the Chinese Government to give up their pastoral life via policies that call for 'returning the pastures to the grassland' (退牧还草). When we got off the bus, I was greeted by a sign that read, 'Kazakh Ethnic Culture Garden', behind which stood dozens of yurts tightly packed against one another. At the entrance to this 'garden', there was a cross-section of a yurt beside an eagle and several replicas of *balbal* statues—ancient anthropomorphic stone stelae that can be found on the Eurasian steppe. Kazakh and Uyghur dancing costumes hung on the yurt wall for tourists to be photographed wearing. As I was taking in this Disneyfied display of Kazakh nomadic culture, a group of Kazakh locals approached the tourists getting off the bus and asked them whether they would like to stay for a night in their yurts. I immediately realised that this was their job—to conduct tourism.

That day, I was the only Kazakh among the Han and foreign tourists who visited Bogda Lake. The tourists were led to see we Kazakhs as simple people clinging to a primitive culture. I saw Kazakh boys the age of my

[*] This article was originally published in *Lausan* on 1 September 2021. The author wishes to thank Sam H. Bass, Darren Byler, Stevan Harrell, as well as the editors at *Lausan* for valuable feedback. Additionally, the author thanks activist Erkin Azat and the Xinjiang Victims Database for their important documentation work on the Xinjiang crisis.

younger cousins renting out their horses for Han tourists to ride, and Kazakh women and men cooking food to serve the tourists, charging them RMB50–100 for food and lodging. They were engaging in a 'Herder Family Happiness' (牧家乐) business model that followed the 'Peasant Family Happiness' (农家乐) model of rural tourism in other Chinese provinces. The lake was unrecognisable from the times I had visited the mountains we call Tengri Tau as a child. On the grassland that herders had once used as their mountain pastures, Chinese-language songs blared from loudspeakers disguised as tree trunks in the woods, and the sound of a bell from a newly built Taoist temple echoed in the mountains. The name 'Flying Dragon Pond' (飞龙潭) was calligraphically carved into the cliff next to the lake, and pavilion-shaped tourist boats explored its waters. Tourist signage designated Bogda Lake as the foot-bathing tub of the mythical Taoist goddess Xiwangmu (西王母的洗脚盆), rendering the landscape of the Central Asian steppe indistinguishable from tourist sites in eastern Chinese provinces.

In 2005, the regional government began to relocate herders, farmers, and miners out of the Bogda Lake area; in the process, more than 1,322 households became 'ecological migrants' (生态移民). In 2012, for the Tianshan region to meet the requirements of its application for designation as a UNESCO World Heritage site, the regional government implemented a grazing ban on 100 square kilometres of pasture around the lake and demolished the shops and buildings there (SCIO 2012; Chinanews.com 2012). Since a state-owned tourism company named Western Regions (西域旅游) took over management of the area, even the locals who used to live there must pay RMB215 to access the lake. Similarly, in 2013, in an effort to develop its tourist industry, the government of the Bortala Mongol Autonomous Prefecture banned grazing on the 110 square kilo-metres surrounding Sayram Lake, displacing 600 households of herders and 120,000 head of livestock (Bortala People's Government 2017). By 2017, the off-limits area had increased to 127 square kilometres (see also Salimjan 2021b). Most of the tourist sites in northern Xinjiang were inha-bited by Kazakh, Mongol, Kyrgyz, and Tuvan herders, on mountainous prairies with rich water resources, such as Sayram Lake, Bogda Lake, Kanas (Qanas) Lake in Altay, and the Narat and Qarajon (Ch: Kalajun, 喀拉峻) prairies in the Ili River Valley. After China's successful applica-tion for World Heritage status in 2013 for the Tianshan region—which includes Qarajon-Qurdnin, Bogda Lake, Bayanbulak Lake, and Tömür Choqqisi (Tomur Peak) in Aksu—tourism boomed.

At the Kazakh Ethnic Culture Garden at Bogda Lake, an old couple who had been relocated from their land told me how their lives had been disrupted by their 'ecological migration' and the boom in the private tourism sector:

> We have been doing tourism for quite a while. Back then we had a better location, quite close to the lake. It was quiet and beautiful; we had a lot of guests. They would stay for a night and hike into the mountains the next day. We had a lot of traveller friends. We had livestock and we had a tourism business. Then … we had to move here. The pastures at the top of the mountain were fenced up, and we had to sell our livestock … many people had to sell livestock. Some people left, some stayed and kept doing tourism. But there are not as many guests as before, and they seldom stay either. We can only rely on tourism now. We used to make about RMB2,000 a day when the business was good, and then most Kazakhs in Sangong County were displaced. Only 100 families were allowed to stay since they had worked in tourism before.

The artificial, manufactured tourist landscape at Bogda Lake, which reduces Kazakhs who have lived on their land for generations to a mere commodity, is only the tip of the iceberg in the systemic dispossession of Turkic peoples and other minorities in Xinjiang. Over the past few years, global attention has focused on the gross violations of human rights such as arbitrary detentions and technological surveillance in Xinjiang. However, there remains a lack of understanding about the relationship between disappearing lifeways and developmental projects that had encroached on native land before the Muslim crackdown even started, let alone attention to the plight of Kazakh pastoralists in northern Xinjiang. In this essay, I delineate a brief history of Kazakh dispossession after China entered its 'ecologically conscious' developmental stage. During this time, not only have Kazakh pastoralists been violently displaced for the sake of the 'ecological restoration' of their grasslands, but also their land and livelihoods have become exploitable resources for the development of ecotourism. The state's crackdown on Muslims, which accelerated from 2017, has facilitated the imprisonment of Kazakh land petitioners as well as the confiscation of their land; Kazakhs have been coerced with the threat of detention to give up their traditional lands and lifeways.

Ecotourism as greenwashing and settler place-making in Xinjiang

The CCP's commitment to achieving an 'ecological civilisation' (生态文明), which was written into China's constitution in 2012 as a response to nationwide environmental problems, undergirds the scientific discourse of 'ecological conservation' (生态保护) as a solution for grassland degradation. In pastoral regions, top-down directives have stimulated state-led conservation work that excludes indigenous populations from being stakeholders in grassland resource management. Most pastoralists in China are state-designated 'minority nationalities' (少数民族) who make up only 1.3 per cent of the national population but who inhabit the vast grasslands that make up 40.9 per cent of the country's territory (Pan 2015). As China entered its more 'ecologically conscious' stage of development, state scientists disproportionately ascribed grassland degradation to 'irresponsible' herders overgrazing their animals, rather than the environmentally destructive operations of state-owned agricultural and extractive industries. After all, 70 per cent of China's domestic coal is exported from its settler colonies in the periphery, such as Inner Mongolia and Xinjiang, to eastern China to fuel its resource demands (Cornot-Gandolphe 2014).

The plight of Kazakh and other nomadic pastoralist communities resonates with the past and present plight of indigenous communities around the world, in that state-led enclosures of Kazakh grassland find their echoes in the colonial land grabs that have taken place globally. For instance, in Norway, the development of wind farms on reindeer-herding lands as part of the government's climate change–mitigation strategy has endangered the life systems and ecological practices of Sami reindeer herders (Fjellheim and Carl 2020; Normann 2021). It has been documented how the United Nations' REDD+ initiative aimed at reducing emissions from deforestation and forest degradation undermines local farmers in countries as diverse as Mozambique, Nigeria, Democratic Republic of Congo, Madagascar, Brazil, Indonesia, Peru, Uganda, and Kenya (WRM and GRAIN 2015). In the United States, the establishment of national parks occurred in the context of the dispossession and genocide of indigenous peoples (Treuer 2021). Before the founding of Yosemite National Park, members of a California state militia razed the villages of, and murdered, the Miwok who had been obstructing the frenzy of extraction brought about by the goldrush. Yellowstone National Park was established in 1872 while the Plains Wars raged around its borders, and the *Yellowstone Act* of 1872 criminalised Shoshone and Bannock peoples' access to the park, barring them from hunting and foraging within its boundaries. In Panama, the Amistad International Biosphere Reserve was established in the aftermath of the US invasion in 1989, after which Naso, Ngobe, and other forest-dwelling communities were removed from the reserve (Landesman 2018). The Panamanian Government granted Texaco drilling rights over 405,000 hectares within the biosphere in 1990. The World Bank's Global Environmental Facility—in tandem with the World Wildlife Fund, Conservation International, and the Nature Conservancy—subsequently took charge of the biosphere's land management program and funded unsuccessful 'alternative livelihood' microprojects and ecotourism initiatives to compensate the impacted forest-dwellers.

In China, state directives sought to extinguish indigenous ways of being on and relating to the land. The ecological civilisation's mandate of scientific conservation and pollution reduction considers mobile pastoralism a backward enterprise that should be abandoned. In this context, herders must adapt to Chinese settler-society norms and settle down, so they can enjoy a 'modern, civilised life' that provides 'stable wages that enable investment in small businesses' (SCIO 2015; Sun 2019). Official media often frame sedentarisation as an improvement of herders' quality of life because they no longer have to seasonally migrate to avoid harsh weather. Moreover, the state has claimed that sedentarisation brings better education, medical care, and employment opportunities. Not only does this paternalistic narrative exaggerate the difficulties of mobile pastoralism, and neglect mobility as an integral part of Kazakh pastoral identity, it also construes pastoralism as incompatible with state modernity and sees sedentarisation as a way to modernise Kazakhs to make them feel grateful towards the Party-State—when, in fact, the Kazakh community in Xinjiang has long cultivated urban and rural social networks to navigate urban life and access urban resources. However, it seems that policies on grazing bans and sedentarisation, which started to be implemented in 2002, have encountered numerous obstacles and therefore have been less successful than expected, at least judging from the central government's insistence that propaganda work is important (see, for instance, National

Forestry and Grassland Administration 2020). It is in this context that the central government set the goal in 2011 of permanently banning grazing on 100,000 square kilometres of land in Xinjiang (Guan and Zhao 2011). In 2015, the Xinjiang Uyghur Autonomous Region (XUAR) Party Committee issued strict environmental assessments and regulatory measures, instituting grazing bans to force the relocation of herders so their grasslands could be rehabilitated (Wang 2017).

Kazakhs' relationship to their land and their mode of land stewardship, mobile pastoralism, have been invalidated according to the paternalistic, legalistic formulations of settler-state sovereignty (Akins and Bauer jr 2021; Moreton-Robinson 2021). Genealogical narratives entangled with land histories are important aspects of Kazakh self-identification. Kazakhs invoke the names of their homeland in turns of phrase such as *ata-babamizding jeri* ('land of our ancestors'), *atameken* ('homeland of our forefathers'), and *kindik qanim tamgan jer* ('land where my umbilical blood was shed'). The names of *khans*, *khojas* ('Islamic missionaries'), and *batirs* ('heroes') who fought for the people are an integral part of local histories and are sometimes kept as placenames. However, these historical markers are often dismissed by the state as folkloric and were even forbidden during high-socialist periods like the Cultural Revolution because they were 'feudalistic' (Salimjan 2021a). To 'restore' nature to its 'original' 'pristine' state (素面朝天, 还其自然), Xinjiang's native community and economy are sidelined and rendered disposable. When a mass internment system was introduced in 2016, the rhythms of removal and theft sped up, proliferating across Kazakh lands.

Coercive ecological conservation came hand in hand with the development of rural tourism and other forms of ecotourism to generate new sources of revenue off land that is undergoing 'ecological rehabilitation'. In Xinjiang, conservation policies to 'return' the land to 'nature' take their cues from the model of de-industrialisation and ecotourism (生态旅游) first pioneered in Anji County, Zhejiang Province, the ethos of which is encapsulated by the slogan 'clear waters and green mountains are mountains of gold and silver' (绿水青山就是金山银山). This slogan is a quote from Xi Jinping when he visited Anji County in 2005, when he was Zhejiang's Party Committee Secretary, and was codified into an aphorism and even written into the Chinese Constitution in 2017 as one of the tenets of the ecological civilisation. It has since featured prominently in the government's calls for the Anji County model to be adopted nationwide. China's Twelfth Five-Year Plan designated Xinjiang as an up-and-coming major tourist destination, with southern Xinjiang to be developed into a showcase for the ancient Silk Road and its folk cultures (XUAR Government 2009; CNTA 2015). As the crackdown on Turkic Muslims has accelerated since 2017, local governments have revamped more and more Uyghur villages in the south into tourist sites in the name of poverty alleviation (see Song 2020; Zero Distance Moyu 2019; YouTube 2021b). Meanwhile, in the north, places from which Kazakh and other pastoralist communities were displaced are branded as locations where tourists can appreciate 'nature', recalling the way in which American national parks were construed as 'virgin' wilderness where settlers could worship the sublime. Many pastoralists—dispossessed by Han settlers or by state authorities enforcing 'ecological conservation'—have had to commodify their culture, just like the Uyghurs in the south, and cater to the tourist gaze to make a living. The violence that undergirds these similar but distinct developments in the north and south is masked with innocuous soundbites from Chinese tourism sites that advise tourists to 'see nature in northern Xinjiang and culture in southern Xinjiang' (北疆看景观, 南疆看人文) (Sohu.com 2020).

Since 2017, counterterrorism campaigns and surveillance technology have engulfed Xinjiang entirely, consolidating what Darren Byler (2022) calls 'terror capitalism', in which cheap, unfree labour is marshalled to secure profits for the region's industrial complexes. Environmental conservation and tourism constitute another site where indigenous land and bodies are capitalised.[1] Tourism in settler societies like the Panamanian Caribbean and Hawai`i often caters to privileged, affluent settlers and foreigners, and is predicated on the disenfranchisement of indigenous peoples (Mollett 2021; Aikau and Gonzalez 2019). This has been the case in the Kazakh region of Xinjiang as well. When landless Kazakhs appealed to the authorities, they were immediately construed as a threat to social stability and punished as rioters. In recent years, the crackdown on Turkic

---

1   In just one month alone in July 2017, the Sayram Lake tourist site had a net income of RMB10 million (~US$1.5 million) from ticket sales. According to the 2020 edition of the Bingtuan statistical yearbook (XUAR Bureau of Statistics 2020), in 2019, tourist numbers reached more than 33 million people, and tourism in Xinjiang generated RMB20.7 billion in income—more than half of the revenue (56.3 per cent) generated by the service industry. Since 2016, in Xinjiang's Ili and Altay regions, the number of 'Herder Family Happiness' tourist services has increased by 40 per cent, compared with the Twelfth Five-Year Plan period of 2011–15. In 2019 alone, rural tourism in Xinjiang served 10.34 million tourists, resulting in RMB400 million in tourist spending. See Ren (2020).

Muslim minorities has created another instance of 'lucrative chaos' for the state to collaborate with corporate entities to appropriate grassland and imprison Kazakh activists, herders, and peasants (Cliff 2016).

By invoking history and geographical narratives to paint northwestern China as a frontier to be tamed, tourism development in Xinjiang is comparable with what indigenous scholar Teresia Teaiwa (2016) calls 'militourism', in which the US military plays a key but clandestine role in establishing the tourism industry in places ravaged by US imperialism. Whereas the US military concealed its activities, the Xinjiang Production and Construction Corps (新疆生产建设兵团)—or Bingtuan, a para-military settler-colonial organisation in Xinjiang—is upfront about its development of Xinjiang's tourism sector. From 2016 to 2020, it made a profit of RMB60 billion from tourism, which is double that made under the previous Five-Year Plan. Bingtuan's tourism services include ecotourism (生态旅游), cultural experiential tourism (文化体验), 'Red' tourism (红色旅游), do-it-yourself road-trips, and wellness vacations, and are mostly offered at tourist sites along the Tianshan range and the Bingtuan towns along the China–Kazakhstan border (Bingtuan Daily 2020). In a China National Tourism Administration bulletin, the state stresses the necessity of tourism for the realisation of the Belt and Road Initiative, as well as the political task of making Xinjiang 'safe' for Han tourists (CNTA 2015).[2] Tourism companies in eastern China are instructed to pair with tourism companies in Xinjiang to assist in setting developmental priorities in a program called Tourism as Xinjiang Aid (旅游援疆). Following a disaster reconstruction development model, Xinjiang Aid (援疆计划) is a state program that requires Chinese provinces and municipalities to aid Xinjiang through human resources, technology, and investment in Xinjiang's industries. As another top-down state project, this program continues to treat Xinjiang as the involuntary recipient of state development and is leading to a greater influx of Han and more resource extraction in the province. A key priority of Tourism as Xinjiang Aid is to further develop the region's transport infrastructure to provide more convenient travel networks, such as express trains that allow tourists to travel directly from sister cities designated by Xinjiang Aid. The Xinjiang

---

2   Incarcerated and exiled Uyghurs and Kazakhs see Han people's ability to enjoy tourism in Xinjiang as a social privilege; only they have such free access and mobility.

Aid program is also heavily involved in a labour transfer program that moves Uyghurs out of Xinjiang and assigns them to factories in the eastern provinces as unfree workers (Xu et al. 2020). Under the state's directive, the tourism narratives propagated by the Bingtuan must champion 'land reclamation culture' (屯垦文化): Chinese settler histories claiming that today's Xinjiang is the fruit of Han settlers' selfless, backbreaking efforts to develop the land while defending its borders from hostile foreign forces. Reminiscent of American settler histories of frontier expansion, this myth-building process is an important process of normalisation and disavowal of the settler-colonial processes of removal and dispossession.

In many global contexts, indigenous peoples' land and bodies become the key sites of settler-colonial violence. Across northern Xinjiang, coercive conservation legitimated by ecological civilisation discourses has not only led to the enclosure of pastures and the dispossession of Kazakh pastoralists, but also—in the cases I present in the following sections— often become the premise for incarcerating resistors under the guise of maintaining social stability.

Displaced by tourism

Qarajon is one of the most beautiful and lush prairies in the Tianshan region, which is under the administration of Tekes County in Ili Kazakh Autonomous Prefecture. The Ili prefectural government reported in 2016 that it had banned grazing on 2.4 million *mu* (1,600 square kilometres) of grassland to restore its ecology (XJYL 2016). While the official report notes that some counties have not fully reimbursed the affected herders and urges local county administrators to refrain from embezzling reimbursement funds, it glosses over the herders' on-the-ground struggles against the authorities. In 2011, the prefectural government implemented the grazing ban without consent from the villagers, and Tekes County officials embezzled the reimbursement money that was supposed to be paid to them. According to a whistle-blower, the banned area in Qarajon (500,000 *mu*, or 333 square kilometres) provided a livelihood for

204 households engaged in animal husbandry.[3] Not only did the herders not receive any state reimbursement (set by the authorities at RMB50/*mu* or 670 square metres), but also the police hastily drove them off their land. Consequently, many livestock starved, were preyed on by wolves, or, when chased by police cars, fell to their death over a cliff. When herders petitioned in May 2012 to be compensated for the enormous economic loss they had suffered, of both land and livestock, they received only RMB13/*mu* for 450,000 *mu* (300 square kilometres) of land—less than one-quarter of the amount they had been promised.

Tekes County's Party Secretary Liu Li claimed that the key to achieving UNESCO World Heritage designation was to ban grazing, and the county had plans to relocate the herders and break their tradition of nomadic pastoralism in favour of rearing livestock in pens (Yuan and Xu 2012). When the prefectural government implemented the grazing ban, it gave Qarajon herders only three days to move, after which they would be driven off the land by force. In a leaked video of the Qarajon incident, Kazakh women were filmed trekking off their land on foot, clinging on to their children and their belongings. They were indignant that the government had sent trucks to demolish their homes, saying their land had already been allocated to tourism sites, and many of their calves had died after being chased by police vans. They complained that state cadres had pressured them to sign the relocation papers, which they refused to do because their husbands were not around. Still, they were evicted, and did not know where to go.

---

3   The Qarajon riots of 2014 (Қаражон оқиғасы; 2014 喀拉峻事件; قاراجون ۋقيعاسى) were documented by an anonymous whistle-blower, whose video on *Youku*, a Mainland Chinese video streaming site, was subsequently censored and removed. The video is now available on YouTube (2021a). This anonymously edited video contains a state media report from *China Central Television* (*CCTV*), screenshots of government documents, a rare clip of herders who have just been evicted from their homes, as well as scenes of protest and subsequent mass arrests in Qarajon. Subtitles that criticise the local government are juxtaposed with the official state narrative. They criticise Tekes County officials' embezzlement of the state funds that are meant to reimburse the dispossessed herders. The video exposes the lies of Tekes County officials. For example, on 3 December 2011, the head of the Grassland Management Office, Meng Gujiang, said on *CCTV* that he had banned pastoralism on 70,000 *mu* (47 square kilometres) of land. He also claimed the government had publicly informed the affected herders of the reimbursements made available to them. However, the real prohibited area was much larger, and the herders were not informed of the reimbursements. The video also notes that state media reports about positive changes in Qaradala village in Tekes County were fabricated. Herder Bahtiyar was instructed to say that his life conditions had improved after sedentarisation measures were implemented, that he had received the RMB50/*mu* reimbursement, and that his livestock numbers had increased. The livestock were actually borrowed from his neighbours for the purpose of shooting the video.

Later in the YouTube video, Kazakh men protesting their evictions tried to reason with the state police and cadres, citing the country's grassland laws to argue for their legal right to access the grassland they had lived on for generations. One of them reproached the cadres:

> Since this country was founded, it has been amiable and kind to us, but regarding the Qarajon issue, the government has committed a crime whose graveness is unheard of! We believe the government's methods in handling us are wrong … the learned intellectuals of law and politics like you in those 50 vehicles that came yesterday had no right to drive people and their livestock off the land! What a crime they have committed! [The work-team leaders] also tried to intimidate our entire Kabsalang Village, scaring our children and wives by saying 'your father misspoke' and 'your father has made a mistake'.

In Xinjiang, work-team leaders, who belong to the lowest level of government, propagandise state policies and hold immense power over the indigenous citizens they 'supervise'. Based throughout the rural areas of the region, they can decide whether a citizen is 'untrustworthy' (不放心人员) and should be sent to the camps for reeducation. This incident happened before the camp system was fully implemented; still, the leaders could have had the herders arrested as a threat to social stability. The Kazakh protester in the YouTube video continued:

> It's been four days that we have been intimidated like this! We have done nothing but arrive at our seasonal pastures quietly. We just want to let our livestock graze and support our families. What crime have we committed? Why do you oppress us? Why are we so oppressed? Why don't the state intellectuals who have learned the laws carefully think this through? Can the government right this wrong or not? If not, we will sue and take legal measures. We will ask for compensation for the psychological damage you inflicted on our people. Alas! Some people's cows died, and our children were frightened … Do you know how many days people haven't had a proper meal here? I haven't even had a cup of water! I've been here day and night! [Asking everyone at the protest:] Do you see anyone set up their tent? Has anyone here sat down to eat?

To quell the protest, the judicial police—led by Ili sub-branch Party Secretary Zhang Zhide, Tekes County Attorney-General Mutallip, and Inspector Serikjan—were accompanied by more than 100 police cars sent by Police Bureau Chief Wang Xinwei to arrest the resisting herders. For three days, the mountains and valleys echoed with the sound of police sirens and the panicked wails of livestock being chased down by police cars. Ili Kazakh Prefecture Animal Husbandry Bureau Party Secretary Hou Jianxin said: 'It just takes arresting five or six herders to shut them all up' (逮捕五六个牧民都全都老实了) (YouTube 2021a).

After the herders' forced relocation, their land was up for grabs. Through an under-the-table deal, the Ili and Tekes officials transferred the rights for 1.28 million *mu* (853 square kilometres) of grassland to Haoxinzhong Tianshan (浩新中天山旅游股份有限公司), a joint venture between the local government and a private tourism development company. The company was renamed Kalajun Investment Company (喀拉峻投资股份有限公司) in March 2012 to manage Qarajon as an 'international ecotourism site' (喀拉峻国际生态旅游区) (Tuniu.com 2006–21).[4] The company then commissioned the XUAR Environment Protection Technology Centre (新疆维吾尔自治区环境保护技术咨询中心)—an institution under the administration of the XUAR Environment Protection Bureau—to assess the Qarajon ecotourism construction project without consulting the herders most affected it. In 2013, Qarajon received designation as a UNESCO World Heritage site and, in 2016, it attained the national 5A title to cement its status as a top ecotourism site in China. It was reported that the company had plans to invest RMB1 billion to develop tourism in the area (Liu 2014).[5]

Disappearance of land petitioners

In July 2013, two years after the Qarajon incident, a Kazakh man named Nurbaqyt Nasihat, who was a student in the Economics Department of Wuxi's Jiangnan University, Jiangsu Province, started to write appeal

---

4   Xinjiang Kalajun Investment Company Limited (新疆喀拉峻投资股份有限公司) has registered capital of RMB130 million. *Xinjiang Morning Post* (2018) reported the story of Chen Gengxin and Wang Guozhi coming to invest in Qarajon. Originally from Guangzhou, Chen attended graduate school in the United States and returned to China to do business. In 2011, the first time he visited Qarajon with Wang, he was impressed and immediately thought of turning the area into 'China's Yosemite' (中国的黄石公园).

5   The company invested RMB1 billion to develop tourism in Qarajon (Liu 2014).

letters on behalf of the herders who had lost their lands in Mori Kazakh Autonomous County (木垒) in the east of Changji Hui Autonomous Prefecture (Xinjiang Victims Database 2018d). The villagers from Shoqpar Tas Village (大石头乡), Bostan Village, and Uzbek Ranch (克木场) sought Nurbaqyt's assistance because he was proficient in Chinese. As was the case in Qarajon, the Mori County Government dispossessed villagers of their land and embezzled large sums of reimbursement funds in the process. In Shoqpar Tas village, 7,000 herders used to steward almost 11.6 million *mu* (7,722 square kilometres) of land. When large tracts of grassland were privatised in the reform era, the Haptik, Dongshan, Hoshur, Kokadir, Salt Lake, and Laojunmiao pastures were enclosed, and the amount of grazing land available shrank to 4,959 square kilometres. As the land use rights for these pastures were held by the Mori Grassland Supervisory Office, the Finance Bureau, the Animal Husbandry Bureau, and various branches of the county government, higher-level officials coordinated to embezzle the reimbursement funds meant for the herders who had to leave their land to make way for mining and road construction projects.[6]

On 10 April 2014, having gathered the signatures of 14,000 herders, Nurbaqyt went with 11 other Kazakhs to petition central government authorities in Beijing. In May, they were taken back to Mori with black hoods over their heads and their ankles in chains, according to the testimony of Nurbaqyt's Kazakhstan-based sister, Mariya Nasihat.[7] Nurbaqyt's family in Mori were unaware of his whereabouts until a police friend told them of his arrest on the third day after his return to Mori. The police interrogated Nurbaqyt as to why he had gone to Beijing, beating him in hopes of securing a confession, but he insisted that he had not committed any crime. He was then detained for eight months, until the court finally opened his case and sentenced him to two years and eight months for 'assembling a crowd to disrupt social order' (聚众扰乱社会秩序罪). On 16 July, Nurbaqyt's application for release on bail pending trial was rejected, as the police claimed he was 'too dangerous to be released' (取保候审后不足以防止发生社会危险性). His appeal letter, signed on 20 July, asked the authorities to investigate the corrupt means by which

---

6 According to Mariya Nusihat's testimony for Nurbaqyt, Mori County leader Kairat sold the 100-year land usage certificate to coal and salt mining companies. Her appeal letter, which outlines the coordinated embezzlement of reimbursements, can be viewed in Nurbaqyt Nasihat's entry on the Xinjiang Victims Database (2018).

7 Her testimony was collected by Serikzhan Bilash, the co-founder of Atajurt Kazakh Human Rights Group.

Mori's officials had enclosed the pastures and displaced the herders. He was confused about why he had been sentenced for simply exercising his civil right to appeal.

The state's intensified crackdown on Muslims in 2016 made it convenient for local authorities to detain petitioners and protesters in Xinjiang who were otherwise not criminalised by the state's Islamophobic policies. As Pittman Potter (2013: 127) points out, 'law and policy on economy and development in Xinjiang reflect tensions between efforts to develop agricultural, petroleum, and mineral resources on the one hand, and security programs aimed at suppressing local dissident and separatist movements on the other'. After 2016, laws and policies in Xinjiang consolidated a highly securitised environment to ensure the stability and profitability of resource extraction. Nurbaqyt was released in October 2016 just as Chen Quanguo began the mass crackdown on ethno-religious minorities in Xinjiang, and he had managed to enjoy only a month of freedom when the police sent him, along with the other 11 Kazakh petitioners, to a detention camp to 'study'.[8] Internal reports from the Ürümqi police department leaked by *The Intercept* show that petitioners are often treated as 'untrustworthy' and subject to detention (Grauer 2021). All the petitioners were subjected to beatings in captivity, according to Mariya. Two were beaten so badly they became disabled and are now reliant on wheelchairs. While Mariya received a phone call from a foreign journalist about Nurbaqyt's release on 24 December 2018, there has been no information about his whereabouts since. The requests by his family, who are currently living in Kazakhstan, for his return remained unanswered. Nurbaqyt's Kazakhstan permanent residency certificate was processed in 2014, but it is not clear whether he will ever be able to get out of Xinjiang.

Land confiscation under crackdown

In 2017, the Chinese Government deemed Kazakhstan one of '26 sensitive countries' (26个涉恐国家)—Muslim-majority and other countries perceived to be 'harbouring religious extremism'.[9] Many Chinese Kazakhs

---

8 According to Mariya Nasihat, the 12 land petitioners are Nurbaqyt, Dalelkhan, Janat, Asai, Sayra (F), Elay, Rasul, Kurpari (F), Muwiq, Jarkingul (F), Rahat, and Qumar. Except for Nurbaqyt, the last names of the 11 other petitioners are unknown.

9 The 26 countries are: Algeria, Afghanistan, Azerbaijan, Egypt, Pakistan, Kazakhstan, Kyrgyzstan, Kenya, Libya, South Sudan, Nigeria, Saudi Arabia, Somalia, Tajikistan, Turkey, Turkmenistan, Uzbekistan, Syria, Yemen, Iraq, Iran, Malaysia, Indonesia, Thailand, United Arab Emirates, and Russia.

in Xinjiang who used to freely travel to Kazakhstan can no longer do so because their passports have been confiscated by the local police. Many Kazakh nationals are detained in the camps, and their families in Kaza-khstan dare not travel to China to visit them. Chinese authorities view Chinese Kazakhs who have visited Kazakhstan as a threat, believing they may publicise the situation in Xinjiang to the international community and undermine bilateral relations. At the same time, the state's expanded repressive capacity has provided authorities with more leverage to coerce Kazakhs and Uyghurs to forfeit their land and assets under threat of being sent to 'study in the camps'.

According to the testimonies collected by the Xinjiang Victims Database, Chinese Kazakhs who have travelled to Kazakhstan, have family in Kaza-khstan, or have Kazakh citizenship or a green card have been intimidated by Xinjiang's local governments into giving up their land.[10] These cases show that the processes that prevented Nurbaqyt from protesting the theft of his land have been accelerated by the internment camp system. Such large-scale theft is no longer an isolated incident; rather, it appears that any Kazakh citizen deemed untrustworthy will be subject to land seizure and detention in the camp system, which has allowed this process to proliferate at a grassroots level.

For example, in 2017, when former farmer Erbolat Zharylqasyn travelled from Kazakhstan to Xinjiang to visit his relatives in Tacheng, the local police demanded he either return the 33 *mu* (2.2 hectares) of farmland he had been cultivating since 1997 or pay a lump sum of RMB160,000 (Xinjiang Victims Database 2018a). Since he refused to give up his farmland and could not pay the exorbitant fee, the authorities made him renounce his Kazakh citizenship. He has been stuck in Xinjiang ever since, separated from his wife and children. Esqat Bekinur had his passport confiscated by the authorities in Zhaosu County in Ili and the village administration demanded he waive title over his farmland to win back his passport (Xinjiang Victims Database 2018b). Esqat, his older sister, and his brother-in-law have been detained in the camps since 2018, leaving his younger sister and elderly parents without financial support in Kazakhstan. Nagima Sultanmurat, a herder in Zhaosu County in Ili, was forced to sign a document giving up her 705 *mu* (47 hectares) of

---

10 Xinjiang Victims Database (2021): 'In numerous documented cases, the state not only detains but also confiscates (land, property, money). We now have a list of (32) entries where this is mentioned.'

pasture, which was valid until 2047, to get her passport back (Xinjiang Victims Database 2018c). However, after she signed the document, the local police refused to return her passport; they would only do so once her Kazakh family members travelled to Xinjiang and went through the deregistration process. When Kunim Zeinolda, a Chinese citizen with a Kazakh residence permit, returned to Wenquan County in Bortala Mongol Autonomous Prefecture to resolve her pension problems, she had her documents confiscated by the authorities on arrival (Xinjiang Victims Database 2019). She kept returning to the local administration offices to try to get her passport back, but the authorities threatened to send her to a camp to 'study' if she persisted. Later, they offered to return her passport on the condition she abandon her family's 30 *mu* (2 hectares) of farmland and give up her retirement pension. She had to give up everything she owned to reunite with her family in Kazakhstan. Many people I have talked to over the past few years faced financial difficulties after fleeing to Kazakhstan from Xinjiang because they were unable to access family assets in China or transfer them to Kazakhstan.

The widespread land grabs and mass detentions associated with the camp system have also been detailed by an anonymous assistant police officer (协警) from Changji Hui Autonomous Prefecture in an interview conducted by activist Erkin Azat (2019). During a '100-day strike-hard' (百日严打) campaign in Xinjiang, he and his Kazakh and Uyghur colleagues were mandated to meet a certain quota of arrests for the camps:

> Around August and September in 2016, a Hui village protested the government's seizure of their land for the construction of a police station and hospital, during which Hui houses and farmlands were demolished without the villagers' knowledge. About 150 people gathered to protest. We arrested them and sent them directly to the detention camps—there weren't any trials or legal procedures. They are still inside now, and I was assigned to guard the prisoners in a heavy, full-body bomb suit. To this day, this incident remains confidential. Starting in 2015, the government bought Kazakh grassland at cheap prices. In 2016, a private company bought the

land for touristic purposes. We attended an opening ceremony
for that private company, and we heard it was operating on land
stolen from the Kazakhs. (Azat 2019)

Disastrous development

Even though China aims to be a global leader in tackling climate change,
ethnic minorities in Xinjiang and their livelihoods have borne the brunt
of top-down policies geared towards intensifying extractive activities
and economic development. Li Yifei and Judith Shapiro (2019) note that
China's version of an ecologically green future is envisioned as being
brought about through authoritarian governance, and this is on full
display in Xinjiang, where coercive conservation proceeds hand in hand
with tourism development that boosts not only national revenue but also
Chinese nationalism.

In response to the international condemnation of human rights violations in Xinjiang, spokespeople for the Chinese Party-State often retort
by pointing out how Xinjiang's development has stabilised the region and
resulted in a booming tourism sector. Though tourism as a development
strategy is endorsed by the United Nations, the World Bank, and many
developmental nongovernmental organisations as a vehicle for poverty
reduction and social advancement for women and minorities, this support
rings hollow, especially in settler-colonial contexts such as Xinjiang and
the other cases discussed in this essay. When the development of Xinjiang's
construction and ecotourism industries is coupled with the CCP's political
priority of maintaining stability, the government inevitably draws on its
expanded policing capabilities to dispossess indigenous communities of
their land and ensnare them in its carceral infrastructure. When the state
introduces a mass internment system for all minority people deemed
untrustworthy, the settler-colonial processes that are already in motion
are amplified. Removal proliferates as a normalised aspect of settler
dispossession of peoples deemed to be detainable primitives.

.

12
Factories of Turkic Muslim internment*

Darren Byler

On 3 November 2018, Yerzhan Qurban, a middle-aged Kazakh man from a small village 50 kilometres from the city of Ghulja in the Xinjiang Uyghur Autonomous Region, was released from the camp where he had been held for nine months. He thought perhaps now he would be free to return to his former life as an immigrant in Kazakhstan. Yet, just a few days later, he was sent to an industrial park in Ghulja to work in a glove factory. For the next 53 days, he experienced life in an internment factory that was built to 'raise the quality' (提高素质) of minority workers.

Yerzhan had been detained soon after he returned to China from Kazakhstan to seek medical treatment for his daughter and care for his ailing mother in early 2018. In a 2019 interview with the German magazine *Die Zeit*, he said:

> On the evening of 8 February 2018, they picked me up in a minibus. It was already dark and they put black plastic sacks over our heads and handcuffs on our hands. There were five young men from my village with me on the minibus. The room in which I had to stay for the next nine months was 5 metres by 5 metres and located on the third floor. On the door, a sign said 'No. 12'. Our floor alone accommodated 260 men. In my room, we were 12. Later I heard that there had been more than 10,000 men detained in our camp. (Die Zeit 2019)

Yerzhan was unsure exactly where the camp was located. It may have been the one built in the fields on the outskirts of the city, just 7 kilometres from the industrial park where he was later forced to work (Die Zeit 2019).

*This chapter is based on an article published in the news journal *SupChina* on 4 September 2019 titled 'How Companies Profit from Forced Labor in Xinjiang' (available from: supchina. com/2019/09/04/how-companies-profit-from-forced-labor-in-xinjiang).

As is often reported by former detainees, conditions in the camp were appalling. Describing the circumstances of his detention, Yerzhan said:

> The toilet was a bucket by the window, there was no running water. In the daytime, we were sitting in rows on our plastic stools. The food was handed to us through an opening in the door. At 7am, we had to sing the Chinese national anthem and then we had three minutes for breakfast. Afterwards, we learned Chinese until 9pm. Our teachers were Kazakhs or Uyghurs. We were watched by four cameras in our room which ensured that we didn't talk to each other. Those who spoke anyway were handcuffed and had to stand by the wall. 'You don't have the right to talk, because you are not humans,' said the guards. 'If you were humans, you wouldn't be here.' (Die Zeit 2019)

Yerzhan said he still does not know why he was taken. Like others detained in Ghulja, his internment was likely because he possessed a passport and had travelled to Kazakhstan—one of 26 Muslim-majority countries on a Chinese state watchlist (see HRW 2019). Over time, the gruelling routine began to change his mental state. He said: 'The first two months, I thought of my wife Maynur and my three children. Sometime later, I only thought about food' (Die Zeit 2019).

About the time Yerzhan was reduced to thinking about his bodily survival, in May 2018, Pan Daojin, the Front Commander and Party Secretary of Yili prefecture, arrived to inspect a newly built industrial park on the other side of town (The Times of Nantong Aiding Xinjiang 2018). He came with a delegation from Jiangsu tasked with providing industrial 'aid' to Xinjiang. Pan, who is also from Jiangsu, was appointed to his position in December 2016, just as the mass detentions of the reeducation system began. During the inspection of the new industrial park, he 'fully affirmed the achievements' of the business leaders from Nantong City in Jiangsu who had funded it. The delegation showed off the new factory of the Jiangsu-based Solamoda Garment Group—a company that partners with Forever 21 and other international brands. They also visited the highly productive glove factory to which Yerzhan would be eventually assigned. This factory was managed by employees of the Luye Shuozi Island Trading Company, a manufacturer based in Baoding City, Hebei Province.

According to the general manager of the glove factory, Wang Xinghua, speaking in a state TV interview released in December 2018: 'With the support of the government, we have already recruited more than 600 people' (Ili Television 2018). One of these 600 government 'recruits' was Yerzhan, who had arrived from the camp less than a month before. General Manager Wang went on to say that since the founding of the new factory in 2017, 'We have generated more than US$6 million in sales. We plan to reach 1,000 workers by the end of this year. We plan to provide jobs to 1,500 people by the end of 2019.' In fact, the glove factory in Ghulja has now far surpassed the capacity of its parent factory, which back in Hebei has less than 200 employees (Alibaba 2019). Moving manufacturing to Xinjiang made economic sense for the company, which sold 96 per cent of its leather gloves across the border in Russia and Eastern Europe.

But there were other reasons why exponential growth was so easy. Since 2018, the state has provided subsidies to build factories in and ship goods from Xinjiang. Construction of the factories was often funded by local governments in eastern China as part of a 'pairing assistance' (配对与援助) program. Up to 4 per cent of new factories' sales volume was subsidised to cover shipping expenses from the new location (People's Government of XUAR 2018). Most importantly, as in every county in Xinjiang, there was a standing labour reserve of tens of thousands of desperate, traumatised detainees like Yerzhan in nearby camps.

A carrier of the economy

Since 2017, factories have flocked to Xinjiang to take advantage of the newly built industrial parks associated with the reeducation camp system and the cheap labour and subsidies that accompany them. In fact, in late 2018, the primary development ministry for the region, the Xinjiang Development and Reform Commission, circulated a statement saying the camps or 'vocational skills education and training centres' (教育培训中心) had become a 'carrier' (载体) of the economy (XJDRC 2018). Because of this system, Xinjiang had attracted 'significant investment and construction from coast-based Chinese companies'. Since China sources more than 80 per cent of its cotton from Xinjiang, there was a special emphasis placed on Chinese textile and garment–related industries (Gro Intelligence 2019). In an effort motivated at least in part by rising labour costs among Han migrant workers on the east coast, the state plans to move more than one million textile and garment industry jobs to the

Xinjiang region by 2023 (Patton 2016). If it succeeds, it will mean that as many as one in every 11 textile and garment industry jobs in China will be in Xinjiang (ILO 2014). The 1,500 jobs at the glove factory in Ghulja are part of that number.

There are three primary tracks through which Uyghurs and other Turkic Muslims are involuntarily assigned to work in the newly built factories as part of the reeducation labour regime. First, many detainees in camps are placed in factories inside or adjacent to camps. They work inside the same camp space in which they are held at night. Second, some new industrial parks built in regional centres host a mix of former detainees and 'rural surplus labourers' who are not former detainees. These surplus labourers are chosen from self-employed populations of rural farmers and peri-urban Kazakhs and Uyghurs who previously found contingent work in heritage trades and service industries. In a new carceral instantiation of what Chris Smith and Pun Ngai (2006) refer to as the 'dormitory labour regime' used to surveil and exploit migrant workers in eastern China, the former detainees who join these surplus labourers in the urban industrial parks are often held in locked dormitories at night, as in the case of Yerzhan. Some 'surplus labourers'—like migrant workers in eastern China—are permitted to return to their own homes at night or to stay in freely chosen accommodation in the regional centre. Third, newly built county-level and smaller-scale 'satellite factories' (卫星工厂) in rural areas host Uyghur workers near their homes. These worker populations of mainly women with young children are assigned by local village and township-level authorities to work while their children are in daycare facilities; their husbands work in the city or are detained in camps. While there are different levels of coercion in these tracks, all three result in forms of family separation and dependence on the state and private industry proxies for training and discipline in Chinese-speaking environments.

In all cases, Turkic Muslim detainees are forcibly assigned to these positions. As documents used by 'neighbourhood watch unit' (社区) and 'village-level work brigade' (大队) workers note, refusing 'poverty alleviation' (扶贫) schemes—a widely used euphemism for assigned factory work and other forms of 'coercive assistance' (Pan 2020)—is regarded as a sign of untrustworthiness and religious extremism (Turki-stan Press 2018). These grassroots-level state workers who partner with police stations and private and state-owned enterprises to implement the campaign are charged with providing employees from populations within their jurisdictions. They often accompany workers to the factories and, at times, act as intermediaries between factory management and the workers. They also enforce discipline on the factory floor and, in some cases, in dormitories. In a radical contravention of the supposed 'freedom' associated with market-based contract law, state authorities assume the only reason a Muslim worker may not want to be separated from their families and work for low wages in a Han-managed factory is because of their aversion to contact with non-Muslims. Forcing Uyghurs and Kazakhs to work in a Chinese-speaking environment can then be framed by state workers and employers as liberating them from their 'native' way of life and traditions. This framing elides the process of state and market dependence that is created by dispossessing Uyghurs and Kazakhs of what Marx (1978) would describe as their own 'means of production' and the radical forms of unfreedom that are produced by forced labour in an alien environment.

The glove factory to which Yerzhan was sent appears to have a mix of both former detainees and involuntarily assigned 'surplus workers'. Many, like Yerzhan, arrived in the factory after briefly being released from the camp. Yet, according to a state report, it appears that more than 1,800 others were sent to work in the industrial park in mid-2017, long before the first detainees were transferred from the camps (Zero Distance Yining 2017). According to Yerzhan and a second worker named Gulzira Auelkhan, whom I interviewed, these early arrivals were 'track two' underemployed rural workers who were determined to be part of the 'normal' population and were assigned to work without first being placed in a camp.

Unfree labour

Several months before Yerzhan arrived at the glove factory, another Kazakh detainee was also transferred from a nearby reeducation camp to work there. Before arriving, Gulzira, a 39-year-old mother of a toddler whom she left with her husband back in Kazakhstan, had endured 15 months of horrific abuse in crowded cells with 18 to 60 other detainees, most of whom were Uyghur (Xinjiang Victims Database 2019). Detainees in her cell were repeatedly shocked in the head with electric batons if they used the bathroom for longer than two minutes. Their closely cropped hair masked some of the visible bruising. Detainees were given dye to darken their hair and scalp before higher-level officials visited the camp (Azat 2019). They were told to smile during the inspections.

Due to the relatively low level of her perceived 'pre-criminal offences'—according to documents supplied to the United Nations by the Chinese Government, many detainees in the camps had not actually committed crimes (UN 2019)—Gulzira was placed in a camp that had the least amount of security. What had marked her as 'untrustworthy' was a previous visit to Kazakhstan and the fact she watched Turkish TV shows in which women wore hijabs. In her section of the camp, there was less of an emphasis on ideological retraining. Instead, the detainees studied Chinese all day, every day. Kazakh and Uyghur languages were not permitted.

Like Yerzhan, when Gulzira was released from the camp, she thought she may be given greater freedom. But within several days, a local village leader appeared with a document saying she must report for work at the glove factory. When she arrived at the plant, she recognised her new boss, General Manager Wang. She had seen him several times in the camp, on tours with camp officials. She surmised that he must have picked her to work in his factory while she was still in the camp. She was told that as a trainee she would be paid 600 *yuan* per month (approximately US$100)—one-third of the 1,800-*yuan* state-mandated minimum wage in the region—for the first three months. She would also be paid a small amount, around 2 jiao (20 Chinese cents), per pair of gloves according to her 'efficiency'. She said: 'The most skilled worker could sew 60 pairs a day. I tried my best, but I could only sew 13 pairs' (Vanderklippe 2019). Since she did not have good eyesight, she found it impossible to improve her productivity. Speaking to Ben Mauk, she said:

> In the end, I worked there for a month and a half. It was piecework. I earned one jiao for every glove I finished. All told, I made more than two thousand gloves and earned 220 *yuan*. So, you see, it was like slavery. (Xinjiang Victims Database 2019)

Although there was less security in the factory than in the camp, the detainees were not allowed to leave. In an interview I did with her in January 2020, months after she had fled across the Chinese border to Kazakhstan, Gulzira spoke of checkpoints at the entrance of the dormitory and factory where her ID and face were scanned. She said:

> We would have our bodies and phones checked when we arrived, and in the middle of the day. When we were leaving for the dormitory at the end of the day they would check again, because they

were worried we might take a [sewing] needle. After we got to
know [the police contractors,] we asked them, 'Why are you still
here watching us?'

While they never replied, she told me she knew the answer was that
the security workers were monitoring whether the detainees were acting
like submissive 'reeducated' industrial workers. She noted that, like every
other Turkic Muslim she knew, her passport had been confiscated and
travel beyond the parameters of their assigned locality—whether it was
an industrial park or the relative freedom of a village—was not permitted.
In addition, like most assigned workers, she had very little money with
which to attempt to pay someone to smuggle her out. Life at the factory
was better than life in the camp, but she understood that in the new space
she was being asked to prove that she had become a truly reeducated
industrial worker.

Outside the discipline of the factory and industrial park, the infrastructure of material walls continued to be a part of her life. Every night
after work, she and other detainees were taken by bus to a makeshift
dormitory around 3 kilometres away. In the dormitory, detainees were
permitted to walk around the campus, but they were not permitted to
leave the premises. According to reporting from *The Globe and Mail*, the
workers 'received readings in the factory before work and, at day's end,
45-minute Chinese lessons in the dormitory, where they were watched
at night by an official' (Vanderklippe 2019).

Both Yerzhan and Gulzira were permitted to visit relatives for several
hours during one day on the weekend. A company bus would ferry them
back and forth from the dormitory to their home villages. A month into
their 'training', however, they found out that these trips were quite costly.
Bosses at the factory, such as General Manager Wang, told them that
because of the cost of the shuttle service and their food expenses, their
600-*yuan* salary would be slashed in half. Yerzhan later recalled: 'I worked
on a production line for 53 days, earning 300 *yuan* in total.'

Government documents show that in Kashgar prefecture in 2018,
100,000 detainees were scheduled to move into and work in the newly
built industrial parks and satellite factories (Kashgar Regional Administrative Office 2018). Other prefectures aimed for similar numbers. In
Kashgar, for each detainee put to work, the factory owners would receive
5,000 *yuan* dispersed over three years. These subsidies were likely put in
place to prevent the type of wage garnishment that Yerzhan and Gulzira

experienced. However, since the factories function as an extension of the camp system, operating in a legal grey zone outside civil and human rights, prevention of worker abuse falls to the moral code of people like General Manager Wang. As an industrialist acting as a proxy for the carceral state, he knew just as well as Yerzhan or Gulzira that any complaint, any slowdown in production, could result in their replacement with other detainees. He could treat them in any way he wanted.

Social implications of reeducation industrial parks

Newly built industrial parks in northwestern China occupy a liminal space between 'reeducation' camps and private industry, proletarianisation and coerced labour. State documents note over and over that the new industrial parks are being built to instil an undefined 'basic quality' (基础素质) in Uyghur and Kazakh detainees and other Muslim surplus labourers. What is often left unsaid in state-approved documents is the way these factory spaces function as an archipelago of near total institutions at the periphery of the Chinese social contract—an implicit agreement that the state will protect its citizens in exchange for their loyalty. For Uyghurs and Kazakh Chinese citizens, this social contract has been shattered, as what Michel Foucault (1975) refers to as the prison archipelago is enlisted in a mode of colonial-capitalist production—a reeducation labour regime—that erodes the vitality of their indigenous social reproduction. The documents of the workers in Xinjiang's internment factories are confiscated or their IDs are marked as invalid, placing them under a pervasive form of unfreedom. This type of coerced labour is subsidised and directed by the state and operationalised by a complex web of surveillance practices and a logistics system that are bringing the Chinese factory to the Uyghur and Kazakh homelands. All this material development is authorised by the threatening presence of hundreds of internment camps that signify the power of the state over Turkic Muslim life.

   Importantly, the effects of this system are not limited to northwestern China, or even to China itself. Nearly all the gloves made by detainees in the satellite factory of the Luye Shuozi Dao Trading Company are sold abroad. On the company's Alibaba distribution site, they note the price of their gloves ranges from US$1.50 to US$24 a pair depending on the style of the glove and quantity purchased. Some are distributed by the upscale Hong Kong–based boutique Bread n Butter, which has outlets in malls around the world where they likely are sold for far more.

In any case, the price at which these gloves are sold is more than, at a minimum, exponentially higher than the price workers are paid per pair. This system of expropriation—a type of state-authorised theft—is justified by the rhetoric of charity, of 'aiding Xinjiang' (援疆) with the gift of the cultural capital provided by knowledge of Chinese language or framed as Han factory owners helping detainees to cultivate the 'quality' (素质) needed to be disciplined industrial workers (for a comparative study in Tibet, see Yeh 2013).

In an essay written in adulation of the internment factory complex, a Ghulja County official wrote that when the Turkic Muslim farmers and herders arrived at the factory, they 'took off their grass shoes, put on leather shoes, and became industrial workers' (Zero Distance Yining 2017). The counterfactual imagery of 'backward' (落后) minority people who wore primitive 'grass' (草) shoes being given the gift of factory discipline through internment precisely captures the spirit of the 'quality' acquisition process as seen by state workers and contractors. In a regional state media video valorising the implementation of a coercive job program, the reporter repeatedly noted that the Turkic Muslim workers did not even pause to look up at the camera during the filming (Ili Television 2018). The reporter interpreted this as a sign of their excellent work ethic as newly trained 'high-quality' workers. This discourse was also instilled by management. Both Yerzhan and Gulzira mentioned that their managers emphasised that they were making gloves for export, so the quality of their sewing had to be very high. The training they received in 'human quality' would be reflected in the quality of the gloves they mass produced.

The introduction of state-directed, Han-exclusive corporate power over Uyghur and Kazakh life has the effect of accelerating the alienating effects of factory labour across ethnic and class difference. Alienation, removing the individual from the ownership of their labour as workers and, in this case, from their autonomy as Turkic Muslim individuals, are in fact primary features of the reeducation factory. The goal of the reeducation industrial parks is to turn Kazakhs and Uyghurs into a deeply controlled proletariat, a newly docile yet productive lumpen class—those without the social welfare afforded to the formally recognised rights-bearing working class. By turning a population of people regarded as undeserving of legal protections into this permanent underclass, state authorities and private industrialists hope they will extend the market expansion of the Chinese textile and garment industry. They are building a colonial frontier in capitalist accumulation—a process that is simultaneously a new iteration of racialised capitalism and contemporary settler colonialism (Goldstein 2017; Byler 2018). This system of controlled labour is 'carried' (载体) forward by a massive reeducation system—a mechanism of infrastructural state power that ensures this new class of interned labourers cannot rise up as a class for themselves. In fact, because of this extralegal system, the only thing that protects Turkic Muslim workers from expropriation and violence is the good will of their Han managers. As indicated by the payment scheme at the glove factory, worker protections often appear as a form of 'investment' in the quality of Turkic workers even while worker wellbeing and indigenous social relationships are viewed as valueless.

At the limit of global capitalism

Since the factories function as an extension of the camp system, outside the rule of law and at the margin of the social contract, factory managers can treat Uyghur and Kazakh workers as disposable. In December 2018, managers at the factory threatened Gulzira with the prospect of being sent back to the camp if she did not sign a one-year work contract (Bunin 2019a). It was only because her husband in Kazakhstan began a campaign for her release—after she managed to text images of the factory to him and he spotted her in a state video promoting the industrial park—that local authorities reluctantly agreed to allow her to return to her family on the other side of the border. They were attempting to silence challenges to the 'aiding Xinjiang' narrative (see also Bunin 2019b). Yet, when these attempts failed, they cut their losses and let her go.

There is a nearly limitless standing reserve of other detainees who do not have advocates for them outside China. The archipelago of the reeducation labour regime continues out of sight—a ghostly presence at the end of global supply chains. In the race to the bottom—the least cost for the most productivity—the reeducation factory in Ghulja is at the limit of contemporary global capitalism.

Part III: Global connections

13

The global age of the algorithm: Social credit, Xinjiang, and the financialisation of governance in China*

Nicholas Loubere and Stefan Brehm

> Beautiful credit! The foundation of modern society. Who shall say that
> this is not the golden age of mutual trust, of unlimited reliance upon
> human promises?

> — Mark Twain and Charles Dudley Warner, *The Gilded Age:*
> *A Tale of Today* (1873)

In recent years, few news items out of China have generated as much anxiety and fear in Western media and public discourse as the Chinese Government's ongoing attempts to create a 'social credit system' aimed at rating the trustworthiness of individuals and companies. Most major Western media outlets have spent significant energy warning about China's efforts to create an Orwellian dystopia. The most hyperbolic of these, *The Economist*, has even run with menacing headlines like 'China Invents the Digital Totalitarian State' and 'China's Digital Dictatorship' (The Economist 2016b, 2016c). These articles both implicitly and explicitly depict social credit as something unique to China—a nefarious and perverse digital innovation that could only be conceived of and carried out by a regime like the Chinese Communist Party (Daum 2017).

Social credit is thus seen as signalling the onset of a dystopian future that could only exist in the Chinese context. But how unique to China is this attempt to 'build an environment of trust', to quote the State Council, using new digital forms of data collection and analysis (General Office of the State Council 2016)? Is this Orwellian social credit system indicative of an inherently Chinese form of digital life, or is it a dark manifestation

*This essay was originally published in the *Made in China Journal* (vol. 3, no. 1, 2018), doi.org/10.22459/MIC.03.01.2018.07. The article has been updated for inclusion in this volume.

of our collective impulses to increase transparency and accountability (at the expense of privacy), and to integrate everyone into a single 'inclusive' system to more easily categorise, monitor, and standardise social activity? In this essay, we propose that the Chinese social credit system should not be exoticised or viewed in isolation. Rather, it must be understood as merely one manifestation of the global age of the algorithm—an age that is sadly coming to maturity through the ongoing experiments with digital social control in Xinjiang and elsewhere.

Engineering a trustworthy society

So, what is social credit, and how is it linked to emerging forms of algorithmic governance? While there have long been discussions about creating an economic and social rating system in China, they took a much more concrete form in 2014, with the publication of a high-level policy document outlining plans to create a nationwide social credit system by 2020 (State Council 2014). At the root of current Chinese social credit ambitions is the fact that China lacks the infrastructure to systematically assess and evaluate risk for both individuals and businesses, which adds to the economic costs of doing business, particularly in the financial sphere. As such, Chinese social credit should be understood, first and foremost, as an attempt to build a comprehensive economic risk-assessment system allowing for smoother economic integration.

Despite the goal of having an integrated, nationwide system by 2020, social credit is still far from being unified or centralised. Like most new policies in China, social credit is being subjected to the country's distinctive policy modelling process (Heilmann 2008), in which local governments produce their own interpretations of policies and then vie to have them become national models. By 2019, approximately 28 localities had been labelled official 'demonstration cities' and were allowed to experiment and innovate within the limitations of the policy framework (Daum 2019). In contrast to other policies, however, eight large internet companies were also initially given licences to run their own pilot programs (Loubere 2017a). The most widely discussed private social credit system was Alibaba's Sesame Credit, which utilised opaque algorithms to arrive at social credit scores for its customers. Those with high scores have been able to access a range of benefits from other Alibaba businesses and their partners (Bislev 2017). However, while Sesame Credit is significant due to the huge amounts of economic data held by Alibaba through Alipay and Ant Financial, the Chinese Government ultimately cancelled its pilot status along with that of the other private companies, and these initiatives now 'essentially function like loyalty rewards programs' (Matsakis 2019).

Financial(ised) inclusion

While social credit can be seen as an outgrowth of our collective impulse to achieve a more trustworthy society, a unified fully functioning social credit system will ultimately turn the quest for trust through transparency and accountability upside down because it will hold citizens responsible vis-a-vis their rulers. At the core of the emerging system, the state and financial actors define, quantify, and calculate trustworthiness and honesty; it is a technocratic fix based on the logic that, with the correct set of algorithms, the good citizen or company can be engineered into society. Social credit therefore seeks to transform individuals into a new 'civilised' (and 'credit conscious') population through the imposition of a system of incentives and disincentives that can mould logical profit-maximising citizens into civilised subjects.

In the case of China's proposed social credit system—as with any credit rating system—these rewards and punishments are meted out through engagement with, and incorporation into, the market. The calculation of credit scores requires market activity, which in turn requires a credit score. Moreover, if social credit is to live up to its technocratic promise of systematically eliminating untrustworthiness, everyone must be assessed equally—that is, everyone must be included in the system. In the absence of a social credit score, the worst must be assumed, meaning that the burden of proving one's trustworthiness falls to the individual. Thus, in a society dominated by social credit, integration into the socioeconomic system is a necessity rather than a choice. In this way, China's social credit resonates with the global financial inclusion project, which seeks to integrate marginal and impoverished populations into the global capitalist system—primarily through expanded access to credit—as a means of promoting economic development and social empowerment.

In the same way that the Chinese social credit system appears poised to extract huge amounts of personal data from individuals in its quest to create a trustworthy society, proponents of financial inclusion justify intrusive methods of assessing creditworthiness to reduce lender risk from untrustworthy borrowers. Indeed, just months before its hyperbolic headlines about China's digital authoritarianism, *The Economist* praised the use of psychometrics and other personal digital data by lenders in developing contexts as being a beneficial financial innovation (The Economist 2016a). In this way, the financial inclusion project depicts the application of financialised logics as the means of producing a more fair and accountable inclusive system, where the trustworthy reap rewards they were denied in the past. However, underpinning this neoliberal fantasy is a glaring contradiction that shatters the illusion of inclusion as being unbiased and fair: those with capital can set the terms of their engagement with the capitalist system much more easily than those without.

This points to the fact that the rich will be able to extract more of the rewards from their participation in financialised rating systems—such as the social credit system—while largely avoiding the sanctions. Moreover, punishments are much more dramatic for those without accumulated capital, as their very existence depends on their continued participation in the capitalist system for daily survival. From this perspective, the spectre of China's financialised social credit system portends a society comprising individual micro-entrepreneurs operating in a shared economic mode in which livelihoods are determined by credit scores. Indeed, Sesame Credit already works with sharing-economy apps, such as Daowei, which provides a platform for a gig economy comprising individuals (with their credit scores listed) advertising the sale of their services or products (Loubere 2017b). Those looking for a plumber in the area can select one with the highest score, just as people in the West choose hotels and restaurants based on Yelp or TripAdvisor reviews.

Financialisation gone wild

In this sense, the emergence of social credit represents an unprecedented climax of the global financialisation project. Financialisation can be broadly defined as 'the increasing role of financial motives, financial markets, financial actors, and financial institutions in the operation of [the] domestic and international economy' (Epstein 2005: 3). Social credit opens the door to financialising social behaviour. To elaborate on this claim, consider the relationship between social and financial capital. The Organisation for Economic Co-operation and Development (OECD), for example, defines social capital as 'networks together with shared norms, values and understandings that facilitate co-operation within or among groups' (Keeley 2007: 103). In the digital age, these networks become the linchpins between the social and the economic spheres. On the one hand, networks are more concrete and easier to observe than the norms and values shaping the perceptions and behaviour of network members. On the other hand, social networks represent a crucial means for both gaining access to material resources and shaping the rules for resource distribution. Thus, analysing and contextualising social networks in a big-data–driven world allows inferences to be made about both the social and the economic attributes of an individual.

Social credit establishes an explicit and tangible link between social behaviour and economic benefits. In this context, the state can assume a new role not dissimilar to that of a corporate shareholder. Social credit creates a market for social capital and transplants the rationale of profit maximisation into the realm of interpersonal relationships. Through managing networks, digital activity, and private action, an individual or organisation can impact social value and, by extension, financial capital. Thus, social credit creates new incentives that can be used to align the interests of citizens and organisations with those of the government. The state, as a shareholder in 'the people', enjoys the dividends of good behaviour and loyalty, which are rewarded through economic privileges. In this all-encompassing financialised system, social action becomes increasingly entrenched within the economic realm, and individual beha-viour is shaped more and more by financial motives. In a nutshell, social credit represents the ultimate marketisation of political control because it provides incentives for maximising citizen value through politically and commercially aligned social behaviour.

Using algorithms to render citizens and organisations compliant with the visions and rationales of the ruling regime reduces the state's infor-mation and monitoring costs dramatically. In the context of China, this has the potential to reshape the 'fragmented authoritarian' model, which is characterised by decentralised decision-making and policy implemen-tation (Mertha 2009). One could envision a future in which the many local officials and bureaucrats who enjoy privileges due to the central leadership's reliance on their support to govern the masses will be subject to the rule of algorithms themselves. Only a small elite would be needed to manage algorithmic rule, entailing a dramatic reconcentration of power. If Chinese experiments are successful, they will certainly serve as a model for many other countries: authoritarian regimes, democratic systems with authoritarian tendencies, and eventually democracies that struggle to maintain legitimacy in an increasingly polarised and fragmented political landscape.

The repressive logics of financialised governance

As noted above, despite the discourse of inclusion resulting in transparency and fairer distribution of resources, social credit and the financialisation of social behaviour are inherently biased and paradoxically result in socioeconomic exclusion within an all-encompassing inclusive system. In addition to being partial to those with capital, social credit will likely also widen other socioeconomic cleavages. Tests and experiments again and again confirm that data and algorithms are just as biased as society is and inevitably reproduce real-life segmentation and inequality (Bodkin 2017). Cathy O'Neil, the author of *Weapons of Math Destruction*, for instance, warns that we need algorithmic audits (O'Neil 2016). After all, algorithms are not some naturally occurring phenomena, but are the reflections of the people (and societies) that create them. For this reason, the rule of algorithms must not be mistaken as an upgraded, more rational, and hyper-scientific rule of law 2.0. This is particularly true in China, where the concept of the rule of law has been increasingly developed and theorised by the Party-State to justify its attempts to consolidate control over society (Rosenzweig et al. 2017).

In recent years, China has already been providing glimpses of the repressive possibilities of algorithmic rule. In particular, the ongoing construction of a sophisticated high-tech surveillance state in the Xinjiang Uyghur Autonomous Region anticipates a near future in which a digital social credit system sits at the core of a coercive security apparatus that is inherently biased against certain segments of society—producing dramatically inequitable and ultimately violent results (HRW 2018). The Xinjiang surveillance state includes police checkpoints, iris scans, mandatory spyware installed on mobile devices, and pervasive closed-circuit television (CCTV) with facial recognition software. These surveillance technologies feed into, and draw on, a large police database developed by the private defence company Landasoft that includes information about personal identity, family and friends, movement, shopping behaviour, and even DNA that is collected at medical check-ups organised by the government (Grauer 2021). Ultimately, these data are run through algorithms that assign residents with public safety scores deeming them 'safe', 'unsafe', or somewhere in between (Millward 2018). Those who are deemed to be a threat are often detained and sent to reeducation centres (Foreign Policy 2018). While this is not the government's proposed social credit system per se—as these types of data are not legally allowed to be collected for public or market information (Daum 2018)—the logic underpinning this type of coercive surveillance infrastructure and the dreams of a nationwide citizen rating system is largely the same.

These developments represent a new reality that, while shocking initially, has become a banal part of everyday existence in a few short years. It is becoming increasingly clear that Xinjiang is a testing ground for technologies and techniques that will soon be rolled out nationwide—and even beyond. China's massive surveillance market is also a global affair, with companies from around the world lining up to develop products for both the Chinese state and private businesses operating in the country (Strumpf and Wenxin 2017). This points to the fact that China is not developing its surveillance capabilities in isolation but is at the forefront of a global push towards increasingly centralised and interconnected surveillance apparatuses. Ratings systems like the proposed social credit system will inevitably sit at the centre of surveillance regimes, providing the basis for how individuals and organisations are monitored and assessed, and what they are able (and not able) to do within society.

Our dark digital futures

China's proposed social credit system and the ongoing construction of a surveillance state in Xinjiang represent the vanguard of more efficient means of socioeconomic control that are being taken up around the globe. They are dark outgrowths of the digital revolution's supposed 'liberation technologies'—underpinned by our very human compulsions for transparency, security, and fairness. Credit systems are, of course, not new, nor are they Chinese in origin. Most industrialised nations have been relying on credit ratings for a long time to quantify the financial risk of countries, firms, and individuals (Yu et al. 2015). Indeed, some of the most disturbing aspects of Chinese social credit, such as its integration into social media, are not uniquely or originally Chinese. In the United States, Affirm, a San Francisco–based lender headed by PayPal co-founder Max Levchin, has been experimenting with social media data to evaluate the credit risk of car buyers since 2013. And Lenddo, a Hong Kong–based company, took an even bolder approach and informed debtors' friends on

Facebook when they did not pay instalments on time. Even the Orwellian nightmare unfolding in Xinjiang has its parallels elsewhere, such as with the recent revelations that in the United States, the New Orleans Police Department and the federal Immigration and Customs Enforcement (ICE) have been working with Peter Thiel's company Palantir Technologies (which also has connections with the Central Intelligence Agency and the Pentagon) to experiment with 'predictive policing' based on data collected from police databases, social media, and elsewhere (Fang 2018; Winston 2018; Hvistendahl 2021). Taken together, these developments reveal a vision of a digital future in which we are all locked in a continuous and banal system of monitoring, accounting, categorising, and tracking—which has potentially far-reaching consequences for those who challenge the hegemony in any way, or even just those who do not have the resources or capacity to participate in the socioeconomic system on the terms mandated.

Big-data–driven social benchmarking sparks entrepreneurs' and politicians' imaginations about the opportunities lying ahead. And even though not all visions will be economically or politically viable in all places in the world, the general trend appears to be global and irreversible. Social credit and the dreams of financialised governance are not Chinese or authoritarian particularities, but are, perhaps, our 'shared destiny' (共同命运)—to use a term employed by President Xi Jinping when talking about the Chinese vision for the future of humanity (Barmé et al. 2014). This, however, makes it not less, but rather more, worrisome. The logical conclusion of society-wide financialisation is the blurring of the border between the political, social, and commercial realms, and the sharpening of the repressive tools wielded by the rich and powerful. In China, this scenario appears to be inevitable. To quote Lucy Peng, the chief executive of Ant Financial, Sesame Credit 'will ensure that the bad people in society don't have a place to go, while good people can move freely and without obstruction' (Hvistendahl 2017).

14
Surveillance, data police, and digital enclosure in Xinjiang's 'Safe Cities'*

Darren Byler

S ometime in the summer of 2019, Vera Zhou, a young college student from the University of Washington, forgot to pretend that she was from the non-Muslim majority group in China, the Han. At a checkpoint at the shopping mall, she put her ID on the scanner and looked at the camera. Immediately, an alarm sounded and the guards manning the equipment pulled her aside. That was when she remembered that when she ventured outside the jurisdiction of her police precinct, she should pretend she had forgotten her ID and hold her head up high, playing the part of a wealthy, urban Han college student who could not be bothered by mall security and face scans.

In fact, as much as Vera could pass as Han—she liked to wear chunky silver earrings, oversized sunglasses, and dress in black—her ID card said she was Hui, a Chinese Muslim group that makes up around one million of the population of 15 million Muslims who are the majority in the Xinjiang region. Now, a surveillance system connected to local police detected that she had ventured out of bounds. As a former detainee in a reeducation camp, she was not permitted to travel to other areas of town without explicit permission from both her neighbourhood watch unit and the Public Security Bureau. Recounting the ordeal several months later, Vera told me that as the alarm went off, she felt she could not breathe. She remembered her father had told her, 'If they check your ID, you will be detained again. You are not like a normal person anymore. You are now one of "those" people.'

Vera was living in her hometown of Kuytun (Kuitun) in Ili Prefecture, an area directly north of the Tian Shan mountains that border Kazakh-stan. She had been trapped there since 2017, when—in the middle of her junior year at the University of Washington, where I was an instructor—she had taken a spur-of-the-moment trip home to see her boyfriend, a

*This essay was originally published in *ChinaFile* on 30 December 2020. It has been updated and edited for style for inclusion in this volume. Jessica Batke provided research for it.

former elementary school classmate. Using digital surveillance tools, the Kuytun police had noticed that Vera had used a Virtual Private Network to access websites such as her university Gmail account. Given her status as a member of a Muslim minority group, this could be deemed a 'sign of religious extremism'.

Police had contacted her boyfriend, who was Han, while the couple was on their way home from a night at the movies, asking him to stop by the nearest police station. Police told him they needed to speak with Vera, so the couple entered the station. There, police explained they would need to take Vera to a larger station for questioning and that her boyfriend could follow the police van in his own car. But once Vera was in the van, safely out of her boyfriend's sight, a man working for the police pulled her hands behind her back and handcuffed her:

> It felt like a horror movie. Like maybe if I said the right things, I would wake up and find that it wasn't happening. That was when I started wailing, half-screaming, half-crying. The lead police officer told me, 'It will be better for you if you shut up.'

Without formal legal proceedings, for the next several months, local police held Vera with 11 other Muslim-minority women in a second-floor cell in a former police station. In whispered conversations, she learned that others in the room had been told they had committed cyber violations or had engaged in other activities indicative of future criminality according to broad interpretations of China's counterterrorism laws, which were established in 2016 (China Law Translate 2018). As Chinese authorities explain in an official document submitted to the United Nations (Government of China 2020), some people detained in this manner are deemed to have participated in 'extremist' activities 'not serious enough to constitute a crime'. Vera told me some of the women had used WhatsApp or registered multiple SIM cards to the same ID. Others had WeChat contacts in Kazakhstan or had travelled to Muslim-majority countries like Malaysia and posted images of visits to famous mosques and of people dressed in identifiably Islamic clothing. Some had been detained for going to mosques too often or for possessing retroactively outlawed religious books or other materials such as DVDs with instructions on how to study the Quran.

Vera spent several months in 'reeducation': chanting rules, singing 'Red songs', writing 'thought reports', and studying elementary Chinese—under the bright lights of her cell and occasionally in a fortified classroom. Then, she was unexpectedly released and placed on a kind of probation. Staff at her neighbourhood watch unit told her she was not permitted to leave her small town. Over time, she told me, she came to understand that the 'smart city' features of Kuytun meant that at key nodes such as train stations or shopping streets (Tianshan Net 2018), ever watchful facial recognition cameras could pick her out of crowds and alert the legions of contract workers employed by the local police that she had ventured out of bounds (Byler 2020a). Fearing that too many of these encounters might result in her being detained again, and aware that many of her friends were afraid to be seen with her, she began to change her behaviour. 'I just started to stay at home all the time,' she said.

'You are not like a normal person anymore. You are now one of "those" people.'

After she had spent several weeks at home, a senior police officer in her neighbourhood learned that she had spent time in the United States as a college student. He asked her to begin tutoring his children in English. She said: 'I thought about asking him to pay me, but my dad said I needed to do it for free. He also made food for the police officer's family, to show how eager he was to please them.' The commander never brought up any form of payment. The reeducation camp and surveillance system left Vera alone and isolated as an unfree, unpaid educator and nanny, responsible for the education of the police officer's family. On many occasions, she stood up in front of her neighbours and confessed the errors of her past, how much she had learned by studying the political thought of President Xi Jinping, and her gratefulness to the government for giving her a second chance.

In an attempt to prove that she could be trusted to continue her education back in the United States, she tried to follow the rules and always demonstrate a good attitude. Getting caught at the mall checkpoint was not part of this plan; since her neighbourhood watch unit was linked to the 'smart city' platform (People's Daily 2019), she knew all her violations would be recorded. Fortunately, the leaders back in her neighbourhood watch unit did not see her unauthorised excursion as a sign of deviance and agreed to let her go with a warning. Eventually, after six months under neighbourhood arrest and after signing numerous documents guaranteeing that she would not talk about what she had experienced, Vera was allowed to reclaim her passport.

When Vera emerged from the escalator into the baggage claim area of Seattle-Tacoma International Airport on 18 September 2019, she smiled weakly at me and the small group that had gathered to welcome her home. She looked exhausted. Her life had been forever changed by her time in the system of confinement and surveillance that had overwhelmed her in Kuytun. And all along, she had been living in what China's government and technology industry calls a 'Safe City' (平安城市).

In combing through hundreds of government documents, I have found that dozens of county-level or larger administrative divisions in Xinjiang have developed 'Safe City' surveillance systems. This network of Safe Cities is a particular instantiation of nationwide Skynet, Smart City, and Sharp Eyes systems (Batke and Ohlberg 2020; Rudolph 2019). Since 2017, when the reeducation campaign intensified, these programs have enveloped the entire region (Sinolink Securities 2018)—pulling Xinjiang's surveillance systems into alignment with and, in some ways, exceeding the capacity of areas in eastern China. Stories like Vera's show how these surveillance systems can control the lives of those they target, but the inner workings of such systems have remained something of a puzzle.

The case of Shawan

Newly uncovered procurement notices for the small town of Shawan and the surrounding county, 64 kilometres from Vera's hometown of Kuytun, now provide a more fine-grained view of how a Safe City surveillance system in Xinjiang can function. As outlined in nearly 400 pages of a 2017 feasibility study and two legal contracts (Chinese Government Procurement Network 2020), the system Shawan's officials hoped to purchase would be supported by the Face++ algorithm designed by the computer vision company Megvii. Megvii denies it did business in Xinjiang, apart from selling facial recognition registration systems that tie hotels to public security bureaus (Byler 2021). But an investigation published in December 2020 by surveillance industry publication *IPVM* revealed that Megvii collaborated with Huawei to develop a 'Uyghur alarm' that would automate the detection of Uyghur faces in video monitoring (IPVM Team 2020).

The Shawan Face++ system would be designed to assess object information such as vehicle licence plates, but also to home in on 'human faces, physical features, accessories, and so on', the feasibility study explained. It would track those identifiers while gathering other social data such as 'communication behaviour, accommodation behaviour, migration behaviour, financial behaviour, consumer behaviour, driving behaviour, and administrative violations'. The accuracy of the system would depend on a base set of images associated with state-issued IDs and comparison technology used to conduct image analysis of other captured images— a system similar to Clearview AI software used by law enforcement agencies in the United States (Mac et al. 2020). It would also use analysis of real-time video—something similar to a London Police pilot project using NEC-supported video facial surveillance (Gallagher 2020). While there are some similarities between American and British policing systems, which also disproportionately harm ethno-racial minorities, according to a study by the American Civil Liberties Union (Crockford 2020) and others in China (Byler and Boe 2020), the high degree of surveillance density in Shawan, as well as the capacity of its detention facilities, shows there are remarkable differences as well.

The Shawan 'Safe City' procurement documents are the first to show in minute detail the design parameters and feasibility of a county-level surveillance system in Xinjiang. In the context of northern Xinjiang, Shawan is an unremarkable, ageing, Han-majority town. According to the *Xinjiang Statistical Yearbook* for 2018, the total population of the county is around 200,000, with 67 per cent of the population between the ages of 18 and 60 years. Almost 80 per cent of the people in the county are employed by the Xinjiang Production and Construction Corps (or Bingtuan) (Statistical Bureau of Xinjiang Uygur Autonomous Region 2018), a paramilitary farming colony that was recently sanctioned by the US Government for its involvement in Xinjiang's detention camps and forced labour (AFP in Washington 2020). Many residents of Shawan are involved in cotton and tomato cultivation (Bureau of Statistics of Shawan County 2019)—two of the primary crops of the region. The ethnic-minority population of the county numbers around 72,000, but only 9,500 are Uyghurs; most are Kazakh and Hui. If demographic trends hold across the entire population, about 48,000 of these Muslims are aged between 18 and 60 years.

Plate 14.1 Images of a detention facility built in Shawan County, accessed on Google Earth, 19 December 2020. Sources: Top image, Google, © Maxar Technologies; centre, Google, © CNES/Airbus; bottom, Google, © Maxar Technologies.

Given the town appears relatively unremarkable—it has no history of violence; it is simply a typical Bingtuan town—the sophistication of the proposed surveillance system is surprising and suggests that even small Han-majority towns are highly invested in the detention and reeducation campaign. Dozens of state media reports and a series of procurement notices from Shawan in 2017 and 2018 make clear that the Shawan Public Security Bureau bought and operationalised significant portions of the surveillance system described in the feasibility study (Ying'an Net 2019; Public Security Bureau of Tacheng Prefecture 2017).

It is also clear that many Muslims in Shawan have been detained. While researching this story in August 2020, I came across a new detention facility (see Plate 14.1), built on the north side of town in 2019. Raphael Sperry, an architect and the secretary of the US-based Architects/Designers/Planners for Social Responsibility, estimates it has the capacity to hold between 7,000 and 20,000 people—roughly 15 to 40 per cent of all Muslim adults in the county. The construction of the new facility flies in the face of the Chinese Government's public line on the detention of Uyghurs. In early 2019, the Governor of Xinjiang, Shohrat Zakir, said everyone held in the camps had 'graduated' (Yanan 2019). The dramatic expansion of the detention facilities in Shawan, after this announcement was made, belies this claim.

Since 2017, Xinjiang has become a limit case even for Chinese surveillance systems (Batke and Ohlberg 2020). In the region, the networks of cameras are denser than systems in other parts of China and are supported by more than 9,000 surveillance hubs—dubbed People's Convenience Police Stations (便民警务站)—and thousands of face-scan and phone-scan checkpoints at jurisdictional boundaries (Yang and Li 2019), and nearly every resident of the region has submitted their biometric data to the authorities in a comprehensive 'public health' initiative (Wee 2019). Because of the fidelity and scale of iris scans and facial image portraits from Xinjiang IDs, which form the baseline of the facial recognition systems, the tools Xinjiang contractors employ are more finetuned and invasive than those of their counterparts elsewhere in the world. The Megvii algorithm—and the algorithms of its principal rivals in China, YITU and Sensetime—run at '1:N', or one-to-many, comparisons with hundreds of millions of images extremely rapidly. Moreover, when partnered with Xinjiang's public security bureaus, these algorithms have access to many high-definition images of the faces of each resident of Xinjiang.

In Shawan, the Megvii system would be designed to match and register the faces and record alarms for up to 300,000 targeted people in 0.8 seconds and, in two-tenths of a second longer, 500,000 people. Matches within such systems are always a probability, but technicians in Shawan would be able to 'set the comparison threshold manually' to finetune the targets of the surveillance algorithm. And the longer the system runs, the more finetuned it would become. Over time, the feasibility study explains, it would automatically 'supplement information for portraits in the base library' with views of residents throughout their daily life and, by collecting online behavioural data, 'enhance person-specific information'.

According to an additional procurement notice in September 2017 (Bidcentre Net 2017a), the Shawan Public Security Bureau began to buy biometric data collection equipment that would 'collect and identify basic personal information and social network data' from populations of 'registered and unregistered people', those who had criminal records, the migrant 'floating population', people from other countries, and 'two types of prisoners'—a phrase that appears to refer to prisoners in the reform through labour and 'reeducation' through labour systems (parts of which were officially abandoned in 2013) (The Economist 2013). Another notice explains explicitly that the Shawan Public Security Bureau would use the system to track 'detainees and people undergoing education transformation' (Bidcentre Net 2017b). Then, on 11 December 2017, in what appeared to be a response to the feasibility study, Shawan issued another major procurement notice announcing the winning bid of the Shawan Safe City project (Bidcentre Net 2017c). The notice outlined how the Shawan Public Security Bureau would pay RMB105 million to Shenzhen Jiaxinjie Technology to construct the Safe City system. In the first year of the project, Jiaxinjie would complete a 'front-end construction, transmission network construction, platform construction, command centre and sub-command centre construction, and monitoring and lighting system construction'. Over the following 10 years, the Shawan Public Security Bureau would pay the Shenzhen company RMB17.7 million per year to maintain the system.

During 2018, the Shawan Public Security Bureau issued a series of additional procurement notices. In another notice, posted in January 2018 (Bidcentre Net 2018a), the bureau declared its intention to purchase 82 sets of iris-scanning equipment from Beijing Wanlihong Technology for RMB1.4 million to use in building a new ID dataset. In yet another procurement notice (Bidcentre Net 2018b), the bureau declared its intention to purchase 52 sets of 'portrait collection devices' and 32 sets of fingerprint collection machines for RMB1.2 million from the Third Research Institute of the Ministry of Public Security.

Surveillance as efficient settler protection

According to much of the framing of state media reports, the design and implementation of the Safe City project in Shawan created greater governance efficiency. In 2018, the Shawan Public Security Bureau administrative services system—responsible for household registration and residential identification documents—transitioned to a smartphone-driven digital model (Xin 2019). A wide array of smartphone-based facial recognition technologies enabled this administrative system to collect individuals' data, a public service announcement explained. The implementation of smartphone-based systems started with a face-scan–centred, state-issued photo ID. By mid-2018, applications to replace lost IDs could be submitted online using a smartphone camera to scan the applicant's face (Public Security Bureau of Shawan County 2018).

To pass through neighbourhood-entrance face-scan checkpoints, residents needed to install another face-scan app on their phones, a government announcement explained (Public Security Bureau of Shawan County 2020). Even agricultural work brigades installed face-scan systems to monitor villagers' work efficiency (Wang and Liu 2018). If the feasibility report was implemented as planned, much, if not all, of this face-scan and phone data from housing areas, work units, and schools would be integrated into the broader three-tiered Safe City system through the 'societal resource integration platform' and funnelled through 14 new neighbourhood watch unit 'subcommand centres'.

As outlined in a recent article by Jessica Batke and Mareike Ohlberg (2020), the proposed Shawan system would use 4,791 networked high-definition cameras, 70 of which were to be facial recognition units:

> [It] would be positioned in crowded places with clear entrances and exits, including mosques, with others to be installed in train stations and bus stations. On the back end: a set of interlocking platforms would span three administrative levels (the village/ township level, the county level, and the prefectural level) and three network layers (the public Internet, a private video network, and the Public Security Bureau's own intranet). Critically, the

system would allow for information to flow from private cameras to the police via a 'societal resource integration platform' that drew from surveillance in 'hotels, Internet cafes, gas stations, schools, hospital monitoring [sic], bicycle rental points, and shops along the street, etc.'

Some locals seemed to welcome the new technology, but newly built forms of surveillance also seemed to inconvenience some residents. For instance, as new systems were put in place in 2017, the Shawan authorities began to conduct 'night patrols' that required drivers to stop and be inspected (Duan 2017). This prompted a resident of Shawan using the surname Hu to complain to his friends on WeChat. According to a state media source called Peaceful Shawan (2019), the Shawan 'Internet Security Police'—a division of the Public Security Bureau stationed in command centres in the Safe City system—discovered these private posts, detained the man for 15 days, and publicly shamed him.

Data police

The Safe City system needs human monitoring to operationalise it and, at times, this human intervention creates friction. As in all complex technology systems, human technicians are required to finetune the data and 'debug' the system. Technology studies scholar Lilly Irani (2015) describes these workers as 'data janitors'. In this context, the data janitors of the Safe City system in Shawan and throughout the region were 90,000 police officers or police assistants (协警) hired at the beginning of 2017 (Byler 2020b). According to job listings (Lintao Focus 2018), most of these recruits would not receive formal training in police academies as Public Security Bureau employees do (Ramzy 2019). Most would not be authorised to carry lethal weapons. In other places in China, they would simply be referred to as 'security guards' (保安) or 'urban management officers' (城管), but in this context they had power over Muslim lives from their positions in the People's Convenience Police Stations. According to research I conducted in Xinjiang in 2018 as well as dozens of online advertisements, local public security bureaus hired many of these workers from Muslim-minority populations. The basic qualification for the job was having a 'trustworthy' (放心) family background, actively opposing 'ethnic division and illegal religious activities' (Peaceful Shawan 2017), and having a basic working knowledge of Chinese. The ads actively recruited the spouses and children of 'Xinjiang Aid' (援疆) personnel. These mostly Han citizens were brought to Xinjiang as part of a 'paired assistance program' that linked wealthy cities and provinces in eastern China with counties and prefectures in Xinjiang (Xinhua 2019). This 'poverty alleviation' scheme brought industries, educators, and labour transfer programs to Xinjiang, but as scholar of Chinese politics Jennifer Pan (2020) points out, it also brought new forms of surveillance and coercion. Shawan's 'sister city' was Anshan, a city of about 3.5 million people in Liaoning Province, in northeastern China.

As one police chief in Ürümqi put it (Yaxin Net 2016), in general, the job of the new contractors was to create a 24-hour 'seamless' security environment. According to Baimurat, a former police contractor who spoke about the system in an interview posted online, assistants conducted spot checks centred on actively profiling passers-by (Byler 2020c), stopping young Turkic people and demanding they provide their state-issued IDs and open their phones for automated inspection via spyware apps and external scanning devices. Policing contractors monitor face-scanning machines and metal detectors at fixed checkpoints. All these activities ensure that information forcibly collected from Uyghur and Kazakh residents continues to feed the system's dataset, making the 'extremism assessments' conducted by neighbourhood watch units more and more precise (Chin and Bürge 2017). As anthropologists such as Joanne Smith Finley (2019) have shown, Muslims determined to be 'untrustworthy' through data checks can be sent to detention centres, where they are interrogated, asked to confess their violations, and name others who are also 'untrustworthy'. In this manner, the parameters of the technopolitical system determine which individuals are slotted for what was referred to in Shawan as a 'centralised closed education training' internment camp (Alecci 2019; Zhang 2019).

Implementing the system

On the edge of Bingtuan farming colonies, in another small town, called Qitai, 370 kilometres directly east of Shawan, Baimurat was one of the police contractors who conducted these checks. He was in one of the first groups of contractors hired from across the region in late 2016. In an extensive, hour-long Kazakh-language interview posted online after he fled across the border to Kazakhstan in early 2019 (Atajurt Kazakh Human Rights 2019), Baimurat provides fine-grained detail on how surveillance systems have overwhelmed small Xinjiang towns and are linked to the camp system. He is one of only a handful of former security workers in the Xinjiang surveillance system who has spoken to researchers and journalists.

In the interview, he says that because he was a college graduate, he was 'considered very well qualified'. As a result, he received the highest-level salary available to the contractors—around RMB6,000 per month, which is far above the local minimum wage of around RMB1,800 (Xinhua 2018). Others in his cohort who were considered less qualified because of their educational background, he says in the interview, were paid closer to RMB2,500. Through research conducted in Kazakhstan in early 2020, I confirmed details of Baimurat's story through an intermediary. Alongside past reporting done by *The New York Times* (Ramzy 2019), I pieced together that, like many highly educated Muslims in northwestern China (Tohti 2015), Baimurat had in the past struggled to find work for which he was qualified, so taking the job was a choice he felt he could not refuse. Not only would he be able to provide for his family, but also he would be able to protect them from the reeducation system. 'We were given uniforms,' he says in the interview. 'Then we started doing different kinds of training. It was really strict, as if we were planning for a war.'

In late 2016, Qitai authorities started building People's Convenience Police Stations, which are a type of surveillance hub erected every several hundred metres in Muslim-majority areas as part of the Safe City grid (Wong 2019). Authorities divided the contractors up and assigned them to the 89 stations that were built in Qitai County (Zhang and Jiao 2017).

According to local media reports and hiring advertisements (Du and Chang 2016; Peaceful Shawan 2017), in Shawan, a similar process played out, with 42 stations erected in 2017 (Public Security Bureau of Tacheng Prefecture 2017). The Public Security Bureau of Shawan recruited at least 490 auxiliary officers (Public Servant Exam Information Website 2017). According to one advertisement (Police Examination Network 2017), 316 officers would be stationed within the town of Shawan along with 48 ethnic-minority recruits, and the remainder would be assigned to rural stations. There is some indication that the force continued to expand. In 2018, Shawan authorities circulated advertisements, first, for 100 more officers in the spring, and another 200 in late summer (Kunlun Human Resources and Social Security Website 2018; Police Officer e-Station 2018). In 2019, Shawan recruited another 200 officers (Career Centre 2019) and, through a series of additional procurement notices, announced that it had awarded bids for close to RMB7 million for equipment and other supplies related to the People's Convenience Police Stations (Ying'an Net 2020). The Shawan feasibility report from 2017 called for 77 stations.

Baimurat recalled in his online interview that, in the Qitai stations, 'initially, we sat facing the TV monitors, and you could see the places where the cameras were pointed'. 'We had to sit there monitoring them all the time. If we failed to notice an alert, or stopped looking, we would be punished.'

Over time, higher-ups in the Public Security Bureau began to assign different types of surveillance work to Baimurat and the other police contractors who were assigned to the People's Convenience Police Stations. First, superiors sorted the contractors based on their Chinese-language ability, demonstration of loyalty, and how well they understood the concept of 'extremism' and its elastic definition in the context of the reeducation system.

'They made us do other exercises like reciting rules about participating in the camp system,' Baimurat said in the interview:

> We had to recite things related to law. There were quotes from Xi Jinping on the walls of the station. We had to learn these by heart. We were not allowed to go out on patrol until we successfully recited the quotes from Xi Jinping.

Then, in the middle of 2017, the police contractors were tasked with actively finetuning the programming of the Safe City system using digital forensic tools. Plugged into smartphones through a USB cable, these devices scanned the phones' files, searching for up to 53,000 markers of Islamic or political activity (Special Equipment Net 2020):

> After I had been working there for six months, they handed out devices to check pedestrians and car drivers. When we scanned their ID card and phone with it, we got information about whether or not the person had worn a veil, had installed WhatsApp, had travelled to Kazakhstan. All sorts of things like that. (Atajurt Kazakh Human Rights 2019)

The officers began to perform night-time checks, like the ones that had upset the person surnamed Hu in Shawan:

> We could stop every car on the street and check them. When we
> stopped them, we asked the people inside to show their phones
> and ID cards. If there was something suspicious like I mentioned
> before, we needed to inform the leaders. (Atajurt Kazakh Human
> Rights 2019)

Around this time, Baimurat learned that although he was a contingent
worker, hired on a contract basis, he was not free to quit:

> If we were tired and wanted to quit, they would tell us if you are
> exhausted you can take a rest, but then you must come back. If you
> quit the job, then you will end up in the 'reeducation camps', too.

Initially, Baimurat and his co-workers felt that despite the long hours
and the confrontational positions they were placed in, being a police
contractor 'was a good job' with a steady paycheque and protection
from police harassment. They saw themselves as being on the side of
the 'good guys'. This began to change around the time they received the
smartphone-scanning equipment. Baimurat said:

> I learned then that they had sent the children from the Kazakh
> Number 3 Middle School in the county seat to the Han school.
> They built an iron gate, high electric fence, and four watchtowers
> around the Kazakh school. If we found anyone suspicious through
> the ID checks, they would send them to the Kazakh school. They
> had suddenly turned it into a prison. They forced all of the people
> who had been visiting mosques, praying, or wearing headscarves
> to go to that school. (Atajurt Kazakh Human Rights 2019)

Initially, it seemed to Baimurat that it was just people who had been
actively religious who were sent to the new 'prison' school. It was close to
six months before he fully realised the implications of the 'rounding up
those that need to be rounded up' policy that the Xi administration had
announced in a speech given by Xinjiang Party Secretary Chen Quanguo
in February 2017 (Ramzy and Buckley 2019). Baimurat said:

> While I was working one day, we had a meeting. It was in early 2018.
> In the meeting, we were told we had to transfer some detainees
> from the jail to the school. We had so many manacles. When we

got there, we saw that they had caught around 600 people. There were rooms inside the building that were like cells. I saw very young women, very old women, and men with beards [over the age of 55] among the detainees. They were mainly minorities, the majority were Uyghurs, then a few Kazakhs and some Hui people. I don't think there were Han people. Maybe one or two, but not more than that. We handcuffed and shackled them and then we gave blankets to them whether they could hold them or not, and we told them to get on the bus. I had to handcuff one person that I had a feeling I had seen before. Then I realised he had worked as a police contractor as well. I had seen him before while I was working. I didn't remember his name, but I knew him. I really wanted to ask what happened to him, but because there were cameras I didn't ask any questions. I thought maybe I could ask later. But I never found a chance. (Atajurt Kazakh Human Rights 2019)

In the interview, Baimurat speaks in a quiet voice without much expression on his face. This begins to change as he discusses this moment of encounter. He holds his hands out in front of him, showing the way the detainees were shackled and how the blankets were thrown on to their bound hands.

Continuing, he explained that sometime later, when he felt it was safe, he asked another Kazakh police contractor about the man he had recognised among the detainees. His co-worker told him:

He came from a village and didn't understand how the CCTV cameras worked. While he was working in the prison, he saw a paper on the floor which said 'get me out of here'. He didn't report it, but the camera saw it, so he was taken 'to study'.

Baimurat said that, hearing this, he for the first time fully realised that any Kazakh or Uyghur could be sent to the camp. No-one was safe, no matter how hard they tried to work within the system. He said:

I felt very bad about being part of the system. There were so many people who made very tiny mistakes and ended up there. As police, we had tasks we were forced to do. Some days the leaders said do this, other days they said do that. Each day, we had to do what they said. (Atajurt Kazakh Human Rights 2019)

Over time, the pressure wore on Baimurat and his wife. He said: 'We couldn't sleep. We were crying all the time, my wife and I. But we didn't show other people that we were crying, because they might think we were dangerous and might inform on us.'

Back in Shawan

Back in Shawan, as the Safe City project was implemented, a similar process appeared to unfold. On the weekend of 7 April 2017, the leaders of Shawan County attended a meeting at which Chen Quanguo declared a new beginning to the ongoing 'de-extremification' campaign (Shawan News 2017). The cadres said they would renew their resolve to 'resolutely oppose the infiltration of religious extremist ideas'. By August 2017, the county jail had been expanded and officially turned into a 'concentration reeducation centre' (Zhang 2019). In early 2018, two of the mosques in the town were destroyed and a third had its Islamic architectural features removed.

In the years since, the Xinjiang Victims Database, an international organisation, has documented more than 100 cases of people detained in Shawan. In most cases, the relatives of Shawan detainees said they had no knowledge of why their relatives were detained. In some cases, detainees or their family members said they were detained for violations that did not rise to the level of criminality and were related to online activity or travel to Kazakhstan to visit their relatives (Atajurt Kazakh Human Rights 2018a, 2018b). The most frequently known reasons for detention, however, were 'praying' and 'visiting a mosque'—the sites where most facial recognition cameras were slated to be installed in Shawan's Safe City project.

Plate 14.2 Nurbai Qunapia and Mahmutjan Abla in an undated wedding photo, provided to the author by Nurbai's sister, Orazhan Qunapia. Source: Courtesy of Orazhan Qunapia.

In Shawan, it appears that, first, they came for the Uyghurs. One of the first people detained was a Uyghur baker named Mahmutjan Abla (Xinjiang Victims Database 2020b). He was taken in the autumn of 2017. The police told his wife it was because of his devotion to Islam. Then in March 2018, they came for his wife, a Kazakh woman named Nurbai Qunapia (Xinjiang Victims Database 2020a). It was around this time that the Shawan Public Security Bureau began to take most of the other documented Kazakh detainees.

When I interviewed Nurbai's sister, Orazhan Qunapia, in January 2020 about what had happened to her family, she said her relatives had been taken for 'no real reason'. They practised Islam and prayed five times a day, but so did most of the 48,000 adult Turkic Muslims living in Shawan County. What may have set them apart was that Mahmutjan was Uyghur and had gone to visit Orazhan's family in Kazakhstan in 2014. 'Actually, they both had gotten their passports, but Nurbai never had a chance to come,' Orazhan said.

The couple met and fell in love when both were working as traders in Ürümqi. Since they were from different ethnic groups, their marriage was a bit unusual; they had a 'love marriage' that was not arranged by their families. 'Nurbai was independent,' Orazhan said. 'She also had a small business when they met. She sold clothes in the market to make money for herself.'

Even more remarkably, given Uyghur patriarchal traditions, Mahmutjan decided to move to Han and Kazakh-dominated Shawan, rather than back to his home village in Khotan Prefecture. He even had his household registration changed to Shawan. Thinking about Mahmutjan's visit to Kazakhstan in 2014, Orzhan remembered: 'He was funny. Since he was a baker, when he came here, he really just wanted to see how people bake bread in Kazakhstan. He loved to learn new things.'

After Nurbai was taken in April 2018, Orzhan's communications with the couple went dark. Then, without warning, Nurbai was released, in December 2018. 'We talked via WeChat in December,' Orzhan told me:

> We talked about her release. She said that Mahmutjan was still in the Shawan camp. I congratulated her on surviving. She said, 'But my health is not good.' We had been careful not to talk about any political or sensitive subjects, so when she said this, I knew that she must have been deeply hurt by her time in the camp.

Within several weeks, Nurbai disappeared again. Orzhan suspects that, like others in Shawan (Feng 2019), she was forced to work in a factory, perhaps at the Shawan Textile and Garment Industrial Park that manufacturers from Anshan City set up as part of their 'Xinjiang Aid' project. In other parts of Xinjiang (Byler 2019) and across the country (Murphy and Elimä 2021), these 'aid' programs have been shown to be part of Muslim forced-labour schemes. In 2019, the broader 'poverty alleviation' scheme in Shawan resulted in county authorities assigning 15,600 'surplus labourers' from Shawan to jobs in places like the industrial park (Shawan News 2019, 2020). As I have shown in other research (Byler 2019), in the context of Xinjiang's camp and surveillance systems, 'poverty alleviation' refers to moving Muslims from farming and self-employment into wage labour, particularly factory work. There are three main tracks used to accomplish this transformation. The first is through the camp system itself, the second is through local authorities assigning underemployed Muslims to work in factories, and the third is by building 'satellite factories' in rural areas. In Shawan, it appears that the first two tracks were the dominant ways Muslims were put to work.

What has troubled Orzhan the most is that Nurbai and Mahmutjan have three children:

> Since December 2018, we have not heard any news about them. No-one knows where the children are. They have two daughters and one son. The oldest is Dilhumar; she is 22. The second is 18 years old, named Dilmira, and the youngest, Enser, is seven years old. The oldest has graduated from school. The second is in school. We don't know where the youngest is. We don't know how he is surviving. It has become almost impossible to find out any information. We can't call our relatives.

Orzhan worries that Enser, the little boy, has been taken to an orphanage as has happened to other children in Shawan (Shawan News 2018). Orzhan also worries that her brother-in-law may have been given a prison sentence like so many other former detainees.

Plate 14.3 An image of Shawan's county seat and surrounding areas, accessed on Google Earth, 17 December 2020. Source: Google, © Maxar Technologies, CNES/Airbus.

Business opportunities

In the feasibility report describing the parameters of the Shawan Safe City project, the assessors argue it will 'greatly improve the local government's ability to quickly respond to major events and ensure economic construction'. At the same time, they suggest it will also foster private business investment and improve social security by protecting private property. 'The indirect economic benefits are immeasurable', they write (Chinese Government Procurement Network 2020).

In April 2017, two months after Party Secretary Chen Quanguo declared the new 'round up those who should be rounded up' campaign and the Shawan procurement notice was posted (Ramzy and Buckley 2019), the Party Secretary of Tacheng Prefecture, Xue Bing, visited Shawan and toured the different facilities involved in the reeducation campaign. According to a report from *Shawan News* (2017), a local state-affiliated weekly news service, he visited the Public Security Bureau command centre to inspect the 'implementation of stability maintenance work'. In his remarks to town officials and state workers, he discussed strengthening the 'education and management services' for mosques—two of which would be destroyed the following year. He described the Shawan Textile and Garment Industrial Park as a key area for future ethnic-minority employment. Meetings conducted at the same time among Shawan Party leaders emphasised 'study transfer' programs and that cadres tasked with village surveillance should fully embrace their role in waving the 'assessment baton ... and enforce strict discipline in the villages' (Shawan News 2017).

Weekly updates in *Shawan News* between April and December 2017 suggest surveillance and political campaigns suffused Shawan. Announcements and advertising from work units and housing complexes make clear that nearly every aspect of the lives of Shawan's residents—from the apps on their phones to the ways they enter and leave their homes—depends on a set of digital codes linked to images of their faces. If the plan laid out in the feasibility study was implemented, these codes would function as flexible systems of monitoring, enclosure, and blockage; the checkpoints could be turned on and off and the sensitivity of watch lists could be manually adjusted. The data collected would then circulate on the regional intranet, among police contractors and Public Security Bureau employees who are themselves surveilled by the system.

As my conversations with Vera make clear, because of this segmentation, the algorithms of face-codes deny the people they target knowing how and why they are being surveilled. Those questions cannot be asked. What is known is that they make people discipline themselves by monitoring deviance in their daily routines. They reroute people, separating sisters from each other and parents from their children. As Baimurat noted, they produce all the feelings of walls and watchtowers but move beyond the sense of being blocked and watched to limiting the ability of Muslim residents to communicate and influence others. Ethnic-minority farmers and self-employed business owners like Nurbai and Mahmutjan have been removed or walled off from the protected population by this system.

At the same time, those who are protected by these systems are, despite minor inconveniences, generally empowered by them. In Shawan, real estate appears to be more valuable because of them. According to the feasibility study, streetlights would have been installed throughout the county, making it harder for people to escape notice when dumping their rubbish.

Taken as a whole, the interlinked surveillance and camp system in Shawan appears to centre on ensuring the movement of 'beneficial' goods, services, and biometric data, while channelling or stopping the movement of objects, bodies, and data that could potentially disrupt this circulation. From the perspective of its designers and purchasers, it would increase the circulation of what the state and its market economy deemed 'good' and cut off the movement of anything and anyone they rejected. The shaping power of this technology would regulate the population to produce lower rates of fear, higher rates of economic growth, and greater power for the right kind of people.

Baimurat recalled that a fellow Kazakh contractor, a 24-year-old Tianjin University graduate with a fancy car, made the mistake of giving a Uyghur detainee a cigarette during his midnight shift at the camp. For young Kazakh and Uyghur men, sharing a cigarette is a basic sign of respect. Baimurat said: 'He thought it wouldn't be a big deal, so he did it. But he forgot about the cameras. Just as the man finished smoking it, the higher-level police came and took my co-worker away. We never saw him again' (Atajurt Kazakh Human Rights 2019). In the controlled society of a Safe City, life is made predictable by maintaining relations of power at a technical remove. It does something more than this, too. When the technology begins to think for people, it starts to strip away their basic humanity. When space for thinking is lost in the black box of a complex technological system, it becomes banal and inhumane, producing profound capacities for cruelty.

15
Transnational carceral capitalism and private paramilitaries in Xinjiang and beyond[*]

Gerald Roche

On 22 January 2019, the innocuously named Frontier Services Group (FSG) announced plans to open a 'training centre' in Tumxuk city in Xinjiang (Shepherd 2019), the 'autonomous region' where hundreds of thousands of people have been held in concentration camps. Although the company has distanced itself from these plans and removed mention of it from its website (Ordonez 2019), this announcement highlighted a vital and underexplored element in the story of Xinjiang's camps: the role of private paramilitary companies and transnational circulations.

Frontier Services Group is a private security firm run by Blackwater founder, Erik Prince (Ciralsky 2009). And although Prince publicly expressed surprise at the 22 January announcement, FSG was in fact already deeply embedded in Xinjiang well before then (Stevenson and Buckley 2019). The company first announced plans to open an office in Xinjiang in March 2017 (Fan 2017). And in November of that year, it appointed Lü Chaohai as head of its northwestern regional operations (Bloomberg 2019; FSG 2017). Previously, Lü was the vice-president of the Xinjiang Construction and Production Corps, the paramilitary-cum-commercial organisation tasked by the CCP with developing Xinjiang's economy.

Hidden linkages

Beyond these clear linkages between FSG and Xinjiang, other plausible but less obvious connections link the company to the region and its camps. For example, since acquiring a stake in Beijing's International

[*]This essay was originally published in the *Made in China Journal* (vol. 4, no. 1, 2019), doi.org/10.22459/MIC.04.01.2019.01. The article has been updated for inclusion in this volume.

Security and Defence College in May 2017, FSG has been working to train private antiterrorism personnel in China (Martina 2017). And although no explicit links between the college and Xinjiang are apparent, its antiterrorist mandate makes these likely and fits a broader pattern in China of importing 'de-extremification' and counterextremism strategies from abroad (see Byler's Chapter 5 in this volume; and Doyon 2019).

In addition to working within the PRC, Prince and FSG are also following China's commercial interests abroad. The company has unambiguously positioned itself as a security provider for the BRI. For example, in December 2018, FSG obtained a licence to operate in Cambodia, which is an enthusiastic supporter of the BRI and a recent recipient of US$600 million in aid from China (FSG 2018b; Mech 2019). And, as we will see below, FSG also began operations in Myanmar in 2019.

These connections highlight how not just FSG and Prince, but also the private paramilitary industry more generally act as conduits between state actors. So, we should not be surprised to learn that while FSG works for China, Prince is simultaneously attempting to exert influence on US policy. In 2016, he addressed then newly elected President Donald Trump in a *South China Morning Post* opinion piece, advocating for the United States to become involved with the BRI (Prince 2016).

But Prince has closer ties to Trump than your average op-ed writer. In addition to having donated a quarter of a million dollars to Trump's presidential campaign, Prince is also the brother of Trump's Secretary of Education, Betsy DeVos (Kirsch 2018). It should not be surprising, then, that in 2017 he met with members of the Trump administration to pitch the privatisation of US operations in Afghanistan and Syria (Hall 2019; Roston 2017). Tellingly, he refers to this strategy as an 'East India Company' approach and suggests it should be led by an 'American viceroy' (Prince 2017).

The private paramilitary industry in Xinjiang

So, Erik Prince is advocating for the United States to roll out mercantile colonialism from Afghanistan to Nigeria, while also helping to train antiterrorism personnel in the PRC, employing political elites from Xinjiang, and opening operations along the BRI. This entanglement of state and private interests across borders has important implications for how we think about, and act against, the Xinjiang camps.

First, it makes clear that we should be paying more attention to private transnational actors—not just Prince and FSG, but also the entire private paramilitary industry. The Xinjiang camps are built and maintained not only by state colonialism, but also by transnational carceral capitalism (Wang 2018). What other connections exist between Xinjiang and security providers from outside the PRC?

Understanding this is important because it will shed light on what techniques are being exchanged and circulated between carceral institutions around the world. This might provide insights into what is going on in Xinjiang when we have such limited access to the realities of the camps.

Researchers have already learnt much about the Xinjiang camps by tracing their evolution from trials elsewhere inside the PRC. Adrian Zenz and James Leibold (2017) have shown how securitisation techniques road-tested in Tibet are now applied in Xinjiang. These include the so-called convenience policing system, which places police at regular intervals throughout the city to implement 'grid-style social management', as well as the practice of placing tens of thousands of CCP officials in villages to 'aid and assist' (and monitor) people (Leibold 2020). Sarah Cook (2019), meanwhile, has shown how the techniques of 'mental transformation' being used in Xinjiang were first tested on members of the Falun Gong.

But missing from this story of the internal circulation of methods and technologies of control within China is the exchange of these things transnationally. Take the camps themselves. We know that concentration camps as a carceral form were first deployed in Cuba by Spain during the Cuban War of Independence (1895–98) (Mühlhahn 2010) and achieved something like their current form under the British in South Africa during the Anglo-Boer War (1899–1902) (Forth 2017). They were then developed through their global circulation and iterative tweaking by a variety of states across the twentieth century (Stone 2017; Pitzer 2017) and obtained new legitimacy in the twenty-first century as a technology of 'carceral humanitarianism' (Oliver 2017).

So, we should be asking, beyond sources within the PRC, what are the transnational precursors to the Xinjiang camps? On what current models might the camps' architects be drawing? What role might private security and logistics companies play in linking these diverse examples, and accelerating the circulation of carceral expertise?

Across borders

Given the way these technologies circulate transnationally, and considering FSG's role as a BRI private security force, we should be concerned with the possibility that camps might spread across borders. In February 2019, FSG began advertising to recruit security personnel in Myanmar and, a month later, registered the company name FSG (Myanmar) Security Services Company Limited (Chau 2019). At this time, Kachin nongovernmental organisation worker Doi Ra expressed concerns to *Asia Times* journalist Bertil Lintner (2019) about the potential role FSG might play in helping the state suppress resistance and force through unpopular infrastructure projects.

We know little about what FSG has been doing in Myanmar since then. However, in 2018, FSG listed news on its website about the memorandum of understanding that was signed in September of that year between Myanmar and the PRC to establish a transnational economic corridor (FSG 2018a). This corridor starts in Yunnan, where FSG has an office, and ends in the Kyaukphyu Special Economic Zone in Rakhine State, where the Myanmar Government carried out ethnic cleansing of Rohingya people in 2017, and where CITIC Group (Myanmar), part of the Chinese state-owned CITIC Group, is currently building a deep-sea port (AFP 2019). We need to worry about how PRC money and private paramilitary expertise might be used to 'help' nations along the BRI solve their domestic problems.

Beyond these concerns, the transnational privatisation of mass detention gives us two good reasons to be sceptical about the effectiveness of lobbying state actors to intervene in the Xinjiang camps. First, most major state players today have an interest in honing their carceral techniques and technologies, and private security firms enable liberal democracies to learn from authoritarian states, where the latitude for trial and error is much greater. In this regard, it is important to remember that it was claimed that President Trump encouraged Chinese President Xi Jinping to build the Xinjiang camps, describing it as 'exactly the right thing to do' (AFP and SBS News 2020). We should also note that since international outcry has been raised about the Xinjiang camps, India has begun building its own camp system to contain Indian residents who have been declared 'foreigners' (Pradhan 2020). Detention facilities thus have an uncanny transnational mobility.

Second, although the BRI has become a source of geopolitical friction, such divisions are worn away by the flow of transnational capital, and the commercial stakes associated with the BRI are vast. It seems unlikely that any states will work against their own political and economic interests to intervene in Xinjiang.

Rather than lobbying states, a more effective strategy would be to address the struggle against the Xinjiang concentration camps to actors who have no vested interests in the camps being maintained: anticolonial, anticapitalist, and prison abolitionist movements.

16
Chinese feminism, Tibet, and Xinjiang*

Séagh Kehoe

hinese feminists are good at making global connections. From showing solidarity with the Stanford Survivor (Phillips 2016) and Zheng Churan's public letter to Donald Trump on 'straight man cancer' (BBC 2016), to supporting the Irish movement for abortion rights (Li 2017), feminists in China have worked hard to reach out, identify shared experiences of oppression, and forge alliances with feminists around the world. More recently, China's #MeToo campaign showed feminists locating their own struggle within an international discourse and joining the international fight against sexual harassment. While the past few years in China have seen increasing government crackdowns on discussions of feminism and civil society more broadly, a commitment to 'walking with women from all over the world' (和全世界的女人一起 散步) remains (Jiayun 2017).

Most of the activists behind China's New Feminist Movement (新女权 运动) are young, urban, middle-class, and university-educated women, several of whom have studied abroad. They are social media savvy and imaginative in bringing campaigns for gender equality to a broader audience. Alongside transnational exchange and a resistance to being anchored in state feminism's conception of women's rights, this movement is also characterised by an explicit concern for intersectionality.

Intersectionality

Intersectionality provides a framework for understanding the ways in which various structures of power converge to produce systems of interlocking oppression and privilege (Crenshaw 1989). By focusing on the experiences of Black women, Crenshaw argued that a single-axis analysis of either feminist theory or antiracist politics tends to distort and even erase the complexity of their experiences. In contrast, taking an inter-

*This essay was originally published in the *Made in China Journal* (vol. 4, no. 1, 2019), doi.org/10.22459/MIC.04.01.2019.12. The article has been updated for inclusion in this volume.

sectional approach allows us to think through the ways in which power works across different institutions and social categories, such as gender, sexuality, race and ethnicity, class, nationality, ability/disability, faith (or lack thereof), and so on.

In China, gender and class constitute one example of how feminists have engaged with intersectional analysis. Organising around class and developing critiques of exploitation under global capitalism are officially frowned on in post-socialist China, but that has not prevented the online platform Pepper Tribe (尖椒部落). The website bears the slogan 'We don't sell pepper, but we make female workers scream louder for their rights' and features stories from women workers across China in which they describe their life in the city, work, and experiences of sexual harassment (Ziyi and Huang 2018). Before being 'harmonised' in July 2018 for 'violating relevant regulations', the site had more than 20,000 followers on Weibo, and it continues to maintain an active account on WeChat. Feminists in different parts of the country have also held workshops with migrant women workers to discuss various issues about their work experiences, advising them on how to access social services and build support networks. A Beijing-based feminist quartet named Jiu Ye (九野) has even been travelling the country performing songs written with migrant women labourers (Yin 2017). All these examples demonstrate a shift away from thinking about power and oppression in single-issue terms.

Intersectionality has been more explicitly applied elsewhere. Feminist Voices (女权之声), one of the most influential online feminist platforms in China, was particularly vocal in problematising notions of the universal experiences of womanhood. It often posted essays on the ways in which gender and sexuality intersect, particularly for queer women, and what this means for marriage and having children, as well as critiques of family life more broadly. Gender was also sometimes discussed in terms of class, disability, age, and *hukou* (household registration) status. Sadly, Feminist Voices was deleted from both Weibo and WeChat around International Women's Day in 2018 for violating 'temporary regulations on the development and management of accounts offering [a] public information service on instant messaging programs' (Jiayun 2018).

Across these various discussions, attention to the convergence of different forms of power and oppression and the importance of global connections are clear in Chinese feminist practice. However, considerably less visible has been the issue of how gender and ethnicity intersect.

Gender and ethnicity in Tibet and Xinjiang

China has 56 officially recognised *minzu* (民族), which is loosely translated as 'nationalities' or 'ethnic groups'. The Han, making up more than 90 per cent of the total population, dominate politically and culturally. They are regularly depicted as the 'big brother', selflessly 'bringing modernity' to 'ethnic minorities' (少数民族) such as Tibetans and Uyghurs. Han superiority is a longstanding narrative reproduced across official propaganda, popular media, and even in educational materials, with the aim of naturalising and legitimising Han hegemony across the country. Indeed, the very language of *minzu* itself plays into this process of flattening disputes about Tibet's and Xinjiang's place within China's national and historical imagination into a question of ethnicity (Lokyitsang 2012).

Though differing in many important ways, Tibet and Xinjiang are broadly similar in their colonial and contested status within the PRC, their international profile, strong religious and cultural practices, and strategic value as borderland regions. All these factors mark them out as points of sensitivity for the Chinese authorities. Since the early 2000s, the Party-State has attempted to resolve ongoing issues of ethnic unrest and marginalisation across the regions through a range of economic development policies. While this shift has created opportunities for some, it has also led to more inward migration, greater competition for employment, economic disparity, and environmental degradation—all of which have fuelled further ethnic discontent, alienation, and resentment. Particularly in the case of Xinjiang, these new policies coincided with the state's adoption of the discourse of the global 'War on Terror' and the recasting of Uyghurs as a 'terrorist threat' in 2001 (Roberts 2018; see also Brophy's Chapter 4 in this volume). Since the protests in Tibet in the spring of 2008 and the riots in Ürümqi in the summer of 2009—and coupled with an ideological turn within the CCP emphasising the consolidation of overall political security (Smith Finley 2018, 2019)—both regions have experienced even greater cultural and religious repression, pressure to assimilate, heightened state security, and widespread and arbitrary detention of people from all walks of life.

As in many Western countries, the internet in China has also played a decisive role in fuelling a politics of fear and facilitating the rise of Islamophobia. While Han supremacism, nationalism, and racism are certainly not new across online spaces in China (Leibold 2010), these discourses have increasingly been informed by the global circulation of extremist rhetoric. Like the ideologies and vocabulary emanating from right-wing populism in Europe and North America, discourses about 'Islamisation' have gained momentum across Chinese social media as a critique of what is perceived to be the excessive 'political correctness' of Western liberals. In echoes of anti-immigrant, anti-refugee, and white nationalist discourses in the West, Muslims across China have been identified as an existential threat to the Chinese nation (Chenchen 2017). Feminism and LGBTQ+ rights are also targeted as part of these discourses, further silencing dissent and consolidating the legitimacy of the Party-State.

In these current conditions, most criticism of the various forms of discrimination 'ethnic minorities' across China face in their everyday lives is generally swiftly silenced. Even in those rare moments when critical Tibetan and Uyghur voices are not immediately erased by censors or attacked by extremists, they are sure to be overwhelmed by calls to maintain 'ethnic harmony' and 'ethnic unity', obsessive deflections referring to Western hypocrisy and conspiracies to divide China, and denials that any problem exists at all.

For Tibetan and Uyghur women, living under a state that is both Han-centric and patriarchal is a double burden, and their bodies have often become an important locus of the state's push for social regulation and control. One example of this includes the launch of 'Project Beauty' (靓丽工程), a five-year campaign encouraging Uyghur women to remove their veils to look 'modern' (see Yi 2019). We have since seen various iterations of this campaign punishing Uyghur women for looking 'too Islamic'. On World Hijab Day in February 2015, a full ban on the veil in public places was enforced across Ürümqi. Similar draconian regulations were later rolled out for men with 'abnormally' long beards (Grose and Leibold 2015).

Experiences of gender and ethnicity overlap in complex and often brutal ways, and it is important to think about the structures of power that produce this, as well as the kind of work that is necessary to dismantle them. Indeed, gender injustice is always part and parcel of broader forms of injustice. Across Tibet and Xinjiang, the heavy police presence, surveillance, travel restrictions, and detention have become everyday realities over the past decade. In response, since 2009, there have been more than 150 cases of self-immolation in Tibet. This has taken an enormous toll on Tibetan society—marked, as recently described by Tashi Rabgey, with a collective 'silent mourning' (Sinica Podcast 2019). Much of this occurred under the intense securitisation and policing strategies of Chen Quanguo, the CPP Secretary in the Tibetan Autonomous Region between 2011 and 2016. In August 2016, Chen took up the same role for Xinjiang and, since his arrival, the situation across the region has deteriorated significantly (Smith Finley 2018).

The mass internment of approximately 1.5 million Uyghurs in 'reeducation' camps as part of the Party-State's efforts in 'de-extremification' has left few lives untouched. Camp survivor Mihrigul Tursun has described her experiences of internment, during which one of her young triplets died in mysterious circumstances while the other two developed health problems (Cockburn 2018). She has detailed how women were forced to take pills that made them faint and to drink a white liquid that caused bleeding in some women and loss of menstruation in others. Her account mirrors that of Gulbahar Jelilova, another Uyghur woman, who has described her experiences of being forced to share a 14-square-metre space with 30 other women and restricted to a starvation diet of 600 calories a day (Byler 2018). There have also been reports of Uyghur women coerced into sterilisation surgeries and threatened with birth quotas (AFP 2020). This, alongside the forced marriages between Uyghur women and Han men, state intrusion into private homes through surveillance by civilian Han 'relatives', disappearances of entire families, separation of children from parents, and reports of torture and death within the camps, reflects the ongoing horror and trauma of everyday state violence in Xinjiang today (Beydoun 2018).

Disconnection in the Chinese feminist movement?

In my conversations with Han feminist activist friends over the years, I have learned that the ways in which gender and ethnicity intersect are rarely, if ever, discussed as a feminist issue within their own circles.

Given the heavy censorship of media coverage about life in Tibet and Xinjiang, and the steady stream of propaganda celebrating state subsidies and preferential policies enabling ethnic minorities to 'reach modernity', it is perhaps not surprising that Tibet and Xinjiang have become a blind spot in the intersectional practices among Han feminists. Indeed, Chinese state media regularly celebrates the state's 'liberation' of Tibetan and Uyghur women. In 2018, for example, the *Global Times* reported that, under the careful guidance of the state, Uyghur women had gained 'respect and self-recognition', while Uyghur men had learned how to 'respect women and admire their contributions to the family' (Liu 2019; Yi 2019). In Tibet, stories of women achieving 'empowerment' through the state's various social, economic, and ecological policies are another regular feature in state media (Global Times 2018). These examples demonstrate how the Chinese state regularly tries to repackage its ongoing violence against both Tibetan and Uyghur societies as a project of social progress. As such, the silence within Han Chinese feminist groups surrounding the specific issues faced by Tibetan and Uyghur women, as well as Tibet and Xinjiang more broadly, in many ways reflects the wider culture of state propaganda, censorship, and Han normativity that pervades Chinese officialdom, education, and media.

There are, however, some Han feminists who are thinking about the place (or lack thereof) of *minzu* politics within China's feminist movement. Should Tibetan and Uyghur feminists and women's rights activists be incorporated under the banner of 'Chinese feminism'? Who gets to decide that? I have also heard a few Han feminists ask how such a cross-cultural feminist solidarity across the PRC could be crafted without reinforcing the hegemony of Han 'Chinese-ness'.

While these are important questions that demand conversation across different *minzu* groups, the gravity of the situation in Tibet and Xinjiang also requires urgent action. But building feminist solidarity and coalitions is far from simple. Amid the ever-intensifying crackdowns across the country in the name of stability, security, and unity, there is a level of fear that can be difficult to fully comprehend for those of us who are not Chinese citizens. Many Han feminists are all too aware of the risks involved in speaking out against state violence. Since 2015, they themselves have faced surveillance, intimidation, and even detention for simply speaking out against sexual harassment on public transport and know what criticising the Party-State's actions in Tibet and Xinjiang will invariably lead to.

The (im)possibility of resistance?

While many might hope that something akin to the #MeTooUyghur movement on Twitter and Facebook will also grace WeChat and Weibo timelines, such a thing is simply impossible right now. Although there are some who are speaking up—and whose messages are promptly 'harmonised' by censors—to conceive of a broader movement, there would need to be so much groundwork done to reverse the decades of endless scaremongering, distortion, and wilful erasure of Tibetan and Uyghur dissent. There would also need to be so much done to change the terms of public discussion about 'ethnic relations' in China, and to challenge the dehumanising discourses that have enabled the pervasive violence against Tibetans and Uyghurs. But currently, the greatest obstacle to any possibility in this sense is that any form of public opposition to what is happening in either Tibet or Xinjiang has become extremely dangerous for anyone in China.

The impossibility of speaking out in China makes it more important for those of us outside China to do so. The support of Chinese citizens abroad is crucial. Despite being afraid and knowing the risks, some of them are already speaking out on social media. Others are educating themselves by going to public talks on what is happening in Xinjiang, asking what they can do to help, and challenging the views of their own friends and family members. Moreover, recently, the Independent Federation of Chinese Students and Scholars, a US-based network founded in response to the Tiananmen Square protests in 1989, condemned the actions of Chinese students who harassed, abused, and threatened Uyghur and Tibetan students at Duke University, the University of Toronto, University College Dublin, the University of Strasbourg, and elsewhere, criticising all efforts to 'suppress the truth about the ongoing genocidal crimes' (RFA 2019).

Non-Chinese citizens can also do a lot. We should remember how influential the international response to the detention of the Feminist Five was in determining their eventual release. Indeed, we have already seen the impact of global pressure in the case of Xinjiang. The diffusion of media reports and satellite images of the 'reeducation' camps has forced the Party-State to shift from a position of totally denying the existence of the camps to trying to justify them. To continue the fight, we must contact our government officials, our embassies and consulates in China, and our local Chinese embassies to firmly express our opposition and call for an immediate halt to the arbitrary detention of Uyghurs. We must contact the long list of companies who continue to do business in Xinjiang and ask them why they do so when they know about the widespread injustice and suffering across the region (ChinaFile 2018). We must call for and practice solidarity with the Institut Ouïghour d'Europe (IODE), the first formal Uyghur feminist advocacy organisation, join the #MeTooUyghur campaign, donate to the Uyghur Human Rights Project (UHRP), organise public talks, and start campaigns at our schools and universities to increase public awareness about what is happening in Xinjiang today (for more, see UHRP n.d.; IODE n.d.).

These are all small but vital steps we can take to keep the pressure on and stop the violence against Tibetans and Uyghurs, but everyone must also challenge Islamophobia, racism, state authoritarianism, the securitisation of borders, the rise of private security firms, and the prison industrial complex within our own communities. We must insist, as Angela Davis (2011) has long argued, on seeing the intersections and interconnectedness of 'local' practices of injustice and what is happening across Xinjiang and Tibet. Without this, there will be no getting to the root of what is in many ways a global problem. Many recognise the intensification of Chinese state patriarchy as part of a growing nationalist strongman politics around the world, but we must also acknowledge how the same politics, alongside transnational online right-wing extremism and carceral capitalism (see Roche's Chapter 15 in this volume), is fuelling state terror across China. We must also see the struggle for liberation in Xinjiang and Tibet as part of the struggle for liberation everywhere.

17
China: Xinjiang :: India: Kashmir*

Nitasha Kaul

Kashmir and Xinjiang share a border. Or, more precisely, the erstwhile princely state of Kashmir that is now divided between India, Pakistan, and China (and officially known as Jammu and Kashmir and Ladakh; Azad Kashmir and Gilgit Baltistan; and Aksai Chin, respectively) shares a border with East Turkestan and Tibet—currently officially called Xinjiang and Xizang. In addition to this geographic proximity, Kashmir and Xinjiang are marked by a complex patchwork of ethnic and religious identities and have borne the weight of contested sovereignty claims throughout most of the modern era.

The specific regions with Muslim-majority populations in Kashmir and Xinjiang (Kashmiri Muslims are concentrated predominantly in the Kashmir Valley, and Uyghur Muslims in East Turkestan) have witnessed a particular form of political power as exercised by the two rising behemoths India and China. This has included systematic human rights violations in the name of curbing separatism and terrorism. The political relationships of these regions with the Indian and Chinese states reveal important similarities and differences. The similarities are occasioned by the fact that these ethno-nationally different Muslim-majority areas have become the focus of assimilation into the evolving Hindu majoritarian nationalism in India and Han majoritarian nationalism in China. Both India and China claim these territories as integral parts of their nation-states.

While Indian Muslims and Hui Muslims in China do not have any overwhelming affinity with the ethnically different Kashmiri and Uyghur Muslim struggles, India and China have still sought to suppress the religious and cultural identities of these peoples by framing them solely as radicalised Muslims; examples include changes to architecture and restricting access to places of worship. This is in line with a broader stigmatisation of their Islamic and ethnic identities as being always already suspect and in need of securitisation. The broader global and regional variants of Islamophobia are an important way to secure justifications

*This essay was originally published in the *Made in China Journal* (vol. 5, no. 2, 2020), doi.org/10.22459/MIC.05.02.2020.05.

for why these people are marginalised (Brophy 2019). The rationale—for putting them into reeducation camps in China, revoking their autonomy without consent in India, imprisoning activists, denying access to the internet and communications, altering the demography of the region, and prohibiting any meaningful Kashmiri or Uyghur dissent in both the Indian and the Chinese cases—is that all this is being done to stamp out terrorism, and to modernise and 'develop' these populations. What this rhetoric has translated into is at best a 'violent paternalism' (Byler 2018), and at worst a prolonged collective punishment of these populations in their own homelands (Anand 2012, 2019).

Although the purported attempts at modernisation and development have proceeded along somewhat different lines in the two contexts, there is a distinct possibility that in the final instance what China is doing today in Xinjiang will be predictive of the Indian trajectory in Kashmir. In this essay, I will provide a background to the Kashmir region and an overview of some of the recent changes, and then theorise why India and China are able to continue acting in this manner towards those in Kashmir and Xinjiang, respectively. I conclude by calling for a greater transregional understanding of these strategies and more solidarity across different contexts.

Kashmir: The background

Over the past two centuries, Kashmiris as a people have had their identities constructed out of prolonged experiences of multiple colonisations—from the Mughal to the Sikh empires, Dogra direct rule, British suzerainty, and contemporary Indian and Pakistani control and administrative claims. These rules were legitimised through a mix of treaty provisions, elite bargains, and securitisations (Kaul 2011). While the precise boundaries and jurisdictions of the erstwhile princely state of Jammu and Kashmir shifted over time, the area nevertheless amalgamated a range of different regional, religious, and ethnic populations—all of which are, with different degrees of volition, able to trace one irreducible element of their identity as Kashmiri, even if, in some cases, this simply means being historically bracketed into the territorial bargains of the former state. The three provinces of the state—Jammu (with several districts), Kashmir (with districts in the Kashmir Valley), and the Frontier Districts (Ladakh, Gilgit, Baltistan, and Poonch/Muzaffarabad)—were carved up following Partition in South Asia, when the independence of British India led to the creation of India and Pakistan. Since their very inception, these two nation-states have been marked internally by the competing and anxious postcolonial nationalisms in their turbulent political dynamics, and externally by the global scenario of the Cold War and its fallout, the ascendant neoliberal consensus, and the protean War on Terror.

Against this setting, Kashmir has remained an unresolved existential issue for India and Pakistan, whose rivalry has played out in a combination of military force, legal impunities, preferred state-centric media framings, cloak-and-dagger politics, and strategic alliances on subsets of economic and political issues with powerful, though problematic, entities (such as China, the United States, and the United Kingdom). Only rarely has this confrontation been conducted through artful diplomacy, let alone by showing any human concern for the Kashmiris affected. By the start of the twenty-first century, with the coming into being of a new global 'Other' via post-9/11 Islamophobia, the rise of Hindu nationalism in India, and following the multiple wars between the two countries, the dominant narrative of the 'Kashmir problem' came to be centred on the Kashmir Valley and its Muslim-majority population. This was in no small measure due to the communalisation of the political dispute because of a number of factors that include: 1) the nationalist Indian position being unable to distinguish between a proxy Pakistan-backed armed insurgency and an anti-Indian uprising with popular support fuelled by decades of accumulated resentment; 2) Pakistan's two-nation theory, which sees Hindus and Muslims as distinct, irreconcilable nations; 3) episodes of anti-minority (anti–Kashmiri Pandit) violence carried out by Islamic militants, and the forced exodus of Kashmiri Pandits under threat of violence and with bafflingly little promised protection to stay put in their homeland from the Indian state; and 4) the overwhelming and multidimensional violence directed at Kashmiri Muslims, combatants and civilians both, by Indian forces, which over the years have killed tens of thousands of Kashmiris and left thousands victimised through enforced disappearances, torture, mass killings, and mass rapes—all of which have been well documented by human rights organisations.

In the past 10 years, newer chasms have opened between the global, the national, the macropolitical, and the micropolitical when it comes to the different facets of Kashmiri identity, human rights, and political aspirations in relation to India and Pakistan. At a global level, the prolonged recession in the West and an aggressively marketed discourse of the 'rising powers' have meant the prioritisation of semantics over substance when it comes to India's democratic credentials. This has also involved an alternating mix of threat and awe regarding China's expanding economic and large-scale infrastructural connectivity through the BRI, including the China–Pakistan Economic Corridor. In this scenario, human rights concerns—whether in Kashmir, Tibet, Xinjiang, Balochistan, or elsewhere—which used to be inserted as a staple into foreign policymaking in the West and were already suffering from substantial critiques of selectivity and hypocrisy, finally fell prey to the rise of powerful and electorally legitimated right-wing leaders in the West, who quite literally mean only business, largely for themselves and their cronies. At the national level in India, the spectacular consolidation of the dream Hindutva project of the Rashtriya Swayamsevak Sangh (RSS), a powerful right-wing nationwide paramilitary organisation, and the rise of the Bharatiya Janata Party (BJP) led by Narendra Modi, with its particular governmentality of 'postcolonial neoliberal nationalism'—which co-constructs ideas of the economy and nation (Kaul 2019a)—have sought to create India, first and foremost, as a Hindu nation akin to a Muslim Pakistan. In these political scripts, the Kashmiris struggling for human rights and/or political self-determination have been essentialised as separatist Muslims who need to be subdued by any means possible, because they are not political human beings, but problematic Muslims *qua* Muslims.

In all this, the issue of Kashmiri Pandits has been weaponised like never before to justify the Hindutva-motivated Indian actions in Kashmir; the Hindutva idea of India sees only Hindu Kashmiri Pandits as 'true' Kashmiris, just as it sees Hindu Brahman Indians as the ideal subjects of the 'pure' Hindu nation. At the macropolitical level, the distance between the imaginaries and mutual cognition of aspirations in the different regions—Jammu, Kashmir, and Ladakh—has increased significantly as a result of policies that consciously foster selective connectivities and relationalities and cultivate rival leaderships. At the micropolitical level, the accumulated resentments of the Kashmiri people, especially of the post-1990 generation, have become multilayered rocks of grievances, symbolically like the rocks that are pelted by masked youths at the soldiers who are seen as the visible human symbols of an unjust and occupying colonial state.

Kashmir today

In 2020, as the world reeled under the impact of the COVID-19 pandemic and different countries staggered through various stages of prolonged lockdowns, the people in Kashmir experienced the fallout of a combination of poor health infrastructure and a fractal version of lockdowns within lockdowns as many of the restrictions on telephony and telecommunications put in place in August 2019 had not yet been fully lifted. This was a direct consequence of the events resembling a 'constitutional coup' that took place the previous year. On 5 August 2019, the Indian Government revoked Article 370 of the Constitution, stripping Jammu and Kashmir (J&K) of its constitutionally guaranteed autonomy over everything except defence, telecommunications, and foreign affairs. In addition to ending autonomy, the statehood of J&K was taken away and it was split into two union territories: Jammu and Kashmir as one, and Ladakh as the other.

This occurred overnight, without the consent of the state legislature or the people of the region. To thwart any dissent, all landline and mobile telephony and internet communications were shut down, curfew-like conditions were imposed, political and civil society leaders from across the spectrum were preventively arrested, no-fly lists were created, and large numbers of people, including children, were imprisoned, sometimes outside the state (Kaul 2019b, 2019c). As the flag of J&K was removed from buildings and police forces were brought under the control of the Union Home Ministry based in New Delhi, Indian opposition leaders were prevented from visiting the region, and a delegation of far-right European parliamentarians was taken on a tour and photographed against scenic backgrounds in the deserted landscape. Foreign media, critical Indian media, and a US Senator were refused access; only state-approved media were permitted to function at media facilitation centres where the chosen few could access the internet for 15 minutes at a time. This internet shutdown continued for months, making it the longest ever internet blockade in any democracy. As of writing, in late autumn 2020, 4G internet services had still not been restored despite the pandemic.

Underlying these developments were clear intentions of a transition to full-throated settler colonialism. As these events were set in motion in 2019, ruling-party politicians in India celebrated the change as something that would allow them to marry 'fair-skinned Kashmiri women'. In the manner of a typical Orientalist fantasy, Kashmir has always been exoticised and feminised in the Indian imagination (Kaul 2018). The Muslim men of Kashmir especially are seen as the cruel Other—latent terrorists who are always already suspect in their politics. In Kashmir, 2020 saw further amendments to the law and policies that confirmed these settler-colonial intentions. The law was changed so that non-citizens of former J&K can now receive fast-tracked domicile status based on residency there. In the middle of the pandemic, in July 2020, masses of Indian workers were brought into Kashmir to work in brick kilns. Also in the same month, the law was changed to allow the designation of any area as strategic, permitting permanent constructions for the use of the armed forces. At the same time, housing and urban development policy has been changed to allow the building of hundreds of thousands of different dwellings, ranging from slum redevelopment to integrated townships, through public–private partnerships, for which contracts will be awarded. Kashmiris fear that these developments, taken together, will result in the mass settlement of outsiders and overwhelming demographic change. That this is not mere doom-mongering is supported by the fact that, in November 2019, the Indian Consul-General in New York was filmed at an event comparing the return of Kashmir's Hindu minority to Israeli settlements: 'If the Israeli people can do it, we can also do it' (Express News Service 2019).

India's camps

China plays a complex role in the Indian public imagination and politics and is often perceived as a very different Other; India is projected as democratic and China as communist authoritarian. Yet, China is also seen as worthy of emulation for its economic and infrastructure growth, and for the ability of its leaders to evade the problems of democratic dissent. India's Prime Minister Modi is portrayed as a 'strong' leader, presented to his masses of followers as someone who can keep democratic noise under control and succeed in the way China has done.

While sections of the Indian media wonder why China hates its Muslim Uyghur minority, they seem comfortable ignoring the ever-increasing and systematic Islamophobic violence in India itself, which is made worse by police inaction or brutality, lack of prompt official condemnation, and inexcusable judicial delays or quietude. It is possible for Indian TV anchors to highlight the plight of the Uyghurs, the lack of religious freedom, and the construction of concentration camps in China; however, the plight of Kashmiri Muslims, the persecution of Indian Muslims, and the construction of detention camps in India receive barely any mainstream attention.

Despite widespread protests, the recent, controversial *Citizenship Amendment Act* succeeded in creating a religious basis for access to Indian citizenship, but Islam is excluded. Furthermore, the Indian Government is planning to establish a National Register of Citizens, and attempts at citizenship verification in certain areas of the country have resulted in the creation of millions of stateless people—often from among those who are already socioeconomically marginalised (for instance, 1.9 million people in Assam, which represents 6 per cent of the state's population; see Rahim 2019). Much to the chagrin of organisations such as the right-wing paramilitary RSS (the ideological parent of the ruling BJP), many Hindus are among the newly stateless people (Rahim 2019). However, while the new *Citizenship Amendment Act* allows these Hindus to find a route back into Indian citizenship, their Muslim counterparts are purposely left in limbo.

An anti-immigrant and Islamophobic agenda is a key staple of the Modi-led BJP, which has been in power since 2014 and has made no secret of endorsing this agenda by refusing to condemn anti-minority violence and indulging in outright hate speech against 'Muslims' and 'foreigners'—both of whom are amalgamated into a composite figure by denying the centuries of Mughal history. In 2014, India's central authorities asked all the provinces to set up at least one detention camp to separate criminals from illegal immigrants or foreigners awaiting deportation after completing their sentences due to the impossibility of confirming their nationality (Kalita 2019). Construction has since begun on several detention camps throughout the country, with the process gathering pace over the past few years (Sen and Singaravelu 2020; Uniyal 2020). While Modi denied the existence of any such camps, lawmakers have accepted they exist (IANS 2019). Also, contrary to the claims by the government that the inmates are housed with dignity and not deprived of basic facilities, there have been reports of numerous deaths in the camps in Assam (Krishnan 2020). The resources needed to set up and run these detention camps make them likely candidates to form a blooming 'sunrise industry' (Balakrishnan 2019).

In the context of Kashmir, a different kind of camp is being proposed. In January 2020, General Bipin Rawat, chief of India's Defence Staff, suggested Kashmiris could be taken away to 'de-radicalisation camps' (Gettleman and Schultz 2020). For many Kashmiris, this echoes the camps in Xinjiang and portends a similar fate for them. The military did not clarify these remarks, but after what was done to Kashmir in the constitutional coup of August 2019, no nightmare is beyond imagination since democratic checks are fast disappearing in the face of a craven judiciary, censored and self-censoring media, targeted attacks on civil society spokespeople and activists, and a wideranging Hindu-majoritarian overhaul of the country's historical, social, cultural, and political identities. A hostile attitude towards the Kashmiri population is nothing new. In 2017, the same general—who at that time was army chief—applauded the use of a Kashmiri civilian tied to the front of a military vehicle as a human shield, calling it an 'innovation'; he also expressed the wish that the Kashmiri people would fire weapons instead of throwing stones so he could do what he wanted with them (Safi 2017).

The moral wound of colonialism and the postcolonial error

Mass internment camps as sites for the deprivation of people's rights and liberties have an inextricable relationship with colonial history and, over the past two centuries, they have been used by many countries across the globe. In fact, governments like those of India and China are only too keen to point to this history of colonial atrocities carried out by Euro-American nations. Added to this are the hypocrisy and selectivity with which 'the West' pursued its human rights agenda during the Cold War, how it has carried out 'humanitarian intervention' in its aftermath through the invasions of Iraq and Afghanistan, and how it has suppressed the rights and liberties of its own citizens under the guise of the War on Terror. Taken together, these add up to a convenient nativist discourse that officials in countries like China and India use to justify their own behaviour in Xinjiang, Kashmir, and elsewhere.

When we think about how large and diverse countries such as China and India are able to create consent among their own majority populations, and globally, to support their actions in Xinjiang and Kashmir, we find two important explanatory variables: media censorship and nation-state–centric media coverage of these issues; and how the ignorance and indifference of the wider world to the fate of these oppressed Muslim populations are tied to access to Indian and Chinese markets and global commodity value chains. However, there is a third, equally important way in which Indian and Chinese—and other non-Western—populations consent to the treatment of Kashmiri and Uyghur people. This relates to the West/non-West divide in the understanding of the history of human rights, and the role of colonial history in this. This third point is my focus here.

It is important to analyse the role of colonial history in the present, and I theorise this through what I call the moral wound of colonialism. Let me explain. To begin with, notwithstanding their geographical proximity, demographic similarity, or strategic treatment, there is a striking paucity of academic work looking at the Kashmir and Xinjiang cases side by side. Such an understanding is often hard to obtain because of the stable sense in which the signifier 'the West' is understood. In the inherited historiography that presents a perennial structuring of colonial power as between 'the haves' of the West and 'the have-nots' of the non-West, there is no place to perceive a colonial exercise of power by the non-West, unless it is seen only as reflective of the divide-and-rule agenda of the West. This is a significant conceptual problem.

It is sustained by thinking that perceives colonialism as a 'moral wound' to the formerly colonised rather than to the colonisers. To have been colonised in the past is understood as a matter of moral shame and humiliation for the colonised, but there is no dominant equivalent narrative of moral shame and humiliation for having been a colonising nation. The idea that a state—interpreted as a political community—is justified in acting colonially over territory and peoples that it seeks to control largely goes unchallenged due to the way in which history is taught in teleological and triumphalist terms. Critical challenges to this rarely make it through to the mass media and wider public consciousness and, when they do, it is in the guise of token appreciation of a handful of secular, humanist, liberated, Western-educated, anticolonial intellectuals. It is certainly the case that what is seen as humiliating is less the carrying out of brutal colonial oppression, and more the inability to have successfully resisted it. In this way, the glory of imperial colonial power is never sufficiently critiqued and the humiliated-yet-virtuous nativist sense of having been colonised is never critically understood either.

This discourse creates the perfect recipe for messianic leaders to manipulate imaginaries of time along the lines of pride and futurity, and to promise the future as a return to a glorious past—either of putative precolonial purity in non-Western countries or of imperious and wide-ranging territorial control in Western countries. In each case, the fantasy is predicated on the idea of making a country great again. Manifest in this—what I call a postcolonial error (in both the formerly colonising and the formerly colonised countries)—is the latent potential for a double bind: the non-West can achieve glory along the colonial lines of the historical West by overcoming its past humiliation, but the non-West has a virtuous inability to be a coloniser because of having been previously colonised. Thus, at the same time, a non-Western country, humiliated through previous formal or informal colonisation, seeks to perform economic and political power in the way of the historical West, and yet is immune to the possibility of playing the role of coloniser in its own peripheries. This is effectively the essence of what the moral wound achieves in political terms in the contemporary era.

When India or China is presented as a 'rising power', this is precisely how 'power' is understood and what is meant by its 'rising'. There is, of course, no logical, historical, biological, or empirical reason to sustain the claim that formerly 'humiliated' or colonised non-Western countries are effectively immunised from acting as colonisers themselves. But attempts to highlight the colonial actions of non-Western countries like India and China are usually answered with the retort that these criticisms are just a regressive, Indophobic or Sinophobic—perhaps even racist—ploy to stop these powers from rising because they are not Western. One might further ask what precisely does being non-Western mean in this context? What is the role of the signifier 'the West' in the idea of 'the non-West'? It certainly does not mean the absence of consumerism, capitalism, and allied infrastructures of conspicuous consumption or urbanisation. When the signifier 'West' is raised in this manner, it refers specifically to the question of liberties and rights and, most specifically, human rights.

This, in a single stroke, relinquishes the global legacy of the evolution of human rights—including anticolonial struggles—to a purported triumphalist West. For the same reason, it also makes the possibility of human rights denial in the West invisible, while enabling the continuation of human rights denial in the non-West to go unchallenged. None of this means there are not regressive Indophobic or Sinophobic—and even racist—voices in Western countries; in fact, many right-wing voices fit this description. However, this weaponisation of the category 'West' to deny rights in the non-West is fundamentally untenable because of the complexity of history, territory, and identity. Be it China's 'century of humiliation' (Callahan 2004) or the imaginary of the 'Golden Bird' that was India before British colonisation, the postcolonial error of conceptualising the moral wound of colonialism serves a very useful purpose in these countries. The Chinese challenge to global human rights discourse is well recognised (Chen 2019). India is on the same path, with the Indian Home Minister recently referring to the inapplicability of 'Western human rights' in India as the country would have its own expanded human rights linked to Indian values (The Wire 2019). Within this framing, the political aspirations, identities, and rights of minority populations in 'restive' regions cannot be framed as struggles; instead, they are seen as targets of patronising development or the repression deserved by traitorous subjects. What is more, the technologies and infrastructure for this development and/or repression in China and India are linked to a global network of profitable corporate interests that work along supra and infrastatal pathways, while simultaneously abetting the denial of rights to marginalise minority populations in the name of Western politicking.

Highlighting commonalities

In both the Indian and the Chinese cases, the uninhibited repression of Muslim-majority regions is aided by the fact that the international community is loath to take any substantive action due to their economic ties with these countries (Ma and Loanes 2019; SupChina 2019). Several Muslim countries refuse to speak up against India and China—for instance, Modi received state honours in the Middle East in August 2019 even as the constitutional coup was under way in Kashmir (Dorsey 2019), and Chinese BRI investments are having a similar silencing effect on Muslim states. At the same time, statements by the United States are seen as hypocritical given that country's own record of human rights abuses, which only worsened under Donald Trump. The global Islamophobia unleashed in the wake of the War on Terror assists in the collective portrayal of Muslims in India as a threat.

In August 2016, the question 'Should India apply the "Chinese model for Xinjiang" in Kashmir?' on a popular web discussion forum received a variety of responses, revealing two common threads (Quora 2016). The first was that doing so was not possible because China was communist authoritarian and India democratic; the second was that Kashmir's autonomous status was guaranteed by Article 370 of the Indian Constitution. Commencing in July 2016, Kashmir was rocked by a massive anti-India uprising in which the mass blinding of people was carried out using pellet guns. By 2020, Article 370 had been revoked and there is an accelerated set of legal and policy moves to bring about demographic, environmental, and infrastructural changes in the region. It is conceivable that where Xinjiang leads, Kashmir may follow.

In 2019, *The New York Times* leaked pages of internal CCP documents, which the journalists described as 'chillingly bureaucratic', including handbooks with questions and model answers prescribed to instruct Uyghur students about their families taken away to camps (Ma 2019). Furthermore, video surveillance firms—like Hikvision from China, a 'national AI champion' according to the CCP and 'either owned or controlled by the Chinese military' according to the US Department of Defense (Dalmia 2020)—have gained increasing prominence in India, including through Indian Government contracts under the 'Make in India' initiative. As others have described, there are evident global linkages in the circulation and export of technologies that enable digital authoritarianism in which China's role is ever expanding (Feldstein 2019; Roche 2019).

Even though the relationship between China and India is marred by strategic rivalry over border issues, which periodically translates into clashes and loss of life, the economic ties between the two countries and the resonances between Xi's and Modi's projects to dominate Xinjiang and Kashmir overshadow these confrontations. The ethnonationalist struggles of the Muslim populations in Kashmir and Xinjiang have a long and complex history; indeed, there is even a small minority of Uyghurs who settled in Kashmir as trans-Himalayan migrants between the 1930s and the 1950s, as communist China took shape. Kashmir today is not the same as Xinjiang, but many developments over the past year indicate that it might become more and more similar. The people in both these regions must contend with a political rule that allows them limited rights or ability to dissent and is marked by deprivation of liberties and lack of accountability. Yet, despite sharing a historical border, the same religion, and fairly similar challenges, these groups are, if not unaware of, at least fairly indifferent to, each other's struggles. However, for those of us—scholars, policymakers, and activists—who can witness the nature of the unfolding political dynamic in the two rising powers of China and India, it is important to highlight the commonalities in terms of strategies, speech acts, and circulations of technology that facilitate such projects. Further and more broadly, as I have argued here, we need to challenge the instrumentalisation of the moral wound of colonialism that translates into a postcolonial error, whereby non-Western countries are able to secure legitimacy and justification for their own exercise of colonial power.

Conclusion

Darren Byler, Ivan Franceschini, and Nicholas Loubere

As we are wrapping up this volume in early November 2021, the ground in Xinjiang is already shifting. In October 2020, concerted pressure from trade unions such as the American Federation of Labor and Congress of Industrial Organizations and advocacy groups such as the Worker Rights Consortium forced ethical trade associations such as the Better Cotton Initiative (BCI) to withdraw their support for Xinjiang carceral institutions—most notably, the Xinjiang Production and Construction Corps, or Bingtuan (BCI 2020). Previously, the BCI—whose stakeholders include dozens of global brands ranging from H&M to Adidas—was a primary partner of the Bingtuan through the latter's Cotton & Linen Company (Mathews 2019). In the year since BCI announced it would no longer work in Xinjiang, most of its affiliated brands declared they would no longer source cotton from Xinjiang or work with suppliers who employed labour from Xinjiang. This, combined with US Government sanctions on Xinjiang cotton, constituted a substantial shock to the Chinese economy, with swings of more than US$100 million from profits to losses among some of China's leading textile companies, prompting a nationwide campaign in China to denounce and boycott companies that refused to use Xinjiang cotton and labour (Dou et al. 2021).

The economic effects of global brands moving away from Xinjiang were accompanied by other material changes on the ground in northwestern China. First, state authorities declared that all 'trainees' in the 'concentrated closed education and training centres' had graduated (Wang 2019). At the same time, local authorities began posting notices of contracts being awarded for the construction of new prisons. Investigative reporters who found their way to former camps discovered that, in some cases—including at the largest facility in the region—the camp had simply been relabelled as a detention facility (Kang 2021a). Other researchers, who wish to remain anonymous, observed that in some places where tourism was encouraged, People's Convenience Police Stations had been disguised as non-police facilities. In some, camera systems had been ripped from their posts; in others, checkpoints remained, but were no longer being used. Another researcher who visited the region in 2020 and who also spoke with us under condition of anonymity was told the reason for this was the locality had run out of money to maintain the technology. But he also found that, at least in the cases he observed, the newly hired grid workers and tens of thousands of police were still employed as intelligence workers, and that, in general, the surveillance systems continued to operate, just a bit further in the background and in more targeted ways. He and others who have visited the region in the past two years surmised that the height of state violence may now be in the past, that fear has been instilled throughout the Muslim population, and people throughout society have begun to adapt to the new norms (see, for instance, Kang 2021b).

Does this mean the Xinjiang emergency is over? That 'we have won', as one overenthusiastic Western commentator recently wrote in response to one such report? Unfortunately, the recent shift is no cause for celebration. While the most visible manifestations of state violence in Xinjiang might be receding from public sight, the situation is far from returning to the status quo ante. Uyghur-language media has been permitted again in the form of television shows and book publication, but only when accompanied with Chinese or as a translation from Chinese. Uyghurs who have emerged from the camps are often not returned to their former positions in society. In fact, many who have been transferred from the camps are still absent from their families, in factories far from home. Still others have been given formal prison sentences and will not be released any time soon. The system appears to be shifting from internment without due process and criminal sentencing to proletarianisation and criminal prosecution and mass imprisonment of former detainees. As we mentioned in the introduction to this volume, state documents show that as many as 533,000 people in Xinjiang were formally prosecuted between 2017 and 2020—a rate around six times higher than the national average (Byler 2021). Official documents also show that around 500,000 children have been assigned to residential boarding schools and, since 2017, the state has hired more than 90,000 new, avowedly non-religious Chinese-speaking teachers (China Education Bureau 2017; Liu 2019). With family separation through processes of removal, incarceration, and coercive proletarianisation still endemic throughout Uyghur and Kazakh society, the process of eliminating and replacing aspects of Muslim social life remains in motion, even if the Chinese authorities are now more cognisant of the economic and moral costs of orchestrating this social engineering project.

What can be done about this? On a practical level, we can think of at least three undertakings. First, we can organise educational and grassroots activities that support truth and reconciliation, such as teach-ins and solidarity events led by both Xinjiang Muslims and Han citizens. Such activities could put those who claim belonging in northwestern China in conversation with global prison abolitionists and those engaged in struggles against settler colonialism in Asia and around the world. Second, we can provide support to initiatives that document and analyse what is happening in Xinjiang, such as the Xinjiang Documentation Project and the Xinjiang Victims Database, either by offering them our time and relevant skills or by simply circulating their materials. Finally, if we work in a university that conducts research that might find application in the repressive activities in Xinjiang or for a company that does business with actors in the region, we can campaign to put an end to these partnerships.

On a theoretical level, we need to fight for a broader epistemological reorientation of the discussion on Xinjiang, especially within the left. It is now more important than ever that we leave behind the frameworks that have dominated the discussion so far—both the 'essentialism' of those who treat the camps as a specifically Chinese phenomenon related to the authoritarian or totalitarian nature of the Chinese Communist Party and the 'whataboutism' of those who maintain that we have no moral authority to criticise the Chinese Government or that the camps, if they exist at all, might not be as bad as people say. So far, the position of the left has been characterised by notable silences and ambiguities on Xinjiang, with several prominent voices engaging in outright denialism in the conviction that criticising the Chinese Government's practices in the region means endorsing its political opponents—most notably, the US Government. It need not be like that. It is obvious that one can be critical of the Chinese authorities without necessarily taking the side of their geopolitical opponents. From this point of view, we believe that a first step for a meaningful critique from the left would be to acknowledge that the Xinjiang camps have been enabled through entangled sets of complicities inherent to the global capitalist system, and recognise how they represent an extreme manifestation of worrying global technological, economic, and political trends that have been unfolding for some time. While not absolving the Chinese Government of any responsibility, such a position might lay the foundation for a more meaningful politics to address the status of the world in which we are living, in China and beyond.

Appendix: Xinjiang timeline

This basic timeline of events in Xinjiang over the past decade is based on several sources. The Xinjiang Documentation Project at the University of British Columbia is the main source for events prior to 2018. Briefs from the *Made in China Journal*, which in turn are based on several media sources, are the key source for events from 2018 onwards.

Date	Event
25–26 June 2009	Allegations of the sexual assault of a Han woman by Uyghur colleagues trigger the lynching of Uyghur workers by Han migrant workers in a toy factory in Shaoguang, Guangdong Province. At least two Uyghur workers are killed and 118 people, mostly Uyghurs, are wounded.
5 July 2009	A lack of government response to the events in Shaoguang triggers mass protests in Ürümqi, which quickly escalate into interethnic violence and police shooting. According to official figures, 197 people are killed and 1,721 injured, the majority of whom are Han. More than 1,000 Uyghurs are arrested or disappeared, mosques are temporarily closed, and internet and phone communications severely restricted.
2010	Following the Ürümqi uprising of July 2009, officials in Xinjiang report that approximately 40,000 riot-proof high-definition surveillance cameras have been installed throughout the region.
28 October 2013	Three Uyghurs drive a truck into a crowd in Tiananmen Square in Beijing, resulting in two deaths and 42 people injured. The three Uyghurs also die. This incident is alleged to be the first act of political violence perpetrated by Uyghurs outside Xinjiang.
19 December 2013	At a Politburo meeting, President Xi Jinping announces a new 'Strategic Plan' for Xinjiang, which the state media calls 'a major altering of the region's strategy'. The plan makes it a primary task to maintain social stability and an enduring peace in Xinjiang. This signals a shift in China's strategy in the region, from concentrating on economic growth to aiming for a combination of maintaining social stability and promoting economic development.
January 2014	Prominent Uyghur Ilham Tohti, a scholar of economics at the Central Minzu University in Beijing and an advocate for the rights of Uyghurs, is arrested in Beijing and transferred to a detention centre in Xinjiang.

1 March 2014   A mass knife attack at a railway station in Kunming, Yunnan Province, kills 31 people and injures more than 140. Local authorities blame 'separatists from Xinjiang' for the attack. This incident is characterised by state media as 'China's 9/11'.

30 April 2014   A bomb and knife attack at a railway station in Ürümqi results in the deaths of the two attackers and one bystander, with 79 people injured. Local authorities describe the event as a 'violent terrorist attack' and blame Uyghurs.

22 May 2014   Four-wheel-drive vehicles carrying explosives collide in a busy street market in Ürümqi, killing 43 people and injuring more than 90, with most of the victims ethnic Han. In response, officials in Beijing promise a merciless campaign against Uyghur separatists, with President Xi pledging to initiate a 'strike first' (先发制敌) strategy through a 'People's War on Terror' (反恐人民战争).

Mid-2014   The reeducation campaign begins when provincial authorities in Xinjiang demand that Uyghur migrants in urban areas within the province return to their hometowns to obtain a new identity card, called the People's Convenience Card (人民便民卡), which is supposed to work as a passbook for these migrants to return to cities. However, it turns out that most rural-born Uyghurs are ineligible for the card, resulting in their mobility within Xinjiang being significantly restricted. The People's Convenience Card is discontinued in May 2016.

28 July 2014   Hundreds of protesting Uyghur civilians are reportedly killed by police in Yarkand County in Xinjiang. The police shooting is believed to be the deadliest incident of state violence in China since the 2009 uprising in Ürümqi. The most reliable accounts suggest that heavy-handed religious restrictions on the eve of one of Islam's most important holy days are the key reason for the violence.

23 September 2014 After a two-day hearing before the Ürümqi People's Intermediate Court, Ilham Tohti is found guilty of 'separatism' and sentenced to life imprisonment. All his assets are seized. According to reports, Tohti is held in solitary confinement until at least early 2016. He is denied the right to communicate with family and friends aside from minimal visits.

December 2014	The Chinese Government publishes a list of '75 behavioural indicators of religious extremism'. While some are considered reasonable examples of incitement to violence, such as 'calling for *jihad*', many are vague and highly questionable—for instance, 'storing large amounts of food at home' and 'suddenly quitting smoking and drinking'. The list also criminalises numerous forms of normative Islamic practice.
29 May 2015	The World Bank approves funding for the Xinjiang Technical and Vocational Education and Training Project, which aims to 'build high-quality teaching and management teams, upgrade school facilities and equipment, offer short-term training programs to rural farmers and urban migrant workers, and provide technical services to local communities and enterprises' in the city of Ürümqi. Given the similarities with the language the Chinese Government later uses to describe reeducation camps in Xinjiang, not to mention the fact that a 'sister school' in Yarkand sponsored by one of the schools funded by the World bank purchases and installs razor wire and other prison/military equipment, in the following years, observers raise concerns that World Bank funding may have been used for surveillance-related activities in Xinjiang.
29 August 2016	Chen Quanguo becomes Party Secretary of Xinjiang Uyghur Autonomous Region. For the previous five years, he was Party Secretary of the Tibet Autonomous Region.
14 February 2017	Five civilians are killed by three Uyghur suicide attackers in a knife assault near Hotan, Xinjiang.
4 March 2017	The Department of Justice in Xinjiang orders that 'educational transformation centres' (教育转化中心) be established throughout Xinjiang. Chinese officials describe these centres as schools where students will learn Mandarin, improve job skills, pursue hobbies, and, most importantly, get rid of 'religious extremist thought'. However, Agence France-Presse later reveals that these centres operate more like jails than schools, where detainees are kept under tight control in locked cells by guards equipped with shackles, tear gas, Tasers, stun guns, and spiked clubs.

Early 2017   Local authorities impose tougher surveillance measures on Uyghurs. More than 7,500 'convenience' police stations are constructed. The Xinjiang Government claims the 'zero-distance proximity' of the convenience police stations will ensure 24-hour surveillance and swift responses to emergencies. The authorities also hire more than 90,000 security workers, most of whom are untrained Uyghur and Kazakh, low-wage assistant police (协警). Their primary role is in the convenience police stations, but they are also assigned to low-level positions in camps and detention centres.

August 2017   A spokesperson for Leon Technology, a Chinese private security technology company, says close to US\$8 billion has been invested in the technology and information industries in Xinjiang, and describes the process of clearing the 'thick atmosphere' of Kashgar with facial recognition cameras. The spokesperson says the security technology industry in Xinjiang has 'unlimited potential' because China's international development strategy includes expansion into markets that contain 60 per cent of the world's Muslim population.

Early 2018   It is reported that Uyghurs in some areas are required to install surveillance apps on their mobile phones and are assigned 'safety scores', with those deemed 'unsafe' sent to reeducation camps.

Mid-2018   It is reported that hundreds of thousands of Uyghurs and other ethnic minorities in Xinjiang are detained in political reeducation camps. Detainees include several prominent Uyghur figures, such as football star Erfan Hezim (detained from April 2018 to March 2019), musician Abdurehim Heyit (detained since April 2017), and Professor Rahile Dawut (detained since December 2017).

August 2018   The UN Committee on the Elimination of Racial Discrimination releases a report in which it expresses concerns about the human rights situation in Xinjiang and calls for the immediate release of all wrongfully and unlawfully detained individuals, as well as the end of ethnoreligious profiling. However, Chinese officials continue to claim that the reeducation centres are 'vocational education and employment training centres' and that Xinjiang is currently 'enjoying overall social stability, sound economic development, and harmonious coexistence of different ethnic groups'.

6 November 2018	The UN Human Rights Council calls on China to address human rights issues, including its treatment of Uyghurs and other minorities in Xinjiang. In response, China's representatives defend the country's human rights record and dismiss the UN assessment as 'politically driven' and 'fraught with bias'.
Mid-November 2018	Led by Canada, 15 Western ambassadors jointly issue a letter requesting a meeting with Xinjiang's Communist Party leaders to provide an explanation of the alleged human rights abuses in the region, but their request is rebuffed by the Chinese Government.
5 December 2018	UN High Commissioner for Human Rights Michelle Bachelet requests permission to visit Xinjiang. Under increasing international pressure, China responds that UN officials are welcome to visit the region on the condition they do not interfere in China's internal affairs.
Early December 2018	International media starts to detail the emergence of a forced labour regime in factories attached to reeducation camps in Xinjiang. It is reported that people detained in the camps are forced to work long hours in factories with no or minimal pay. They are also required to learn Mandarin and study party propaganda, while not being allowed to leave the factories or contact their families without permission.
February 2019	In an attempt to dispel international criticism of its treatment of Uyghurs in Xinjiang, China releases a proof-of-life video of Abdurehim Heyit, a Uyghur musician who disappeared in 2017 and was rumoured to be dead. However, this action backfires, prompting other Uyghurs abroad to take to social media to demand the Chinese Government disclose the whereabouts of their loved ones.
February 2019	Ethical hacker Victor Gevers exposes a data breach suffered by SenseNets, a former subsidiary of the Chinese company Sensetime that specialises in facial recognition and crowd analysis technology and works with the Chinese police. The breach reveals that SenseNets has been assisting Chinese authorities in closely tracking the locations and identities of almost 2.6 million people in Xinjiang.
14 June 2019	Prominent Uyghur writer Nurmuhammad Tohti dies. He was detained in an internment camp in Xinjiang from November 2018 to March 2019. His granddaughter, who is based in Canada, reveals that Tohti was denied treatment for diabetes and heart disease, and was only released from the internment camp after he became incapacitated due to his medical condition.

June 2019

American universities begin reevaluating their collaborations and partnerships with Chinese companies after media reports that the Massachusetts Institute of Technology and at least one other American university are still in partnerships with iFlytek, a Chinese AI company whose voice recognition software is used to securitise Xinjiang.

11 July 2019

Twenty-two states, including Australia, Canada, Germany, and the United Kingdom, co-sign a letter to the UN High Commissioner for Human Rights condemning China's actions in Xinjiang. In response, ambassadors of 37 other countries, including Pakistan, Saudi Arabia, and North Korea, pen a letter praising China's 'achievements in the field of human rights', including its treatment of Uyghurs and other Muslim minorities in Xinjiang.

16 August 2019

China's State Council Information Office releases a white paper that details the necessity and effectiveness of vocational education and training centres in Xinjiang in helping China counter the threat of terrorism.

August 2019

Some officials in China claim that up to 90 per cent of Uyghurs have been released from the centres and 'returned to society', but there is little evidence to support these claims as camps continue to operate.

13 September 2019

Scholars at Risk, a US-based international network of academic institutions organised to support and defend the principles of academic freedom and the human rights of scholars around the world, issues a letter to Chinese officials, calling for the halt of the execution of Tashpolat Tiyip, a renowned Uyghur academic who was abducted and sentenced to death following a secret trial in 2017.

Late September 2019

A video emerges showing hundreds of men blindfolded and bound during what is geolocated as a mass transfer in April 2019 at a train station in Korla, Xinjiang. At roughly the same time, at an event on the sidelines of a UN summit, Chinese Foreign Minister Wang Yi claims China has not seen a single case of violent terrorism in the past three years, and defends the camps on the grounds that they 'are schools that help the people free themselves from terrorism and extremism and acquire useful skills'.

30 September 2019

Jailed Uyghur scholar Ilham Tohti is awarded the Vaclav Havel Prize, which honours outstanding civil society action in defence of human rights.

Early October 2019   The United States imposes visa restrictions on Chinese officials implicated in repression in Xinjiang and begins blocking
US companies from trading with tech companies that support
violations of human rights in Xinjiang.

Late October 2019   Competing statements on China's practices in Xinjiang are
issued by two groups of UN member countries, with a British
representative raising human rights concerns and a Belarusian
delegate endorsing China's approach to 'combating terrorism'.

Early November   The World Bank decides to downscale its project supporting
2019   vocational schools in Xinjiang (see the entry for 29 May 2015).
It discontinues funding for partner schools in southern Xinjiang
while continuing to fund the five schools in Ürümqi that are
directly supported by the project.

16 November 2019   *The New York Times* analyses 403 pages of internal Chinese
Government documents on Xinjiang, which provide insight
into the secretive policy decisions on the mass incarceration
of Uyghurs and other ethnic minorities in the area. One of the
most striking revelations concerns the downfall of Wang Yongzhi,
a veteran Han official in Xinjiang who prioritised economic
growth in his locality over increased mass detention. The documents also discuss how officials should explain the disappearance of parents to Uyghur students returning from residential
boarding schools. Discussions among Chinese officials about
the mass detention of Muslim minorities are also disclosed,
with Chen Quanguo, Party Secretary of Xinjiang, demanding
his staff 'round up everyone who should be rounded up'. More
strikingly, the documents link the reeducation campaign in
Xinjiang directly to President Xi through previously unpublished
speeches that he delivered to local officials in 2014. In these, Xi
calls for 'absolutely no mercy' in a crackdown on 'terrorism
and separatism'.

Late November   The International Consortium of Investigative Journalists
2019   leaks another trove of Chinese official documents on Xinjiang,
including a secret directive on the inner workings and manage-
ment of detention centres in Xinjiang. It is disclosed that Zhu
Hailun, Deputy Party Secretary of Xinjiang, mandated that the
reeducation camps be run like high-security prisons, with strict
discipline, punishment, no 'abnormal deaths', and no escapes.

Early December   Scientific journal publishers Springer Nature and Wiley
2019   announce the reevaluation of some of their previous publica-
                  tions related to ethnic minorities in China due to growing ethical
                  concerns. Specifically, there are worries that scientists backed by
                  the Chinese Government have been using DNA or facial-reco-
                  gnition technology to study vulnerable ethnic minority groups
                  in China—most notably, Uyghurs in Xinjiang—without free,
                  informed consent.

December 2019   Chinese state media launches personal attacks on foreign experts
                  on Xinjiang, including Darren Byler, and threatens Asiye Abdu-
                  laheb, a Uyghur woman in the Netherlands who helped leak
                  documents to the International Consortium of Investigative
                  Journalists.

January 2020   More documents are leaked detailing the surveillance and incar-
                  ceration of hundreds of Muslim individuals from the Karakax
                  region in Xinjiang. They show that as many as 10 per cent of
                  detainees were detained due to violations of family planning
                  policies as part of the 'zero illegal births' program.

March 2020   The Australian Strategic Policy Institute (ASPI) releases a report
                  on the labour conditions of Uyghur and other ethnic minority
                  individuals who are transferred from Xinjiang to factories across
                  China. ASPI estimates that at least 80,000 Uyghurs were relocated
                  from Xinjiang to factories between 2017 and 2019, where they
                  worked 'under conditions that strongly suggest forced labour'.
                  These factories include suppliers of well-known brands such as
                  Apple, Nike, Amazon, Samsung, Zara, H&M, Microsoft, Merce-
                  des-Benz, and Uniqlo.

May 2020   The US Senate and House of Representatives overwhelmingly
                  pass a bill calling for targeted sanctions against Chinese officials
                  responsible for the oppression of Uyghurs in Xinjiang.

May 2020   The Chinese Government is reported to have resumed its job
                  placement scheme for tens of thousands of Uyghurs who have
                  completed compulsory programs at reeducation camps in
                  Xinjiang, as the outbreak of COVID-19 seems to have been
                  brought under control within the country. Under the job place-
                  ment scheme, many Chinese provinces are required to meet a
                  quota for the number of Uyghurs whom they will take in to
                  work in their factories.

Late June 2020	Associated Press (AP) investigates birth-control practices in Xinjiang. Based on government statistics, state documents, and interviews with ex-detainees, family members, and a former detention camp instructor, AP finds that forced birth control in Xinjiang is far more widespread and systematic than previously known and mass detention is used both to deter minority families from having children and to punish those who have failed to comply with birth-control policies in the past.
20 July 2020	The US Commerce Department blacklists another 11 Chinese textile and technology companies that are implicated in forced labour and DNA collection and analysis targeting Uyghurs. This is the third group of Chinese companies and institutions that has been added to the US blacklist over human rights violations in Xinjiang.
23 July 2020	More than 190 organisations from 36 countries call for formal commitments from clothing brands to sever ties with suppliers implicated in using forced labour in Xinjiang and to stop sourcing anything from Xinjiang in the next 12 months.
31 July 2020	The US Treasury Department blacklists the Xinjiang Production and Construction Corps (Bingtuan), due to its involvement in the detention camp and forced labour system in Xinjiang.
Early August 2020	Merdan Ghappar, a Uyghur fashion model for the Chinese online retailer Taobao, sends a video and multiple text messages directly from the inside of a reeducation camp. His testimony provides rare firsthand insights into the conditions inside the camp and the situation during the COVID-19 pandemic.
1 September 2020	In response to questions from *CNN* about forced birth control in Xinjiang, Chinese officials acknowledge via fax that birth rates in Xinjiang declined by nearly one-third in 2018 compared with 2017 but deny any forced sterilisation or genocide by authorities in the region, claiming the significant reduction in birth rates is related to 'the comprehensive implementation of the family planning policy'.
Early September 2020	Disney's new movie *Mulan* provokes a global backlash over its links to Xinjiang when it is revealed the film was partly shot in the region and its credits include thanks to authorities responsible for camp operations in the area. Amid intensifying calls overseas to boycott the movie, Chinese authorities are reported to have told major domestic media outlets not to cover the release of the movie.

14 September 2020   The US Customs and Border Protection agency issues five separate Withhold Release Orders imposing restrictions on cotton, computer parts, and hair products made by six entities in Xinjiang.

15 September 2020   Swedish clothing brand H&M announces that, due to concerns about alleged forced labour in Xinjiang, it will phase out its business relationships with producers in the area within the next 12 months and will no longer source cotton from the region.

16 September 2020   In her first State of the Union address, new President of the European Commission, Ursula von der Leyen, singles out China's human rights abuses in Xinjiang and Hong Kong, and announces the European Union will overhaul its sanctions scheme, which may include changing sanctions implementation from unanimous decisions among all EU members to qualified majority voting.

17 September 2020   China's State Council releases a white paper on employment and labour rights in Xinjiang, which is largely perceived as an attempt to defend its approach to Uyghurs and other minority peoples amid growing international criticism of its human rights abuses in Xinjiang. The white paper provides figures on the 'employment-oriented training program' in Xinjiang. It reports that an average of 1.3 million workers, including 415,400 from southern Xinjiang, went through 'vocational training' every year between 2014 and 2019 and the average annual 'relocation of surplus rural labour' exceeded 2.76 million people, with more than 60 per cent coming from southern Xinjiang. Researchers argue that the figures amount to a tacit admission of forced labour in Xinjiang and hint at the scope of internment camps in the region.

22 September 2020   The US House of Representatives passes the *Uygur Forced Labor Prevention Act*, which prevents importers from sourcing goods produced either wholly or in part in Xinjiang unless the US Government can verify with 'clear and convincing' evidence that the goods are not produced using forced labour.

22 September 2020   French President Emmanuel Macron calls for an international mission under the aegis of the United Nations to visit China's Xinjiang over growing concerns in the international community about the Muslim Uyghur minority in the region.

24 September 2020   The ASPI, a think tank based in Canberra, releases a new report documenting the detention system in Xinjiang. Based on satellite imagery, the report finds there are more than 380 'suspected detention facilities' in Xinjiang—approximately 40 per cent more than previously estimated. The report also finds that thousands of mosques in Xinjiang have been damaged or destroyed over the past three years, leaving fewer than 15,000 mosques in the region. These findings contradict Chinese authorities' claims that 'trainees in education and vocational training centres' in Xinjiang had 'graduated' by late 2019 and that religious beliefs in the region were protected and respected. In response to the release of the new report, China's Foreign Ministry spokesman Wang Wenbin accuses ASPI of being 'imbued with ideological prejudice' and 'practically an anti-China "vanguard"', which he claims publishes 'a concoction of lies against China' with the support of foreign funding.

26 September 2020   At the third central symposium on work related to Xinjiang, President Xi asserts that 'practice has proven that the party's strategy for governing Xinjiang in the new era is completely correct', claiming that current policies in Xinjiang have brought 'unprecedented achievements' in economic growth, social development, and improvement in people's livelihoods and that 'the sense of gain, happiness, and security among the people of all ethnic groups has continued to increase'. Xi adds that China's Xinjiang strategy 'must be adhered to in the long term'. He asks the whole party to 'treat the implementation of the Xinjiang strategy as a political task' and to 'work hard to implement it completely and accurately to ensure that the Xinjiang work always maintains in the correct political direction'. He also emphasises the importance of 'continuing the direction of Sinicising Islam to achieve the healthy development of religion' and the necessity of 'telling the story of Xinjiang in a multilevel, all-round, and three-dimensional manner, and confidently propagate the excellent social stability of Xinjiang'.

30 September 2020   The US House of Representatives passes a second Bill relating to forced labour that, if enacted, would require publicly listed companies in the United States to disclose in their annual reports whether they or their affiliated entities have imported goods originating from Xinjiang or containing materials sourced from the region.

Late September
2020

It is reported that at least five organisations will no longer assist companies in auditing their supply chains in Xinjiang, indicating that increasingly tight government surveillance and control in the region have made it too hard to assess whether entities in Xinjiang are using forced labour.

6 October 2020

During a meeting on human rights at the United Nations, Germany leads a group of 39 countries urging China to respect the rights of its Muslim minorities in Xinjiang and allow UN rights observers 'immediate, meaningful, and unfettered access' to Xinjiang. The 39 countries include most of the EU member states and countries such as the United States, Canada, Japan, Australia, and New Zealand. At the same meeting, Cuba issues a statement on behalf of 45 countries in support of China's policy in Xinjiang. Turkey, having joined neither group, makes a separate statement expressing its concern about the human rights situation in Xinjiang.

Early October 2020

The Chinese Government confirms to the United Nations the death of Abdulghafur Hapiz, a Uyghur man believed to have been held in an internment camp in Xinjiang since 2017. Although Hapiz's disappearance was registered with the UN Working Group on Enforced or Involuntary Disappearances (WGEID) in April 2019, the Chinese Government only recently responded to formal inquiries about this man's circumstances, informing WGEID that Hapiz died of 'severe pneumonia and tuberculosis' on 3 November 2018.

13 October 2020

China is reelected to the UN Human Rights Council amid sustained international concerns about the Chinese Government's human rights violations in Xinjiang. However, its reelection is achieved with 139 votes—41 fewer than its previous tally.

15 October 2020

US Customs and Border Protection says a shipment of 1,900 pairs of gloves will be held at the Port of Los Angeles unless Overland, the American company seeking to import the gloves, can prove they were not made with forced labour. The gloves are believed to have been made by Yili Zhuowan Garment Manufacturing Company—the factory described in Chapter 12 of this volume, which is among the companies shown to use forced labour and prohibited from importing goods into the United States.

Mid-October 2020   The Business, Energy, and Industrial Strategy Committee of the British House of Commons issues individual letters to key stakeholders in the fashion, retail, and information technology industries—including Adidas, H&M, Amazon, and the Walt Disney Company—as part of its inquiry into the issue of forced labour in Xinjiang. The committee requests written feedback on how each company manages their supply chains to maintain visibility and combat modern slavery, and invites a representative from each company to present oral evidence at a public hearing.

20 October 2020   The Xinjiang Development Research Centre of the Chinese Academy of Social Sciences releases an investigative report on the 'Employment of Ethnic Minorities in Xinjiang'. The report states that 'people of all ethnic groups in the Xinjiang Uyghur Autonomous Region voluntarily choose their jobs and they are never forced to work outside the region' while dismissing the allegation by Western think tanks of 'large-scale forced labour in Xinjiang' as being 'profoundly untrue, unreasonable, and untenable'. The report says the investigation team made field trips to more than 70 enterprises, rural labour cooperatives, and business startups in Ili Kazak and Kezilesu Kirgiz autonomous prefectures and Kashgar, Hotan, and Aksu prefectures, and visited cities outside Xinjiang, including Beijing and Tianjin.

21 October 2020   The Better Cotton Initiative (BCI), which had already suspended licensing and assurance activities in Xinjiang in March 2020, decides to cease all field-level activities in Xinjiang effective immediately, including capacity-building, data monitoring, and reporting. The decision follows an external review of cotton sourcing in Xinjiang, commissioned by the BCI, amid increasing international scrutiny of forced labour and other human rights abuses in Xinjiang.

Late October 2020   A Canadian parliamentary committee report concludes that China's treatment of Uyghurs in Xinjiang constitutes genocide and calls for the Canadian Government to sanction officials implicated in the Chinese Government's policies in Xinjiang. In response, China's Foreign Ministry dismisses the committee's report as 'full of lies and disinformation'. It also warns Canadian lawmakers to stop their 'blatant interference' in China's internal affairs.

Late October 2020   The Solar Energy Industries Association calls for companies to move their supply chains out of Xinjiang due to growing concerns about human rights abuses in the region.

Late October 2020   According to an official of the Aksu Huafu Textile Factory, a branch of Huafu Fashion Company Limited in the Aksu prefecture in Xinjiang, approximately 20,000 former internment camp detainees are working at the factory, which appears to be one of the largest facilities in the entire Aksu prefecture.

Late October 2020   As part of their fight against the spread of COVID-19, officials at the European Parliament and the European Commission purchase thermal-imaging cameras produced by Hikvision, a Chinese firm that has been implicated in the suppression of Uyghurs and other Muslim minorities in Xinjiang. While the United States blacklisted Hikvision in October 2019 over human rights and national security concerns, the Chinese company has yet to be sanctioned or blacklisted by the European Union.

Late October 2020   Two ethnic Kazakhs from Xinjiang who illegally crossed the border are granted temporary refugee status in Kazakhstan. Thirty-seven-year-old Malikuly entered Kazakhstan illegally in 2017 after Chinese authorities confiscated his Kazakh permanent residence permit during his visit to Xinjiang in 2015. Forty-four-year-old Aqan illegally crossed the border into Kazakhstan in May 2018 after local authorities in Xinjiang threatened to put her in an internment camp.

12 November 2020   Jailed Uyghur scholar Rahile Dawut, who disappeared from Xinjiang in December 2017 and is believed to be currently held in an internment camp, is honoured with the Courage to Think Award 2020 by New York–based rights group Scholars at Risk. The award is presented at a virtual conference and Dawut's daughter, Akeda Pulati, accepts the award on her mother's behalf.

15 November 2020   Bob Rae, Canada's Ambassador to the United Nations, says he has called on the UN Human Rights Council to investigate whether China's treatment of the Uyghurs since 2017 should be considered an act of genocide. Rae tells *CBC* chief political correspondent Rosemary Barton: 'There's no question that there's aspects of what the Chinese are doing that fit into the definition of genocide in the genocide convention. But that then requires you to go through a process of gathering information and of making sure that we've got the evidence that would support that kind of an allegation.' The Chinese Foreign Ministry dismisses Rae's comments as ridiculous, claiming that, based on long-term population growth statistics, Canada itself better fits the description of having perpetrated genocide.

Mid-November 2020	Volkswagen defends its decision to continue operating its car factory in Xinjiang, despite increasing international concerns about human rights abuses in the region. In an interview with the *BBC*, Stephen Wollenstein, Volkswagen's CEO in China, says the company 'does not have forced labour' in its workforce but when asked how certain he is about this claim, he adds: 'We could never reach 100 per cent certainty.'
Late November 2020	Two US Congressional staffers reveal that Apple lobbyists are trying to water down the *Uyghur Forced Labor Prevention Act*, a new law aimed at preventing forced labour in Xinjiang. The new bill would hold American companies accountable for using imprisoned or coerced Uyghur labour. Apart from Apple, several other American companies, including Nike and Coca Cola, are also reported to be opposing the bill in its current formulation.
27 November 2020	In answering a question from *CNN*, Eljan Anayt, spokesperson of the Xinjiang Provincial Government, tells a press conference that some locations that have been identified as 'concentration camps' by Western media and institutions, especially the ASPI, are civilian institutions, such as administration buildings, nursing homes, logistics centres, or schools. This confirms the claims of numerous detainees who reported being held in administrative buildings and nursing homes that had been converted into fortified camps with locked cells.
10 December 2020	Following years of media coverage and lobbying by the Australian Government and human rights activists, Sadam Abudusalamu, an Australian Uyghur, is reunited with his wife and son, who had been held against their will in Xinjiang since 2017.
11 December 2020	French football star Antoine Griezmann announces he is immediately ending his sponsorship deal with Huawei following a report released by US-based surveillance research firm IPVM that shows Huawei is involved in testing facial recognition software in China that can be used by authorities to identify Uyghurs.
12 December 2020	*The Washington Post* reports that Huawei has worked with at least four partner companies to develop surveillance technologies that could monitor people according to their ethnicity, including multiple AI-powered facial recognition tools that could identify members of the Uyghur community and alert Chinese authorities.

17 December 2020	In an online statement, Alibaba, a leading Chinese technology company, says it is 'dismayed to learn' that Alibaba Cloud, its cloud computing unit, developed a facial recognition software feature that can help users to identify members of the Uyghur community in China. It says the technology feature was used for capability testing only rather than being deployed by any customer, and it does not and will not allow its technology to be used to target or identify specific ethnic groups.
18 December 2020	The European Parliament passes the Resolution on Forced Labour and the Situation of the Uyghurs in the Xinjiang Uyghur Autonomous Region, which will allow the European Union to sanction Chinese officials implicated in human rights abuses in Xinjiang. The resolution also calls for expediting asylum applications from Uyghurs and other oppressed minorities in China and suspending extradition treaties with the country.
Late December 2020	Franck Riester, France's Minister Delegate for Foreign Trade and Economic Attractiveness, says France will oppose the proposed EU–China investment agreement over concerns about the use of forced labour in Xinjiang. Riester remarks: 'We cannot facilitate investment in China if we do not commit to abolishing forced labour', adding that other European countries such as Belgium, Luxembourg, the Netherlands, and Germany share France's position.
Late December 2020	During its National People's Congress, China ratifies an extradition treaty with Turkey. While the Turkish Government is yet to ratify the treaty, human rights groups are worried that, once adopted, it could endanger Uyghur families and activists who have fled to Turkey to avoid persecution by Chinese authorities. Critics of the treaty urge the Turkish Government to discard it to prevent it from 'becoming an instrument of persecution'.
6 January 2021	British retailer Marks & Spencer signs a call to action initiated by the Coalition to End Forced Labour in the Uyghur Region (which consists of civil society organisations and trade unions) and becomes one of the first major brands to back the action to cut ties with suppliers in Xinjiang that use forced labour of Uyghurs and other ethnic Muslim minorities.
Early January 2021	Documents discovered by the Tech Transparency Project show that Lens Technology, Apple's long-time supplier, is using forced Uyghur labour transferred from Xinjiang. While Apple says that Lens Technology has not received any transfers of forced Uyghur labour from Xinjiang, Lens Technology refuses to comment on the issue.

19 January 2021   On the last full day of the Trump administration, the US Department of State declares the Chinese Government is committing genocide and crimes against humanity by repressing Uyghurs and other Muslim ethnic minorities in Xinjiang. While Anthony J. Blinken—the nominee as incoming Secretary of State—agrees with the declaration at a Senate confirmation hearing, the Chinese Embassy in the United States dismisses the genocide claims as a 'lie'.

Late January 2021   Twitter locks the account of China's Embassy in the United States over a tweet posted earlier in the month saying that Uyghur women were no longer 'baby-making machines' based on a study quoted in Chinese state-owned newspaper *China Daily*. Twitter explains that the embassy's tweet violated the firm's policy against 'dehumanisation' and therefore has been removed from the platform.

22 February 2021   The Canadian Parliament passes a non-binding motion that declares China's treatment of Uyghurs in Xinjiang 'genocide'.

25 February 2021   The Dutch Parliament passes a non-binding motion that declares China's treatment of Uyghurs in Xinjiang 'genocide'. This is the first such declaration made by a European legislature.

Late March 2021   The European Union places sanctions on Chinese officials over human rights violations in Xinjiang. In response, China blacklists 10 European individuals (including politicians and scholars) and four entities.

Late March 2021   H&M and other foreign companies experience a backlash from Chinese consumers for expressing concern about forced labour in Xinjiang and banning cotton imports from the region. The backlash, seeded and promoted by state media and the Communist Youth League, creates new business opportunities for Chinese domestic brands, such as Li Ning and Anta, whose share prices increase.

22 April 2021   The British Parliament passes a non-binding motion declaring China's treatment of Uyghurs in Xinjiang 'genocide'.

12 and 13 May 2021   During a virtual meeting held by the United Nations, Western countries led by the United States, the United Kingdom, and Germany, as well as human rights groups, accuse China of massive human rights abuses against Uyghurs in Xinjiang and demand unimpeded access to Xinjiang for UN experts.

Mid-May 2021   A new report by scholars at Sheffield Hallam University, entitled 'In Broad Daylight: Uyghur Forced Labor and Global Solar Supply Chains', shows the production in Xinjiang of key components needed for solar panels involves exploitation of Uyghurs and other peoples.

20 May 2021	The Lithuanian Parliament declares China's treatment of Uyghurs in Xinjiang 'genocide' and votes to call for a UN investigation of the human rights situation in the region and to demand the European Commission review its relations with China.
4 June 2021	A series of hearings starts in London to collect evidence from about 30 witnesses on China's treatment of Uyghurs and other peoples in Xinjiang. The four-day Uyghur Tribunal is conducted by an independent eight-member panel, chaired by prominent British barrister Sir Geoffrey Nice, and comprises academics, lawyers, and a former British diplomat. The publicly available hearings offer the most comprehensive English-language testimonies of a wide range of former detainees and camp workers to date.
21 July 2021	The *Associated Press* reports that some concentrated close education and training centres have been relabelled as detention centres and that some 'trainees' have become formal 'prisoners'. State procurator reports show that more than 500,000 people have been formally prosecuted in the region since 2017.
10 October 2021	A report from the *Associated Press* confirms that state authorities have begun to wind back some aspects of the surveillance systems in urban centres in Xinjiang. Uyghur-language books begin to appear on bookstore shelves but seem to be translations from Chinese rather than texts by Uyghur authors.
Mid-November 2021	A report published by Sheffield Hallam University provides evidence that more than 100 global brands continue to buy cotton sourced in Xinjiang from second-party intermediaries. Canada seizes products made with forced labour in Xinjiang, marking the first instance of a government other than that of the United States seizing Xinjiang-produced goods. Canadian legislators introduce a bill to ban all imports from Xinjiang.
29 November 2021	The Uyghur Tribunal receives 300 pages of classified documents that had been examined and verified as authentic by *The New York Times*. These previously unpublished documents include classified speeches by Xi Jinping and other central party leaders concerning the Xinjiang issue as well as other internal government documents marked 'top secret'. These documents are the clearest evidence to date of the goals of the mass internment campaign.

Author biographies

Zenab Ahmed is a writer, activist, and graduate student currently finishing her doctoral studies at SOAS, University of London. She specialises in bodily politics, economics of underdevelopment, and state and anti-state violence in Northwest Pakistan. She has been published in *The Guardian*, *Verso Blog*, *The New Arab*, and *Souciant*, where she was an associate editor. She also works at Reprocare Healthline, an emotional support service for self-managed abortion.

Stefan Brehm is a Researcher at the Centre for East and South-East Asian Studies, Lund University, and co-founder of Globalworks Lund AB, a start-up specialising in big-data analytics for social and environmental governance. Stefan is an economist by training and has studied modern Chinese in Germany and Taiwan.

David Brophy is a Senior Lecturer in Modern Chinese History at the University of Sydney. He studies the social and political history of the Xinjiang Uyghur Autonomous Region. His first book was *Uyghur Nation* (Harvard University Press, 2016), on the politics of Uyghur nationalism between China and the Soviet Union. His most recent book is *China Panic: Australia's Alternative to Paranoia and Pandering* (Black Inc., 2021), a critique of Australia's hawkish policy turn towards the People's Republic of China.

Darren Byler is an Assistant Professor of International Studies at Simon Fraser University in Vancouver, British Columbia. He is the author of an ethnography titled *Terror Capitalism: Uyghur Dispossession and Masculinity in a Chinese City* (Duke University Press, 2022) and a narrative-driven book titled *In the Camps: China's High-Tech Penal Colony* (Columbia Global Reports, 2021). His current research interests are focused on infrastructure development and global China in the context of Xinjiang and Malaysia.

Tom Cliff is a Senior Lecturer in Anthropology and Chinese Political Economy in the School of Culture, History and Language at The Australian National University. Tom is currently investigating non-state welfare and public goods provision in rural China, research that is centrally concerned with charity 'model' innovation and dissemination, industrial organisation, and popular mobilisation. In 2018, Tom's first book, *Oil and Water: Being Han in Xinjiang* (Chicago University Press, 2016), won the Association for Asian Studies' prestigious E. Gene Smith Prize for Best Book on Inner Asia.

Ivan Franceschini is a Postdoctoral Fellow at The Australian National University. His research mainly focuses on labour activism in China and on the social impacts of Chinese engagements in Cambodia. He is the founder and co-editor of the *Made in China Journal* and *The People's Map of Global China*. His latest books are the co-edited volumes *Afterlives of Chinese Communism: Political Concepts from Mao to Xi* (ANU Press and Verso Books, 2019), *Xinjiang Year Zero* (ANU Press, 2022), and *Proletarian China: A Century of Chinese Labour* (Verso Books, 2022). With Tommaso Facchin, he co-directed the documentaries *Dreamwork China* (2011) and *Boramey: Ghosts in the Factory* (2021).

Timothy A. Grose is an Associate Professor of China Studies at Rose-Hulman Institute of Technology in Indiana. His research on expressions of Uyghur ethno-national identities and public performances of Islamic piety has been published in *The China Journal*, *Journal of Contemporary China*, *China File*, and *Dissent*. Timothy's commentary on ethnic policy in Xinjiang has appeared in *Al Jazeera*, *The Atlantic*, *CNN*, *The Diplomat*, *The Economist*, *Foreign Policy*, *The Guardian*, and *Vox*, among others. His book on boarding schools for Uyghur students, *Negotiating Inseparability*, was published by Hong Kong University Press in 2019.

Nitasha Kaul is a novelist, economist, poet, and a Reader (Associate Professor) in Politics and International Relations at the Centre for the Study of Democracy, University of Westminster, UK. Her books include *Imagining Economics Otherwise* (Routledge, 2007); *Future Tense* (HarperCollins, 2020); *Residue* (Rainlight, 2014, shortlisted for the Man Asian Literary Prize); and *Can You Hear Kashmiri Women Speak?* (Kali for Women Press, 2020). Links to all work can be found at www.nitashakaul.com.

Séagh Kehoe is a Lecturer in Chinese Studies at the School of Humanities, University of Westminster. Their research interests include ethnicity, gender, media, and the internet in contemporary China. They tweet at @seaghkehoe.

Nicholas Loubere is an Associate Professor in the Study of Modern China at the Centre for East and South-East Asian Studies, Lund University. His research examines socioeconomic development in rural China, with a particular focus on microcredit and migration. He co-edits the *Made in China Journal*.

Andrea Pitzer is the author of *One Long Night: A Global History of Concentration Camps* (2017) and . She has also written for the *New York Review of Books*, *The Washington Post*, *The Daily Beast*, *GQ*, and *Lapham's Quarterly*, among other publications.

Gerald Roche is an anthropologist and Senior Research Fellow in the Department of Politics, Media, and Philosophy at La Trobe University. His research on Tibetan-language politics has led him to an interest in contemporary colonialism, resistance by Indigenous and minority peoples, and transnational social movements.

Guldana Salimjan is the Ruth Wynn Woodward Junior Chair at the Gender, Sexuality, and Women's Studies Department at Simon Fraser University in Burnaby, Canada (2019–22). Her research focuses on the intersectionality of gender, colonialism, the politics of memory, and environmental justice. Her works have appeared in *Central Asian Survey*, *Asian Ethnicity*, *Human Ecology*, *Lausan*, and the *Made in China Journal*. She is also the co-director of the Xinjiang Documentation Project, and the founder of the media art project Camp Album.

Rian Thum is a Senior Lecturer at the University of Manchester. His research and teaching are generally concerned with the interpenetration of China and the Muslim World. Since 1999, he has regularly conducted field research in Xinjiang and other areas of China with large Muslim populations, both Uyghur and Chinese-speaking. His book, *The Sacred Routes of Uyghur History* (Harvard University Press, 2014) was awarded the Fairbank Prize for East Asian History (American Historical Association) and the Hsu Prize for East Asian Anthropology (American Anthropological Association). Thum's current book project, *Islamic China*, is a reexamination of Chinese Islam that takes full account of the numerous Persian and Arabic sources that Chinese-speaking Muslims have used and written.

Sam Tynen holds a PhD in Human Geography from the University of Colorado, Boulder. They lived in China for five years between 2009 and 2017 and in Xinjiang for two of those years. Their research focuses on state-building, nationalism, and ethnic conflict in Asia. Their goal is to better understand how we can create more inclusive, equitable, and sustainable communities. To do so, they look at China in a global context and the effects of authoritarian state-building. Their publications have appeared in *Territory, Politics, and Governance*, *Eurasian Geography and Economics*, *Space and Culture*, *Geographical Review*, and *Geopolitics*, among others.

Ye Hui (pseudonym) studies decolonisation, and, through poetry and community organising, is committed to practicing non-nationalist modes of history, politics, and care.

Bibliography

Xinjiang year zero: An introduction (DARREN BYLER, IVAN FRANCESCHINI, AND NICHOLAS LOUBERE)

Byler, Darren. 2021a. 'Chinese Infrastructures of Population Management on the New Silk Road.' In *Essays on the Rise of China and Its Implications*, edited by Abraham M. Denmark and Lucas Myers, 7–34. Washington, DC: Wilson Center for International Scholars.

Byler, Darren. 2021b. *In the Camps: China's Hi-Tech Penal Colony*. New York, NY: Columbia Global Reports.

Byler, Darren. 2022. *Terror Capitalism: Uyghur Dispossession and Masculinity in a Chinese City*. Durham, NC: Duke University Press. doi.org/10.2307/j.ctv21zp29g.

Cliff, Tom. 2016. *Oil and Water: Being Han in Xinjiang*. Chicago, IL: University of Chicago Press. doi.org/10.7208/chicago/9780226360270.001.0001.

Franceschini, Ivan and Nicholas Loubere. 2020. 'What about Whataboutism? Viral Loads and Hyperactive Immune Responses in the China Debate.' *Made in China Journal* 5(2): 18–30. doi.org/10.22459/MIC.05.02.2020.01.

Franceschini, Ivan and Nicholas Loubere. (Forthcoming). *Global China as Method*. Cambridge, UK: Cambridge University Press.

Li, Xiaoxia 李晓霞. 2021. '新疆地区人口变动情况分析报告 [Analysis Report on Population Changes in Xinjiang].' Ürümqi: Xinjiang Development Research Centre. Available from: archive.md/O1vOg.

Millward, James. 2021. *Eurasian Crossroads: A History of Xinjiang*. Rev. edn. London: Hurst Publishers.

Pitzer, Andrea. 2017. *One Long Night: A Global History of Concentration Camps*. New York, NY: Little, Brown & Company.

Xinjiang Victims Database. 2021. 'Village/Township Analytics.' Xinjiang Victims Database. Available from: shahit.biz/eng/#village.

1. Nation-building as epistemic violence (YE HUI)

Anderson, Benedict. 2006. *Imagined Communities: Reflections on the Origin and Spread of Nationalism*. London: Verso Books.

Asad, Talal. 2003. *Formations of the Secular: Christianity, Islam, Modernity*. Redwood City, CA: Stanford University Press.

Asad, Talal. 2006. 'Trying to Understand French Secularism.' In *Political Theologies: Public Religions in a Post-Secular World*, edited by Hent de Vries and Lawrence Eugene Sullivan, 494–526. New York, NY: Fordham University Press. doi.org/10.5422/fso/9780823226443.003.0026.

Brophy, David. 2019. 'Good and Bad Muslims in Xinjiang.' *Made in China Journal* 4(2): 44–53. doi.org/10.22459/MIC.04.02.2019.05.

Byler, Darren. 2019. 'Ghost World.' *Logic*, No. 7, 1 May. Available from: logicmag.io/china/ghost-world/.

Byler, Darren. 2021. *Terror Capitalism: Uyghur Dispossession and Masculinity in a Chinese City*. Durham, NC: Duke University Press.

Chakrabarty, Dipesh. 2002. *Habitations of Modernity: Essays in the Wake of Subaltern Studies*. Chicago, IL: University of Chicago Press.

Chinese Communist Party United Front Work Department (CCP UFWD). 1991. 民族问题文献汇编 [*The Minzu Question Anthology*]. Beijing: Zhonggong Zhongyang Dangxiao Chubanshe.

Chinese Soviet Republic. 1931. '中华苏维埃共和国宪法大纲 [Outline of the Constitution of the Chinese Soviet Republic].' Adopted at the First National Congress of the Chinese Soviet, 7 November 1931. In *Selected*

Works of the Central Committee of the Communist Party of China. Volume Seven. Available from: www.marxists.org/chinese/reference-books/ccp-1921-1949/07/066.htm.

Duara, Prasenjit. 1995. *Rescuing History from the Nation: Questioning Narratives of Modern China.* Chicago, IL: University of Chicago Press. doi.org/10.7208/chicago/9780226167237.001.0001.

Fabian, Johannes. 2014. *Time and the Other: How Anthropology Makes its Object.* New York, NY: Columbia University Press. doi.org/10.7312/fabi16926.

Hua, Chunying. 2021. 'Foreign Ministry Spokesperson Hua Chunying's Regular Press Conference on March 26, 2021.' Press release, 27 March. Beijing: Ministry of Foreign Affairs of the People's Republic of China. Available from: www.fmprc.gov.cn/mfa_eng/xwfw_665399/s2510_665401/t1864659.shtml.

Leibold, James. 2006. 'Competing Narratives of Racial Unity in Republican China.' *Modern China* 32(2): 181–220. doi.org/10.1177/0097700405285275.

Liu, Andrew. 2020. 'We Need to Think about Xinjiang in Internationalist Terms.' *The Nation*, 28 October. Available from: thenation.com/article/world/xinjiang-uigher-camps/.

Liu, Xiaoyuan 刘晓原. 2018. 边缘地带的革命–中共民族政策的崛起 [*Frontier Passages: Ethnopolitics and the Rise of Chinese Communism, 1921–1945*]. Translated by Wan Zhiyun. Hong Kong: Chinese University of Hong Kong Press.

Mamdani, Mahmood. 2020. *Neither Settler nor Native.* Boston, MA: Harvard University Press. doi.org/10.4159/9780674249998.

Mao, Zedong 毛泽东. 1938. '论新阶段 [On the New Phase].' October. *In Long Live Mao Zedong Thought.* Available from: www.marxists.org/chinese/maozedong/1968/2-120.htm.

Massad, Joseph. 2018. 'Against Self-Determination.' *Humanity Journal* 9(2): 161–91. Available from: doi.org/10.1353/hum.2018.0010.

'Memorandum of Conversation between Stalin and CCP Delegation.' 27 June 1949. History and Public Policy Program Digital Archive. APRF: F. 45, Op. 1, D. 329, Ll. 1-7. Reprinted in Andrei Ledovskii, Raisa Mirovi-tskaia, and Vladimir Miasnikov, *Sovetsko–Kitaiskie Otnosheniia* [*Soviet–Chinese Relations*]. *Volume 5, Book 2: 1946 – February 1950*, 148–51. Translated by Sergey Radchenko. Moscow: Pamiatniki Istoricheskoi Mysli, 2005. Available from: digitalarchive.wilsoncenter.org/document/113380.

Millward, James. 1998. *Beyond the Pass: Economy, Ethnicity, and Empire in Qing Central Asia, 1759–1864.* Redwood City, CA: Stanford University Press. doi.org/10.1515/9780804797924.

Millward, James. 2007. *Eurasia Crossroads: A History of Xinjiang.* New York, NY: Columbia University Press.

Mosca, Matthew. 2013. *From Frontier Policy to Foreign Policy: The Question of India and the Transformation of Geopolitics in Qing China.* Redwood City, CA: Stanford University Press. doi.org/10.11126/stan-ford/9780804782241.001.0001.

Mullaney, Thomas. 2010. *Coming to Terms with the Nation: Ethnic Classification in Modern China.* Oakland, CA: University of California Press.

Schluessel, Eric. 2020. *Land of Strangers: The Civilizing Project in Qing Central Asia.* New York, NY: Columbia University Press. doi.org/10.7312/schl19754.

Scott, David. 1999. *Refashioning Futures: Criticism after Postcoloniality.* Princeton, NJ: Princeton University Press. doi.org/10.1515/9781400823062.

Stewart, Phil and Ben Blanchard. 2018. 'Xi Tells Mattis China Won't Give Up "Even One Inch" of Territory.' *Reuters*, 27 June. Available from: www.reuters.com/article/us-china-usa-defence/xi-tells-mattis-chi-na-wont-give-up-even-one-inch-of-territory-idUSKBN1JN03T.

Sun, Yat-sen. 2006 [1924]. '三民主义之民族主义—讲 [The Three People's Principles: Nationalism—Lecture 1].' 27 January 1924. In *Selected Works of Sun Wen. Volume 1*, edited by Huang Yan, 11. Guangzhou: Guangdong People's Publishing House. Available from: www.sunyat-sen.org/index.php?m=content&c=index&a=show&catid=46&id=6638.

2. Revolution and state formation as oasis storytelling in Xinjiang (ZENAB AHMED)

Agence France-Presse (AFP). 2019. 'More than 20 Ambassadors Condemn China's Treatment of Uighurs in Xinjiang.' *The Guardian*, 10 July. Available from: www.theguardian.com/world/2019/jul/11/more-than-20-ambassadors-condemn-chinas-treatment-of-uighurs-in-xinjiang.

Brophy, David. 2019. 'Good and Bad Muslims in Xinjiang.' *Made in China Journal* 4(2): 44–53. doi.org/10.22459/MIC.04.02.2019.05.

Calabrese, John. 2019. 'China–Iraq Relations: Poised for a "Quantum Leap"?' *All About China*, 8 October. Washington, DC: Middle East Institute. Available from: www.mei.edu/publications/china-iraq-relations-poised-quantum-leap.

Jacobs, Justin M. 2016. *Xinjiang and the Modern Chinese State*. Seattle, WA: University of Washington Press.

Kerimkhanov, Abdul. 2019. 'China Remains Uzbekistan's Largest Trading Partner.' *AzerNews*, [Baku], 25 April. Available from: www.azernews.az/region/149606.html.

Liu, Zhen. 2019. 'China, Iran to Forge Closer Ties Due to Common Threat from the United States, Analysts Say.' *South China Morning Post*, [Hong Kong], 23 May. Available from: www.scmp.com/news/china/diplomacy/article/3011573/china-iran-forge-closer-ties-due-common-threat-united-states.

Pitzer, Andrea. 2017. *One Long Night: A Global History of Concentration Camps*. London: Little, Brown & Company.

Reuters. 2019. 'Pompeo Says Orwell's "1984" Coming to Life in China's Xinjiang Region.' *Reuters*, 11 October. Available from: www.reuters.com/article/us-usa-china-muslims-pompeo/pompeo-says-orwells-1984-coming-to-life-in-chinas-xinjiang-region-idUSKBN1WQ27U.

Shams, Shamil. 2019. 'Has China–Pakistan Economic Corridor Lived Up to the Hype?' *Deutsche Welle*, 30 September. Available from: www.dw.com/en/has-china-pakistan-economic-corridor-lived-up-to-the-hype/a-50644617.

South China Morning Post. 2020. 'Mike Pompeo Demands China End "Uygur Sterilisations in Xinjiang".' *South China Morning Post*, [Hong Kong], 30 June. Available from: www.scmp.com/news/china/article/3091112/mike-pompeo-demands-china-end-reported-uygur-sterilisations-xinjiang.

Thum, Rian. 2012. 'Beyond Resistance and Nationalism: Local History and the Case of Afaq Khoja.' *Central Asian Survey* 31(3): 293–310. doi.org/10.1080/02634937.2012.722366.

Thum, Rian. 2014. *The Sacred Routes of Uyghur History*. Cambridge, MA: Harvard University Press. doi.org/10.4159/harvard.9780674736238.

US State Department. 2020. *Xinjiang Supply Chain Business Advisory*. 1 July. Washington, DC: US Department of State. Available from: www.state.gov/wp-content/uploads/2020/07/Xinjiang-Supply-Chain-Business-Advisory_FINAL_For-508-508.pdf.

Zhang Dong 张栋. 2017. '数百亿的新疆安防市场，集成巨头告诉你如何才能从中分杯羹 [Xinjiang's Tens-of-Billion-Scale Security Market, the Integration Giant Tells You How to Get Your Share].' 雷锋网 [*Lei Feng Net*], 31 August. Available from: web.archive.org/web/20190406231923/https://www.leiphone.com/news/201708/LcdGuMZ5n7k6sepy.html.

3. Blood lineage (GULDANA SALIMJAN)

Biebuyck, Daniel P. 1966. 'On the Concept of Tribe.' *Civilisations* 16(4): 500–15.

Bulag, Uradyn E. 2019. 'Nationality.' In *Afterlives of Chinese Communism: Political Concepts from Mao to Xi*, edited by Christian Sorace, Ivan Franceschini, and Nicholas Loubere, 149–54. Canberra: ANU Press and Verso Books. doi.org/10.22459/ACC.2019.24.

Bulag, Uradyn E. 2000. 'From Inequality to Difference: Colonial Contradictions of Class and Ethnicity in "Socialist" China.' *Cultural Studies* 14(3–4): 531–61. doi.org/10.1080/09502380050130437.

Byler, Darren. 2021. *Terror Capitalism: Uyghur Dispossession and Masculinity in a Chinese City*. Durham, NC: Duke University Press.

Chin, Josh and Clément Bürge. 2017. 'Twelve Days in Xinjiang: How China's Surveillance State Overwhelms Daily Life.' *The Wall Street Journal*, 9 December. Available from: www.wsj.com/articles/twelve-days-in-xinjiang-how-chinas-surveillance-state-overwhelms-daily-life-1513700355.

Dikötter, Frank. 2015. *The Discourse of Race in Modern China*. New York: Oxford University Press.

Dutton, Michael. 2004. 'Mango Mao: Infections of the Sacred.' *Public Culture* 16(2): 161–87. doi.org/10.1215/08992363-16-2-161.

Fried, Morton. 1966. 'On the Concepts of "Tribe" and "Tribal Society".' *Transactions of the New York Academy of Sciences* 28: 527–40. doi.org/10.1111/j.2164-0947.1966.tb02369.x.

Hoshur, Shohret. 2018. 'Chinese Authorities Jail Four Wealthiest Uyghurs in Xinjiang's Kashgar in New Purge.' [Translated by Alim Seytoff and Mamatjan Juma.] *Radio Free Asia Uyghur Service*, [Washington, DC], 5 January. Available from: www.rfa.org/english/news/uyghur/wealthiest-01052018144327.html.

Human Rights Watch (HRW). 2018. 'China: Big Data Fuels Crackdown in Minority Region.' *News*, 26 February. New York: Human Rights Watch. Available from: www.hrw.org/news/2018/02/26/china-big-data-fuels-crackdown-minority-region.

Mozur, Paul. 2019. 'One Month, 500,000 Face Scans: How China is Using A.I. to Profile a Minority.' *The New York Times*, 14 April. Available from: www.nytimes.com/2019/04/14/technology/china-surveillance-artificial-intelligence-racial-profiling.html.

Ramzy, Austin and Chris Buckley. 2019. '"Absolutely No Mercy": Leaked Files Expose How China Organized Mass Detentions of Muslims.' *The New York Times*, 16 November. Available from: www.nytimes.com/interactive/2019/11/16/world/asia/china-xinjiang-documents.html.

Roberts, Sean R. 2020. *The War on the Uyghurs: China's Internal Campaign against a Muslim Minority*. Princeton, NJ: Princeton University Press. doi.org/10.1515/9780691202211.

Smith Finley, Joanne. 2013. *The Art of Symbolic Resistance: Uyghur Identities and Uyghur–Han Relations in Contemporary Xinjiang*. Leiden: Brill. doi.org/10.1163/9789004256781.

Wee, Sui-Lee and Paul Mozur. 2019. 'China Uses DNA to Map Faces, with Help from the West.' *The New York Times,* 10 December. Available from: www.nytimes.com/2019/12/03/business/china-dna-uighurs-xinjiang.html.

Woeser, Tsering, Robert Barnett, and Susan T Chen. 2020. *Forbidden Memory*. Lincoln, NE: Potomac Books. doi.org/10.2307/j.ctvzxxbdk.

Wong, Edward. 2014. 'To Temper Unrest in Western China, Officials Offer Money for Intermarriage.' *The New York Times*, 2 September. Available from: www.nytimes.com/2014/09/03/world/asia/to-temper-unrest-china-pushes-interethnic-marriage-between-han-and-minorities.html.

4. Good and bad Muslims in Xinjiang (DAVID BROPHY)

Auslin, Michael R. 2018. 'The Long Encounter: China and Islam's Irreconcilable Tensions.' *The Caravan*, No. 1819, 9 October. Stanford, CA: Hoover Institution. Available from: www.hoover.org/research/long-encounter-china-and-islams-irreconcilable-tensions.

Avni, Benny. 2018. 'China Is Inventing a Whole New Way to Oppress a People.' *New York Post*, 17 September. Available from: nypost.com/2018/09/17/china-is-inventing-a-whole-new-way-to-oppress-a-people.

Brophy, David. 2013. 'Correcting Transgressions in the House of Islam: Yang Zengxin's Buguozhai wendu on Xinjiang's Muslims.' In *Islam, Society and States across the Qazaq Steppe (15th – Early 20th Centuries)*, edited by Niccolò Pianciola and Paolo Sartori, 267–96. Vienna: Austrian Academy of Sciences Press. doi.org/10.2307/j.ctt1vw0r3p.13.

Chaguan. 2019. 'History Shows the Folly of China's Paranoia about Islam.' *The Economist*, 19 January. Available from: www.economist.com/china/2019/01/19/history-shows-the-folly-of-chinas-paranoia-about-islam.

China Central Television (CCTV). 2019. '新疆的反恐去极端化斗争 [China's Counter-Terrorism and De-radicalisation Struggle].' *China Central Television*, 19 March. Available from: www.youtube.com/watch?v=3xyMloesl58.

Doyon, Jérôme. 2019. '"Counter-extremism" in Xinjiang: Understanding China's Community-Focused Counter-Terrorism Tactics.' *War on the Rocks*, 14 January. Available from: warontherocks.com/2019/01/counter-extremism-in-xinjiang-understanding-chinas-community-focused-counter-terrorism-tactics.

Fletcher, Joseph. 1978. 'The Heyday of the Ch'ing Order in Mongolia, Sinkiang, and Tibet.' In *The Cambridge History of China. Volume 10: Late Ch'ing 1800–1911, Part 1*, edited by John K. Fairbank, 351–408. Cambridge, UK: Cambridge University Press. doi.org/10.1017/CHOL9780521214476.009.

Goldberg, Jeffrey. 2016. 'What Obama Actually Thinks about Radical Islam.' *The Atlantic*, 15 June. www.theatlantic.com/international/archive/2016/06/obama-radical-islam/487079.

Halevi, Leor. 2019. 'Is China a House of Islam? Chinese Questions, Arabic Answers, and the Translation of Salafism from Cairo to Canton, 1930–1932.' *Die Welt des Islams* [*International Journal for the Study of Modern Islam*] 59: 33–69. doi.org/10.1163/15700607-00591P03.

Hunerven, Adam. 2019. 'Spirit Breaking: Capitalism and Terror in Northwest China.' *Chuang* 2: 485–525.

Hussain, Javed. 2018. 'Religious Affairs Minister Discusses Treatment of Xinjiang Muslims with Chinese Envoy.' *Dawn*, [Karachi], 19 September. Available from: www.dawn.com/news/1433886.

Israeli, Raphael. 1977. 'Muslims in China: The Incompatibility between Islam and the Chinese Order.' *T'oung Pao* 63(4–5): 296–323. doi.org/10.1163/156853277X00105.

Jamshidi, Maryam. 2019. 'The War on Terror's Reeducation Camps.' *Jacobin*, 12 January. Available from: jacobinmag.com/2019/01/uyghur-ree-ducation-camps-china-war-on-terror.

Johnson, Ian. 2018. 'The Uighurs and China's Long History of Trouble with Islam.' *The New York Review of Books*, 23 November. Available from: www.nybooks.com/daily/2018/11/23/the-uighurs-and-chinas-long-history-of-trouble-with-islam.

Karp, Paul. 2018. 'MPs Widely Condemn Fraser Anning's "Final Solution" Speech.' *The Guardian*, 15 August. Available from: www.theguardian.com/australia-news/2018/aug/15/mps-widely-condemn-fraser-annings-final-solution-speech.

Kundnani, Arun. 2014. *The Muslims are Coming! Islamophobia, Extremism, and the Domestic War on Terror*. London: Verso.

Leibold, James. 2016. 'Creeping Islamophobia: China's Hui Muslims in the Firing Line.' *China Brief* 16(10): 12–15. Available from: jamestown.org/program/creeping-islamophobia-chinas-hui-muslims-in-the-firing-line.

Liu, Menggang. 2018. '有效谋划和推进新疆"去极端化"研究 [A Study on Effectively Planning and Implementing "Deradicalisation" in Xinjiang].' 新西部 [*The New Western Region*], March: 31–32.

Millward, James. 2019. '"Reeducating" Xinjiang's Muslims.' *The New York Review of Books*, 7 February. Available from: www.nybooks.com/articles/2019/02/07/reeducating-xinjiangs-muslims.

National People's Congress Ethnic Affairs Committee (ed.). 1956. 新疆维吾尔自治区若干调查材料汇编 [*A Compilation of Certain Survey Materials on the Xinjiang Uyghur Autonomous Region*]. Beijing: National People's Congress.

Remeikis, Amy. 2017. 'Pauline Hanson Says Islam is a Disease Australia Needs to "Vaccinate".' *Sydney Morning Herald*, 24 March. www.smh.com.au/politics/federal/pauline-hanson-says-islam-is-a-disease-australia-needs-to-vaccinate-20170324-gv5w7z.html.

Ross, Alice. 2016. 'Academics Criticize Anti-Radicalisation Strategy in Open Letter.' *The Guardian*, 29 September. Available from: www.theguardian.com/uk-news/2016/sep/29/academics-criticise-prevent-anti-radicalisation-strategy-open-letter.

Shakman Hurd, Elizabeth. 2015. *Beyond Religious Freedom: The New Global Politics of Religion*. Princeton, NJ: Princeton University Press. doi.org/10.23943/princeton/9780691166094.001.0001.

Shih, Gerry. 2017. 'Uighurs Fighting in Syria Take Aim at China.' *Associated Press*, 23 December. apnews.com/79d6a427b26f4ee-ab226571956dd256e.

State Council Information Office. 2019. *The Fight Against Terrorism and Extremism and Human Rights Protection in Xinjiang*. White Paper. Beijing: State Council of the People's Republic of China. Available from: english.gov.cn/archive/white_paper/2019/03/18/content_281476567813306.htm.

Wang, Hui. 2017. '两洋之间的新大同想象 [Imagining a New Great Unity between the Two Oceans].' 爱思想 [*Aisixiang*], 12 November. Available from: www.aisixiang.com/data/106828.html.

Wang, Xin. 2018. '反极端主义视角下的中外去极端化比较研究 [A Comparative Study of Chinese and Foreign Deradicalisation from the Point of View of Anti-Extremism].' 中国人民公安大学学报 [*Journal of the People's Public Security University of China*] 3: 47–59.

Zhang, Lijuan. 2017. '关于新疆伊斯兰教中国化的若干思考 [Some Thoughts on the Sinicisation of Islam in Xinjiang].' 中国宗教 [*China's Religions*] 6: 46–47.

5. Imprisoning the open air: Preventative policing as community detention in northwestern China (DARREN BYLER)

Buckley, Chris. 2018. 'China Is Detaining Muslims in Vast Numbers. The Goal: "Transformation".' *The New York Times*, 8 September. Available from: www.nytimes.com/2018/09/08/world/asia/china-uighur-muslim-deten-tion-camp.html.

Byler, Darren. 2018. 'Violent Paternalism: On the Banality of Uyghur Unfreedom.' *Asia-Pacific Journal: Japan Focus* 16(24/4): 1–15. Available from: apjjf.org/2018/24/Byler.html.

Doyon, Jérôme. 2019. '"Counter-Extremism" in Xinjiang: Understanding China's Community-Focused Counter-Terrorism Tactics.' *War on the Rocks*, 14 January. Available from: warontherocks.com/2019/01/counter-extremism-in-xinjiang-understanding-chinas-community-focused-counter-terrorism-tactics.

Enders, David. 2008. 'Camp Bucca: Iraq's Guantánamo Bay.' *The Nation*, 8 October. Available from: www.thenation.com/article/archive/camp-buc-ca-iraqs-guantaacutenamo-bay.

Greer, Tanner. 2018. 'Forty-Eight Ways to Be Sent to a Chinese Concentration Camp.' *Foreign Policy*, 13 September. Available from: foreignpolicy.com/2018/09/13/48-ways-to-get-sent-to-a-chinese-concentration-camp.

Gregory, Derek. 2008. 'The Rush to the Intimate: Counterinsurgency and the Cultural Turn.' *Radical Philosophy* (150)(July–August). Available from: www.radicalphilosophy.com/article/the-rush-to-the-intimate.

Grose, Timothy. 2019. "'Once Their Mental State Is Healthy, They Will Be Able to Live Happily in Society": How China's Government Conflates Uighur Identity with Mental Illness.' *China File*, 2 August. Available from: www.chinafile.com/reporting-opinion/viewpoint/once-their-mental-state-healthy-they-will-be-able-live-happily-society.

Harcourt, Bernard E. 2018. *The Counterrevolution: How Our Government Went to War against Its Own Citizens*. New York, NY: Basic Books.

Hunerven, Adam. 2019. 'Spirit Breaking: Capitalism and Terror in Northwest China.' *Chuang* 2: 485–525.

Iraq Body Count (IBC). 2019. 'Documented Civilian Deaths from Violence.' *IBC Database*. [Online.] Available from: www.iraqbodycount.org/database.

ITV. 2019. 'Undercover: Inside the Chinese Digital Gulag.' *Financial Times*, 3 July. Available from: www.ft.com/content/b3ecae28-a304-11e9-974c-a-d1c6ab5efd1.

Ji, Yantao 姬艳涛 and Yin Wei 伟尹. 2016. '反恐社区警务的理论与实践 [The Theory and Practice of Antiterrorism Community Policing].' 中国人民公安大学学报: 社会科学版 [*Journal of the Chinese People's Public Security University: Social Science Edition*] (1): 144–51.

Kelly, John D., Beatrice Jauregui, Sean T. Mitchell, and Jeremy Walton (eds). 2010. *Anthropology and Global Counterinsurgency*. Chicago, IL: University of Chicago Press. doi.org/10.7208/chicago/9780226429953.001.0001.

Kundnani, Arun and Ben Hayes. 2018. *The globalisation of countering violent extremism policies: Undermining human rights, instrumentalising civil society*. Report. Amsterdam: Transnational Institute. Available from: www.tni.org/files/publication-downloads/the_globalisation_of_countering_violent_extremism_policies.pdf.

Liu, Xin. 2019. 'Refuting 22 Western Nations, 37 Governments Laud China's Human Rights Achievements.' *Global Times*, [Beijing], 13 July. Available from: www.globaltimes.cn/content/1157728.shtml.

Lowe, David. 2017. 警务反恐: 反恐侦查专题研究 [*Policing Terrorism: Research Studies into Police Counterterrorism Investigations*]. Translated by Cao Xuefei 曹雪飞 and Li Yongtao 李永涛. Beijing: Zhongguo Renmin Gong'an Daxue Chubanshe.

Lu, Peng 芦鹏 and Cao Xuefei 雪飞曹. 2014. '浅析以色列反恐战略及对中国新疆反恐启示 [An Analysis of Israel's Antiterrorism Strategy and How it Inspires China's Xinjiang Antiterrorism].' 中国刑警学院学报 [*Journal of the National Police University of China*] (1): 19–21.

Mahmut, Dilmurat. 2019. 'Controlling Religious Knowledge and Education for Countering Religious Extremism: Case Study of the Uyghur Muslims in China.' *FIRE: Forum for International Research in Education* 5(1): 22–43. doi.org/10.32865/fire201951142.

Wang, Ding 王定 and Shan Dan 丹山. 2016. '反恐研究与新疆模式 [Studies on Antiterrorism and the Xinjiang Mode].' 情报杂志 [*Journal of Intelligence*] 35(11): 20–26.

Wolfe, Patrick. 2006. 'Settler Colonialism and the Elimination of the Native.' *Journal of Genocide Research* 8(4): 387–409. doi.org/10.1080/14623520601056240.

Yang, Qingchuan 杨晴川. 2007. '美"儒将"彼得雷乌斯能拯救伊拉克战局吗 [Can the US "Sage" Petraeus Save the Iraq War]?' 瞭望新闻周刊 [*Outlook Weekly*], 18 February. Available from: news.sohu.com/20070218/n248296000.shtml.

Zhang, Wande 张万得. 2016. '乌鲁木齐市大街小巷将建949个便民警务站 [949 People's Convenience Police Stations Have Been Built in the Streets of Urumqi].' 亚心网 [*Yaxin Net*], 27 October. Available from: kknews.cc/society/2a4mrng.html.

Zucchino, David. 2019. 'U.S. and Afghan Forces Killed More Civilians than Taliban Did, Report Finds.' *The New York Times*, 24 April. Available from: www.nytimes.com/2019/04/24/world/asia/afghanistan-civilian-casualties-united-nations.html.

7. Recruiting loyal stabilisers: On the banality of carceral colonialism in Xinjiang (GULDANA SALIMJAN)

[Advertisement No. 1] 2018. '新疆生产建设兵团招2364人! [Xinjiang Bingtuan Is Recruiting 2,364 People!]' 西安高新技术职业学院 [*Xi'an High Tech University Employment Information*], 4 April. Available from: Available from: archive.ph/ZM5EK.

[Advertisement No. 2] 2019. '2019年新疆生产建设兵团面向内地高校毕业生招录公务员公告 [Xinjiang Bingtuan is Recruiting Civil Servants from Inner China Universities in 2019].' 延安大学西安创新学院就业信息网 [*Xi'an Innovation College of Yan'an University Employment Information*], 1 April. Available from: archive.ph/Gmd7b.

[Advertisement No. 3] Anhui Provincial Personnel Examination Network. 2018. '2018年新疆生产建设兵团招录111名公务员公告 [Xinjiang Bingtuan is Recruiting 111 Civil Servants in 2018].' 国家公务员考试网 [*National Public Servant*], 9 November. Available from: archive.ph/SgH6N.

[Advertisement No. 4] 2018. '新疆兵团面向部分内地省（区、市）招录237名公务员 [Xinjiang Bingtuan is Recruiting 237 Civil Servants from Inner China].' 中国新闻网 [*China News*], 12 December. Avaliable from: archive.ph/DOIaz.

[Advertisement No. 5] Dingxi Human Resources and Social Security Bureau. 2018. '2018年新疆和田面向定西市招录乡镇机关公务员简章 [Xinjiang Bingtuan in Hotan is Recruiting County-Level Civil Servants from Dingxi City in 2018].' 国家公务员考试网 [*National Public Servant*], 5 November. Available from: archive.ph/TIOwn.

[Advertisement No. 6] Jilin City Human Resources and Social Security Bureau. 2018. '2018年新疆和田面向吉林省招录人才信息公告 [Xinjiang Hotan is Recruiting Civil Servants from Jilin Province in 2018].' 国家公务员考试网 [*National Public Servant*], 30 October. Available from: archive.ph/pjnVx.

[Advertisement No. 7] Inner Mongolia Personnel Examination Information Network. 2018. '2018年新疆和田面向内蒙古招录乡镇机关公务员简章 [Xinjiang Hotan is Recruiting County-Level Civil Servants from Inner Mongolia in 2018].' 国家公务员考试网 [*National Public Servant*], 5 November. Available from: archive.ph/I7W8I.

[Advertisement No. 8] Bengbu Personnel Network. 2018. '2018年新疆和田面向安徽省招录人才公告 [Xinjiang Hotan is Recruiting Civil Servants from Anhui Province in 2018].' 国家公务员考试网 [*National Public Servant*], 26 October. Available from: archive.ph/KUx5K.

[Advertisement No. 9] Shanxi Personnel Examination Network. 2018. '2018年新疆生产建设兵团面向河北、山西招录公务员48人公告 [Xinjiang Bingtuan is Recruiting 48 Civil Servants from Hebei and Shanxi in 2018].' 国家公务员考试网 [*National Public Servant*], 9 November. Available from: archive.ph/6Orkj.

[Advertisement No. 10] Hubei Personnel Examination Network. 2018. '2018年新疆兵团面向湖北_甘肃招录公务员61人公告 [Xinjiang Bingtuan is Recruiting 61 Civil Servants from Hubei and Gansu in 2018].' 国家公务员考试网 [*National Public Servant*], 9 November. Available from: archive.ph/EbBGv.

[Advertisement No. 11] 2019. '兵团面向内地招录620名公务员 [Xinjiang Bingtuan is Recruiting 620 Civil Servants from Inner China].' 兵团日报 [*Bingtuan Daily*], 26 March. Available from: archive.ph/j8dJw.

[Advertisement No. 12] 2018. '新疆兵团公务员面试-一本正经的胡说八道 [Xinjiang Bingtuan Civil Servant Interview: Speaking Nonsense in a Serious Manner].' 腾讯网 [*Tencent*], 22 September. Available from: v.qq.com/x/page/a0713ul070i.html.

[Advertisement No. 13] 2018. '新疆兵团公务员面试真题答题示范 [Xinjiang Bingtuan Civil Servant Interview: Real Questions and Exemplar Answers].' 腾讯网 [*Tencent*], 14 September. Available from: v.qq.com/x/page/x0702dkzt74.html.

[Advertisement No. 14] Public Examination Information Network. 2018. '2018年新疆生产建设兵团招录公务员公告 [Notice for Xinjiang Bingtuan Civil Servant Recruitment in 2018].' 国家公务员考试网 [*National Public Servant*], 4 April. Available from: archive.ph/5zLzN.

[Advertisement No. 15] 2019. '2019年新疆生产建设兵团面向内地高校毕业生招录监狱人民警察500人公告 [Xinjiang Bingtuan is Recruiting 500 Prison Police from Inner China Colleges in 2019].' 中公警法 [*Police Exam*], 20 May. Available from: archive.ph/bAUT9.

[Advertisement No. 16] 2019. '2019新疆兵团招录狱警简章解读与备考指导 [Xinjiang Bingtuan Police Recruitment Strategy Analysis and Exam Preparation for 2019].' 腾讯网 [*Tencent*], 15 May. Available from: v.qq.com/x/page/f08714f7lzc.html.

[Advertisement No. 17] Sichuan Personnel Examination Network. 2017. '2017年新疆兵团面向四川省高校招录113名监狱人民警察公告 [Xinjiang Bingtuan is Recruiting 113 Prison Police from Colleges in Sichuan Province in 2017].' 国家公务员考试网 [*National Public Servant*], 3 July. Available from: archive.ph/PgRku.

[Advertisement No. 18] Xinjiang Corps Personnel Examination Information Network. 2017. '2017年新疆兵团招录执法勤务类人民警察公告 [Xinjiang Bingtuan is Recruiting Police for Law Enforcement Service in 2017].' 国家公务员考试网 [*National Public Servant*], 8 December. Available from: archive.ph/fD7Gb.

[Advertisement No. 19] Xinjiang Corps Personnel Examination Network. 2018. '2018年新疆兵团公务员考试公告(1348人) [Announcement of 2018 Xinjiang Bingtuan Public Servant Examination (1,348 People)].' 国家公务员考试网 [*National Public Servant*], 11 August. Available from: archive.ph/ChWQ5.

[Advertisement No. 20] Xinjiang Corps Examination Information Network. 2019. '2019年新疆兵团面向公安院校招录人民警察公告 [Xinjiang Bingtuan is Recruiting Police from Public Security Institutes in 2019].' 国家公务员考试网 [*National Public Servant*], 19 March. Available from: archive.ph/YbP5E.

[Advertisement No. 21] 2019. '兵团招49人,提供住宿! [Xinjiang Bingtuan is Recruiting 49 People, and Provides Accommodation!]' 新浪网 [*Sina.com*], 15 April. Available from: archive.ph/GA4Hu.

[Advertisement No. 22] 2019. '新疆建设兵团铁门关市第二师二二三团在河北省招录辅警岗位330人 [Xinjiang Bingtuan 2nd Division is Recruiting 330 Demobilised Soldiers from Hebei Province].' 搜狐网 [*Sohu.com*], 29 April. Available from: archive.ph/WPptI.

[Advertisement No. 23] 2018. 'Xinjiang Bingtuan 6th Division 50th Regiment's Recruitment Plan.' 华图教育 [*Huatu.com*], 16 May. Accessed from: ha.huatu.com/2018/0516/1528331.html [page discontinued].

[Advertisement No. 24] Xiji County Culture, Tourism, Radio, Film and Television Bureau. 2017. '西吉县举行向新疆建设兵团转移就业 安置职工欢送大会 [Xiji County Held a Farewell Ceremony for the Relocating Employees of Xinjiang Bingtuan].' 西吉县人民政府 [*Xiji County People's Government*], 24 October. Available from: archive.ph/bdVXo.

[Advertisement No. 25] 2017. 'Xinjiang Bingtuan is Recruiting New Employees.' 腾讯网 [*Tencent*], 13 October. Accessed from: v.qq.com/x/page/t05608gg97g.html [page discontinued].

Bunin, Gene A. 2019. 'From Camps to Prisons: Xinjiang's Next Great Human Rights Catastrophe.' *Art of Life in Chinese Central Asia*, 5 October. Available from: livingotherwise.com/2019/10/05/from-camps-to-prisons-xinjiangs-next-great-human-rights-catastrophe-by-gene-a-bunin.

Byler, Darren. 2019. 'How Companies Profit from Forced Labor in Xinjiang.' *SupChina*, 4 September. Available from: supchina.com/2019/09/04/how-companies-profit-from-forced-labor-in-xinjiang.

Cliff, Thomas. 2009. 'Neo Oasis: The Xinjiang Bingtuan in the Twenty-First Century.' *Asian Studies Review* 33(1): 83–106. doi.org/10.1080/10357820802714807.

Cliff, Thomas. 2016. *Oil and Water: Being Han in Xinjiang.* Chicago, IL: University of Chicago Press. doi.org/10.7208/chicago/9780226360270.001.0001.

Doman, Mark, Stephen Hutcheon, Dylan Welch, and Kyle Taylor. 2018. 'China's Frontier of Fear.' *ABC News*, 1 November. Available from: www.abc.net.au/news/2018-11-01/satellite-images-expose-chinas-network-of-re-education-camps/10432924.

Jiang, Tao. 2019. 'Over 2,000 Uyghurs Secretly Relocated to Prisons in Henan.' *Bitter Winter: A Magazine on Religious Liberty and Human Rights in China*, 21 July. Available from: bitterwinter.org/over-2000-uyghurs-secretly-relocated-to-prisons.

Kuo, Lily. 2019. 'China Footage Reveals Hundreds of Blindfolded and Shackled Prisoners.' *The Guardian*, 23 September. Available from: www.theguardian.com/world/2019/sep/23/china-footage-reveals-hundreds-of-blindfolded-and-shackled-prisoners-uighur.

Li, Wensheng. 2019. '"Hanification" of Xinjiang through False Promises and Threats.' *Bitter Winter: A Magazine on Religious Liberty and Human Rights in China*, 27 June. Available from: bitterwinter.org/hanification-of-xinjiang-through-false-promises-and-threats.

McMillen, Donald H. 1979. *Chinese Communist Power and Policy in Xinjiang, 1949–1977*. Boulder, CO: Westview Press.

Ministry of Justice. 2018. '新疆生产建设兵团监狱管理局 强化"忠诚教育" 铸就忠诚警魂 [Xinjiang Bingtuan Prison System Reinforces "Loyalty Education" and Builds Police Spirit of Loyalty].' 11 December. Beijing: Ministry of Justice of the People's Republic of China. Available from: archive.ph/Jk5Qf.

Moseley, George. 1966. *A Sino-Soviet Cultural Frontier: The Ili Kazakh Autonomous Chou*. Cambridge, MA: Harvard University Press. doi.org/10.2307/j.ctt1tg5n34.

Seymour, James D. 2000. 'Xinjiang's Production and Construction Corps, and the Sinification of Eastern Turkestan.' *Inner Asia* 2(2): 171–93. doi.org/10.1163/146481700793647805.

Sina.com. 2018. '跨越3000公里去安家 [Make a Home Across 3,000 Kilometres].' *Sina.com*, 5 June. Available from: photo.sina.cn/album_1_89251_281252.htm, or archive.ph/15G4M.

Zenz, Adrian and James Leibold. 2019. 'Securitizing Xinjiang: Police Recruitment, Informal Policing and Ethnic Minority Co-optation.' *The China Quarterly* 242: 324–48. doi.org/10.1017/S0305741019000778.

Zhu, Yuchao and Dongyan Blachford. 2016. '"Old Bottle, New Wine"? Xinjiang Bingtuan and China's Ethnic Frontier Governance.' *Journal of Contemporary China* 25(97): 25–40. doi.org/10.1080/10670564.2015.1060760.

8. Triple dispossession in northwestern China (SAM TYNEN)

Alexander, Peter and Anita Chan. 2006. 'Does China Have an Apartheid Pass System?' *Journal of Ethnic and Migration Studies* 30(4): 609–29. doi.org/10.1080/13691830410001699487.

Byler, Darren. 2018. Spirit breaking: Uyghur dispossession, culture work and terror capitalism in a Chinese global city. PhD dissertation, University of Washington, Seattle.

Byler, Darren 2021. *In the Camps: China's High Tech Penal Colony.* New York, NY: Columbia Global Reports.

Cliff, Tom. 2009. 'Neo Oasis: The Xinjiang Bingtuan in the Twenty-First Century.' *Asian Studies Review* 33(1): 83–106. doi.org/10.1080/10357820802714807.

Cliff, Tom. 2016. *Oil and Water: Being Han in Xinjiang.* Chicago, IL: University of Chicago Press. doi.org/10.7208/chicago/9780226360270.001.0001.

Coulthard, Glen. 2014. *Red Skin, White Masks: Rejecting the Colonial Politics of Recognition.* Minneapolis, MN: University of Minnesota. doi.org/10.5749/minnesota/9780816679645.001.0001.

Das, Veena. 2007. *Life and Words: Violence and the Descent into the Ordinary*. Berkeley, CA: University of California Press. doi. org/10.1525/9780520939530.

Dautcher, Jay. 2009. *Down a Narrow Road: Identity and Masculinity in a Uyghur Community in Xinjiang, China*. Cambridge, MA: Harvard University Asia Center Press. doi.org/10.2307/j.ctt1x07w8b.

Han, Dong. 2009. 'Policing and Racialization of Rural Migrant Workers in Chinese Cities.' *Ethnic and Racial Studies* 33(4): 593–610. doi. org/10.1080/01419870903325651.

Hessler, Peter. 2006. *Oracle Bones: A Journey through Time in China*. New York: HarperCollins.

Honig, Emily. 1992. *Creating Chinese Ethnicity: Subei People in Shanghai 1850–1980*. New Haven, CT: Yale University Press. doi.org/10.2307/j. ctt211qx9h.

Marx, Karl. 1867. 'Capital. Volume One: Part VIII: Primitive Accumulation.' In *The Marx–Engels Reader*, edited by R. Tucker, 431–38. 2nd edn. New York, NY: W.W. Norton & Company.

Moreton-Robinson, Aileen. 2015. *The White Possessive: Property, Power, and Indigenous Sovereignty*. Minneapolis, MN: University of Minnesota Press. doi.org/10.5749/minnesota/9780816692149.001.0001.

Perdue, Peter. 2005. *China Marches West: The Qing Conquest of Central Eurasia*. Cambridge, MA: Harvard University Press.

Pun, Ngai. 2005. *Made in China: Women Factory Workers in a Global Workplace*. Durham, NC: Duke University Press. doi. org/10.1515/9780822386759.

Roberts, Sean. 2020. *The War on the Uyghurs: China's Campaign against Xinjiang's Muslims*. Princeton, NJ: Princeton University Press.

Roy, Ananya. 2019. 'Racial Banishment.' In *Keywords in Radical Geography: Antipode at 50*, edited by Antipode Editorial Collective, 227–30. Hoboken, NJ: Wiley Blackwell. doi.org/10.1002/9781119558071. ch42.

Ryan, Caitlin and Sarah Tynen. 2019. 'Fieldwork under Surveillance: Rethinking Relations of Trust, Vulnerability, and State Power.' *Geographical Review* 110(1–2): 38–51. doi.org/10.1111/gere.12360.

Schluessel, Eric. 2016. The Muslim emperor of China: Everyday politics in colonial Xinjiang, 1877–1933. PhD dissertation, Harvard University, Cambridge, MA.

The Economist. 2016. 'The Race Card.' *The Economist*, 3 September. Available from: www.economist.com/china/2016/09/03/the-race-card.

Tynen, Sarah. 2019. Uneven state territorialization: Governance, inequality, and survivance in Xinjiang, China. PhD dissertation, University of Colorado, Boulder.

Tynen, Sarah. 2020. 'Dispossession and Displacement of Migrant Workers: The Impact of State Terror and Economic Development on Uyghurs in Urban Xinjiang.' *Central Asian Survey* 39(3): 303–23. doi.org/10.1080/026 34937.2020.1743644.

Wu, Lili 武丽丽. 2020. '新疆少数民族流动人口法律意识的现状分析 [An Analysis of the Legal Awareness among Migrants from Xinjiang Ethnic Minorities].' *Netease News*, 17 August. Available from: c.m.163. com/news/a/FK7R622R0541LBHV.html.

Xinjiang Statistics Bureau. 2016. '2015年新疆住人口为2359.73万人 [The Resident Population of Xinjiang in 2015 was 23,597,300].' *Chinaxinjiang.cn*, 29 July. Available from: www.chinaxinjiang.cn/zixun/ xjxw/201607/t20160729_536093.htm.

Yan, Hairong. 2008. *New Masters, New Servants: Migration, Development, and Women Workers in China*. Durham, NC: Duke University Press. doi. org/10.2307/j.ctv11hphh4.

Zenz, Adrian. 2020. *Sterilizations, IUDs, and mandatory birth control: The CCP's campaign to suppress Uyghur birthrates in Xinjiang*. Working Paper, 21 July. Washington, DC: The Jamestown Foundation. Available from: jamestown.org/wp-content/uploads/2020/06/Zenz-Internment-Steriliza-tions-and-IUDs-UPDATED-July-21-Rev2.pdf?x58715.

Zhang, Li. 2001. *Strangers in the City: Reconfigurations of Space, Power, and Social Networks within China's Floating Population*. Stanford, CA: Stanford University Press.

9. Replace and rebuild: Chinese colonial housing in Uyghur communities (TIMOTHY A. GROSE)

Beh, Yuen Hui. 2017. 'Xi Jinping's Quest to Build a Beautiful China.' *The Star Online*, [Malaysia], 30 October. Available from: www.thestar.com.my/opinion/columnists/colours-of-china/2017/10/30/xi-jinpings-quest-to-bu-ild-a-beautiful-china-the-premiers-continuing-initiative-for-conserva-tion-and.

Buckley, Chris. 2019. 'China's Prisons Swell After Deluge of Arrests Engulfs Muslims.' *The New York Times*, 31 August. Available from: www.nytimes.com/2019/08/31/world/asia/xinjiang-china-uighurs-prisons.html.

Byler, Darren. 2018. 'China's Government Has Ordered a Million Citizens to Occupy Uighur Homes. Here's What They Think They're Doing.' *China File*, 24 October. Available from: www.chinafile.com/reporting-opinion/postcard/million-citizens-occupy-uighur-homes-xinjiang.

Child, Brenda. 1998. *Boarding School Seasons*. Lincoln: University of Nebraska Press.

China Kashgar Net. 2018. '咱们农村大变样 幸福生活"秀"出来 [Our Village Has Undergone Big Changes, Happy Lives Are "Coming Forth"].' 中国喀什网 [*China Kashgar Net*], 3 March. Available from: archive.vn/uyogx.

Cliff, Tom. 2016. *Oil and Water: Being Han in Xinjiang.* Chicago, IL: University of Chicago Press. doi.org/10.7208/chicago/9780226360270.001.0001.

Dautcher, Jay. 2009. *Down a Narrow Road: Identity and Masculinity in a Uyghur Community in Xinjiang China.* Cambridge, MA: Harvard University Press. doi.org/10.2307/j.ctt1x07w8b.

Dovey, Kim. 1999. *Framing Places: Mediating Power in Built Form.* London: Routledge. doi.org/10.4324/9780203267639 [page discontinued].

Foucault, Michel. 1984. *The Foucault Reader.* New York, NY: Pantheon Books.

Foucault, Michel. 1991 [1978]. 'Governmentality.' In *The Foucault Effects: Studies in Governmentality*, edited by Graham Burchell, Colin Gordon, and Peter Miller, 87–104. Chicago, IL: University of Chicago Press.

Glover, William. 2007. *Making Lahore Modern.* Minneapolis, MN: University of Minnesota Press.

Healy, Sianan. 2019. 'From Riverbank Humpy to White House: Spatial Assimilation at Rumbalara in 1950s Victoria.' In *Interdisciplinary Unsettlings of Place and Space: Conversations, Investigations, and Research*, edited by Sarah Pinto, Shelley Hannigan, Bernadette Walker-Gibbs, and Emma Charlton, 233–50. Singapore: Springer. doi.org/10.1007/978-981-13-6729-8_15.

Khotan Daily. 2018. '农村把这件事做好了 [Villages Have Done This Well].' 和田日报 [*Khotan Daily*], 5 March. Available from: freewechat.com/a/MzIwMzE3NjkxNQ==/2651909044/1.

Kobi, Madlen. 2016. *Constructing, Creating, and Contesting Cityscapes: A Socio-Anthropological Approach to Urban Transformation in Southern Xinjiang, People's Republic of China.* Wiesbaden, Germany: Harrassowitz Verlag. doi.org/10.2307/j.ctvc7717d.

Kobi, Madlen. 2018. 'Building Transregional and Historical Connections: Uyghur Architecture in Urban Xinjiang.' *Central Asian Survey* 37(2): 208–27. doi.org/10.1080/02634937.2018.1427555.

Livestock Office of the Xinjiang Uyghur Autonomous Region (XUAR). 2018. 经验交流 [*Experience Exchange*]. 3 September. Ürümqi: Livestock Office of the XUAR. Available from: web. archive.org/web/20190822215211/www.xjxmt.gov.cn/article/ C038/20180903111525632.html.

Ma, Long 马龙 and Lin Shuang 霜林. 2018. '"三新生活"乡村振兴战略 引领群众过上新生活 [The "Three New Lives" Rural Revitalisation Strategy Leads Masses to a New Life].' 疏附零距离 [*Zero Distance Konashähär*], 26 March. Available from: freewechat.com/a/MzAwNzA5N-DUyOQ==/2651777724/4.

Mähsut, Alimjan and Abdushükür Mähsut. 2000. *Uyghur Binakarliq Tarixi* [*A History of Uyghur Architecture*]. Ürümqi: Xinjiang Renmin Chubanshe.

Mitchell, Timothy. 1991. *Colonising Egypt*. Berkeley, CA: University of California Press. doi.org/10.1525/9780520911666.

Moreno, Aran. 2018. 'From Process of Civilization to Policy of Civilization: A Holistic Review of the Chinese Concept Wenming.' *(Con)textos: Revista d'Antropologia i Investigació Social* (8): 23–36.

People's Daily. 2018. '莎车开展"三新"活动 贯彻落实十九大精神 [Yarkand Launches the "Three New Campaign" to Carry Out the Spirit of the Nineteenth People's Congress].' 人民日报海外网 [*People's Daily Overseas Online*], 12 December. Available from: web.archive.org/ web/20200211155659/m.haiwainet.cn/middle/457197/2017/1205/ content_31197241_1.html.

Radio Free Asia. 2019. 'Uyghurs Ordered to Destroy Muslim Architecture Deemed "Extremist" by Authorities.' *Radio Free Asia*, [Washington, DC], 10 July. Available from: www.rfa.org/english/news/uyghur/architecture-07102019140830.html.

Steenberg, Rune. 2014. 'Transforming Houses: The Changing Concept of the House in Kashgar.' *Internationales Asienforum* 45(1–2): 171–91.

Stoler, Ann Laura. 2010. *Carnal Knowledge and Imperial Power: Race and the Intimate in Colonial Rule*. Berkeley, CA: University of California Press.

Tursuntohti, Abdukerimjan. 2013. *Uyghur Örp-Ädätliri wä Salamätlik* [*Uyghur Customs and Health*]. Ürümqi: Xinjiang Renmin Chubanshe.

Wolfe, Patrick. 2006. 'Settler Colonialism and the Elimination of the Native.' *Journal of Genocide Research* 8(4): 387–409. doi. org/10.1080/14623520601056240.

Yarkand County Radio and TV. 2018a. '三新活动 [The "Three New" Activities].' 莎车县广播电视台 [*Yarkand County Radio and TV*], 13 March. Available from: freewechat.com/a/MzA4NjMyNTgyNQ==/2650232622/2.

Yarkand County Radio and TV. 2018b. '三新活动: 莎车居民迈入新生活 [The 'Three New' Activities: Yarkand's Residents March into a New Life].' 莎车县广播电视台 [*Yarkand County Radio and TV*], 19 March. Available from: freewechat.com/a/MzA4NjMyNTgyNQ==/2650232925/4.

Zenz, Adrian. 2019. '"Thoroughly Reforming Them towards a Healthy Heart Attitude": China's Political Re-education Campaign in Xinjiang.' *Central Asian Survey* 38(1): 102–28. doi.org/10.1080/02634937.2018.1507997.

Zero Distance Kashgar. 2018. '聚焦三新: 真帮实扶暖人心文明新风进乡村 [Focus on the "Three New": Help Support the Will of the People and Bring Civilisation into the Countryside].' 喀什零距离 [*Zero Distance Kashgar*], 4 September. Accessed from: www.sohu.com/a/256385039_697224 [page discontinued].

Zero Distance Konashähär. 2018. '"三新生活"转变思想观念 村民圆梦幸福生活 ["Three New Living": Change Ways of Thinking, Villagers Dream about Happy Lives].' 疏附零距离 [*Zero Distance Konashähär*], 1 January. Available from: freewechat.com/a/MzAwNzA5NDUyOQ==/2651774801/4.

Zero Distance Maralbeshi. 2018. '"Güzäl hoyla-aram" bärpa qilish täshäbbusamisi [The "Beautify Spaces" Initiative Document].' 巴楚零距离 [*Zero Distance Maralbeshi*], 15 March. Available from: freewechat.com/a/ MzAwNjU3NjM5NA==/2653084532/3.

Zero Distance Päyzawat. 2018. '三新活动 [The Three New Campaign].' 伽师零距离 [*Zero Distance Päyzawat*], 7 August. Available from: web. archive.org/web/20190821020410/www.jinciwei.cn/d297460.html.

10. The spatial cleansing of Xinjiang: *Mazar* desecration in context (RIAN THUM)

Abdu Vali Akhon. 1905. Māzārlārgha Bārādūrghānlārnīng Yaʿnī Ziyārat-gāhnīng Bayāni [On those who go to *mazars*, that is to say, on pilgrimage sites]. Gunnar Jarring Collection, Lund University Library, Sweden.

Agence France-Presse (AFP). 2019. '"No Space to Mourn": The Destruction of Uygur Graveyards in Xinjiang.' *South China Morning Post*, [Hong Kong], 12 October. Available from: www.scmp.com/news/china/ politics/article/3032646/no-space-mourn-destruction-uygur-graveyards-xinjiang.

Brophy, David and Rian Thum. 2015. 'Appendix: The Shrine of Muḥammad Sharīf and its Qing-Era Patrons.' In *The Life of Muhammad Sharif: A Central Asian Sufi Hagiography in Chaghatay*, edited by Jeff Eden, 55–76. Vienna: Verlag der Österreichischen Akademie der Wissenschaften.

Byler, Darren. 2018. 'China's Government Has Ordered a Million Citizens to Occupy Uighur Homes. Here's What They Think They're Doing.' *China-File*, 24 October. Available from: www.chinafile.com/reporting-opinion/ postcard/million-citizens-occupy-uighur-homes-xinjiang.

Dawut, Rahilä. 2001. *Uyghur Mazarliri* [*Mazars of the Uyghurs*]. Ürümqi: Shinjang Khälq Näshriyati.

Dūghlāt, Mīrzā Haydar. 1996 [1543]. *Mirza Haydar Dughlat's Tarikh-i Rashidi: A History of the Khans of Moghulistan*. Translated by W.M. Thackston. Cambridge, MA: Department of Near Eastern Languages and Civilizations, Harvard University.

Gansu Daily Net. 2019. '平川区完成土炕改造2563铺 [Pingchuan District Completes Reform of 2,563 *Kangs*].' 每日甘肃网 [*Gansu Daily Net*], 21 January. Available from: by.gansudaily.com.cn/system/2019/01/21/017124756.shtml.

Google Earth. 2020. 'Satellite Image Showing Former Location of Ordam Padishah Mazar.' *Google Earth*. Available from: earth.google.com/web/@38.91253865,76.65675727,1614.22900131a,0d,35y,-0.0105h,28.7197t,0r.

Grose, Timothy. 2020. 'If You Don't Know How, Just Learn: Chinese Housing and the Transformation of Uyghur Domestic Space.' *Ethnic and Racial Studies* 44(11): 2052–73. doi.org/10.1080/01419870.2020.1789686.

Harris, Rachel and Rahilä Dawut. 2002. 'Mazar Festivals of the Uyghurs: Music, Islam and the Chinese State.' *British Journal of Ethnomusicology* 11(1): 101–18. doi.org/10.1080/09681220208567330.

Hoshur, Shohret. 2016. 'Under the Guise of Public Safety, China Demolishes Thousands of Mosques.' *Radio Free Asia*, [Washington, DC], 19 December. Available from: www.rfa.org/english/news/uyghur/udner-the-guise-of-public-safety-12192016140127.html.

Jarring, Gunnar. 1935. 'The Ordam-Padishah-System of Eastern Turkistan Shrines.' *Geografiska Annaler* 17: 348–54. doi.org/10.2307/519870.

Kemal, Ahmet. 1925. *Çīn Türkistān Hatıraları* [*Memoir of Chinese Turkistan*]. Izmir, Turkey: Marifet Matbaası.

Khotan Government. 2019. 'Notice Regarding the Removal of Sultanim Mazar and Graveyard.' See author's Twitter thread at: twitter.com/Rian-Thum/status/1255146071258349574.

Kobi, Madlen. 2016. *Constructing, Creating and Contesting Cityscapes: A Socio-Anthropological Approach to Urban Transformation in Southern Xinjiang, People's Republic of China.* Wiesbaden, Germany: Harrassowitz Verlag. doi.org/10.2307/j.ctvc7717d.

Kuo, Lily. 2019. 'Revealed: New Evidence of China's Mission to Raze the Mosques of Xinjiang.' *The Guardian*, 7 May. Available from: www.theguardian.com/world/2019/may/07/revealed-new-evidence-of-chinas-mission-to-raze-the-mosques-of-xinjiang.

Lesté-Lasserre, Christa. 2020. 'Scientists Are Leading Notre Dame's Restoration—and Probing Mysteries Laid Bare by Its Devastating Fire.' *Science*, 12 March. Available from: www.sciencemag.org/news/2020/03/scientists-are-leading-notre-dame-s-restoration-and-probing-mysteries-laid-bare-its. doi.org/10.1126/science.abb6744.

Liu, Tianyang and Zhenjie Yuan. 2019. 'Making a Safer Space? Rethinking Space and Securitization in the Old Town Redevelopment Project of Kashgar, China.' *Political Geography* 69: 30–42. doi.org/10.1016/j.polgeo.2018.12.001.

Manzi, Su. 2013. 'An Interview with Rahilä Dawut.' In *Living Shrines of Uyghur China*, Photographs by Lisa Ross, 121–23. New York, NY: The Monacelli Press.

MarcelTraveller. 2018. 'Imam Asim's Tomb, Hotan.' Review on *Tripadvisor*, June. Available from: www.tripadvisor.com/Attraction_Review-g528737-d8705159-Reviews-Imam_Asim_s_Tomb-Hotan_Xinjiang_Uygur.html.

Millward, James. 2009. *Eurasian Crossroads: A History of Xinjiang.* New York, NY: Columbia University Press.

Ministry of Civil Affairs. 2018. '民政部等9部门联合发文部署开展殡葬领域突出问题专项整治行动 [The Ministry of Civil Affairs and Nine Other Departments Jointly Issue a Document Launching a Special Rectification Campaign for Outstanding Problems in the Field of Funerals and Burials].' 2 July. Beijing: Ministry of Civil Affairs of the People's Republic of China. Available from: www.mca.gov.cn/article/xw/tzgg/201807/20180700009909.shtml.

Pawan, Sawut and Abiguli Niyazi. 2016. 'From Mahalla to Xiaoqu: Transformations of the Urban Living Space in Kashgar.' *Inner Asia* 18(1): 121–34. doi.org/10.1163/22105018-12340056.

Rivers, Matt. 2020. 'More Than 100 Uyghur Graveyards Demolished by Chinese Authorities, Satellite Images Show.' *CNN*, 2 January. Available from: www.cnn.com/2020/01/02/asia/xinjiang-uyghur-graveyards-china-intl-hnk/index.html.

She County People's Government. 2020. '殡葬整治工作半年总结 [Mid-Year Summary of Funeral and Burial Rectification Work].' 3 July. Handan: She County People's Government. Available from: web.archive.org/web/20200809152743/www.ahshx.gov.cn/BranchOpennessContent/show/1745160.html.

Sintash, Bahram. 2019. *Demolishing Faith: The Destruction and Desecration of Uyghur Mosques and Shrines*. Washington, DC: Uyghur Human Rights Project.

Sugawara, Jun. 2016. 'Opal, a Sacred Site on the Karakoram Highway.' In *Mazar: Studies on Islamic Sacred Sites in Central Eurasia*, edited by Sugawara Jun and Rahile Dawut, 153–74. Tokyo: Tokyo University of Foreign Studies Press.

Thum, Rian. 2014. *The Sacred Routes of Uyghur History*. Cambridge, MA: Harvard University Press. doi.org/10.4159/harvard.9780674736238.

Tuck, Eve and K. Wayne Yang. 2012. 'Decolonization Is Not a Metaphor.' *Decolonization: Indigeneity, Education & Society* 1(1): 1–40.

Wang, Jianping. n.d. Islam in Kashgar in the 1950s. Unpublished paper.

Xiao, Eva and Pak Yiu. 2019. 'China Disturbs Even the Uighur Dead in "Development" of Xinjiang.' *The Japan Times*, [Tokyo], 11 October. Accessed from: www.japantimes.co.jp/news/2019/10/11/asia-pacific/social-issues-asia-pacific/death-uighurs-long-reach-china [page discontinued].

Xinjiang Civil Affairs Department. 2018. '和静县召开殡葬领域突出问题专项整治动员大会 [Hejing County Held a Special Rectification Mobilisation Meeting for Prominent Issues in the Area of Funerals and Burials].' 2 September. Ürümqi: Xinjiang Civil Affairs Department. Available from: web.archive.org/web/20201115152910/mzt.xinjiang.gov.cn/xjmca/dfxx/201809/5ae7347ed0344a92adc955205ba99b3c.shtml.

Xinjiang Daily. 2018. '雪克来提·扎克尔到喀什开展"四同"活动时强调: 深入促进各族干部群众交往交流交融打牢新疆社会稳定和长治久安的坚实基础 [When He Went to Kashgar for the "Four Sames" Activities, Shohret Zakir Emphasised: Thoroughly Promote the Intermingling and Communication between Cadres of All Ethnic Groups and the Masses in Order to Establish a Firm Base for Social Stability and Long-Term Security in Xinjiang].' 新疆日报 [*Xinjiang Daily*], 14 February. Available from: wap.xjdaily.com/xjrb/20180214/99479.html.

Xinjiang Minsheng Net. 2018. '工作队引导村民建设美丽庭院 [Work Team Guides Villagers in Constructing Beautiful Households].' 新疆民生网 [*Xinjiang Minsheng Net*], 5 June. Available from: www.xjmsw.cn/xxzl/20180605/2018060548831.html.

Xinjiang United Front Work Department. 2017a. '非法宗教活动的26种表现 [26 Manifestations of Illegal Religious Activities].' 19 June. Ürümqi: Xinjiang United Front Work Department. Available from: web.archive.org/web/20200624135746/www.xjtzb.gov.cn/2017-06/19/c_1121167392.htm.

Xinjiang United Front Work Department. 2017b. '新疆启动民族团结结亲周百万干部职工分批下基层 [A Million Cadres and Workers Go to the Grassroots as Xinjiang Kicks Off the "Weeklong Becoming Family" Campaign for Ethnic Unity].' 19 December. Beijing: Central United Front Work Department. Available from: web.archive.org/web/20180521023148/http://www.zytzb.gov.cn/tzb2010/S1824/201712/029ea48103254b359c754152e005c302.shtml.

Xu, Qian 许倩. 2018. '喀什盘橐城免费开放 各地游客争相一睹班超风采_西域 [Kashgar's Pantou City Opens Free of Admissions Charges: Tourists from Everywhere Fall Over Each Other to Get a Glimpse of

Ban Chao's Elegant Bearing].' 新疆晨报 [*Xinjiang Chenbao*], 28 August. Available from: web.archive.org/web/20200808183201/www.sohu. com/a/250604268_100034331.

Zenz, Adrian. 2020. 'The Karakax List: Dissecting the Anatomy of Beijing's Internment Drive in Xinjiang.' *The Journal of Political Risk* 8(2). Available from: www.jpolrisk.com/karakax.

Zero Distance Awat. 2019. ' 【乡村振兴】阿克切克力片区召开群众 宣传教育暨美丽庭院'建设现场工作推进会_生活 [Village Revita-lisation: Akeqiekeli Area Held a Propaganda and "Beautiful Courtyard" Construction Work Promotion Meeting].' 阿瓦提零距离 [*Zero Distance Awat*], 31 March. Available from: www.sohu.com/a/305042908_752235.

Zero Distance Yining. 2019. ' 【公告】伊宁县墩麻扎镇墩麻扎 村坟墓搬迁事宜公告_墓地 [Announcement of the Removal of Graves at Dunmaza Village, Dunmaza Town, Yining County].' 伊宁 县零距离 [*Zero Distance Yining*], 8 May. Available from: www.sohu. com/a/312763996_120056900.

Zhang, Shicai. 2016. 'The Waqf System and the Xinjiang Uyghur Society from the Qing Dynasty to the Republic of China Period.' In *Mazar: Studies on Islamic Sacred Sites in Central Eurasia*, edited by Sugawara Jun and Rahile Dawut, 127–40. Tokyo: Tokyo University of Foreign Studies Press.

Zheng, Chaohua 郑朝华. 2017. '"土炕"改"电炕"干净又节能—甘州区 农村改炕工作纪实 [Changing Earthen *Kang*s to Electric *Kang*s Is Clean and Energy-Saving: An Account of *Kang* Reform Work in Rural Gansu].' 1 December. Beijing: Ministry of Agriculture of the People's Republic of China. Available from: web.archive.org/web/20200819200640/jiuban.moa. gov.cn/fwllm/qgxxlb/qg/201712/t20171201_5959814.htm.

11. Camp land: Settler ecotourism and Kazakh removal in contemporary Xinjiang (GULDANA SALIMJAN)

Aikau, Hōkūlani K. and Vernadette Vicuña Gonzalez (eds). 2019. *Detours: A Decolonial Guide to Hawai`i.* Durham, NC: Duke University Press. doi. org/10.1215/9781478007203.

Akins, Damon B. and William J. Bauer jr. 2021. *We Are the Land: A History of Native California.* Berkeley, CA: University of California Press. doi. org/10.1525/9780520976887.

Azat, Erkin. 2019. '我是协警: 他们为了充人数把协警都关进去了 [I Am an Associate Policeman: They Even Arrested Associate Police to Meet the Quotas].' *Medium*, 19 February. Available from: erki-nazat2018.medium.com/我是协警-他们为了充人数把协警都关进去-b5cbe93e8489.

Bingtuan Daily. 2020. '十三五期间兵团旅游总收入将突破600亿元 [Bingtuan Tourism Revenue Will Exceed RMB60 Billion during the Thirteenth Five-Year Plan Period].' 兵团日报 [*Bingtuan Daily*], 28 September. Available from: news.ts.cn/system/2020/09/28/036447755.shtml.

Bortala People's Government. 2017. 赛里木湖生态环境保护完成情况 [*A Report on Ecological Environmental Protection of Sayram Lake*]. 3 August. Bortala People's Government. Accessed from: www.xjboz.gov.cn/info/1343/35739.htm [page discontinued].

Byler, Darren. 2022. *Terror Capitalism: Uyghur Dispossession and Masculinity in a Chinese City.* Durham, NC: Duke University Press.

China National Tourism Administration (CNTA). 2015. '旅游局发布《关于进一步推进旅游援疆工作的指导意见》 [Regarding Guiding Instructions on the Further Development of the Tourism Xinjiang Aid Program].' 21 July. Beijing: State Council of the People's Republic of China. Available from: web.archive.org/web/20210329222315/http://www.gov.cn/xinwen/2015-07/21/content_2899951.htm.

Chinanews.com. 2012. '新疆天山天池景区禁牧拆除建筑保护自然生态 [Xinjiang Tianshan Tianchi Implemented Demolition and Grazing Ban to Protect Natural Ecology]. 中国新闻网 [*Chinanews.com*], 8 June. Available from: www.chinanews.com/df/2012/06-08/3950352.shtml.

Cliff, Tom. 2016. 'Lucrative Chaos: Interethnic Conflict as a Function of the Economic "Normalization" of Southern Xinjiang.' In *Ethnic Conflict and Protest in Tibet and Xinjiang: Unrest in China's West*, edited by Ben Hillman and Grey Tuttle, 122–50. New York, NY: Columbia University Press. doi.org/10.7312/columbia/9780231169981.003.0005.

Cornot-Gandolphe, Sylvie. 2014. *China's Coal Market: Can Beijing Tame 'King Coal'?* OIES Paper: CL 1. Oxford, UK: Oxford Institute for Energy Studies. Available from: doi.org/10.26889/9781784670177.

Fjellheim, Eva Maria and Florian Carl. 2020. '"Green" Colonialism is Ruining Indigenous Lives in Norway.' *Al Jazeera*, 1 August. Available from: www.aljazeera.com/opinions/2020/8/1/green-colonialism-is-ruining-indigenous-lives-in-norway.

Grauer, Yael. 2021. 'Revealed: Massive Chinese Police Database.' *The Intercept*, 29 January. Available from: theintercept.com/2021/01/29/china-uyghur-muslim-surveillance-police.

Guan, Qiaoqiao and Zhao Chunhui. 2011. '新疆将对全区1.5亿亩荒漠草原实行永久性禁牧 [Xinjiang Will Permanently Ban Grazing on 150 Million mu of Arid Steppe].' *Xinhua News Agency*, 11 March. Available from: web.archive.org/web/20210726045115/http://www.gov.cn/jrzg/2011-03/11/content_1822809.htm.

Landesman, Nash. 2018. 'Escape from Protection: The Catastrophe of Conservation in Panama.' *Foreign Policy Journal*, 18 April. Available from: www.foreignpolicyjournal.com/2018/04/18/escape-from-protection-the-catastrophe-of-conservation-in-panama.

Li, Yifei and Judith Shapiro. 2019. *China Goes Green: Coercive Environmentalism for a Troubled Planet*. Cambridge, UK: Polity Press.

Liu, Jian 刘建. 2014. '新疆喀拉峻国际生态旅游区索道站项目正在加紧施工 [Construction of Sky Gondola is Under Way in the Xinjiang Kalajun International Ecotourism Site]. 天山网 [*Tianshan Net*], 8 July. Available from: news.sina.com.cn/c/2014-07-08/092230486094.shtml.

Mollett, Sharlene. 2021. Land, servitude and embodied histories-of-the-present: Troubling residential tourism space-making on the Panamanian Caribbean. Social Justice Institute Noted Scholars Series Public Lecture, University of British Columbia, Vancouver, 24 March.

Moreton-Robinson, Aileen. 2021. 'Incommensurable Sovereignties: Indigenous Ontology Matters.' In *Routledge Handbook of Critical Indigenous Studies*, edited by Brendan Hokowhitu, Aileen Moreton-Robinson, Linda Tuhiwai-Smith, Chris Andersen, and Steve Larkin, 257–68. London: Routledge. doi.org/10.4324/9780429440229-23.

National Forestry and Grassland Administration. 2020. '国家林业和草原局关于进一步加强草原禁牧休牧工作的通知,林草发 (2020) 40号 [National Forestry and Grassland Administration Notice: Further Work on Grazing Ban of Grassland (2020), No. 40].' 13 April. Beijing: State Council of the People's Republic of China. Available from: www.gov.cn/zhengce/zhengceku/2020-04/13/content_5501822.htm.

Normann, Susanne. 2021. 'Green Colonialism in the Nordic Context: Exploring Southern Saami Representations of Wind Energy Development.' *Journal of Community Psychology* 49(1): 77–94. doi.org/10.1002/jcop.22422.

Pan, Jiahua 潘家华. 2015. 中国的环境治理与生态建设 [*China's Environmental Governance and Ecological Civilisation*]. Beijing: Zhongguo Shehui Wenxue Chubanshe.

Potter, Pittman B. 2013. *China's Legal System*. Cambridge, UK: Polity Press.

Ren, Jiang 任江. 2020. '农家乐牧家乐, 旅游发展乡村乐! [Peasant Family Happiness Herder Family Happiness, Tourism Development Rural Happiness!]' *Sina.com*, 29 October. Available from: k.sina.com.cn/article_2275883675_87a73a9b01900ubc0.html.

Salimjan, Guldana. 2021a. 'Mapping Loss, Remembering Ancestors: Gene-alogical Narratives of Kazakhs in China.' *Asian Ethnicity* 22(1): 105–20. doi.org/10.1080/14631369.2020.1819772.

Salimjan, Guldana. 2021b. 'Naturalized Violence: Affective Politics of China's "Ecological Civilization" in Xinjiang.' *Human Ecology: An Interdisciplinary Journal* 49(1): 59–68. doi.org/10.1007/s10745-020-00207-8.

Sohu.com. 2020. '北疆看风景, 南疆看人文! [See Nature in Northern Xinjiang and Culture in Southern Xinjiang]!' 搜狐 [*Sohu.com*], 9 June. Available from: www.sohu.com/a/400712743_100126287.

Song, Yawen 宋雅文. 2020. '墨玉县加汗巴格乡达拉斯喀勒村: 村民家门口吃上"旅游饭" [Villagers in Karakax County Benefit from Tourism].' 新疆日报 [*Xinjiang Daily*], 10 January. Available from: archive.is/8PRla.

State Council Information Office (SCIO). 2012. '新疆借助"天山申遗" 保护草原自然景观 [Xinjiang Protects Natural Grassland Landscape by Applying for "World Heritage for Tianshan"].' 26 June. Beijing: State Council Information Office. Available from: www.scio.gov.cn/zhzc/8/2/Document/1177972/1177972.htm.

State Council Information Office (SCIO). 2015. '新疆游牧民定居工程提前一年完成规划任务 [Xinjiang Nomad Sedentarisation Project Achieving the Goal One Year Ahead of Schedule].' 24 September. Beijing: State Council Information Office. Available from: www.scio.gov.cn/zhzc/8/2/Document/1450272/1450272.htm.

Sun, Zhe 孙哲. 2019. '新疆: 生态移民助推艾比湖湿地再现生机 [Xinjiang: Ecological Migration Boosts Vitality of Aibi Lake Wetland].' 新华网 [*Xinhua News Agency*], 3 July. Available from: web.archive.org/web/20210726045525.

Teaiwa, Teresia. 2016. 'Reflections on Militourism, US Imperialism, and American Studies.' *American Quarterly* 68(3): 847–53. doi.org/10.1353/aq.2016.0068.

Treuer, David. 2021. 'Return the National Parks to the Tribes: The Jewels of America's Landscape Should Belong to America's Original Peoples.' *The Atlantic*, May. Available from: www.theatlantic.com/magazine/archive/2021/05/return-the-national-parks-to-the-tribes/618395.

Tuniu.com. 2006–21. '新疆喀拉峻国际生态旅游区 [Xinjiang Kalajun International Ecotourism Site].' 途牛 [*Tuniu*]. Available from: www.tuniu.com/menpiao/2027361#/index.

Wang, Yayun 王亚芸. 2017. '让天蓝地绿水更清: 新疆维吾尔自治区生态文明建设综述 [Make the Sky Bluer and the Water Clearer: A Summary of Xinjiang Uyghur Autonomous Region's Ecological Civilisation Construction].' 新疆日报 [*Xinjiang Daily*], 5 August. Available from: cpc.people.com.cn/n1/2017/0805/c412690-29451726.html.

World Rainforest Movement (WRM) and GRAIN. 2015. *How REDD+ Projects Undermine Peasant Farming and Real Solutions to Climate Change.* Report, 29 October. Barcelona: GRAIN. Available from: grain.org/article/entries/5322-how-redd-projects-undermine-peasant-farming-and-real-solutions-to-climate-change.

Xinjiang Ili Kazakh Autonomous Prefecture People's Government (XJYL). 2016. '伊犁州实施新一轮草原生态保护补助奖励政策 [Ili Prefecture Solidifies the Implementation of Grassland Ecological Protection Subsidy].' 31 August. Xinjiang Ili Kazakh Autonomous Prefecture People's Government. Available from: www.xjyl.gov.cn/info/1746/303394.htm.

Xinjiang Morning Post. 2018. '一眼定缘喀拉峻 85后海归从广东来到新疆 [First Sight Love for Kalajun: Overseas-Educated Guangdong Man Born after 1985 Came to Xinjiang].' 新疆晨报 [*Xinjiang Morning Post*], 31 May. Available from: news.sina.cn/gn/2018-05-31/detail-ihcikce-v2634234.d.html.

Xinjiang Uyghur Autonomous Region (XUAR) Bureau of Statistics. 2020. 新疆生产建设兵团统计年鉴2020年 [*Xinjiang Production and Construction Corps Statistical Yearbook 2020*]. Beijing: Zhongguo Tongji Chubanshe.

Xinjiang Uyghur Autonomous Region (XUAR) Government. 2009. '新疆维吾尔自治区国民经济和社会发展十二五规划纲要 [Outline of the Twelfth Five-Year Plan for National Economic and Social Development of Xinjiang Uyghur Autonomous Region]'. 中国国情 [*Zhongguo Guoqing*], 6 July. Available from: archive.ph/VAgkI.

Xinjiang Victims Database. 2018a. 'Erbolat Zharylqasyn'. Entry 255 of 24750. Available from: shahit.biz/eng/#255.

Xinjiang Victims Database. 2018b. 'Esqat Bekinur'. Entry 272 of 24750. Available from: shahit.biz/eng/#272.

Xinjiang Victims Database. 2018c. 'Nagima Sultanmurat'. Entry 1337 of 24750. Available from: shahit.biz/eng/#1337.

Xinjiang Victims Database. 2018d. 'Nurbaqyt Nasihat'. Entry 1461 of 24460. Available from: shahit.biz/eng/#1461.

Xinjiang Victims Database. 2019. 'Kunim Zeinolda'. Entry 2734 of 24750. Available from: shahit.biz/eng/#2734.

Xinjiang Victims Database. 2021. 'Confiscation of Assets'. Public testimony data exported from Xinjiang Victims Database on 11 October 2021. Available from: t.co/inFzABhyyE?amp=1.

Xu, Vicky Xiuzhong, Danielle Cave, James Leibold, Kelsey Munro, and Nathan Ruser. 2020. *Uyghurs for Sale: 'Re-Education', Forced Labour and Surveillance beyond Xinjiang*. Policy Brief No. 26. Canberra: Australian Strategic Policy Institute. Available from: www.aspi.org.au/report/uyghurs-sale.

YouTube. 2021a. '2014 Kalajun Riots'. *YouTube*, 28 April. Available from: www.youtube.com/watch?v=z5ALhhhmGno.

YouTube. 2021b. 'Uyghur Village in Tuyuq Valley, Turpan'. *YouTube*, 31 July. Available from: www.youtube.com/shorts/NZs34nFFsv4.

Yuan, Jing 袁晶 and Xu Yunfeng 许云峰. 2012. '新疆"八卦城"特克斯县借"申遗" 还原草原风貌 [Xinjiang Tekes County's "Bagua City" Restoring Grassland through "Application for World Heritage Site"].' 中国新闻网 [*China News Network*], 6 August. Available from: www.chinanews.com/df/2012/08-06/4085854.shtml.

Zero Distance Moyu. 2019. '墨玉县: 乡村风貌改造增强群众幸福感 [Karakax County: Village is Renovated Anew and People's Happiness Enhanced].' 墨玉零距离 [*Zero Distance Moyu*], 16 December. Available from: archive.is/m6CXq.

12. Factories of Turkic Muslim internment (DARREN BYLER)

Alibaba. 2019. 'Lixian Huawei Gloves Factory.' Company Profile, Alibaba. Available from: web.archive.org/web/20191229054241/huaweiglove.en.alibaba.com/company_profile.html.

Azat, Erkin. 2019. 'Gulzira Auelkhan's Records in a Chinese Concentration Camp: "I Worry about the Lives of Those Eight Who Have Not Signed a Contract in the Factory."' Online post. *Medium*, 4 March. Available from: medium.com/@erkinazat2018/gulzira-auelkhan-s-records-in-a-chinese-concentration-camp-i-worry-about-the-lives-of-those-c18a2038a5a2.

Bunin, Gene A. 2019a. 'Detainees Are Trickling Out of Xinjiang's Camps.' *Foreign Policy*, 18 January. Available from: foreignpolicy.com/2019/01/18/detainees-are-trickling-out-of-xinjiangs-camps.

Bunin, Gene A. 2019b. 'Making the Xinjiang Authorities Dance: 40 Examples of Publicized Cases.' *Art of Life in Chinese Central Asia*, 17 May. Available from: livingotherwise.com/2019/05/17/making-xinjiang-authorities-dance-40-examples-generally-positive-outcomes-publicized-cases.

Byler, Darren. 2018. Spirit breaking: Uyghur dispossession, culture work and terror capitalism in a Chinese global city. PhD dissertation, University of Washington, Seattle. Available from: digital.lib.washington.edu/researchworks/bitstream/handle/1773/42946/Byler_washington_0250E_19242.pdf.

Die Zeit. 2019. 'Ihr seid keine Menschen [You Are Not Human].' *Die Zeit*, [Hamburg], 31 July. Available from: www.zeit.de/2019/32/zwangsla-ger-xinjiang-muslime-china-zeugen-menschenrechte/seite-2.

Foucault, Michel. 1975. *Discipline and Punish: The Birth of Prison*. Translated by Alan Sheridan. London: Penguin.

Goldstein, Alyosha. 2017. 'On the Reproduction of Race, Capitalism, and Settler Colonialism.' In *Race and Capitalism: Global Territories, Transnational Histories*, edited by Ananya Roy, 42–51. Los Angeles, CA: Institute on Inequality and Democracy at UCLA Luskin. Available from: challengeinequality.luskin.ucla.edu/wp-content/uploads/sites/16/2018/04/Race-and-Capitalism-digital-volume.pdf.

Gro Intelligence. 2019. 'Provincial Data Shows China's Shifting Agricultural Trends.' *Insights*, 6 March. New York, NY: Gro Intelligence. Available from: gro-intelligence.com/insights/articles/provincial-data-shows-chinas-shifting-agricultural-trends - Cotton [page discontinued].

Human Rights Watch (HRW). 2019. *China's Algorithms of Repression: Reverse Engineering a Xinjiang Police Mass Surveillance App*. Report, 1 May. New York, NY: Human Rights Watch. Available from: www.hrw.org/report/2019/05/01/chinas-algorithms-repression/reverse-enginee-ring-xinjiang-police-mass-surveillance [page discontinued].

Ili Television. 2018. '州直纺织服装产业敲开群众"就业门"' [The State Direct Textile and Garment Industry Knocks on "Employment Door" of the Masses].' 伊犁电视台 [*Ili Television*], 4 December. Available from: archive.md/KSe5r.

International Labour Organization (ILO). 2014. *Wages and working hours in the textiles, clothing, leather and footwear industries*. Issues Paper for discussion at the Global Dialogue Forum on Wages and Working Hours in the Textiles, Clothing, Leather and Footwear Industries, Geneva, 23–25 September 2014. Geneva: International Labour Office, Sectoral Activities Department, ILO. Available from: www.ilo.org/wcmsp5/groups/public/@ed_dialogue/@sector/documents/publication/wcms_300463.pdf.

Kashgar Regional Administrative Office. 2018. '关于印发《喀什地区困难群体就业培训工作实施方案》的通知 [Notice on Issuing the "Implementation Plan for Employment Training for Disadvantaged Groups in Kashgar"].' 10 August. Kashgar: Kashgar Regional Administrative Office. Available from: web.archive.org/web/20181204024839/http:/kashi.gov.cn/Government/PublicInfoShow.aspx?ID=2963.

Marx, Karl. 1978. *The Marx–Engels Reader*. Edited by Robert Tucker. New York, NY: W.W. Norton & Company.

Pan, Jennifer. 2020. *Welfare for Autocrats: How Social Assistance in China Cares for Its Rulers*. Oxford, UK: Oxford University Press. doi.org/10.1093/oso/9780190087425.001.0001.

Patton, Dominique. 2016. 'Xinjiang Cotton at Crossroads of China's New Silk Road.' *Reuters*, 12 January. Available from: www.reuters.com/article/us-china-xinjiang-cotton-insight-idUSKCN0UQ00320160112.

People's Government of the Xinjiang Uyghur Autonomous Region (XUAR). 2018. '关于进一步完善自治区纺织服装产业政策的通知 [Notice on Further Improving the Textile and Apparel Industry Policy of the Autonomous Region].' 6 April. Ürümqi: People's Government of the Xinjiang Uyghur Autonomous Region. Available from: archive.fo/ZBsk8.

Smith, Chris and Pun Ngai. 2006. 'The Dormitory Labour Regime in China as a Site for Control and Resistance.' *The International Journal of Human Resource Management* 17(8): 1456–70. doi.org/10.1080/09585190600804762.

The Times of Nantong Aiding Xinjiang. 2018. '江苏援伊前沿指挥部领导研究南通市对口援疆工作 [Leaders of Jiangsu Aid to Yining Front Headquarters Investigate the Paired Aid to Xinjiang from Nantong City].' 南通援疆进行时 [*The Times of Nantong Aiding Xinjiang*], 31 May. Available from: archive.md/f490v.

Turkistan Press. 2018. 'Çin'in Yeni Planlarinin Yazili Emri İfşa Oldu [Written Order of China's New Plans Revealed].' *Turkistan Press*, 23 July. Available from: turkistanpress.com/page/cin-39-in-yeni-planlarinin-yazili-emri-ifsa-oldu/247.

United Nations (UN). 2019. *Information Received from China on Follow-Up to the Concluding Observations on its Combined Fourteenth to Seventeenth Periodic Reports*. 8 October. Geneva: Committee on the Elimination of Racial Discrimination. Available from: undocs.org/CERD/C/CHN/FCO/14-17.

Vanderklippe, Nathan. 2019. '"I Felt Like a Slave": Inside China's Complex System of Incarceration and Control of Minorities.' *The Globe and Mail*, [Toronto], 31 March. Available from: www.theglobeandmail.com/world/article-i-felt-like-a-slave-inside-chinas-complex-system-of-incarceration.

Xinjiang Uyghur Autonomous Region Development and Reform Commission (XJDRC). 2018. '自治区经济结构稳中有活 发展良好 [The Economic Structure of the Autonomous Region Is Stable, Alive and Well Developed].' 5 December. Ürümqi: Xinjiang Uyghur Autonomous Region Development and Reform Commission. Available from: web.archive.org/web/20190520143306/http:/www.xjdrc.gov.cn/info/9923/23516.htm.

Xinjiang Victims Database. 2019. 'Gulzira Aeulkhan.' *Xinjiang Victims Database*. [Online.] Available from: shahit.biz/eng/viewentry.php?entryno=1723.

Yeh, Emily T. 2013. *Taming Tibet: Landscape Transformation and the Gift of Chinese Development*. Ithaca, NY: Cornell University Press. doi.org/10.7591/9780801469787.

Zero Distance Yining. 2017. '伊宁县"轻纺产业区"的产业工人: 幸福是奋斗出来的 [Industrial Workers in the "Textile Industry Zone" of Yining County: Happiness Comes from Struggle]!' 伊宁县零距离 [*Zero Distance Yining*]. Available from: archive.md/Cv6w5 - selection-23.14-31.7 [page discontinued].

Zhu, Hailun. 2017. 'Opinions on Further Strengthening and Standardising Vocational Skills Education and Training Centres' Work.' *Autonomous Region State Organ Telegram: New Party Politics and Law* (419). Available from: www.documentcloud.org/documents/6558510-China-Cables-Telegram-English.html - text/p1 [page discontinued].

13. The global age of the algorithm: Social credit, Xinjiang, and the financialisation of governance in China (NICHOLAS LOUBERE AND STEFAN BREHM)

Barmé, Geremie R., Linda Jaivin, and Jeremy Goldkorn (eds). 2014. *Shared Destiny: China Story Yearbook 2014*. Canberra: ANU Press. doi. org/10.26530/OAPEN_607531.

Bislev, Ane. 2017. 'Contextualizing China's Online Credit Rating System.' *The Asia Dialogue*, 4 December. Available from: theasiadialogue. com/2017/12/04/contextualizing-chinas-online-credit-rating-system.

Bodkin, Henry. 2017. 'AI Robots Are Sexist and Racist, Experts Warn.' *The Telegraph*, [London], 24 August. Available from: www.telegraph.co.uk/ news/2017/08/24/ai-robots-sexist-racist-experts-warn.

Daum, Jeremy. 2017. 'Giving Credit.' *China Law Translate*, 4 January. Available from: www.chinalawtranslate.com/giving-credit/?lang=en.

Daum, Jeremy. 2018. 'Giving Credit 3: Inputs and Outputs.' *China Law Translate*, 15 January. Available from: www.chinalawtranslate.com/giving-credit-3-inputs-and-outputs.

Daum, Jeremy. 2019. 'What Is a Social Credit Demonstration City?' *China Law Translate*, 16 August. Available from: www.chinalawtranslate.com/en/ what-is-a-social-credit-demonstration-city.

Epstein, Gerald A. 2005. 'Introduction: Financialization and the World Economy.' In *Financialization and the World Economy*, edited by Gerald A. Epstein, 3–16. Cheltenham, UK: Edward Elgar.

Fang, Lee. 2018. 'ICE Used Private Facebook Data to Find and Track Criminal Suspect, Internal Emails Show.' *The Intercept*, 26 March. Available from: theintercept.com/2018/03/26/facebook-data-ice-immigration.

Foreign Policy [Special Correspondent]. 2018. 'A Summer Vacation in China's Muslim Gulag.' *Foreign Policy*, 28 February. Available from: forei-gnpolicy.com/2018/02/28/a-summer-vacation-in-chinas-muslim-gulag.

General Office of the State Council. 2016. '国务院办公厅关于加强个人诚信体制建设的指导意见 [The General Office of the State Council's Guiding Opinion on the Strengthening of the Establishment of the Personal Creditworthiness System].' 30 December. Beijing: State Council of the People's Republic of China. Available from: www.gov.cn/zhengce/content/2016-12/30/content_5154830.htm.

Grauer, Yael. 2021. 'Revealed: Massive Chinese Police Database.' *The Intercept*, 29 January. Available from: theintercept.com/2021/01/29/china-uyghur-muslim-surveillance-police.

Heilmann, Sebastian. 2008. 'From Local Experiments to National Policy: The Origins of China's Distinctive Policy Process.' *The China Journal* 59: 1–30. doi.org/10.1086/tcj.59.20066378.

Human Rights Watch (HRW). 2018. 'China: Big Data Fuels Crackdown in Minority Region.' *News*, 26 February. New York, NY: Human Rights Watch. Available from: www.hrw.org/news/2018/02/26/china-big-data-fuels-crackdown-minority-region.

Hvistendahl, Mara. 2017. 'Inside China's Vast New Experiment in Social Ranking.' *WIRED*, 14 December. Available from: www.wired.com/story/age-of-social-credit.

Hvistendahl, Mara. 2021. 'How the LAPD and Palantir Use Data to Justify Racist Policing.' *The Intercept*, 30 January. Available from: theintercept.com/2021/01/30/lapd-palantir-data-driven-policing/.

Keeley, Brian. 2007. *Human Capital: How What You Know Shapes Your Life*. Paris: OECD Publishing. doi.org/10.1787/9789264029095-en.

Loubere, Nicholas. 2017a. 'China's Internet Finance Boom and Tyrannies of Inclusion.' *China Perspectives* 2017(4): 9–18. doi.org/10.4000/chinaperspectives.7454.

Loubere, Nicholas. 2017b. 'Cyber Loan Sharks, Social Credit, and New Frontiers of Digital Control.' In *China Story Yearbook 2016: Control*, edited by Jane Golley, Linda Jaivin, and Luigi Tomba, 213–23. Canberra: ANU Press. doi.org/10.22459/CSY.06.2017.06A.

Matsakis, Louise. 2019. 'How the West Got China's Social Credit System Wrong.' *WIRED*, 29 July. Available from: www.wired.com/story/china-social-credit-score-system.

Mertha, Andrew. 2009. '"Fragmented Authoritarianism 2.0": Political Pluralization in the Chinese Policy Process.' *The China Quarterly* 200: 995–1012. doi.org/10.1017/S0305741009990592.

Millward, James A. 2018. 'What It's Like to Live in a Surveillance State.' *The New York Times*, 3 February. Available from: www.nytimes.com/2018/02/03/opinion/sunday/china-surveillance-state-uighurs.html.

O'Neil, Cathy. 2016. *Weapons of Math Destruction: How Big Data Increases Inequality and Threatens Democracy*. New York, NY: Crown.

Rosenzweig, Joshua, Ewan Smith, and Susan Treveskes. 2017. 'Forum: Interpreting the Rule of Law in Xi Jinping's China.' In *Made in China Yearbook 2016: Disturbances in Heaven*, edited by Ivan Franceschini, Kevin Lin, and Nicholas Loubere, 98–105. Canberra: ANU Press. doi.org/10.22459/MIC.02.2017.16.

State Council. 2014. '关于印发社会信用体系建设规划纲要(2014–2020年) [Planning Outline for the Construction of a Social Credit System (2014–2020)].' *China Copyright and Media*, 14 June. Available from: china-copyrightandmedia.wordpress.com/2014/06/14/planning-outline-for-the-construction-of-a-social-credit-system-2014-2020.

Strumpf, Dan and Wenxin Fan. 2017. 'Who Wants to Supply China's Surveillance State? The West.' *The Wall Street Journal*, 1 November. Available from: www.wsj.com/articles/who-wants-to-supply-chinas-surveillance-state-the-west-1509540111.

The Economist. 2016a. 'Tests of Character.' *The Economist*, 29 September. Available from: www.economist.com/news/finance-and-economics/21707978-how-personality-testing-could-help-financial-inclusion-tests-character.

The Economist. 2016b. 'China Invents the Digital Totalitarian State.' *The Economist*, 17 December. Available from: www.economist.com/news/briefing/21711902-worrying-implications-its-social-credit-project-china-invents-digital-totalitarian.

The Economist. 2016c. 'China's Digital Dictatorship.' *The Economist*, 17 December. Available from: www.economist.com/news/leaders/21711904-worrying-experiments-new-form-social-control-chinas-digital-dictatorship.

Winston, Ali. 2018. 'Palantir Has Secretly Been Using New Orleans to Test Its Predictive Policing Technology.' *The Verge*, 27 February. Available from: www.theverge.com/2018/2/27/17054740/palantir-predictive-policing-tool-new-orleans-nopd.

Yu, Lean, Xinxie Li, Ling Tang, Zongyi Zhang, and Gang Kou. 2015. 'Social Credit: A Comprehensive Literature Review.' *Financial Innovation* 1(6): 1–18. doi.org/10.1186/s40854-015-0005-6.

14. Surveillance, data police, and digital enclosure in Xinjiang's 'Safe Cities' (DARREN BYLER)

AFP in Washington. 2020. 'US Imposes Sanctions on Chinese "State-within-a-state" Linked to Xinjiang Abuses.' *The Guardian*, 1 August. Available from: www.theguardian.com/world/2020/jul/31/us-sanctions-china-xinjiang-uighurs.

Alecci, Scilla. 2019. 'How China Targets Uighurs "One by One" for Using a Mobile App.' *Investigations: China Cables*, 24 November. Washington, DC: International Consortium of Investigative Journalists. Available from: www.icij.org/investigations/china-cables/how-china-targets-uighurs-one-by-one-for-using-a-mobile-app/.

Atajurt Kazakh Human Rights. 2018a. 'Қытай Сауан ауданында тұтқындалғандардың Баспасөзі [Press Conference of Detainees in Shawan County of China].' *YouTube*, 15 September. Available from: www.youtube.com/watch?v=qdVV82gnsH8.

Atajurt Kazakh Human Rights. 2018b. 'Сұхбат-23 [Interview Number 23].' *YouTube*, 28 November. Available from: www.youtube.com/watch?v=IA-mEG2xEfTE.

Atajurt Kazakh Human Rights. 2019. 'Сұмдық СҰХБАТ [Terrifying Interview].' *YouTube*, 12 January. Available from: www.youtube.com/watch?-v=p8rVTEStmY8.

Batke, Jessica and Mareike Ohlberg. 2020. 'State of Surveillance.' *ChinaFile*, 30 October. Available from: www.chinafile.com/state-surveillance-china.

Bidcentre Net. 2017a. '沙湾县公安局一体化信息采集工作台项目采用单一来源方式采购公示 [Notice on Public Security Bureau of Shawan County Using Single-Source Procurement Method for its Integrated Information Collection Workstation Project].' *Bidcentre Net*, 11 September. Available from: archive.fo/txXKx#selection-1319.28-1319.30.

Bidcentre Net. 2017b. '新疆沙湾县智慧(平安)项目中标公告 [Announcement on the Tender Outcome of Xinjiang Shawan County's Smart (Safety) Project].' *Bidcentre Net*, 11 December. Available from: archive.fo/MAt0q#selection-1307.0-1307.17.

Bidcentre Net. 2018a. '虹膜信息采集设备招标公告 [Bidding Announcement for Iris Information Collection Equipment].' *Bidcentre Net*, 17 January. Available from: archive.fo/qw2AQ#selection-1117.17-1117.29.

Bidcentre Net. 2018b. '居民身份证人像、平面十指指纹信息采集设备拟采用招标公告 [Provisional Bidding Announcement for Equipment Collecting Information on Resident Identity Card Portrait and Full Sets of Fingerprints].' *Bidcentre Net*, 17 January. Available from: archive.fo/RtZB9#selection-1323.33-1323.39.

Bureau of Statistics of Shawan County. 2019. 沙湾县*2018年国民经济和社会发展统计公报* [*Statistical Communiqué of Shawan County's 2018 National Economic and Social Development*]. 30 April. Shawan: Bureau of Statistics of Shawan County. Available from: www.xjswx.gov.cn/info/1655/47725.htm.

Byler, Darren. 2019. 'How Companies Profit from Forced Labor in Xinjiang.' *SupChina*, 4 September. Available from: supchina.com/2019/09/04/how-companies-profit-from-forced-labor-in-xinjiang/.

Byler, Darren. 2020a. 'Do Coercive Reeducation Technologies Actually Work?' *Blog, Los Angeles Review of Books*, 1 June. Available from: blog.lareviewofbooks.org/provocations/coercive-reeducation-technologies-actually-work/.

Byler, Darren. 2020b. 'The Global Implications of "Re-Education" Technologies in Northwest China.' *Terrain Analysis*, 8 June. Washington, DC: Center for Global Policy. Available from: newlinesinstitute.org/china/the-global-implications-of-re-education-technologies-in-northwest-china/.

Byler, Darren. 2020c. 'The Xinjiang Data Police.' *Noema*, 8 October. Available from: www.noemamag.com/the-xinjiang-data-police/.

Byler, Darren. 2021. *In the Camps: China's Hi-Tech Penal Colony*. New York, NY: Columbia Global Reports.

Byler, Darren and Carolina Sanchez Boe. 2020. 'Tech-Enabled "Terror Capitalism" is Spreading Worldwide. The Surveillance Regimes Must Be Stopped.' *The Guardian*, 24 July. Available from: www.theguardian.com/world/2020/jul/24/surveillance-tech-facial-recognition-terror-capitalism.

Career Centre. 2019. '沙湾县公安局招聘公告 [Recruitment Announcement by Public Security Bureau of Shawan County].' 就业指导中心 [*Career Centre*], 30 April. Available from: archive.fo/a3kXl#selection-293.3-293.9.

Chin, Josh and Clément Bürge. 2017. 'Twelve Days in Xinjiang: How China's Surveillance State Overwhelms Daily Life.' *The Wall Street Journal*, 19 December. Available from: www.wsj.com/articles/twelve-days-in-xinjiang-how-chinas-surveillance-state-overwhelms-daily-life-1513700355.

China Law Translate. 2018. 'Opinions on Several Issues on the Application of Law in Cases of Terrorist Activities and Extremism Crimes.' *China Law Translate*, 12 June. Available from: www.chinalawtranslate.com/en/opinions-on-several-issues-on-the-application-of-law-in-cases-of-terrorist-activities-and-extremism-crimes/.

Chinese Government Procurement Network. 2020. 'Xinjiang Shawan County Smart (Safe) Project Feasibility Study.' *ChinaFile*, 30 December. Available from: www.chinafile.com/library/reports/xinjiang-shawan-county-smart-safe-project-feasibility-study.

Crockford, Kade. 2020. 'How is Face Recognition Surveillance Technology Racist?' *News and Commentary*, 16 June. New York, NY: American Civil Liberties Union. Available from: www.aclu.org/news/privacy-technology/how-is-face-recognition-surveillance-technology-racist/.

Du, Hong 杜红 and Chang Yi 常乙. 2016. '便民警务站: 步步为民 事 事连心 [People's Convenience Police Station: Doing Everything for the People, Keeping the People's Welfare in Mind].' 沙湾新闻 [*Shawan News*], 26 October. Available from: archive.vn/wp1cK#selection-205.3-205.7.

Duan, Jiangxi 段江玺. 2017. '沙湾新闻: 我县开展交通整治夜检夜查行动 [Shawan News: Our County Rolled Out Traffic Regulation and Night Patrols].' *WeChat*, 15 August. Available from: archive.fo/oqY7K#selection-41.64-41.83.

Feng, Emily. 2019. '"Illegal Superstition": China Jails Muslims for Practicing Islam, Relatives Say.' *NPR*, 8 October. Available from: www.npr.org/2019/10/08/764153179/china-has-begun-moving-xinjiang-muslim-detainees-to-formal-prisons-relatives-say.

Gallagher, Sean. 2020. 'London to Deploy Live Facial Recognition to Find Wanted Faces in a Crowd.' *Ars Technica*, 29 January. Available from: arstechnica.com/information-technology/2020/01/london-to-deploy-live-facial-recognition-to-find-wanted-faces-in-crowd/.

Government of China. 2020. '中国提供的关于其第十四至第十七次合并定期报告结论性意见后续行动的资料 [Information Received from China on Follow-Up to the Concluding Observations on its Combined Fourteenth to Seventeenth Periodic Reports].' Document No. CERD/C/CHN/FCO/14-17, 5 February. Geneva: Committee on the Elimination of Racial Discrimination, International Convention on the Elimination of All Forms of Racial Discrimination. Available from: undocs.org/Home/Mobile?FinalSymbol=CERD%2FC%2FCHN%2FFCO%2F14-17&Language=E&DeviceType=Desktop.

IPVM Team. 2020. 'Huawei/Megvii Uyghur Alarms.' *IPVM*, 8 December. Available from: ipvm.com/reports/huawei-megvii-uygur.

Irani, Lilly. 2015. 'Justice for "Data Janitors".' *Public Books*, 15 January. Available from: www.publicbooks.org/justice-for-data-janitors/.

Kunlun Human Resources and Social Security Website. 2018. '招100名辅警!2018新疆这里便民警务站、公安检查站、培训中心招聘100人公告 [Recruiting 100 Auxiliary Police Officers! Announcement on Xinjiang Recruiting 100 Staff Members in 2018 for People's Convenience Police Stations, Public Security Inspection Stations, and Training Centres].' 昆仑人社网 [*Kunlun Human Resources and Social Security Website*], 1 March. Available from: archive.fo/cbink#selection-49.25-49.30.

Lintao Focus. 2018. '2018年新疆喀什地区招聘县聘事业编制便民警务站工作人员招聘简章 [Recruitment Brochure for 2018 Recruitment of Staff Members (Affiliated with Public Institution) for People's Convenience Police Stations in Kashgar, Xinjiang].' *WeChat*, 19 December. Available from: archive.fo/OUfAC#selection-41.64-41.96.

Mac, Ryan, Caroline Haskins, and Logan McDonald. 2020. 'Clearview's Facial Recognition App Has Been Used by the Justice Department, ICE, Macy's, Walmart, and the NBA.' *BuzzFeed News*, 27 February. Available from: www.buzzfeednews.com/article/ryanmac/clearview-ai-fbi-ice-global-law-enforcement.

Murphy, Laura and Nurala Elimä. 2021. *In Broad Daylight: Uyghur Forced Labour and Global Solar Supply Chains*. Sheffield, UK: Helena Kennedy Centre for International Justice, Sheffield Hallam University.

Pan, Jennifer. 2020. *Welfare for Autocrats: How Social Assistance in China Cares for its Rulers*. Oxford, UK: Oxford University Press. doi.org/10.1093/oso/9780190087425.001.0001.

Peaceful Shawan. 2017. '沙湾县公安局招聘100名事业编制便民警务站工作人员 [Public Security Bureau of Shawan County Recruiting 100 Staff Members (Affiliated with Public Institution) for People's Convenience Police Stations].' *WeChat*, 22 August. Available from: archive.fo/sjWJJ#selection-41.64-41.89.

Peaceful Shawan. 2019. '新疆一男子发朋友圈辱骂民警, 喜提拘留所"15日游"! 网友: 活该 [A Man in Xinjiang Insulted Police on his WeChat Account and was Awarded a "15-Day Tour" in the Detention Centre! Netizens: He Deserved It]!' *WeChat*, 1 March. Available from: archive.fo/9SdxQ#selection-41.64-41.96.

People's Daily. 2019. '新疆奎屯市: 智慧平台, 让社区治理更加精准高效 [Kuitun City in Xinjiang: Smart Platform Makes Community Governance More Precise and Efficient].' 人民网 [*People's Daily Online*], 23 July. Available from: archive.fo/pMuMg#selection-209.0-209.3.

Police Examination Network. 2017. '2017年新疆塔城沙湾县公安局招聘专职警务辅助人员报考条件 [Application Requirements for Special-Duty Auxiliary Police Officers Recruited by Public Security Bureau of Shawan County, Tacheng, Xinjiang, in 2017].' 易考吧 [*eTest8*], 5 April. Available from: archive.vn/GYoTX#selection-657.19-659.5.

Police Officer e-Station. 2018. '招警3162人! 公务员编制(附职位表), 不限户籍, 不限性别, 快转给身边需要的人 [Recruiting 3,162 Police Officers! Positions Affiliated with Public Institution (Position Descriptions Attached), No Restrictions on Household Registration, No Restrictions on Gender. Please Quickly Share Around].' 小警E站 [*Police Officer e-Station*], 13 August. Available from: archive.fo/m27mf#selection-53.25-53.29.

Police Officer Liu Online. 2019. '智慧小区人脸识别门禁系统登记方法(新) [Method for Registering for Facial Recognition Access Control System Used in Smart Residential Compounds (New)].' *WeChat*, 12 February. Available from: archive.fo/vG7TY#selection-41.64-41.83.

Public Security Bureau of Shawan County. 2018. '重磅!新疆户籍居民身份证丢失补领可网上自助办理了!附操作指南 [Important! Online Self-Services Available for Xinjiang Residents Who Need to Replace their Lost Resident Identity Cards. Instructions Attached].' *WeChat*, 12 October. Available from: archive.vn/a6Rhm#selection-41.64-41.94.

Public Security Bureau of Tacheng Prefecture. 2017. '42个便民警务站"团组织"全覆盖 ["Youth Leagues" Established at All 42 People's Convenience Police Stations].' *WeChat*, 30 March. Available from: archive.fo/R5KWI#selection-41.78-41.81.

Public Servant Exam Information Website. 2017. '沙湾县公安局2017年招聘事业单位工作人员岗位设置一览表 [A List of Positions Affiliated with Public Institutions Recruited by Public Security Bureau of Shawan County in 2017].' 公务员考试信息网 [*Public Servant Exam Information Website*], 30 May. Available from: archive.fo/HSz61#selection-1039.3-1039.12.

Ramzy, Austin. 2019. 'He Needed a Job. China Gave Him One: Locking Up His Fellow Muslims.' *The New York Times*, 2 March. Available from: www.nytimes.com/2019/03/02/world/asia/china-muslim-detention-uighur-kazakh.html.

Ramzy, Austin and Chris Buckley. 2019. '"Absolutely No Mercy": Leaked Files Expose How China Organised Mass Detentions of Muslims.' *The New York Times*, 16 November. Available from: www.nytimes.com/interactive/2019/11/16/world/asia/china-xinjiang-documents.html.

Rudolph, Josh. 2019. 'Sharper Eyes: Surveilling the Surveillers (Part 1).' *China Digital Times*, 9 September. Available from: chinadigitaltimes.net/2019/09/sharper-eyes-surveilling-the-surveillers-part-1/.

Shawan News. 2017. '2017年4月24号沙湾新闻 [Shawan News Dated 24 April 2017].' *WeChat*, 24 April. Available from: archive.fo/bhPnC#selection-41.64-41.78.

Shawan News. 2018. '2018年1月2号沙湾新闻 [Shawan News Dated 2 January 2018].' *WeChat*, 2 January. Available from: archive.fo/Y1qVj#selection-41.64-41.77.

Shawan News. 2019. '2019年12月20号沙湾新闻 [Shawan News Dated 20 December 2019].' *WeChat*, 20 December. Available from: archive.fo/O8J0T#selection-41.64-41.79.

Shawan News. 2020. '2020年4月14号沙湾新闻 [Shawan News Dated 14 April 2020].' *WeChat*, 14 April. Available from: archive.vn/V0adL#selection-41.64-41.78.

Sinolink Securities. 2018. 证券研究报告: 公司深度研究 [*Securities Research Report: In-Depth Corporate Analysis*]. 12 March. Chengdu: Innovative Technology and Corporate Service Research Centre of Sinolink Securities Research Institute 国金证券研究所创新技术与企业服务研究中心. Available from: pg.jrj.com.cn/acc/Res/CN_RES/STOCK/2018/3/12/604dacbe-8f48-4847-958a-bfafcd09c3af.pdf.

Smith Finley, Joanne. 2019. 'Securitization, Insecurity and Conflict in Contemporary Xinjiang: Has PRC Counter-Terrorism Evolved into State Terror?' *Central Asia Survey* 38(1): 1–26. doi.org/10.1080/02634937.2019.1586348.

South China Morning Post. n.d. 'Chengguan.' [Topic page], *South China Morning Post* [Hong Kong]. Available from: www.scmp.com/topics/chengguan#:~:text=Chengguan%20are%20an%20urban%20management,city%20sanitation%2C%20landscaping%20and%20parking.

Special Equipment Net. 2020. '反恐利剑 [Useful Anti-Terrorism Equipment].' 特种装备网 [*Special Equipment Net*], 9 January. Available from: archive.fo/tGaiw#selection-1727.0-1727.5.

Statistical Bureau of Xinjiang Uygur Autonomous Region. 2018. 新疆统计年鉴2018 [*Xinjiang Statistical Yearbook 2018*]. Beijing: Zhongguo Tongji Chubanshe.

The Economist. 2013. 'Long Overdue.' *The Economist*, 12 January. Available from: www.economist.com/china/2013/01/12/long-overdue.

Tianshan Net. 2018. '奎屯为美好生活插上智慧翅膀 [Kuitun Leverages Smart Technologies in Pursuit of a Beautiful Life].' 中国农业信息网 [*China Agricultural Information Network*], 22 June. Available from: archive. fo/bCrux.

Tohti, Ilham. 2015. *Present-Day Ethnic Problems in Xinjiang Uighur Autonomous Region: Overview and Recommendations*. [Online.] Translated by Cindy Carter. Hosted by the Xinjiang Documentation Project. Available from: xinjiangdocumentation.sites.olt.ubc.ca/files/2020/11/ilham-tohti_present-day-ethnic-problems-in-xinjiang-uighur-autonomous-region-overview-and-recommendations_complete-translation3.pdf.

Wang, Tingting 王婷婷 and Liu Decheng 刘德成. 2018. '沙湾县: 合作社拓宽致富路 小农户迈向大农业 [Shawan County: Cooperatives Expanding the Pathway to Prosperity, Small Peasant Households Transitioning into Large-Scale Agriculture].' *WeChat*, 14 December. Available from: archive.fo/aX1VS#selection-41.71-41.93.

Wee, Sui-Lee. 2019. 'China Uses DNA to Track its People, with the Help of American Expertise.' *The New York Times*, 21 February. Available from: www.nytimes.com/2019/02/21/business/china-xinjiang-uighur-dna-thermo-fisher.html.

Wong, Chun Han. 2019. 'China's Hard Edge: The Leader of Beijing's Muslim Crackdown Gains Influence.' *The Wall Street Journal*, 7 April. Available from: www.wsj.com/articles/chinas-hard-edge-the-leader-of-beijings-muslim-crackdown-gains-influence-11554655886.

Xin, Man 辛曼. 2019. '着力打造"最亲民"服务窗口 [Strive to Provide the "Most People-Friendly" Services].' *WeChat*, 24 May. Available from: archive.fo/mPF40#selection-49.25-49.29.

Xinhua. 2018. 'Xinjiang Hikes Minimum Wage by 10 pct.' *Xinhua*, 28 March. Available from: www.xinhuanet.com/english/2018-03/28/c_137072135.htm.

Xinhua. 2019. 'China Highlights Support to Xinjiang through Pairing Assistance.' *Xinhua*, 16 July. Available from: www.xinhuanet.com/english/2019-07/16/c_138231911.htm.

Xinjiang Victims Database. 2020a. 'Nurbai Qunapia.' *Xinjiang Victims Database*, 22 August. Available from: shahit.biz/eng/viewentry.php?entryno=1483.

Xinjiang Victims Database. 2020b. 'Mahmutjan Abla.' *Xinjiang Victims Database*, 2 September. Available from: shahit.biz/eng/viewentry.php?entryno=2696.

Yanan, Wang. 2019. 'China Claims Everyone in Xinjiang Camps Has "Graduated".' *AP News*, 9 December. Available from: apnews.com/article/27f00e4feaa2755f25ab514cecda7add.

Yang, Rui 杨睿 and Li Na 李娜. 2018. '新疆农村警务工作的隐忧与建议 [Recommendations and Concerns on Policing Work in Rural Xinjiang].' 广西警官高等专科学校学报 [*Journal of Guangxi Police College*] 31. Available from: archive.ph/6SRpk.

Yaxin Net. 2016. '烏魯木齊市大街小巷將建949個便民警務站 [949 People's Convenience Police Stations will be Established across Ürümqi].' 亞心網訊 [*Yaxin Net*], 27 October. Available from: archive.fo/a9LTE#selection-49.0-49.4.

Ying'an Net. 2019. '2018年新疆地区警用装备采购中标统计报告 [Statistical Report on 2018 Police Equipment Procurement Outcomes in Xinjiang Region].' *WeChat*, 12 March. Available from: archive.vn/xcLfK#-selection-41.68-41.89.

Ying'an Net. 2020. '2019年新疆地区警用装备采购中标统计报告 [Statistical Report on Tender Outcomes of Police Equipment Procurement in Xinjiang in 2019].' 搜狐 [*Sohu*], 3 May. Available from: archive.fo/V2jAI#selection-609.25-609.46.

Zhang, Hui 张惠 and Jiao Wenqiang 焦文强. 2017. '昌吉州民政局向奇台县89个便民警务站赠送户外防护器材 [Civil Affairs Bureau of Changji Prefecture Donated Outdoor Protective Equipment to 89 People's Convenience Police Stations in Qitai County].' 2 August. Civil Affairs Bureau of Changji Hui Autonomous Prefecture. Available from: archive.fo/GsTas#selection-401.3-401.9.

Zhang, Shawn. 2019. 'Satellite Imagery of Xinjiang "Re-Education Camp"'. *Medium*, 19 May. Available from: medium.com/@shawnwzhang/satellite-imagery-of-xinjiang-re-education-camp-83-377e9453db7a.

15. Transnational carceral capitalism and private paramilitaries in Xinjiang and beyond (GERALD ROCHE)

Agence France-Presse (AFP). 2019. 'Former Blackwater Contractor in Myanmar Security Venture.' *France24*, 21 March. Available from: www.france24.com/en/20190321-former-blackwater-contractor-myanmar-security-venture.

Agence France-Presse (AFP) and SBS News. 2020. 'Donald Trump Told China's Xi Jinping Detaining Uighurs Was "Right Thing to Do", New Book Claims.' *SBS News*, 18 June. Available from: www.sbs.com.au/news/donald-trump-told-china-s-xi-jinping-detaining-uighurs-was-right-thing-to-do-new-book-claims.

Bloomberg. 2019. 'Lv Chaohai. Head: Northwest, Frontier Services Group Ltd.' *Bloomberg*. Available from: www.bloomberg.com/profile/person/20593608.

Chau, Thompson. 2019. 'Ex-Blackwater Boss Moves into Myanmar Security.' *Myanmar Times*, 18 March. Available from: www.mmtimes.com/news/ex-blackwater-boss-moves-myanmar-security.html.

Ciralsky, Adam. 2009. 'Tycoon, Contractor, Soldier, Spy.' *Vanity Fair*, 2 December. Available from: www.vanityfair.com/news/2010/01/blackwater-201001.

Cook, Sarah. 2019. 'The Learning Curve: How Communist Party Officials Are Applying Lessons from Prior "Transformation" Campaigns to Repression in Xinjiang.' *China Brief* 19(3). Available from: jamestown.org/program/the-learning-curve-how-communist-party-officials-are-applying-lessons-from-prior-transformation-campaigns-to-repression-in-xinjiang.

Doyon, Jérôme. 2019. 'Counter-Extremism in Xinjiang: Understanding China's Community-Focused Counter-Terrorism Tactics.' *War on the Rocks*, 14 January. Available from: warontherocks.com/2019/01/counter-extremism-in-xinjiang-understanding-chinas-community-focused-counter-terrorism-tactics.

Fan, Lingzhi. 2017. 'Blackwater Founder to Open Bases in Xinjiang.' *Global Times*, [Beijing], 21 March. Available from: www.globaltimes.cn/content/1038847.shtml.

Forth, Aidan. 2017. *Barbed-Wire Imperials: Britain's Empire of Camps, 1876–1903*. Oakland, CA: University of California Press. doi.org/10.1525/california/9780520293960.001.0001.

Frontier Services Group (FSG). 2017. *Annual Report 2017*. Hamilton, Bermuda: Frontier Services Group. Available from: doc.irasia.com/listco/hk/frontier/annual/2017/ar2017.pdf.

Frontier Services Group (FSG). 2018a. 'China Signs CMEC MOUs with Myanmar.' *News*, 28 September. Hamilton, Bermuda: Frontier Services Group. Available from: www.fsgroup.com/en/news/show-427.html.

Frontier Services Group (FSG). 2018b. 'FSG Obtained Cambodian Security License.' *News*, 13 December. Hamilton, Bermuda: Frontier Services Group. Available from: www.fsgroup.com/en/news/show-436.html.

Hall, Richard. 2019. 'US Troops in Syria Could Be Replaced by Private Contractors, Blackwater Founder Erik Prince Says.' *The Independent*, [London], 15 January. Available from: www.independent.co.uk/news/world/middle-east/syria-us-troop-withdrawal-private-contractors-blackwater-erik-prince-trump-military-a8729121.html.

Kirsch, Noah. 2018. 'Blackwater's Dark Prince Returns.' *Forbes*, 4 April. Available from: www.forbes.com/return-of-erik-prince/#7315a18b50aa.

Leibold, James. 2020. 'Surveillance in China's Xinjiang Region: Ethnic Sorting, Coercion, and Inducement.' *Journal of Contemporary China* 29(121): 46–60. doi.org/10.1080/10670564.2019.1621529.

Lintner, Bertil. 2019. 'Controversial Security Firm Moving into Myanmar.' *Asia Times*, [Hong Kong], 19 March. Available from: asiatimes. com/2019/03/controversial-security-firm-moving-into-myanmar.

Martina, Michael. 2017. 'Blackwater Founder's FSG Buys Stake in Chinese Security School.' *Reuters*, 30 May. Available from: www.reuters.com/ article/us-china-silkroad-companies/blackwater-founders-fsg-buys-sta-ke-in-chinese-security-school-idUSKBN18Q0WR.

Mech, Dara. 2019. 'Hun Sen and Xi Herald Continued Strong Ties.' *The Phnom Penh Post*, 23 January. Available from: www.phnompenhpost.com/ national/hun-sen-and-xi-herald-continued-strong-ties.

Mühlhahn, Klaus. 2010. 'The Concentration Camp in Global Historical Perspective.' *History Compass* 8(6): 543–61. doi.org/10.1111/j.1478-0542.2010.00687.x.

Oliver, Kelly. 2017. *Carceral Humanitarianism: Logics of Refugee Detention*. Minneapolis, MN: University of Minnesota Press. doi. org/10.5749/9781452958507.

Ordonez, Victor. 2019. 'Erik Prince's Company Plans Business in China Province under Human Rights Scrutiny According to Financial Disclosure.' *ABC News*, 10 October. Available from: abcnews.go.com/International/erik-princes-company-plans-business-china-province-human/ story?id=66139535.

Pitzer, Andrea. 2017. *One Long Night: A Global History of Concentration Camps*. London: Little, Brown & Company.

Pradhan, Bibhudatta. 2020. 'Millions in India Could End Up in Modi's New Detention Camps.' *Bloomberg*, 26 February. Available from: www. bloomberg.com/features/2020-modi-india-detention-camps.

Prince, Erik. 2016. 'What the Chinese Approach to Overseas Infra-structure Can Teach the World.' *South China Morning Post*, [Hong Kong], 27 December. Available from: www.scmp.com/comment/insight-opi-nion/article/2056883/what-chinese-approach-overseas-infrastructu-re-can-teach.

Prince, Erik. 2017. 'The MacArthur Model for Afghanistan.' *Wall Street Journal*, 31 May. Available from: www.wsj.com/articles/the-macarthur-model-for-afghanistan-1496269058.

Roston, Aran. 2017. 'Private War: Erik Prince Has His Eye on Afghanistan's Rare Metals.' *BuzzFeed News*, 7 December. Available from: www.buzzfeednews.com/article/aramroston/private-war-erik-prince-has-his-eye-on-afghanistans-rare#.esG7JBV8Q.

Shepherd, Christian. 2019. 'Erik Prince Company to Build Training Centre in China's Xinjiang.' *Reuters*, 31 January. Available from: www.reuters.com/article/us-china-xinjiang/erik-prince-company-to-build-training-center-in-chinas-xinjiang-idUSKCN1PP169.

Stevenson, Alexandra and Chris Buckley. 2019. 'Blackwater Founder's New Company Strikes Deal in China. He Says He Had No Idea.' *The New York Times*, 1 February. Available from: www.nytimes.com/2019/02/01/business/erik-prince-xinjiang-china-fsg-blackwater.html.

Stone, Dan. 2017. *Concentration Camps: A Short History*. Oxford, UK: Oxford University Press.

Wang, Jackie. 2018. *Carceral Capitalism*. South Pasadena, CA: Semiotext(e).

Zenz, Adrian and James Leibold. 2017. 'Chen Quanguo: The Strongman Behind Beijing's Securitization Strategy in Tibet and Xinjiang.' *China Brief* 17(12). Available from: jamestown.org/program/chen-quanguo-the-strongman-behind-beijings-securitization-strategy-in-tibet-and-xinjiang.

16. Chinese feminism, Tibet, and Xinjiang (SÉAGH KEHOE)

Agence France-Presse (AFP). 2020. 'China Sterilising Ethnic Minority Women in Xinjiang, Report Says.' *The Guardian*, 29 June. Available from: www.theguardian.com/world/2020/jun/29/china-sterilising-ethnic-minority-women-in-xinjiang-report-says.

BBC. 2016. 'Chinese Activist Zheng Churan: "Hey Trump, Feminists Are Watching You".' *BBC*, 15 December. Available from: www.bbc.co.uk/news/world-asia-china-38325121.

Beydoun, Khaled A. 2018. 'China Holds One Million Uighur Muslims in Concentration Camps.' *Al Jazeera*, 13 September. Available from: www.aljazeera.com/indepth/opinion/china-holds-million-uighur-muslims-con-centration-camps-180912105738481.html.

Byler, Darren. 2018. '"As If You've Spent Your Whole Life in Prison": Starving and Subdued in Xinjiang Detention Centers.' *SupChina*, 5 December. Available from: supchina.com/2018/12/05/starving-and-subdued-in-xinjiang-detention-centers.

Chenchen, Zhang. 2017. 'The Curious Rise of the "White Left" as a Chinese Internet Insult.' *Open Democracy*, 11 May. Available from: www.opendemocracy.net/en/digitaliberties/curious-rise-of-white-left-as-chine-se-internet-insult.

ChinaFile. 2018. 'Here Are the Fortune 500 Companies Doing Business in Xinjiang.' *ChinaFile*, 2 October. Available from: www.chinafile.com/reporting-opinion/features/here-are-fortune-500-companies-doing-busi-ness-xinjiang.

Cockburn, Harry. 2018. 'Muslim Woman Describes Torture and Beatings in China Detention Camp: "I Begged Them to Kill Me."' *The Independent*, [London], 28 November. Available from: www.independent.co.uk/news/world/asia/uighur-muslim-china-mihrigul-tursun-torture-reeduca-tion-camps-a8656396.html.

Crenshaw, Kimberle. 1989. 'Demarginalizing the Intersection of Race and Sex: A Black Feminist Critique of Antidiscrimination Doctrine, Feminist Theory and Antiracist Policies.' *University of Chicago Legal Forum* 1989(1): 139–67.

Davis, Angela. 2011. *Abolition Democracy: Beyond Empire, Prisons, and Torture*. New York, NY: Seven Stories Press.

Grose, Timothy and James Leibold. 2015. 'China's Ban on Islamic Veils Is Destined to Fail.' *Foreign Policy*, 5 February. Available from: foreignpolicy.com/2015/02/05/chinas-ban-on-islamic-veils-is-destined-to-fail.

Institut Ouïghour d'Europe (IODE). n.d. 'Let's Defend Uyghur Culture in Europe!' Institut Ouïghour d'Europe website. Available from: www.uyghur-institute.org/index.php/en.

Jiayun, Feng. 2017. 'Hard Time for Feminists in China.' *SupChina*, 8 March. Available from: supchina.com/2017/03/08/hard-times-feminists-china.

Jiayun, Feng. 2018. 'Chinese Social Media Censors Feminist Voices.' *SupChina*, 9 March. Available from: supchina.com/2018/03/09/chinese-social-media-censors-feminist-voices.

Leibold, James. 2010. 'More Than a Category: Han Supremacism on the Chinese Internet.' *The China Quarterly* 203: 539–59. doi.org/10.1017/S0305741010000585.

Li, Maizi. 2017. 'I Went to Jail for Handing Out Feminist Stickers in China.' *The Guardian*, 8 March. Available from: www.theguardian.com/commentisfree/2017/mar/08/feminist-stickers-china-backash-women-activists.

Li, Ruohan. 2019. 'Tibet Records Double-Digit GDP Growth for 26 Consecutive Years.' *Global Times*, [Beijing], 11 January. Available from: www.globaltimes.cn/content/1135465.shtml.

Liu, Xin. 2018. 'Xinjiang Women Gain Respect and Self-Recognition.' *Global Times*, [Beijing], 24 October. Available from: www.globaltimes.cn/content/1124253.shtml.

Lokyitsang, Dawa. 2012. 'The Art of (China's) Colonialism: Constructing Invisibilities in (Tibetan) History and Geography.' *Lhakar Diaries*, [Blog], 19 December. Available from: lhakardiaries.com/2012/12/19/the-art-of-chinas-colonialism-constructing-invisibilities-in-tibetan-history-and-geography.

Phillips, Tom. 2016. 'Chinese Feminists Post Selfies in Solidarity with Stanford Assault Victim.' *The Guardian*, 10 June. Available from: www.theguardian.com/world/2016/jun/10/chinese-feminists-selfies-solidarity-stanford-assault-victim.

Radio Free Asia (RFA). 2019. 'Independent Students Slam China-Backed Intimidation on Overseas Campuses.' *Radio Free Asia*, [Washington, DC], 15 February. Available from: www.rfa.org/english/news/china/campuses-02152019094958.html.

Roberts, Sean. 2018. 'The Biopolitics of China's "War on Terror" and the Exclusion of the Uyghurs.' *Critical Asian Studies* 50(2): 232–58. doi.org/10.1080/14672715.2018.1454111.

Sinica Podcast. 2019. 'Sinica Podcast: Tashi Rabgey and Jim Millward on China's Ethnic Policy in Xinjiang and Tibet.' *SupChina*, 15 February. Available from: supchina.com/2019/02/15/sinica-podcast-tashi-rabgey-and-jim-millward-on-chinas-ethnic-policy-in-xinjiang-and-tibet/.

Smith Finley, Joanne. 2018. 'Islam in Xinjiang: "De-Extremification" or Violation of Religious Space?' *The Asia Dialogue*, 15 June. Available from: theasiadialogue.com/2018/06/15/islam-in-xinjiang-de-extremification-or-violation-of-religious-space.

Smith Finley, Joanne. 2019. 'Securitization, Insecurity and Conflict in Contemporary Xinjiang: Has PRC Counter-Terrorism Evolved into State Terror?' *Central Asian Survey* 38(1): 1–26. doi.org/10.1080/02634937.2019.1586348.

Uyghur Human Rights Project (UHRP). n.d. 'What You Can Do.' Website. Washington, DC: Uyghur Human Rights Project. Available from: uhrp.org/what-you-can-do.

Yi, Xiaocuo. 2019. '"Saved" by State Terror: Gendered Violence and Propaganda in Xinjiang.' *SupChina*, 14 May. Available from: supchina.com/2019/05/14/saved-by-state-terror-gendered-violence-and-propaganda-in-xinjiang.

Yin, Yijun. 2017. 'Feminist Folk Quartet Gives Voice to China's Migrant Workers.' *Sixth Tone*, 29 March. Available from: www.sixthtone.com/news/2128/feminist-folk-quartet-gives-voice-china s-migrant-workers.

Ziyi, Tang and Echo Huang. 2018. 'A Platform for Female Factory Workers Has Disappeared from China's Twitter.' *Quartz*, 16 July. Available from: qz.com/1328627/a-chinese-platform-for-female-factory-workers-rights-has-been-blocked-on-weibo.

17. China: Xinjiang :: India: Kashmir (NITASHA KAUL)

Anand, Dibyesh. 2012. 'China and India: Postcolonial Informal Empires in the Emerging Global Order.' *Rethinking Marxism: A Journal of Economics, Culture & Society* 24(1): 68–86. doi.org/10.1080/08935696.2012.635039.

Anand, Dibyesh. 2019. 'Colonization with Chinese Characteristics: Politics of (In)security in Xinjiang and Tibet.' *Central Asian Survey* 38(1): 129–47. doi.org/10.1080/02634937.2018.1534801.

Balakrishnan, Paran. 2019. 'Detention Camps as Growth Model.' *The Hindu Business Line*, [Chennai], 20 September. Available from: www.thehindubusinessline.com/opinion/columns/from-the-viewsroom/detention-camps-as-growth-model/article29460978.ece.

Byler, Darren. 2018. 'Violent Paternalism: On the Banality of Uyghur Unfreedom.' *The Asia-Pacific Journal* 16(4): 1–15.

Callahan, William A. 2004. 'National Insecurities: Humiliation, Salvation, and Chinese Nationalism.' *Alternatives: Global, Local, Political* 29(2): 199–218. doi.org/10.1177/030437540402900204.

Chen, Yu-Jie. 2019. 'China's Challenge to the International Human Rights Regime.' *NYU Journal of International Law and Politics* 51: 1179–222.

Dalmia, Vinayak. 2020. 'China's Hikvision Controls India's Surveillance Market: Modi Needs to Do More than Ban Apps.' *ThePrint*, [New Delhi], 1 July. Available from: theprint.in/opinion/chinas-hikvision-controls-indias-surveillance-market-modi-needs-to-do-more-than-ban-apps/452014.

Dorsey, James M. 2019. *Diverging Gulf responses to Kashmir and Xinjiang reflect deep divisions*. BESA Center Perspectives Paper No. 1,299, 25 September. Ramat Gan, Israel: Begin-Sadat Center for Strategic Studies, Bar-Ilan University. Available from: besacenter.org/perspectives-papers/gulf-states-kashmir-xinjiang.

Express News Service. 2019. 'Indian Diplomat Compares Return of Kashmiri Pandits with Israeli Settlements, Sparks Row.' *The Indian Express*, [Noida], 28 November. Available from: indianexpress.com/article/india/indian-diplomat-compares-return-of-kashmiri-pandits-with-israeli-settlements-sparks-row-6140271.

Feldstein, Steven. 2019. *The global expansion of AI surveillance*. Working Paper, 17 September. Washington, DC: Carnegie Endowment for International Peace. Available from: carnegieendowment.org/2019/09/17/global-expansion-of-ai-surveillance-pub-79847.

Gettleman, Jeffrey and Kai Schultz. 2020. 'Indian General Talks of "Deradicalization Camps" for Kashmiris.' *The New York Times*, 17 January. Available from: www.nytimes.com/2020/01/17/world/asia/india-kashmir-camps.html.

Indo-Asian News Service (IANS). 2019. 'Modi Says No Detention Camps, Minister Accepted 6 in Assam.' *Outlook India*, [New Delhi], 23 December. Available from: www.outlookindia.com/newsscroll/modi-says-no-detention-camps-minister-accepted-6-in-assam/1692393.

Kalita, Prabin. 2019. 'India's Biggest Detention Centre to House "Foreigners" by 2020.' *The Times of India*, 8 September. Available from: timesofindia.indiatimes.com/city/guwahati/indias-biggest-detention-centre-to-house-foreigners-by-2020/articleshow/71030993.cms.

Kaul, Nitasha. 2011. 'On Loving and Losing Kashmir.' *India International Centre Quarterly* 37(3–4): 42–53.

Kaul, Nitasha. 2018. 'India's Obsession with Kashmir: Democracy, Gender, (Anti-)nationalism.' *Feminist Review* 119: 126–43. doi.org/10.1057/s41305-018-0123-x.

Kaul, Nitasha. 2019a/B. 'The Political Project of Postcolonial Neoliberal Nationalism.' *Indian Politics & Policy* 2(1): 3–30. doi.org/10.18278/inpp.2.1.2.

Kaul, Nitasha. 2019b/A. 'Kashmir Is Under the Heel of India's Colonialism.' *Foreign Policy*, 13 August. Available from: foreignpolicy.com/2019/08/13/kashmir-is-under-the-heel-of-indias-colonialism.

Kaul, Nitasha. 2019c. 'Written Testimony of Dr Nitasha Kaul, Associate Professor, Centre for the Study of Democracy University of Westminster, London, UK for Hearing on "Human Rights in South Asia: Views from the State Department and the Region, Panel II". US House of Representatives, Subcommittee on Asia, the Pacific and Nonproliferation (Committee on Foreign Affairs), Washington, DC, 22 October. Available from: docs.house.gov/meetings/FA/FA05/20191022/110143/HHRG-116-FA05-Wstate-KaulN-20191022.pdf. [For the oral testimony, see www.youtube.com/watch?v=b-S8xyn1cgY.]

Krishnan, Vidya. 2020. '"Gov't Killed My Husband": Why Are Detainees Dying in Assam?' *Al Jazeera*, 3 March. Available from: www.aljazeera.com/features/2020/03/03/govt-killed-my-husband-why-are-detainees-dying-in-assam.

Ma, Alexandra. 2019. 'China Tells Uighur Muslims They Are Abducting Their Families so They Can Cleanse Their Brains Like They Have a Disease, Leaked Documents Show.' *Business Insider*, 18 November. Available from: www.businessinsider.com/china-uighur-detention-camps-cleanse-religion-leaked-documents-nyt-2019-11?r=US&IR=T.

Ma, Alexandra and Ellen Loanes. 2019. 'China and India Are Using the Same Playbook to Trample on Their Minorities, and the Rest of the World Is Too Powerless to Stop Them.' *Business Insider*, 23 November. Available from: www.businessinsider.com/china-uighur-india-kashmir-assam-oppression-parallels-2019-11?r=US&IR=T.

Quora. 2016. 'Should India Apply the "Chinese Model for Xinjiang" in Kashmir?' Quora, [Online]. Available from: www.quora.com/Should-India-apply-the-Chinese-model-for-Xinjiang-in-Kashmir.

Rahim, Zamira. 2019. 'India Builds Detention Camps for up to 1.9m People "Stripped of Citizenship" in Assam.' *The Independent*, [London], 11 September. Available from: www.independent.co.uk/news/world/asia/assam-india-detention-camps-bangladesh-nrc-list-a9099251.html.

Safi, Michael. 2017. 'India Army Chief Defends Soldiers Who Tied Man to Vehicle and Used Him as a Human Shield.' *The Guardian*, 29 May. Available from: www.theguardian.com/world/2017/may/29/india-army-chief-kashmir-protests-man-tied-to-vehicle.

Sen, Sumant and Naresh Singaravelu. 2020. 'Data: Where Are Detention Centres in India?' *The Hindu*, [Chennai], 1 January. Available from: www.thehindu.com/data/data-where-are-detention-centres-in-india/article30451564.ece.

SupChina. 2019. 'Is Kashmir the Next Xinjiang?' *SupChina*, 21 October. Available from: supchina.com/2019/10/21/is-kashmir-the-next-xinjiang.

The Wire. 2019. 'Western Standards on Human Rights Can't Be Blindly Applied to India: Amit Shah.' *The Wire*, [New Delhi], 13 October. Available from: thewire.in/politics/western-standards-on-human-rights-cant-be-blindly-applied-to-india-amit-shah.

Uniyal, Ruchika. 2020. 'What Are Detention Centres?' *The Times of India*, 12 February. Available from: timesofindia.indiatimes.com/india/what-a-re-detention-centres/articleshow/72975067.cms.

Conclusion (DARREN BYLER, IVAN FRANCESCHINI, AND NICHOLAS LOUBERE)

Better Cotton Initiative (BCI). 2020. 'BCI to Cease all Field-Level Activities in the Xinjiang Uyghur Autonomous Region of China.' *Announcements*, 21 October. Geneva: Better Cotton Initiative. Available from: web.archive.org/web/20210107110309/https://bettercotton.org/bci-to-cease-all-field-level-activities-in-the-xinjiang-uyghur-autonomous-region-of-china.

Byler, Darren. 2021. *In the Camps: China's High-Tech Penal Colony*. New York, NY: Columbia Global Reports.

China Education Bureau. 2017. 全国统筹县域内城乡义务教育一体化 改革发展现场推进会 [*National Overall Planning for the Integration of Urban and Rural Compulsory Education in Counties Reform and Development On-Site Promotion Meeting*]. China Education Bureau's Department of Basic Education, December. Available from: http://www. moe.gov.cn/jyb_xwfb/xw_zt/moe_357/jyzt_2016nztzl/ztzl_xyncs/ztzl_xy_dxjy/201801/W020180109353888301306.pdf [page discontinued].

Dou, Eva, Jeanne Whalen, and Alicia Chen. 2021. 'U.S. Ban on China's Xinjiang Cotton Fractures Fashion Industry Supply Chains.' *The Washington Post*, 22 February. Available from: www.washingtonpost.com/world/asia_pacific/china-cotton-sanctions-xinjiang-uighurs/2021/02/21/a8a4b128-70ee-11eb-93be-c10813e358a2_story.html.

Kang, Dake. 2021a. 'Room for 10,000: Inside China's Largest Detention Center.' *Associated Press*, 21 July. Available from: apnews.com/article/business-religion-china-only-on-ap-f89c20645e69208a416c64d229c072de.

Kang, Dake. 2021b. 'Terror & Tourism: Xinjiang Eases its Grip, but Fear Remains.' *Associated Press*, 10 October. Available from: apnews.com/article/coronavirus-pandemic-lifestyle-china-health-travel-7a6967f-335f97ca868cc618ea84b98b9.

Liu, Yuguang 刘玉光. 2019. '新疆举行教育脱贫攻坚工作新闻发布会 [Xinjiang Holds Press Conference on Educational Poverty Alleviation Work].' 10 May. Beijing: State Council Information Office of the People's Republic of China. Available from: web.archive.org/web/20201001035511/https://www.scio.gov.cn/xwfbh/gssxwfbh/xwfbh/xinjiang/Document/1654083/1654083.htm.

Mathews, Brett. 2019. 'BCI Ditches Chinese Partner with Prison Labour Links.' *Apparel Insider*, 27 November. Available from: apparelinsider.com/bci-ditches-chinese-partner-with-prison-labour-links/.

Wang, Yanan. 2019. 'China Claims Everyone in Xinjiang Camps Has "Graduated". *Associated Press*, 9 December. Available from: apnews. com/article/religion-terrorism-ap-top-news-international-news-politics-27f00e4feaa2755f25ab514cecda7add.

www.ingramcontent.com/pod-product-compliance
Lightning Source LLC
Chambersburg PA
CBHW040154270326
41929CB00041B/3396